The Actual and the Rational

THE ACTUAL
AND
THE RATIONAL

Hegel and Objective Spirit

Jean-François Kervégan

Translated by Daniela Ginsburg and Martin Shuster

The University of Chicago Press

Chicago and London

The University of Chicago Press, Chicago 60637
The University of Chicago Press, Ltd., London
© 2018 by The University of Chicago
All rights reserved. No part of this book may be used or reproduced in any manner
whatsoever without written permission, except in the case of brief quotations in critical
articles and reviews. For more information, contact the University of Chicago Press,
1427 E. 60th St., Chicago, IL 60637.
Published 2018
Printed in the United States of America

27 26 25 24 23 22 21 20 19 18   1 2 3 4 5

ISBN-13: 978-0-226-02380-9 (cloth)
ISBN-13: 978-0-226-02394-6 (e-book)
DOI: https://doi.org/10.7208/chicago/9780226023946.001.0001

Originally published as *L'effectif et le rationnel. Hegel et l'esprit objectif*
© Librairie Philosophique J. Vrin, Paris, 2008.
http://www.vrin.fr

Cet ouvrage a bénéficié du soutien des programmes d'aide à la publication de l'Institut
français. This work, published as part of a program of aid for publication, received support
from the Institut français. Published with the cooperation of the Université Paris I
Panthéon-Sorbonne and of the University Institute of France.

Library of Congress Cataloguing-in-Publication Data
Names: Kervégan, Jean-François, author. | Ginsburg, Daniela, translator. |
Shuster, Martin, translator.
Title: The actual and the rational : Hegel and objective spirit / Jean-François Kervégan ;
translated by Daniela Ginsburg and Martin Shuster.
Other titles: Effectif et le rationnel. English
Description: Chicago ; London : The University of Chicago Press, 2018. | Includes
bibliographical references and index. | Originally published: Paris : Librairie philosphique
J. Vrin. © 2008 under title L'effectif et le rationnel: Hegel et l'esprit objectif.
Identifiers: LCCN 2017059969 | ISBN 9780226023809 (cloth : alk. paper) |
ISBN 9780226023946 (pbk.)
Subjects: LCSH: Hegel, Georg Wilhelm Friedrich, 1770–1831. | Law—Philosophy. |
Political science—Philosophy. | Objectivity. | Subjectivity.
Classification: LCC K230.H432 K4713 2018 B2948 | DDC 193—dc23
LC record available at https://lccn.loc.gov/2017059969

♾ This paper meets the requirements of ANSI/NISO Z39.48-1992 (Permanence of Paper).

CONTENTS

Hegel without Metaphysics?

It is not necessary to justify the special interest one takes in a certain area of an author's thought (in my case, Hegel's legal, social, and political thought, to which a large part of my research over the last twenty-five years has been dedicated). The reasons for one's interest may be partly external to that thought or to philosophy on the whole. On the other hand, the *way* one studies an area of thought, the presuppositions of one's reading, must be exposed and justified, which means one must be clearly aware of them, being able to measure their effects. For me, coming to this realization was a slow process, one that to a certain degree modified the rules by which I had undertaken my study of Hegel. After years spent reading and commenting on the *Science of Logic* as part of a group led by the late André Lécrivain,[1] I naturally approached the study of the doctrine of objective spirit with that long, collective labor in mind. I was, and remain, convinced that the logical-speculative perspective opened relatively unprecedented hermeneutic possibilities and that it was important to read Hegel's legal-political writings not as the expression of opinions or even theoretical positions in political philosophy but as elements of a system, of an

---

1. See J. Biard et al., *Introduction à la lecture de la science de la logique de Hegel*, vol. 1, *L'être* (Paris: Aubier-Montaigne, 1987).

"Encyclopedia of Philosophical Sciences," of which the *Science of Logic* is the center and nexus of meaning. Moreover, this conviction comes from a basic reading of the texts. In the *Philosophy of Right*,[2] Hegel constantly emphasizes the interdependence between the doctrine of objective spirit and the *Logic*, to which he makes some twenty explicit references. He writes, for example, in the preface,

> It will readily be noticed that the work as a whole, like the construction of its parts, is based on the logical spirit. It is also chiefly from this point of view that I would wish this treatise to be understood and judged. For what it deals with is *science*, and in science, the content is essentially inseparable from the *form*.[3]

It is indisputable that for Hegel the doctrine of objective spirit, like every part of the system, rests not only on the "spirit" of the *Logic* but on its letter; if that were not the case, there would be no sense in speaking of a Hegelian system. For Hegel, as for Kant, a system is fundamentally distinct from a mere "aggregate" of knowledge.[4] Moreover, for Hegel, the systematic project is not at all incompatible with attention to the concrete aspect of things and with the concern for the "life of men," as he wrote to Schelling:

> In my scientific development, which started from [the] more subordinate needs of man, I was inevitably driven toward science, and the ideal of [my] youth had to take the form of reflection and thus at once of a system. I now ask myself, while I am still occupied at it, what return to intervention in the life of men can be found.[5]

2. I accept the usual translation of *Philosophie des Rechts* as "Philosophy of Right." But there are good reasons for choosing "Philosophy of Law" instead, inasmuch as on my view in the Hegelian context the "subjective" meaning of *Recht* (right) depends on the "objective" meaning of the word (law).

3. *RPh, GW* 14.1, p. 6 (*Elements*, 10; see *Outlines*, 4).

4. "By an architectonic I understand the art of systems. Since systematic unity is that which first makes ordinary cognition into science, i.e., makes a system out of a mere aggregate of it, architectonic is the doctrine of that which is scientific in our cognition in general" (*KrV, Ak.* 3, B 860 / 1C, p. 691).

5. G. W. F. Hegel, *Hegel: The Letters*, trans. Clark Butler and Christiane Seiler (Bloomington: Indiana University Press, 1984), 64. Letter dated November 2, 1800.

The problem—raised quite early on, in particular by Marx—is the following: must we believe Hegel, and to what extent, when he maintains that all the philosophy of law and right (e.g.) is an extension of his *Logic*? If the answer is yes, don't we risk having to consider that "the entire philosophy of right is only a parenthesis to *Logic*"?[6] It must, moreover, be noted that the young Marx's position on the matter evolved greatly, for in the end he (along with Engels) considered the *Logic* to constitute the "rational kernel"—revolutionary because dialectic—of Hegelianism. Strangely enough, that had already been the position of Rudolf Haym, who so greatly contributed to establishing the bad reputation of the "philosopher of the Prussian state" when he asserted that the system is "revolutionary in its logical part" though "conservative in its practical part."[7] The opposite position, which was adopted by a good number of later commentators, consists in separating the argument of the *Philosophy of Right* as much as possible from its logical-systematic context in an attempt to render it more acceptable at a time and in a context where absolute spirit no longer enjoys very good press. If we wanted to summarize this alternative crudely, we might say, with the help of a historical nod, that either, like the "old Hegelians," one opts for an orthodox reading of the system and runs the risk of helping discredit it, or, like the "young Hegelians," one pits the spirit of the work against its letter and tries to rid it of its metaphysical dross at the risk of depriving it of what gives it its power and coherence.

It must be noted that recently, though some eminent commentators continue to take the "old Hegelian" position of a reading faithful to Hegelianism's explicit systematic program (even if this means nourishing the suspicions that some burden it with—e.g., the suspicion of totalitarianism popularized by Popper), others increasingly choose a "young Hegelian," nonmetaphysical reading of Hegel—a reading that, no matter how it breaks with the letter of the system, implies pushing away or relativizing some of its strongest ambi-

6. Karl Marx, *Critique of Hegel's "Philosophy of Right"* (Cambridge: Cambridge University Press, 1977), 18. "*Logic* is not used to prove the nature of the state, but the state is used to prove the *Logic*" (ibid.).

7. Rudolf Haym, *Hegel und seine Zeit: Vorlesungen über Entstehung und Entwicklung, Wesen und Werth der Hegel'schen Philosophie* (Berlin: Rudolph Gaertner, 1857), 368–69. We find the same argument in Engels; see Friedrich Engels, *Socialism: Utopian and Scientific* (New York: Pathfinder, 1972), 67–70; Friedrich Engels and Karl Marx, *Ludwig Feuerbach and the Outcome of Classical German Philosophy* (New York: International, 1941).

tions at the obvious risk of thus depriving it of what is most powerful in it. I would like, with the help of several examples, to show what is interesting and risky in such iconoclastic attempts, which, at bottom, amount to distinguishing once again "what is living" and "what is dead" in Hegel,[8] even at the risk of being suspected of doing arbitrary violence to the coherence of this thought.

When one considers the disrepute that has followed Hegel within the dominant strand of Anglo-Saxon philosophy ever since Russell's break with neo-Hegelian idealism, it is surprising to observe that for some ten years now, Hegel has once again become a significant point of reference within what one no longer dares call analytic philosophy, given that it is now so diverse and renounces some of the distinctive traits of its original identity—in particular, its distrust of continental philosophy and especially of German idealism. It is not only that important, now-classic contributions to the study of Hegel have been born in the Anglo-American world, which had previously lagged behind in this area (I am thinking, e.g., of the innovative works of Robert Pippin[9] and Terry Pinkard).[10] We have even seen analytic philosophers seize Hegelianism (certainly in a very liberal way that would be problematic for a historian of philosophy in the European tradition) and even what is apparently most suspect within it—that is, its idealism—in order to try to raise, on the analytic continent itself, new, post-Wittgensteinian, post-Quinean, or neopragmatist questions. I am thinking here of the works of Robert Brandom[11] and John McDowell,[12] which have caused quite a commotion, and not only because of

8. See Benedetto Croce, *What Is Living and What Is Dead of the Philosophy of Hegel*, trans. Douglas Ainslie (New York: Macmillan, 1915).

9. See in particular Robert B. Pippin, *Hegel's Idealism: The Satisfactions of Self-Consciousness* (Cambridge: Cambridge University Press, 1989); *Idealism as Modernism: Hegelian Variations* (Cambridge: Cambridge University Press, 1997); *Hegel's Practical Philosophy* (Cambridge: Cambridge University Press, 2008).

10. See Terry Pinkard, *Hegel's Phenomenology: The Sociality of Reason* (Cambridge: Cambridge University, 1996); *Hegel: A Biography* (Cambridge: Cambridge University Press, 2001); *Hegel's Naturalism* (Oxford: Oxford University Press, 2012); Terry Pinkard and H. Tristram Engelhardt, *Hegel Reconsidered: Beyond Metaphysics and the Authoritarian State* (Dordrecht: Kluwer, 1994).

11. Robert Brandom, *Making It Explicit: Reasoning, Representing, and Discursive Commitment* (Cambridge, MA: Harvard University Press, 1994); Robert B. Brandom, "Some Pragmatist Themes in Hegel's Idealism: Negotiation and Administration in Hegel's Account of the Structure and Content of Conceptual Norms," *European Journal of Philosophy* 7, no. 2 (1999): 164–89.

12. John McDowell, *Mind and World* (Cambridge, MA: Harvard University Press, 1996); *Meaning, Knowledge, and Reality* (Cambridge, MA: Harvard University Press, 1998); *Having the*

the doubly iconoclastic use they make of Hegel (iconoclastic in relation to classic readings of Hegel and in relation to the analytic mainstream).

However, these works deal with problems of philosophy of knowledge and philosophy of language. Since my subject is different, I will highlight instead Axel Honneth's effort to update the Hegelian doctrine of *Sittlichkeit*. In a book titled *Suffering from Indeterminacy*, he proposes a "reactualization of Hegel's philosophy of right"[13] in order to show that here, too, a return to Hegel, comparable to the return occurring in the field of theories of knowledge, is fruitful. Honneth does not claim that the *Philosophy of Right* offers answers to the questions raised by contemporary social and political philosophy, but he does maintain that a nonmetaphysical reading of the text makes it possible to confront and even resolve certain difficulties encountered by contemporary philosophy—for example, in the debate between liberals and communitarians. After dismissing the usual political objections (Hegel is an enemy of democracy) and methodological objections (the system's logical-speculative presuppositions are unacceptable), Honneth shows that the doctrine of objective spirit, adequately reconstructed, can be fruitful for post-Habermasian discussions on three subjects. First of all, the Hegelian theory of right and law, centered as it is on the idea of a "universally free will," can be understood as a theory of justice in the contemporary (post-Rawlsian) sense of the term—as a theory that exposes the intersubjective conditions of individual autonomy and distinguishes different spheres of self-realization. Second, in direct line with his earlier works on recognition and "social suffering," Honneth seeks within the doctrine of *Sittlichkeit* the ingredients for a "therapeutic for social pathologies." Finally—and on this point there is convergence with Pippin— he proposes understanding this doctrine as a normative theory of modernity; a theory whose limits, nevertheless, stem from its "superinstitutional" character. This, by the way, is a point whose demonstration can be debated; doesn't it fall prey to the anti-institutional disposition common to large sections of contemporary political philosophy? Whatever the case may be, these analyses show the potential inventiveness and fecundity of nonmetaphysical readings of Hegel. But of course, Honneth, like the other authors mentioned,

---

World in View: Essays on Kant, Hegel, and Sellars (Cambridge, MA: Harvard University Press, 2009.

13. Axel Honneth, *Suffering from Indeterminacy: An Attempt at a Reactualization of Hegel's Philosophy of Right; Two Lectures*, trans. Jack Ben-Levi (Assen, Netherlands: Van Gorcum, 2000).

must answer the prejudicial question, do Hegelian statements (here, those concerning objective spirit) still make sense when one abstracts them from the logical-speculative context of their justification? There is material here for fruitful debates.

As for me, I confess that on this essential question my opinion is, if not wavering, at least nuanced. Having started off from an orthodox (old Hegelian) position nourished by long contact with the *Logic*, I gradually realized that what interested me the most and seemed most relevant in the doctrine of objective spirit did *not always* need to be correlated with the logical-metaphysical infrastructure of the system in order to be judged valid. A good part of the doctrine of abstract law—which I aim to reevaluate in a positive manner—can be coherently understood independently of Hegelian metaphysics (by which I mean first and foremost the *Logic*, which Hegel explicitly tells us "takes the place of the former *metaphysics*").[14] But this is not always the case. On one decisive point, the question of the rabble (*Pöbel*), I believe I have shown that the solution Hegel seems to support (there *must* be a social and political solution to the social question) presupposes what I call a meta-ethical and metaobjective guarantee: the spirit of the world, the worldly figure of absolute spirit.[15] Moreover, this is what is suggested by the final paragraph of the *Philosophy of Right*, which in a sense places the principle of the internal opening of objective spirit in the direction of absolute spirit (religion, philosophy) and affirms—counterintuitively—that "the present has cast off its barbarism" and that, as a result, the state appears as "the image and actuality of reason."[16] Indeed, the doctrine of *Sittlichkeit* and even the doctrine of objective spirit in its entirety do not by themselves offer the means for thinking civil society's reconciliation (*Versöhnung*) with itself as *necessary*; they show, rather, the unavoidable nature of social fracture, as we would say today, and the ultimately aporetic character of the solutions that civil society and the state can implement to remedy it (such as aid for the poor or the policy of colonial expansion). But what does the idea that the structural contradictions of objective spirit can be resolved only from the point of view of absolute spirit mean if not that Hegel's metaphysics is the ultimate guarantee of the coherence of his philosophy of finite spirit and in particular of the doctrine of objective spirit?

14. *WdL* 1[1], *GW* 11, p. 32, or *WdL* 1[2], *GW* 21, p. 48 (*Science of Logic*, 42).
15. See below, chapter 6.
16. *RPh*, § 360, *GW* 14.1, p. 281 (*Elements*, 380; see *Outlines*, 323).

An anecdote recounted by Heine seems to confirm this: to the question, "Do you really believe that everything that is *wirklich* is *vernünftig*?" Hegel is said to have answered, smiling, "It could also be put: 'Everything that is rational, must be!'"[17]

Having arrived at this point, we must examine what exactly the term *metaphysics* refers to in the Hegelian context, where its meaning is obviously transformed.[18] I am aware that in the foregoing remarks I mentioned interpretations that are neither synonymous nor necessarily compatible with one another. I do not know exactly what Hegel thought about this question. (When it comes to his explicit formulations, I know, of course, like everyone else; what is less clear to me is the definition of a position in keeping with the overall intention of Hegelianism as I perceive or reconstruct it.) But I can attempt to define the spectrum of acceptable positions. They seem to me to fall between two extremes: (1) Hegel's metaphysics is his *Logic*; (2) Hegel's metaphysics is his doctrine of absolute spirit. It is not my goal here to choose between these two positions — there are good arguments for either one — but instead to show the stakes of these interpretive choices.

If it is true that the *Logic* "takes the place of" and at the same time "takes over for" traditional (precritical) metaphysics, then it must be said that it *is* the true metaphysics. So what is the intention of Hegelian logic? It is to show — in accordance with a strong understanding of what *logos* is[19] — that rational discourse is the very discourse of being, that logic is an onto-logic. According to its explicit ambition, Hegelian logic, setting itself apart from all that is said or thought by means of this word, including from the point of view of transcendental philosophy, claims to be not a discourse on being but

17. Günter Nicolin, *Hegel in Berichten Seiner Zeitgenossen* (Hamburg: Meiner, 2013), document 363, p. 235: "It could also mean: 'everything that is rational, must be.'"

18. See Hans Friedrich Fulda, "Spekulative Logik als die eigentliche Metaphysik: Zu Hegels verwandlung des neuzeitlichen Metaphysikverständnisses," in *Hegels Transformation der Metaphysik*, ed. Detlev Pätzold (Cologne: Dinter, 1991); Emmanuel Renault, "La Métaphysique entre logique et sciences particulières," in *Logique et sciences concrètes dans le système Hégélien*, ed. Jean-Michel Buée, Emmanuel Renault, and David Wittman (Paris: L'Harmattan, 2006). The state of the debate is summarized in Frederick Beiser, *The Cambridge Companion to Hegel* (Cambridge: Cambridge University Press, 1993), 1–20. Discussions with Bernard Mabille helped me to clarify my own position.

19. On this point, see the illuminating observations — in spite of the radically anti-Hegelian conclusions drawn from them — of Dominique Dubarle, *Logos et formalisation du langage* (Paris: Klincksieck, 1977), chaps. 1, 8–10.

rather the discourse *of* being. Hegel is then "just" a secretary taking dictation from the World Spirit, which through him thinks its own actuality. If this is the case (I mean, if one agrees not to disqualify this program immediately as paranoid or hypocritical), then Hegel's logic/metaphysics defines not only the conditions of possibility for thinking the thinkable (as does Kant's transcendental logic) but also the very regime of being engaged in a unique process of verification. To say that logic replaces metaphysics, understood as the science of being as being and not as the description of existents or as regional ontology, is thus to affirm that the program for a theory of (true) discourse of *substance* raising itself into *subject*—to use the terms of the preface to the *Phenomenology of Spirit*—must replace the program for a theory of the conditions of possibility of experience.

This hardly helps us assess the other position, the interpretation of metaphysics as the philosophy or science of absolute spirit in its triple register: art, religion, philosophy. My hypothesis is that this interpretation and everything that derives from it is of course required by Hegelianism's own self-representation but is not necessarily part of the development of "real [philosophical] sciences"—in any case, of the philosophy of nature and of finite spirit. In other words, the doctrine of objective spirit undoubtedly cannot be thought coherently without the *Logic* but perhaps can be without the philosophy of religion. However, on certain key points, this position is no longer tenable: once again, the way Hegel deals with the problem he highlights—the structural crisis of civil society—must give us pause. We know the solution he retains: the institutionalization of social life through corporations and proper enforcement by the rational state supplemented by an adroit policy of using the poor for colonial expansion allows for the gradual resolution of the fundamental contradiction of civil society (which here must be called *bourgeois* civil society) on the ground of world history, which is expressly mentioned in section 247 of the *Philosophy of Right* in order to emphasize the increasing role played by the globalization of trade, including at the cultural level. Now, the reasons for this speculative optimism[20] cannot be found in the doctrine of

---

20. To speak of speculative optimism obviously does not mean ascribing to Hegel the naive faith in the progress of the human spirit proclaimed by the *Aufklärung*; for him, it is the "work of the negative" that causes history, like any process, to advance. "Optimism" here designates only the proclaimed conviction that there will be an ultimate resolution of social and political contradictions.

objective spirit *alone*, although Hegel does not seem willing to admit as much. Here, we might read the half-worried, half-furious observations he makes over the course of the 1820s regarding the harmful effects of the freedom of enterprise[21] and of the suppression of corporations[22] as well as his tirade, at the end of the 1830 course on the philosophy of history, against the dangers liberalism (here, *political* liberalism of the French type) poses for old Europe. Obviously, old Hegel wasn't very optimistic about the health of *Sittlichkeit*! Consequently, what I, in the interest of simplicity, have named his speculative optimism can only be a *metaphysical*, counterintuitive optimism, the very optimism that caused him, in his lectures, to give the expression from the 1820 preface, "The rational is actual and the actual is rational," the sense of historical process — "the rational becomes actual and the actual becomes rational"[23] — and even of a speculative necessity: "it must be so!"

Which position to choose? Mine is the following, which I openly admit is *debatable*: when Hegel's speculative optimism (at least within the doctrine of objective spirit) seems to be contradicted by the state of the world or to contrast with what we are given to know of it, it is rooted not simply in the *Logic* as a theory of discourse and of being (onto-logic) but also in the doctrine of absolute spirit, or at least in that which within objective spirit echoes absolute spirit ("the spirit of the world"). If our concern is to discern the effective truth of Hegelian discourse and to make good use of it — in other words, if we read Hegel from a perspective that is neither historical nor "technological" in Martial Gueroult's sense — a good rule would seem to be to practice an *epokhè* toward statements whose strength of conviction seems exhausted as well as toward the context of meaning they belong to and to separate them (as much as possible, which can only be measured on a case by case basis) from the rest of the analysis. To return to my earlier example, we can take advantage of Hegel's analyses of the tensions of civil society and "social suffering" without thereby believing that the institutionalization of social life and good government policy necessarily provide a positive and definitive solution to these tensions. This amounts to considering that it is dialecticity that

---

21. See *W* 11, p. 567. See also chapter 6 below.

22. See G. W. F. Hegel, *Vorlesungen über Rechtsphilosophie* (Stuttgart: Frommann-Holzboog, 1974), 4:619.

23. G. W. F. Hegel, *Philosophie des Rechts: Die Vorlesung von 1819/20 in einer Nachschrift* (Frankfurt am Main: Suhrkamp, 1983), 51. See Dieter Henrich's commentary in his Introduction, 14–16.

constitutes the living, and possibly topical, element of Hegelian analyses but also that we probably must renounce what was perhaps for Hegel himself a purely metaphysical conviction: faith in a "true reconciliation that has become objective"[24] woven into the fabric of the human world. No doubt in doing so we sacrifice what is most ambitious in Hegel's metaphysics—that which, from his point of view, guarantees the "positively rational" coherence of the system: not only the doctrine of absolute spirit but also a significant part of the teaching of the *Logic*. It seems to me that this sacrifice is necessary because of what we are and what our world is: we no longer live up to the heights of absolute spirit. But to pronounce this diagnosis is still to be Hegelian in a certain way, by accepting the congruence of the rational and the actual.

---

24. *RPh*, § 360, *GW* 14.1, p. 281 (*Elements*, 380; see *Outlines*, 323).

The Actual and the Rational

"Was vernünftig ist, das ist wirklich; und was wirklich ist, das ist vernünftig."[1] This is undoubtedly the most often quoted expression in the entire Hegelian corpus and also the one that has most contributed to Hegel's bad reputation—perhaps we should say, to his bad reputations. Doesn't it contain within it all the ambiguities of *speculative dialectics*, to use the term that constantly reappears in the writings of Hegel's enemies? This, in any case, is what some of the most perspicacious first readers the *Philosophy of Right* already suspected, first and foremost Nikolaus von Thaden, a worthy representative of the Prussian administration that the work in question allegedly aims to glorify. In a letter to Hegel dated August 8, 1821, von Thaden presents "what was displeasing in [its] politics" to him, "a faithful soul, a zealous disciple."[2] There follows a long list of criticisms that constitute the first and nearly definitive version of the liberal argument against the *Philosophy of Right*. The disappointed disciple suspects Hegel of having, "out of enthusiasm for the princes," "justified the

---

1. "What is rational is actual; and what is actual is rational." *RPh*, *GW* 14.1, p. 24 (*Elements*, 20; see *Outlines*, 14).

2. Johannes Hoffmeister, ed. *Briefe von und an Hegel* (Hamburg: Meiner, 1952–1960), 2:278. For an English excerpt, see Hegel, *The Letters*, 462–65.

reality that exists in most states,"[3] and in particular in the Prussian state — in contradiction with the teachings that can and must be drawn from his philosophy and with the views that he had presented in the "famous article" of 1817 on the states of Wurtemberg. Von Thaden suggests that this piece, considered the most liberal of Hegel's texts (even if some, e.g., Niethammer, find it too "governmental" — according to him, it "defends a bad cause with great wit"[4]), might well contain Hegel's "true" political philosophy, meaning the only philosophy that conforms to the requirements of the system. Thus, the expression from the preface to the *Philosophy of Right* deserves special treatment. For von Thaden, this proposition, admittedly "the greatest, highest, and most important of all" is "philosophically true," but it is also "politically false,"[5] since it amounts to giving philosophical approval — Haym says "benediction" — to the most contingent and contestable aspects of reality: for example, the repressive and conservative policy of the Prussian state in applying the Carlsbad decisions after 1819. But the letter discusses only this latter aspect of the question. Von Thaden admits that this phrase from the preface is, in general, faithful to the broad lines of Hegelian philosophy; however, although he explains why it seems to him politically false or inappropriate, he does not say how it is philosophically true. So what then, exactly, does the equivalence of the actual and the rational mean when measured against the logical-systematic requirements of Hegelian philosophy?

The Real and the Actual

According to the common translation — which corresponds to the most frequent interpretation and, it would seem, to the obvious meaning of the words — the phrase from the 1820 preface means "what is rational is real and what is real is rational." It is easy to see where such an interpretation leads, for the vision of Hegelian philosophy that remains most widespread rests on it. When Hegel postulates that "*all* that is real is rational," doesn't he radically deny contingency, and in this way doesn't he sacrifice freedom — which he nevertheless constantly invokes — to a costly necessitarianism? Of course, we can note in passing the unconscious addition of a universal qualifier that

---

3. Hoffmeister, *Briefe von und an Hegel*, 2:278.
4. Letter to Hegel, dated December 27, 1817 (ibid., 2:172).
5. Hoffmeister, *Briefe von und an Hegel*, 2:279; Hegel, *The Letters*, 463.

is absent from the text, as well as the omission—or at least relegation to the rank of a mere indirect filler—of the other half of the couplet, which proclaims the actuality of the rational. But, at bottom, this does not change much. In the eyes of nearly all, Hegel remains the philosopher for whom being is but the garb of the concept and who thus embodies the most extreme version of idealism's mad ambition to "deduce" or "construct" everything that exists, including—as Krug perfidiously noted—the pen used to refute it.[6] From this fundamental and fundamentally false position follow the other vices of such a philosophy: first and foremost, what Haym and others called its quietism, its irresistible tendency to accord the "benediction of the concept" to everything that exists and everything that is done, including the most revolting acts. And from there comes the imputation of conservatism that among Hegel's opponents is so often associated with metaphysical suspicion of what is perceived as blind necessitarianism. Thus, Haym writes in the fifteenth chapter of his book on Hegel:

> In contrast with a politics of progress [embodied by Fries], the preface gives classical expression to the spirit of the Restoration, it pronounces *the absolute formula of political conservatism, quietism, and optimism*: . . . what is rational is actual, and what is actual is rational.[7]

In the century that followed, interpretations went even further, to the point of seeing in Hegelian philosophy an early anticipation of Nazi or Stalinist totalitarianism. The move from the tyranny of the concept to tyranny tout court would appear plausible: certain interpretations—though not necessarily the strongest ones—bluntly proclaimed it.[8]

---

6. See *W* 2, p. 195–97. On the question of contingency, see Dieter Henrich, "Hegels Theorie des Zufalls," in *Hegel im Kontext* (Frankfurt am Main: Suhrkamp, 1971); Jean-Marie Lardic, "La contingence chez Hegel," in G. W. F. Hegel, *Comment le sens commun comprend la philosophie*, trans. Jean-Marie Lardic, 63–114 (Arles: Actes Sud, 1989); Bernard Mabille, *Hegel: L'épreuve de la contingence* (Paris: Aubier, 1999).

7. Haym, *Hegel und Seine Zeit*, 365. Haym also says that "the Hegelian system became the scientific home of the spirit of the Prussian Restoration" (359).

8. See Karl Popper, *The Open Society and Its Enemies*, 2 vols. (Princeton, NJ: Princeton University Press, 1966); Hubert Kiesewetter, *Von Hegel zu Hitler: Die politische Verwirklichung einer totalitaren Machtstaatstheorie in Deutschland, 1815–1945* (Frankfurt am Main: Lang, 1995); Ernst Topitsch, *Die Sozialphilosophie Hegels als Heilslehre und Herrschaftsideologie*, 2nd ed. (Munich: Piper, 1981).

It is sometimes forgotten that in the second edition of the *Encyclopedia* (1827), Hegel formally contests such an interpretation of the dictum from the preface to the *Philosophy of Right* while at the same time conceding that "these simple propositions have seemed shocking to many."[9] To read him as saying that "[all] the real is rational" is to ignore the conceptual distinction that the *Science of Logic* establishes between *Realität* and *Wirklichkeit*, between the reality of empirical, contingent *Dasein*, as it is analyzed in the first section of the logic of being, and actuality, as it is presented in the third section of the logic of essence. There, Hegel specifies:

> But when I spoke of actuality, it should have been evident in what sense I am using this expression, since I treated actuality in my more extensive Logic, too. There I directly distinguished it not only from what is contingent (which, afterall, exists as well), but also and more specifically and precisely from existence [*Dasein*], concrete existence [*Existenz*] and other determinations.[10]

The real in the sense of the *Logic* is that which, characterized by the finitude of its qualitative determination and the variability of its quantitative limit, can always be other than what it is and even—this is the meaning of the famous being-nothing-becoming sequence with which the *Logic* opens— necessarily and incessantly *becomes* other than it is. Existence (*Dasein*), whose reflected expression is "reality," is "*being* with a *non-being*":[11] it suffers from an insurmountable negativity that identifies its positivity as a mix of being and nonbeing, being-self and being-other. However, within what is commonly called the real, this negativity remains enveloped, so to speak, within the massive and "naive" positivity of the existent, of what merely exists.

> In *reality*, as quality with the accent on being an existent, that it is determinateness and hence also negation is concealed; reality only has, therefore, the value of something positive from which negating, restriction, lack, are excluded.[12]

---

9. *Enzykl*, § 6 Anmerkung, *GW* 20, p. 45 (*Encyclopedia* 34).
10. *Enzykl*, § 6, *GW* 20, p. 45 (*Encyclopedia* 34).
11. *WdL* 1¹, *GW* 11, p. 67.
12. *WdL* 1², *GW* 21, p. 99 (*Science of Logic*, 85).

Thus, the real is existence in its insurmountable contingency and its factuality but also in the deceptive obviousness of its presence: it is *there*.

Actuality, on the other hand, is "essence which is one with its appearance,"[13] "the unity, become immediate, of essence and existence, or of what is inner and what is outer."[14] The result is that in the reality of immediate concrete existence, mediation, which is constantly hidden, can only manifest itself in the corrupting form of alteration and change, whereas what is actual is "exempted from *passing-over*."[15] But it is exempted precisely because its exteriority, its phenomenality or concrete existence (*Existenz*, as opposed to simple *Dasein*), do not presuppose any *Hintergrund*, any background on which its being and meaning would depend. From a Hegelian point of view, it is thus obvious that reality is something quite different from actuality: the two correspond to different levels of thought about what is. It is quite possible that actuality could be entirely rational, though the *Logic* does not specifically say so. On the other hand, reality cannot be absolutely rational, and the (empirical) real is often not rational at all: "Who is not smart enough to be able to see around him quite a lot that is not, in fact, how it ought to be?"[16] No doubt reality cannot be assigned any coefficient of rationality inasmuch as instability, variability, and inequality are inherent to it.

The Logical Status of Actuality

However, we are not out of the woods yet. Not satisfied with the *Encyclopedia*'s clarification, Rudolf Haym formulated a weighty objection. The dictum from the preface to the *Philosophy of Right* "contains in concentrated form all the duplicity of the system" in that, through conscious play on the "empirical" and "ideal" meanings of the term *wirklich*, it leads either to a contradictory conclusion or to a tautological one. If the term *wirklich* is taken as it is usually understood, in the sense of empirical reality, then the Hegelian thesis is contradictory, for it is obvious — Hegel himself agrees — that the real is saturated with irrationality. One could then just as easily write "the real is not real." But if we distinguish between *Realität* and *Wirklichkeit*, as the *Logic* tells us to, then the

---

13. *WdL* 2, *GW* 11, p. 243 (*Science of Logic*, 339).
14. *Enzykl*, § 142, *GW* 20, p. 164 (*Encyclopedia* 213).
15. *Enzykl*, § 142 Anmerkung, *GW* 20, p. 164 (*Encyclopedia* 214).
16. *Enzykl*, § 6 Anmerkung, *GW* 20, p. 46 (*Encyclopedia* 30).

preface's slogan becomes a tautology pure and simple: for what is the actual in the Hegelian sense if not precisely that which, within the real, is able to reveal its rationality? The famous catchphrase "what is actual is rational," then, says nothing more than "what is rational is rational."[17] In one case, one insists on the *actuality* that the rational has or must have, and the Hegelian dictum takes on a revolutionary cast: the real must be made to conform to what the philosopher considers to be rational. In the other case, one emphasizes the *rationality* of the actual (in the sense of what is given), and one arrives at conservative conclusions: the real, as it is, must be credited with rationality for, as Hegel says, "*what is* is reason."[18] But this cultivated ambiguity comes at the cost of an unacceptable doubling of the concept of *Wirklichkeit*: there would be an "empirical, phenomenal" actuality and a "true, rational" actuality.[19]

Is it possible—and if so, how—to respond to this objection, one of the strongest ever made against the 1820 preface's formulation and perhaps even against Hegelian philosophy overall, of which it stands as an emblem? To find out, it is necessary to return to the analysis of actuality developed in the *Logic*. If we want to avoid not only Haym's conclusions but above all the suspicion of inconsistency that they cast over the system (the same term has two distinct *and* incompatible meanings), we should of course maintain the conceptual unity of *Wirklichkeit*, which does not rule out recognizing within it a specific semantic thickness analogous to that of other terms Hegel seizes onto in order to reproduce—thanks to lexical suppleness and in spite of the limitations of the propositional form—the very movement, the processuality, that constitutes all reality. The best example of the lexical polyvalence that Hegelian philosophy acquires by exploiting the lexical resources of natural language is of course the famous *Aufheben*, which as Hegel emphasizes has, in ordinary language, the double meaning of "to preserve" and "to put an end to." He adds the following specification, which seems to apply to all the other terms that speculative philosophy uses in order to think the real in its processuality:

17. Haym, *Hegel und Seine Zeit*, 368 ff.

18. *RPh, GW* 14.1, p. 15 (*Elements*, 21; see *Outlines*, 15). See Haym, *Hegel und Seine Zeit*, 369: "Revolutionary in its logical part, the system is conservative in its practical part." This judgment is identical to Engels's in *Ludwig Feuerbach*, where, however, the intention is the opposite: to valorize the system's revolutionary potential.

19. Haym, *Hegel und Seine Zeit*, 368.

It must strike one as remarkable that a language has come to use one and the same word for two opposite meanings. For speculative thought it is gratifying to find words that have in themselves a speculative meaning.[20]

We can in fact consider that it is the suppleness of natural languages (a word never has *one* meaning or *one* context of use) that makes them more suitable than formalized language for expressing dialecticity or processuality. But it is clear that mobilizing the resources of language is quite different from passively accepting its ambiguities. We then assert that there is no confusion between "reality" and "actuality" in Hegel's texts, or between the trivial meaning and the philosophical meaning of "actuality," though this does not mean that Hegel does not play on the proximity between these terms and these meanings in common language.

So what then of *Wirklichkeit* within Hegelian logic? We must first consider where the examination of *Wirklichkeit* takes place: not within the doctrine of being, like the examination of reality, but rather within the doctrine of essence. It is not part of the study of thought in its immediacy but rather of thought "in its *reflection* and *mediation*."[21] This placement indicates that the actual, unlike simple, real *Dasein*, is from the outset given a depth that has to do with the fact that within it the inessential and the essential, contingency and necessity, are intertwined: there is, in actuality, a distance of self from self, a mobility, an active reflexivity that contrasts with the immediate coincidence with itself or with its own determinacy that is the hallmark of concrete existence, of the real in its immediacy. Essence designates in general the negativity and reflexivity that are always inherent to being in the apparent immediacy of its positivity or existence: "essence is past — but timelessly past — being."[22] Consequently, within *actuality* in the logical sense of the term, immediacy and mediation, exteriority and interiority, negativity and positivity are copresent, and each expresses itself in the terms of the other. The actual is an immediacy that carries within itself the present trace of the mediation that structures it: it is an exterior term that is entirely inhabited by the interiority toward which it points; a positive saturated with negativity. But this distance from self, this reflexivity,

---

20. *WdL* 1², *GW* 21, p. 94 (*Science of Logic*, 82).
21. *Enzykl*, § 83, *GW* 20, p. 120 (*Encyclopedia* 133).
22. *WdL* 2, *GW* 11, p. 241 (*Science of Logic*, 337).

is here — contrary to the first two sections of the logic of essence — grasped in the movement of its reduction and not any longer in the movement of its emergence. This is the sense of the distinction between the shining (*Scheinen*) of essence, or its reflection within itself, and the appearance (*Erscheinen*) of this essence, understood as interiority, within the externality of a concrete existence or a phenomenon (*Erscheinung*) and the (self)-manifestation of actuality.[23] *Wirklichkeit* in its totality designates the mobile, processual coincidence of the inner and outer, whatever name they go by: substance and accident, necessity and contingency, cause and effect. This process is what Hegel calls *manifesting* or *revealing*, where revealing is understood as the fact that essential "interiority" "is, in and for itself, nothing *but this: to express itself*."[24] Thus, unlike the forms of immediacy previously encountered (being, existence, phenomenon), "the actual is therefore *manifestation*. . . . This means that in its externality, and only in *it*, it is *itself*."[25]

We must be more precise. Actuality is the culmination of the dialectics of essence, and Hegel, outlining a comparison between the structures of essence and the structures of being, suggests that actuality is in a sense the being for self of essence, just as existence and phenomenon are essence's concrete existence:

> Absolute essence in this simple unity with itself has *no existence* [*Dasein*]. But it must pass over into existence, for it is *being-in-and-for-itself*; that is to say, it *differentiates* the determinations which it holds *in itself*. . . . Since essence is at first *simple* negativity, in order to give itself existence and then being-for-itself, it must now posit in *its* sphere the determinateness which it contains in principle only *in itself*.[26]

With actuality, essence bends back on itself, so to speak, or rejoins itself after having exposed itself to the risk of externality. But this does not mean that the actual has absorbed the essential figures of externality (existence, ap-

---

23. On these three dialectical modalities of essence and the relation between them, see *WdL* 2, *GW* 11, p. 380–81 (*Science of Logic*, 477–78).

24. *WdL* 2, *GW* 11, p. 368 (*Science of Logic*, 464).

25. *WdL* 2, *GW* 11, p. 381 (*Science of Logic*, 478). See *Enzykl*, § 142, *GW* 20, p. 164 (*Encyclopedia* 213): "The utterance [*Äusserung/extériorisation*] of the actual is the actual itself."

26. *WdL* 2, *GW* 11, p. 242 (*Science of Logic*, 338–39).

pearance) into a pure interiority; to the contrary, actuality is in a sense nothing but externality; its interiority is exhausted in its external expression. This is explained by the specific characteristics of essence's process. Born out of the initial and massive duality of "indeterminate" essence and the appearance to which being is temporarily reduced with regard to essence, the process by which essence *posits* its determinations—identity and difference, foundation and what is founded, essence and existence, essentiality and phenomenon, inner and outer—can be understood as a way of confronting, in order to overcome it, the dualistic tendency of the metaphysics Hegel is combating. The thought of actuality, "essence which is one with its appearance,"[27] requires abandoning all understanding of what is on the basis of a presupposed background; it manifests the full coincidence of being and reason for being in a movement in which what is revealed is not united with the medium of being within which it manifests itself. Thus, what Hegel says about the necessary in his presentation of absolute necessity can be applied to the actual in general: it "only *is* because it *is*."[28] It *is* absolutely, without remainder—this is its dimension of externality or existence—but it is *because* it is, it is the raison d'être of its being—this is its dimension of inwardness or reflexivity.

The end of the second book of the *Logic* and the beginning of the third teach us that this process of constituting a surface without depth—or rather, a surface that is its own depth—leads from essence, which is an inwardness "glowing" or "appearing" within a network of external configurations, to *concept*, which is the free subject of infinite self-affirmation and is its own "development."[29] Consequently, the actual, capable of manifesting itself from itself and not within a foreign or predetermined milieu is, at bottom, nothing other than the prefiguration of the concept, freedom expressing itself—and it *must* do so—in the vocabulary of necessity. In other words, its process guarantees the conversion of necessity into freedom. But, insofar as actuality still bears the trace of the dualities whose *Aufhebung* it constitutes, it still only stands "on the threshold of the Concept."[30]

27. *WdL* 2, *GW* 11, p. 243 (*Science of Logic*, 339).

28. *WdL* 2, *GW* 11, p. 391 (*Science of Logic*, 487).

29. "The progression of the Concept is no longer either passing-over or shining into another, but *development*." *Enzykl*, § 161, *GW* 20, p. 177 (*Encyclopedia* 237). The addition to this paragraph clarifies that with this development, "only that is posited which is already implicitly present."

30. *Enzykl*, § 156 Zusatz, *W* 8, p. 302 (*Encyclopedia* 231).

Wirklichkeit is thus the becoming concept of being, always already mediated by the negativity of essence — and only this becoming. Let us admit that in the Hegelian system, the rational is identified with the concept. Strictly speaking, this is true only of the idea, which corresponds to "the proper philosophical meaning of 'reason.'"[31] But the idea, which itself is only "the unity *in-itself* of the subjective and the objective . . . posited as *being-for-itself*,"[32] is at bottom nothing other than the coming to expression of the immanent rationality of the actual, of its being-concept.

> As distinct from mere appearance [*Erscheinung*] actuality, being initially the unity of inward and outward, is so far from confronting reason as something other than it, that it is, on the contrary, what is rational through and through; and what is not rational must, for that very reason, be considered not to be actual.[33]

But the rationality of the actual stands in need of an explanation: the word *concept* is the *name* for this explanation.

We may thus say that the analysis of *Wirklichkeit*, as it is carried out at the end of the objective logic, describes the movement of the rational arriving at the position of *subject* of the *real* or of objectivity, where subjectivity is understood not as an anthropological determination but as the very vitality of the concept — the concept, "which, being dialectical, breaks through its own barrier, and opens itself up into objectivity"[34] — and where reality is understood as the infinitely open field in which "objective thought" — a thinking production of being by itself — is deployed. This last formulation expresses nothing other than the immanence of thought to the world, to actuality in the logical sense of the term. By its constitution, actuality thus testifies to the congruence of the "rational" and the "real":

> To say that there is understanding, or reason, in the world is exactly what is contained in the expression "objective thought." But this expression is inconvenient precisely because "thought" is all too commonly used as if it

---

31. *Enzykl*, § 214, *GW* 20, p. 216 (*Encyclopedia* 88).
32. *Enzykl*, § 212, *GW* 20, p. 214 (*Encyclopedia* 86).
33. *Enzykl*, § 143 Zusatz, *W* 8, p. 280 (*Encyclopedia* 214).
34. *Enzykl*, § 192 Zusatz, *W* 8, p. 345 (*Encyclopedia* 268).

belonged only to spirit, or consciousness, while "objective" is used primarily just with reference to what is unspiritual.[35]

In a sense, then, Haym is not wrong to judge the Hegelian identification of the rational with the real and the real with the rational to be either tautological or grossly contradictory. However, there is one crucial caveat: this identity is neither a fact nor a given but rather both the stakes and the result of an infinite process of adjustment between the concept and being, a process whose fundamental constitution the *Logic* exposes and whose concrete figures are presented, in all their diversity, by the "real sciences," in particular the doctrine of objective spirit. This is why in the 1819–1820 course on the philosophy of right, we find the equation from the 1820 preface expressed in terms of movement: "what is rational *becomes* actual, and what is actual *becomes* rational."[36]

"Reason That Is"

What does the phrase whose speculative content I have just presented imply for the "real [philosophical] sciences" and in particular for the doctrine of objective spirit? This is the question of the "relation of philosophy to actuality," which gives rise to "misunderstandings." The principled answer that Hegel gives to this question comes out of his understanding of actuality but also exceeds it in part. Here is his answer:

> Since philosophy is *exploration of the rational*, it is for that very reason the
> *comprehension of the present and the actual*, not the setting up of a *world
> beyond* which exists God knows where.[37]

This sentence highlights another aspect of the thesis of the rationality of the actual, one that the rest of the preface forcefully emphasizes, with clearly polemical intent:[38] the refusal of all *normativism*. It is not philosophy's task to prescribe what reality must or should be, for *beyond* the real or being there is

---

35. *Enzykl*, § 24 Anmerkung, *GW* 20, p. 67–68 (*Encyclopedia* 56).

36. Hegel, *Philosophie des Rechts*, 51. There is no need to indulge in haphazard conjectures about why Hegel did not, in the end, retain the preface's formulation.

37. *RPh*, *GW* 14.1, p. 13 (*Elements*, 20; see *Outlines*, 13).

38. I do not deal with this aspect here. Information on the context can be found in the "Présentation" section of my translation of the *Philosophy of Right* as well as in Adriaan Peperzak's

nothing; in any case, nothing other than the void of an incantatory and self-referential discourse. Philosophy's task is rather to "to comprehend *what is* ... for *what is* is reason."[39] *What is*: not, of course, immediate concrete *Dasein* insofar as it is empirical, or even existence or phenomenon, which are always as if at a distance from the essentiality they reflect, but rather the actual, the present as the presence and actuality of the rational. *Reason*: not an abstractly normative reason claiming to teach the world how "it ought to be"[40] but rather reason that is the "*thought* of the world,"[41] or the self-thought of a world that discovers that it bears truth, and learns to regard itself as such. But then, if the equation of the actual and the rational signifies nothing other than the congruence of rationality with itself, the concordance of "reason as self-conscious spirit" and "reason as present actuality,"[42] then isn't Haym's suspicion that the Hegelian formula is a flat-out tautology justified in spite of what I have just tried to claim?

To answer this question, it is useful to refer to what Hegel says about Plato's *Republic* in the *Philosophy of Right* and in the lectures on the history of philosophy. His argumentation should be compared with Kant's on the same subject;[43] the comparison shows that although the two philosophers have different strategies, when it comes to the relationship between ideality and normativity, they both seek to do justice to what, in Plato, falls under the "tension of the concept." What does Hegel say? The Platonic city is "a proverbial example of an *empty ideal*"[44] because it rules out choosing one's social position (which is imposed) or one's spouse (sexual communism) as well as private property: it eliminates everything that modern mankind demands in the name of the idea of freedom. These measures do indeed consistently exclude "the principle of subjective freedom."[45] But this exclusion is not some whim

---

meticulous commentary in the preface to *Philosophy and Politics* (Norwell, MA: Kluwer Academic, 1987).

39. *RPh, GW* 14.1, p. 15 (*Elements*, 21; see *Outlines*, 15).

40. *RPh, GW* 14.1, p. 15 (*Elements*, 21; see *Outlines*, 15).

41. *RPh, GW* 14.1, p. 16 (*Elements*, 23; see *Outlines*, 16).

42. *RPh, GW* 14.1, p. 15 (*Elements*, 22; see *Outlines*, 1).

43. See *KrV, Ak.* 3, A 316, B 372–73.

44. *RPh, GW* 14.1, p. 14 (*Elements*, 20; see *Outlines*, 13).

45. *GdP, W* 19, p. 123 (*Lectures on the History of Philosophy*, 109). Hegel also speaks of "repression of the principle of individuality."

of Plato's or the trait of a totalitarian fantasy. It proves that he, better than his contemporaries, understood just how much the principle of autonomy—which philosophy was the first to valorize by proclaiming everyone's right to think for himself—contradicted the very essence of Greek *Sittlichkeit*, whose purest expression is democracy:

> Established ethicality [*Sittlichkeit*] has in general the relation of the substantial, and therefore is maintained as divine. This is without question the fundamental determination. The determination which stands in contrast to this substantial relation of the individual to established morality is the subjective will of the individual.[46]

The *Republic* declares the incompatibility of Greek *Sittlichkeit* and the "substantial" rationality around which it was ordered with subjective self-determination; in imagistic terms, it demonstrates the necessity of Socrates' execution and perhaps also—though developing this point would lead us too far astray—Christ's. It was Plato's great merit to have foreseen—precisely in trying to eliminate it—the political effect that the emergence of "subjective freedom"[47] would necessarily have. It is the hallmark of modern *Sittlichkeit* to hold that the universal cannot truly be universal unless it welcomes within itself the principle of particularity and recognizes the right of subjects to think and desire for themselves and that the state must let develop within itself a civil society that carries its "unilateral principle" to its logical conclusion. Indirectly, Plato helps us think through this. In a single movement, the author of the *Republic* grasped "the nature of Greek ethics" and discerned that it was "being penetrated by a deeper principle"[48] that would rattle and then replace it: he exposes the essence, in all its rationality, of the *polis*, pointing out the historical limits of this rationality and, consequently, the inscription of *all* rationality within a *history*. Thus, he simultaneously demonstrates the rationality of the actual (the *Republic* is an ideal-type that captures the deep meaning of

---

46. *GdP, W* 19, p. 113–14 / (G. W. F. Hegel, *Lectures on the History of Philosophy*, vol. 3, *Medieval and Modern Philosophy*, trans. Frances H. Simson and E. S. Haldane (Lincoln: University of Nebraska Press, 1995), 98 modified.

47. *RPh*, § 124 Anmerkung, *GW* 14.1, p. 110 (*Elements*, 151 see *Outlines*, 122).

48. *RPh, GW* 14.1, p. 14 (*Elements*, 20; see *Outlines*, 13).

Greek historical reality) and the actuality of the rational (what this philosophy proscribes is precisely "the pivot on which the impending world revolution turned"[49]).

The equivalence of the rational and the actual, of reason that thinks and reason that is, is thus no more tautological when it is grasped in the domain of objective spirit than it is in a strictly logical context: moreover, who would claim that the *Republic* proposes a copy of the Athenian city or even a simple inverted image of it? The identity between them is of the order of a process or a history. As Plato's example shows with perfect clarity, this history is the history by which objective spirit as ethicality (*Sittlichkeit*) produces an image of itself in *thought* and in so doing works toward its own transformation. Hence, it becomes clear that Hegel's resolute refusal of normativism — philosophy always comes too late to tell the world what it *must* be — does not at all prevent the concept from having intrinsic normative power. To the contrary, philosophy demands it if it is true that the idea "is not so impotent that it merely ought to be, and is not actual."[50] But this normativity remains immanent to the field of objectivity to which it applies. It is therefore necessary to stop representing the concept or norm as the product of a subjectivity defined at an anthropological level, freely disposing of its productions. The norm of the true — the "rational" — far from any separation between *Sollen* and *Sein*, which, according to Hans Kelsen,[51] is the precondition of any coherent normativism, is present at the heart of the historical world — the "actual" — "as the rose in the cross of the present,"[52] to quote the enigmatic expression from the 1820 preface. In my opinion, we may take this to mean that the true — the speculative — is something like an indicator of the fact that, within a world not yet reconciled with itself, a world prey to suffering and contradiction, the dimension of *Versöhnung* is not only present in the mode of the implicit or potential but is truly actual inasmuch as it is this alone that makes it possible to conceive of a *future* for the world. But, at bottom, is this future of a historical world itself historical in nature? Is it *another* figure of the world or *another* world?

49. *RPh, GW* 14.1, p. 14 (*Elements*, 20; see *Outlines*, 13).

50. *Enzykl*, § 6 Anmerkung, *GW* 20, p. 46 (*Encyclopedia* 30).

51. "The difference between is and ought cannot be explained furthermore. We are immediately aware of the difference." Hans Kelsen, *Pure Theory of Law* (Gloucester, MA: Smith, 1989), p. 5.

52. *RPh, GW* 14.1, p. 15–16 (*Elements*, 22; see *Outlines*, 15).

The Object of the Doctrine of Objective Spirit

What does the doctrine of objective spirit as a "real science" deal with? With the real, of course, or rather with the actual, whose immanent rationality or concept this doctrine brings to expression. As the example of the *Republic* has very clearly shown, this does not mean that it is a mere copy of the real: to grasp the rationality of the actual is to reveal the drive that moves the real and carries it beyond itself; it is to think the contradiction that will usher in a new world. The 1820 preface contains famous, though enigmatic, remarks on this topic. Let us first highlight two judgments that at first seem contradictory at the very least: philosophy "is *its own time comprehended in thoughts*,"[53] and "what matters is to recognize in the semblance of the temporal and transient the substance which is immanent and the eternal which is present."[54] How can philosophy simultaneously be the "daughter of its time" and the expression of a timeless truth—even when its object is intrinsically historical? What, indeed, can a political *philosophy* speak of if it has no normative vocation and if its object—the state—is by its nature engaged in history and exposed to contingency?

A passage from the preface can put us on the path to answering these questions:

> This treatise, therefore, in so far as it deals with political science, shall be nothing other than an attempt to *comprehend and portray the state as an inherently rational entity.* . . . Such instruction as it may contain cannot be aimed at instructing the state on how it ought to be, but rather at showing how the state, as the ethical universe, should be comprehended.[55]

It should henceforth be understood that it is not philosophy's role to imagine what the state should be: as we have seen, Hegel judges all forms of normativism to be incompatible with the subordination of thought to the present or the actual. But in what sense is it philosophy's task to present how the state *must be comprehended*? According to a perspective such as that of Haym or

53. *RPh, GW* 14.1, p. 15 (*Elements*, 21; see *Outlines*, 15).
54. *RPh, GW* 14.1, p. 14 (*Elements*, 20, modified; see *Outlines*, 14).
55. *RPh, GW* 14.1, p. 15 (*Elements*, 21, modified; see *Outlines*, 14–15).

Ilting, this affirmation proves Hegel's political "quietism," or, to put it harshly, his servility; didn't he write to chancellor Hardenberg in 1821 that the *Philosophy of Right* was "the immediate auxiliary to the government's beneficent intentions"?[56] But it seems to me that this statement can be understood in another way if we agree to take seriously the stated claim of Hegel's philosophy to be both "exploration of the rational" and "comprehension of the present and the actual."

Philosophy is a thinking of the present. Its vocation is thus to be the rational knowledge of actuality, or rather to let actuality arrive, within itself, at awareness of its own degree and shape of rationality. But just as actuality is not identical with reality, the present that philosophy thinks is not what occurs contingently; it is the timeless presence of the rational within the time of the event:

> In philosophy . . . we are concerned not with what belongs exclusively
> to the past or to the future, but with that which *is*, both now and eter-
> nally — in short, with reason. And that is quite enough to occupy our
> attention.[57]

We must add that this eternity of the rational, emphasized quite provocatively at the beginning of the *Science of Logic*,[58] has no place that is distinct from the real: it *reveals* itself in the real not as a masked inwardness but rather as the mediation that binds the real to itself. Despite the preface's recourse to a metaphorical register that evokes the essentialist representation of a background truth (there is a "brightly colored covering" that one must "penetrate" in order to find the "core" of truth),[59] in the "real science" of objective spirit, Hegel maintains the teaching of speculative logic: that is, that the revelation or manifestation that is proper to the actual in its rationality (in its becoming-

---

56. Hoffmeister, *Briefe von und an Hegel*, 2:214. Cf. Hegel, *The Letters*, 459.

57. G. F. W. Hegel, *Die Vernunft in der Geschichte* (Hamburg: Felix Meiner, 1955), 210; *Lectures on the Philosophy of World History*, trans. Hugh Barr Nisbet (Cambridge: Cambridge University Press, 1975), 171.

58. "This content [of logic] is *the exposition of God as he is in his eternal essence before the creation of nature and of a finite spirit.*" WdL 1¹, GW 11, p. 17, or WdL 1², GW 21, p. 34 (*Science of Logic*, 29).

59. RPh, GW 14.1, p. 14 (*Elements*, 21; see *Outlines*, 14).

concept) is not that of an "Other" of the actual; its "being-there is only the *manifestation of itself,* not of an other."[60]

In these circumstances, what is the object of political philosophy (in Hegelian terms, the doctrine of objective spirit) given that this object can be defined analogously to that of other "real sciences"? What is it to teach "how the state must be recognized"? It is to show, within the real, the presence of what both "actually" structures it and what attests to its immanent limitation. To think the political — but also law, civil society, and history itself — as "the image and actuality of reason"[61] is to measure what, within its *own* constitution, exceeds it. Not in the sense that there would be, beyond the state and history, an absolute, intangible, metaphysical truth: infinite spirit has no space distinct from the space of spirit in its subjective and objective finitude. But rather in the sense that the thought of truth — and also the thought of the truth of the state and history — is that which assigns them a limit from within simply because it is of the order of knowledge. Philosophy, as the thought of the rational in actuality, indicates the insurmountable limit of every form or degree of actuality, which stems from the fact that its thought logically precedes its being (which is paradoxically expressed as a chronological delay):

> When philosophy paints its grey in grey, a shape of life has grown old, and it cannot be rejuvenated, but only recognized, by the grey in grey of philosophy; the owl of Minerva begins its flight only with the onset of dusk.[62]

The thought of spirit in its actuality only comes at dusk, precisely when one of its figures ceases to be actual. This is why this thought only becomes complete in transgressing its object — that is, in revealing itself to be philosophy tout court. The conjunction of the rational and the actual, the cornerstone of Hegel's philosophy, demonstrates the "relativity of political philosophy"[63] at the same time as it defines its task.

---

60. *Enzykl,* § 142, *GW* 20, p. 164 (*Encyclopedia* 393).

61. *RPh,* § 360, *GW* 14.1, p. 281 (*Elements,* 380; see *Outlines,* 323).

62. *RPh, GW* 14.1, p. 16 (*Elements,* 23; see *Outlines,* 16).

63. Bernard Bourgeois, *La pensée politique de Hegel* (Paris: Presses Universitaires de France, 1969), 6.

PART I

The Law

The Positivity of Abstraction

Because of the adjective Hegel attaches to it, abstract law is generally considered to be secondary within the economy of objective spirit, just as (although for different reasons) morality is. If *Sittlichkeit* is the concrete milieu in which "freedom, as the *substance*, exists no less as *actuality* and *necessity* than as *subjective* will,"[1] law and morality are *abstract*, which in the Hegelian context means at the very least that they are not fully intelligible by themselves. For many commentators, antilegalism is a characteristic trait of Hegelianism, which thus finds itself far from the dominant opinion within postrevolutionary political philosophy, which saw rights as the inalienable condition of political freedom. Against this common interpretation, I would like to establish here that *because of its very abstraction*, abstract law is judged positively by Hegel to the extent that it is indispensable for adequately thinking the concept of law in a way that accounts for social and political modernity and history as the history of the actualization and concretization of law. This is what I show, at a general level, in the first chapter, which seeks to explain the expansion that the concepts of law and right undergo in Hegel's treatment. The second chapter shows that this expansion makes it possible to overcome the difficulties of modern theories of natural law by thinking of law as "between nature and his-

1. *RPh*, § 33, *GW* 14.1, p. 48 (*Elements*, 62; see *Outlines*, 50).

1

tory." The third chapter studies Hegel's discussion of the concept of contract: far from being a necessary tool for understanding the nature of the *political* relationship, as in the dominant current of modern thought (culminating with Fichte), the contract is what makes it possible to connect abstract law and modern *civil*, "bourgeois" society, which actualizes its principles by making it possible to think the juridical conditions of the social.

The Objectivity of Willing

> Will making itself its own object is the basis of all Right
> and Obligation.[1]

Let us begin with this paragraph from the introduction to the *Philosophy of Right*:

> *Right* is any existence [*Dasein*] in general which is the *existence* of the *free will*. Right is therefore in general freedom, as Idea.[2]

The first thing to take from this passage — to which we could add a parallel paragraph from the *Encyclopedia*[3] — is that there is a strong equivalence between *freedom, will*, and *right*. This equivalence makes it possible to define the position of what Hegel calls *objective spirit*. But what exactly do these concepts cover? In particular, what does the conjunction of will and right signify? This is what we must specify. One thing, however, is clear from the outset: within

---

1. *W*, 12:524; *Lectures on the Philosophy of World History*, 442.
2. *RPh*, § 29, *GW* 14.1, p. 45 (*Elements*, 58; see *Outlines*, 46).
3. *Enzykl*, § 486, *GW* 20, pp. 479–80 (*Encyclopedia* 243).

Hegelian philosophy the content of such concepts is different from their usual understanding, so it would be hasty, to say the least, to classify Hegel as a legal voluntarist, as sometimes has been done, on the grounds that he defines right as "the *existence* of the *free will*." There are several indications of this. First of all, following Kant—at least Kant of the *Doctrine of Right*[4]—Hegel clearly distinguishes will (*der Wille*) from free choice (*die Willkür*): free choice, as the power to choose between possibilities, is only an aspect or moment—a moment of extreme tension[5]—of the will, which is a force of *rational* self-determination. Second, Hegel is consistent in his rejection of the usual definition (which is also Kant's) of law as a *limitation* of the will or free choice of each individual according to a universal rule. Indeed, that definition makes the will or free choice of the particular individual the primary principle of law rather than the "rational will which has being in and for itself,"[6] and thus it entails an irremediable deficit of universality. Finally, we must insist on the originality of the Hegelian definition of *freedom*: understood in general as "being at home with oneself in the other,"[7] it can in no case be understood as the predicate of an isolated subjectivity, closed in on itself; it is rather a movement of objectification by an interiority that does not preexist this movement but constitutes itself thanks to it. Not only is freedom not the opposite of necessity, but the former necessarily passes through the latter, and in it, freedom "acquires the *form of Necessity*."[8] A notion such as that of "objective will,"[9] used to introduce the concept of objective spirit or law in the broad sense, illustrates the shifts that the Hegelian definition of law presupposes.

4. Kant, *MdS*, Einleitung, *AA* VI, pp. 213, 226; *Practical Philosophy* [*PP*], pp. 374, 380.

5. "Instead of being the will in its truth, arbitrariness is rather the will as *contradiction*." *RPh*, § 15 Anmerkung, *GW* 14.1, p. 39 (*Elements*, 48; see *Outlines*, 38). See *Enzykl*, § 145 Zusatz, *W* 8, p. 285 (*Encyclopedia* 206).

6. *RPh*, § 29 Anmerkung, *GW* 14.1, p. 80 (*Outlines*, 47, see *Elements*, 58).

7. The "thinking of necessity" (that is, freedom) "is its going-together with *itself* in the other" (*Enzykl*, § 159 Anmerkung, *GW* 20, p. 176 [*Encyclopedia* 234]). "To be sure, necessity as such is not yet freedom; but freedom presupposes necessity and contains it sublated within itself" (*Enzykl*, § 158 Zusatz, *W* 8, p. 303 [*Encyclopedia* 233]).

8. *Enzykl*, § 484, *GW* 20, p. 478 (*Encyclopedia* 241). The second edition of the *Encyclopädie* (1827 [*Enzykl*]) says "realize its concept . . . in the externally objective realm" (§ 485, *GW* 19, p. 353). See also *Enzykl*, § 385, *GW* 20, p. 383 (*Encyclopedia* 20): "a *world* produced and to be produced by it [spirit]."

9. *Enzykl*, § 486, *GW* 20, p. 480 (*Encyclopedia* 242).

The Strata of Willing

The distinction between understanding (or reason) and will plays a constitutive role in modern philosophy, at least its dominant strand. As Descartes, who did not invent the distinction but did give it decisive significance, says,

> All the modes of thinking that we experience within ourselves can be brought under two general headings: perception, or the operation of the intellect, and volition, or the operation of the will.[10]

Of course, Kant complicated the schema by distinguishing between understanding and reason and by adding a third term, the faculty of judgment, to the "powers of the mind." But knowing and willing, thinking and wanting are still the two fundamental powers of the mind. The will, explains Kant, is "a power [of all rational beings] to determine their causality by the presentation of rules,"[11] and one cannot conceive of reason determining the will (that is to say, of reason being "practical in-itself") unless one has an adequate concept of the freedom of the will—in this case, the concept of autonomy, "the sole principle of all moral laws."

Hegel rejects this dualism between theory and practice, between knowledge and will, and he thus sets "practical philosophy" (which in his work no longer goes by that name) on a new path. In both the *Logic* (the penultimate chapter of which deals with "the idea of cognition") and in the *Encyclopedia*'s theory of subjective spirit, Hegel insists on the fundamental continuity—a continuity, it is true, that is less linear than circular, and less consecutive than dialectical—between thinking and willing, between theory and practice. Thus, we read in an Addition in the *Encyclopedia*,

> For ordinary thinking, thought and will fall outside of each other. But in truth . . . thought determines itself into will and remains the substance of the latter; so that without thought there can be no will.[12]

---

10. René Descartes, *The Principles of Philosophy*, I, art. 32, in René Descartes, *The Philosophical Writings of Descartes*, trans. John Cottingham, Robert Stoothoff, Dugald Murdoch, and Anthony Kenny (Cambridge: Cambridge University Press, 1985), 1:204.

11. Kant, *KpV, Ak.* 5, p. 32.

12. *Enzykl*, § 468 Zusatz, *W* 10, p. 288 (*Encyclopedia* 227–28). See also *Enzykl*, §§ 443–44,

Two aspects of this continuity should be emphasized. First, practical spirit (the will) is less the complement or competitor of theoretical spirit than the result of theoretical spirit going deeper within itself: thinking intelligence takes complete ownership of the object it believed it would merely find and meet as a given and posits itself as the reason that produces this objectivity (and thus is practical):

> But when intelligence is aware that it is determinative of the content, which is *its* mode no less than it is a mode of being, it is Will.[13]

Second, the will is not solely the outcome of theoretical spirit or intelligence. The will itself, at least from the philosopher's point of view, includes a dynamism that tends to reproduce in it the element from which it results (thinking, the intellectual act). With what the third edition of the *Encyclopedia* calls "free spirit,"[14] there is, at the transition point between subjective spirit and objective spirit—thus, at the point of contact between the finite subject and the juridical and ethical-political objectivity of a common world—a resurgence of knowledge within the will in the form of the *universal*:

> Actual free will is the unity of theoretical and practical spirit: a free will, which realizes its own freedom of will. . . . This universalism, the will has as its object and aim, only so far as it thinks itself, knows this [as] its concept, and is *will* as free *intelligence*.[15]

Let us not be fooled into thinking that this is an empty dialectical game. To the contrary, we must convince ourselves that the reciprocal implication and copenetration of knowing and willing are essential to the project of a "philosophy of spirit"—an expression, we must remember, created by Hegel, as was the doublet *Naturwissenschaften-Geisteswissenschaften*. In brief, this project as-

---

GW 20, pp. 437–39 (*Encyclopedia* 227) and WdL 3, GW 12, p. 177–78, 231–32 (*Science of Logic*, 675, 728–30).

13. *Enzykl*, § 468, GW 20, p. 465 (*Encyclopedia* 227).

14. *Enzykl*, §§ 481–82, GW 20, p. 476 (*Encyclopedia* 238–40). These two paragraphs correspond, in the first edition, to the two first paragraphs of the section on objective spirit (*Enzykl* 1817, §§ 400–401, GW 13, p. 224 [*Encyclopedia* 1817, 201]).

15. *Enzykl*, § 481, GW 20, p. 476 (*Encyclopedia* 238–39, modified).

pires to make objective spirit (*objectivity* in law, morality, and ethical-political institutions) — that is, this *"world* produced and to be produced by"[16] spirit — appear as the outcome, or rather as the always necessary presupposition of subjectivity (in the ordinary sense of the term). In other words, the reciprocal implication of the theoretical and the practical, of knowing and willing (which are here anything but "faculties" of an empirical or transcendental subject), is what allows Hegel to develop a nonsubjective concept of spirit, which includes an objective moment that is just as necessary as its subjective moment. And only such a concept — which in reality is only consistent insofar as, beyond these two finite moments, it fits into the infinite processual totality of *absolute spirit* — makes it possible to give meaning to the following statement, which disrupts the idea we have of both spirit and knowledge:

> If to be aware of the Idea . . . is a matter of *speculation*, still this very Idea itself is the actuality of men — not something which they *have*, as men, but which they *are*.[17]

However, although the Hegelian doctrine of will excludes the usual dichotomy between knowing and willing, theoretical and practical, it also endeavors to *integrate* the various classical conceptions of will by relativizing them and making them into moments, partial and, as such, nonindependent aspects of a *unified* and speculative concept of will. This concept is itself considered under the aforementioned conception — perhaps the guiding idea of Hegelian philosophy — of freedom as *Beisichsein im Anderen*, as being at home with oneself in and thanks to what is other than oneself or through alienation from oneself. It is appropriate here to mention quickly the stratification of the concept of the will as it is presented in detail (more so than in the *Encyclopedia*) in paragraphs 5 to 28 of the introduction to the *Philosophy of Right*.[18] Indeed, this stratification is what accounts for the necessity of the objectivization of the

---

16. *Enzykl*, § 385, *GW* 20, p. 383 (*Encyclopedia* 20).

17. *Enzykl*, § 482 Anmerkung, *GW* 20, p. 477 (*Encyclopedia* 240).

18. This passage (*RPh*, *GW* 14.1, p. 32–45; *Elements*, 37–58; see *Outlines*, 28–46) must be read in parallel with §§ 388–401 of the 1817 *Encyclopedia* (*Enzykl* 1817, *GW* 13, p. 217–24 [*Encyclopedia* 1817, 235–41]) or with *Enzykl* §§ 469–82, *GW* 20, p. 466–77 (*Encyclopedia* 228–41; or, in the second edition, *GW* 19, p. 344–52). A very detailed commentary on the introduction to the *Philosophy of Right* can be found in Adriaan Peperzak, "Zur Hegelschen Ethik," in *Hegels Philosophie des*

will—in other words, the transition from subjective spirit to what Hegel calls objective spirit.

The text first presents (§§ 5–10) what we may call the determinants of the process of the will. These consist of the three moments—the universal, the particular, and the individual—of the not-yet-developed concept of the will (§§ 5–8) as well as the principles of the differentiation or particularization of "abstract" or "formal" will, which *"finds* an external world outside itself" (§§ 8–10):[19] an active relation to the given that is the world and the (necessary) determination that consists in giving this abstract will a content or purpose, which is a matter of "translat[ion] . . . into objectivity."[20] In a second phase, which corresponds to the bulk of the passage, Hegel studies in succession the three figures the will takes when it leaves abstraction. These are less separate forms of the will than integrative moments whose dynamic totalization alone gives access to the fully developed idea of the will: "the *immediate* or *natural* will" (§§ 11–13); free choice (*Willkür*), "the commonest idea [*Vorstellung*] we have of freedom,"[21] which is analyzed in its constitutive "contradiction" or in the dialectical tension that sets it against drives, desires, and passions (§§14–20); and finally, the "will which is free in and *for itself,*" which is "truly infinite" (§ 22, p. 54) and which, as actual infinity (*infinitum actu*), is universal and objective as well as subjective (§§ 21–28).

Without going into a detailed examination of this difficult passage, which attests to the innovativeness of the Hegelian conceptualization of the will, it must be emphasized that the passage clearly aims to *integrate* the various competing conceptions of freedom into a concept that can house all of them but that can also relativize them by highlighting what is unilateral in them: the concept of a freedom that has only itself as object (the "free will which wills the free will," says § 27) and not out of autism but because it finds itself in its object and only in this way can it access its identity, which is inseparably both subjective and objective. There can only be a willing subject insofar as that subject seeks to gain its own subjectivity in things and knows that only in this way can it constitute its subjectivity:

Rechts: Die Theorie der Rechtsformen und ihre Logik, ed. Dieter Henrich and Rolf-Peter Horstmann (Stuttgart: Klett-Cotta, 1982).

19. *RPh,* § 8, *GW* 14.1, p. 35 (*Elements,* 42–43; see *Outlines,* 33).

20. *RPh,* § 9, *GW* 14.1, p. 35 (*Elements,* 43; see *Outlines,* 34).

21. *RPh,* § 15 Anmerkung, *GW* 14.1, p. 38 (*Elements,* 48; see *Outlines,* 37).

The activity of the will consists in cancelling [*aufheben*] the contradiction between subjectivity and objectivity and in translating its ends from their subjective determination into an objective one, while at the same time remaining *with itself* in this objectivity. . . . This activity is the *essential development* of the substantial content of the Idea, a development in which the concept determines the *Idea*, which is *itself* at first *abstract* to [produce] the totality of its system. This totality, as the substantial element, is independent of the opposition between a merely subjective end and its realization, and is *the same* in both of these forms.[22]

Let us retain from this brief analysis that one does not really *think* the will, in the complexity of its being and manifestations, when it is reduced to one of its *moments*, given that in Hegel a moment is always a nonindependent aspect of a totality. The will cannot be identified with either the natural will, which is immediate and finite and exhausts itself in a singular, prejudgmental decision that takes into consideration one or another of our contradictory affects, or with free choice (*Willkür*), the reflexive power to make a deliberate choice between the abstract possibilities represented by one's drives and desires, or even with the will that is free in and for itself, taken in isolation (which nevertheless wills itself *objectively* in the world of objectivity that it encounters and inhabits). So what, then, is the will? Nothing other than the dynamic *system* of these different moments, which can be identified within common representations and which certain philosophies (it is not difficult to put names to the descriptions Hegel gives) have taken unilaterally to be the entirety of the will. The Hegelian concept of the will is not the concept of a thing or the concept of a faculty that would be a thing ("the soul") that produces certain effects. It designates, rather, a process inseparable from the process of thought, which links together and relativizes the partial meanings that can be attributed to this process and which carries as if to its conclusion the idea of an *objectivization* of the will—an objectivization that is less the effect of action by subjectivity than the apparently given presupposition of action: the "way of the will" consists in "mak[ing] itself objective spirit."[23]

22. *RPh*, § 28, *GW* 14.1, p. 45 (*Elements*, 57–58; see *Outlines*, 46).
23. *Enzykl*, § 469, *GW* 20, p. 466 (*Encyclopedia* 228).

Objectivization: Law

From the beginning, what distinguishes practical spirit and theoretical spirit, will and intelligence, is that the latter presupposes its object (the world to be known, which it takes in or seems to take in as a given), whereas the will, as Kant indicates, is the power to "produce objects corresponding to one's presentations"[24]: it engenders its objects, which are neither things nor ideas but actions, or rather schemata of actions, that include a normative claim. It is thus normal that the development of practical spirit, whose different strata I have just presented (and which are all moments of a dynamic conception of willing), should culminate in an objectivization of initially (apparently) merely subjective will. In reality, it will appear that, in keeping with the progressive-regressive structure of the Hegelian method,[25] this objectivization of the will in legal, social, and political norms and institutions is *presupposed* by the constitution of subjective will while this subjective will at the same time *posits*, from itself, the necessity of this objectivization. Finite subjectivity (which is finite precisely because it is *only* subjective), in going to its limit, is led to find or recognize itself in the "actuality of a world,"[26] in which it encounters the ends it posits as its own, in the objective form of institutionalized norms.

This is carefully presented in Hegel's development of the idea of the good in the penultimate chapter of the *Logic*. The paradox or contradiction—but we must remember that "the thought of contradiction is the essential moment of the concept"[27]—of what Hegel calls the syllogism of action is that action supposes both (1) that the purpose it prescribes for itself has not been realized (otherwise there would be no need to act) and (2) that in a certain way it is always already realized in the sense that the world is in some way disposed to receive the purposes of the acting subject (otherwise action would always shatter against the resistance of the world). But this contradiction must be thought in its productive dynamic: to grasp its fecundity, one needs merely

24. Kant, *KpV, Ak.* 5, p. 15.

25. On this point, see the methodological considerations in the last chapter of the *Science of Logic*. For example, "each step of the *advance* in the process of further determination, while getting away from the indeterminate beginning, is also a *getting back closer* to it" (*WdL* 3, GW 12, p. 251 [*Science of Logic*, 750]).

26. *Enzykl*, § 484, GW 20, p. 478 (*Encyclopedia* 241).

27. *WdL* 3, GW 12, p. 246 (*Science of Logic*, 745).

to bring together the two premises of the syllogism and to accept (this is the paradox inherent to all acting and all willing) that "the *purpose of* [*the action*] is being achieved and equally is not being achieved."[28] Hegel specifies this idea in his lectures and shows how it implies overcoming Kantian and Fichtean normativism:

> The good ought to be realised; we have to work at this, to bring it forth, and the will is simply the good that is self-activating. But then if the world were as it ought to be, the result would be that the activity of willing would disappear. Therefore the will itself also requires that its purpose shall not be realised. This correctly expresses the finitude of willing. . . . The will knows the purpose as what is its own, and intelligence interprets the world as the Concept in its actuality. This is the genuine position of rational cognition.
>
> What is null and vanishing constitutes only the surface of the world, not its genuine essence. This essence is the Concept that is in and for itself, and so the world is itself the Idea. Unsatisfied striving vanishes when we [re]cognise that the final purpose of the world is just as much accomplished as it is eternally accomplishing itself.[29]

The transition from subjective spirit to objective spirit (from will to law and rights) corresponds to the discovery that individual subjectivity and universal objectivity are in a way preordained for one another. But it should be added, as Hegel immediately does, that "this agreement between is and ought is not rigid and unmoving, however, since the final purpose of the world, the good, only *is*, because it constantly brings itself about."[30] Contrary to a commonly raised suspicion, the concept of objective spirit does not imply any quietism, any "benediction of what exists" (Rudolf Haym); it does not mean that all good purposes are always already realized, and even less that the good is always already accomplished in a world eternally identical to what it must be. Far from subscribing to such a conservative metaphysics, Hegel considers that action, always necessary, always urgent, must reside in the space of play that separates and binds an unbridled subjectivity, supremely ignorant of the "right of the world," and an objectivity that is illusorily believed to be closed

---

28. *Enzykl*, § 234, *GW* 20, p. 227 (*Encyclopedia* 301).
29. *Enzykl*, § 234 Zusatz, *W* 8, p. 387 (*Encyclopedia* 302).
30. *Enzykl*, § 234 Zusatz, *W* 8, p. 387 (*Encyclopedia* 302).

in on itself, autotelic. The world of objective spirit is, however, neither soft wax nor impenetrable granite; this is what is established by the analysis of *Sittlichkeit* in its twofold subjective and objective dimension.[31] The world is disposed to receive the effort that is always demanded of subjectivity while at the same time it constantly reminds subjectivity of the conditions of objectivity of its acting. Thus, actual will can only exist within a world open even to the will's most anarchical expressions because they are secretly congruent with it.

Why then does Hegel assign the name *law* to segments of objective spirit, giving this term a meaning that deliberately goes beyond its legal usage? This metonymical function of law has something to do with the *institutionalism* of the Hegelian doctrine of objective sprit.[32] The legal order, even reduced to abstract law alone (the private law of jurists, or at least its rational substructure), is in a way the paradigm of an *institutional system*: it is a set of universal and objective determinations that, escaping the grasp of actors (law is unavailable to them) nevertheless appears as that which can provide a meaning, or at least a description, to their acts. In other words, it is because Hegel thinks that abstract law founds an "objective individuality" and institutes "rights without subjects"[33] that he can make it a *blueprint* for objective freedom. It is true that only ethical institutions (familial, social, and political institutions) form "developed and actualized rationality."[34] But this ethical "second nature," this set of institutional configurations that the "political disposition"[35] of individuals invigorates and structures, does nothing more than carry out and realize the formal structure defined by abstract law: the institutional conversion of subjectivity into *personality*, the indefinite thing into a legally classified thing, in which "I, as free will, am an object [*gegenständlich*] for myself."[36] In short, the objectification of freedom, the sole motive for the entire doctrine of objective

---

31. "The identity—which is accordingly *concrete*—of the good and the subjective will, the truth of them both, is *ethicality*. . . . The *ethical* is a subjective disposition, but of that law which has being in itself" (*RPh*, § 141 and Anmerkung, *GW* 14.1, p. 135 (*Elements*, 185–86, modified; see *Outlines*, 152).

32. See below, part 4, preliminary, and chapter 12.

33. These terms are taken from Maurice Hauriou, representative par excellence of legal institutionalism; see Maurice Hauriou, *Principes du droit public* (Paris: Sirey, 1916), 93 ff.

34. *RPh*, § 265, *GW* 14.1, p. 211 (*Elements*, 287; see *Outlines*, 239).

35. *RPh*, § 268, *GW* 14.1, p. 211 (*Elements*, 288; see *Outlines*, 240). See also chapter 11, below.

36. *RPh*, § 45, *GW* 14.1, p. 57 (*Elements*, 76; see *Outlines*, 61).

spirit, finds its fundamental organization in law in the narrow sense, in the "abstract law" of jurists.

One of the main reasons for the exemplary value accorded to abstract law is its promotion of a "subjectless" concept of the will. Hegel—and I am aware that here I am going against the still-dominant opinion according to which he is mistaken about the intellectual construction of law[37]—bases himself on what can be called an immanent philosophy of the formal legal order all in order to contest the *subjectivist* understanding of the concept of the will dominant among philosophers. When Hegel talks about "objective will,"[38] when he talks about the reciprocal institution of persons and things, his argument outrages philosophers trained in the Kantian or Fichtean tradition. But his argument would be much less shocking to a jurist, who is used to defining, for example, property as the objectification of a will (*animus*) through material indexes (*corpus*). If, as an eminent historian maintains, "the Romans did not consider *corpus* and *animus* as two independent established facts, one objective, the other subjective, but rather grasped two sides of a process represented as one unit,"[39] then we can agree that the Hegelian conception of objective spirit (of law in the broad sense), like the objectification of will, is in general terms in accord with Roman law (of which it is at most an extrapolation—and this also obviously does not mean that Hegel subscribes to the dominant interpretation of the Roman theory of property law, which was put forward in 1803 by Savigny in *Das Recht des Besitzes*).

To conclude, let us summarize what we have seen so far.

(1) The will cannot be conceived as a faculty of a subject, nor can an act of willing be conceived as a simple exercise of decision by this faculty; the *objectification* of the will must therefore be thought of as the necessary culmination of the dialectical deployment of its components. The will is only fully adequate to itself, is only a free will willing its own freedom, by investing things and being invested in things, which it first does *qua* legal will.

---

37. This point of view is exemplified by Michel Villey, "Le droit romain dans la philosophie du droit de Hegel," *Archives de Philosophie du Droit* 16 (1971).

38. *RPh*, § 13 Anmerkung, *GW* 14.1, p. 37, and § 26, p. 44 (*Elements*, 47 and 55. See *Outlines*, 36, 44).

39. Max Kaser, *Das römische Privatrecht* (Munich: Beck, 1955), 1:331.

(2) Thanks to the operators of person, property, and contract, abstract law is the paradigm of such an objectification of the will. It is entirely a system of institutional objectification of freedom, and this is why it can be regarded as a formal sketch of the sphere of objective spirit in its entirety.

(3) But legal will is not only objective will: it is also, or tends to be, a universal and rational will. However, it only *tends* toward this, and this is what, for Hegel, marks the limit of the law in general and of objective spirit: it contains only "the *existential* side of reason."[40] If, as the preface to the *Philosophy of Right* indicates, there must be congruence between reason that thinks and reason that is,[41] then it seems that the sphere of objective reason has an impassable limit. Indeed, following the teaching of the *Logic*, for Hegel, the reconciliation between objective rationality (law, ethics) and rational thought (philosophy) cannot take place in the field of objectivity. In other words, objective spirit ("law") cannot develop the rationality inherent to it except by going beyond its limits both as law and as will. This limit is the limit that constitutes for objective spirit its objectivity, and going beyond it constitutes the transition from objective spirit to absolute spirit: "genuine objectivity," Hegel writes, "is only in the medium of *thought*."[42]

---

40. *Enzykl*, § 482, *GW* 20, p. 476 (*Encyclopedia* 239).
41. See *RPh*, *GW* 14.1, p. 15 (*Elements*, 21; see *Outlines*, 15).
42. *Enzykl*, § 562 Anmerkung, *GW* 20, p. 548 (*Encyclopedia* 297).

Law

Its Concept and Actualizations

There is one point on which, with few exceptions, partisans, adversaries, casual readers, and recognized specialists of Hegel have all agreed: Hegel's philosophy does not look favorably on the notion of law. Thus, an established specialist writes, "Law is not Hegel's God . . . Hegel hardly prizes law or freedom of the person."[1] Indeed, doesn't Hegel constantly describe law—at least, the law he calls "limited juristic law"[2]—as formal and abstract?[3] And doesn't the *Phenomenology of Spirit*, as well as the *Lectures on the Philosophy of History* (in the section on the Roman world), paint a merciless picture of the state of law or legal status (*Rechtzustand*)?[4] And isn't it necessary to go beyond the sphere of abstract law in order to arrive at the essential truth of the human world, which is an ethical-*political* truth? From this point of view, law in the strict sense—which in Kantian practical philosophy is foundational and, in a

1. Jacques d'Hondt, "La personne et le droit abstrait selon Hegel," in *Droit et liberté selon Hegel*, ed. Guy Planty-Bonjour (Paris: Presses Universitaires France, 1986).

2. *Enzykl*, § 486, *GW* 20, p. 479 (*Encyclopedia* 218).

3. See in particular *RPh*, *GW* 14.1, § 30, p. 46; § 33, p. 48; § 36, p. 52 (*Elements*, 59, 62, 69; see *Outlines*, 47, 50, 55). See also *Enzykl*, *GW* 20, § 486, p. 479; § 487, p. 481; § 529, p. 501.

4. See *PhG*, *GW* 9, pp. 260–64 (*Phenomenology*, ¶¶ 477–83). The courses on the philosophy of history describe the *Rechtszustand* as the "complete absence of law and right" (*vollendete Rechtslosigkeit*). See *Geschichte*, *W* 12, p. 387.

way, insurmountable: *fiat justitia, pereat mundus* (let there be justice, though the world perish)[5] — seems instead like a bad moment to be passed through. Of course, in 1820, when Hegel published an amply fleshed-out version of the part of the system that, since the first 1817 edition, the *Encyclopedia* had somewhat esoterically termed *objective spirit*,[6] Hegel titled the version *Elements of the Philosophy of Right* — a remarkable expression, all the more remarkable as it was unusual at the time. But this innovation, which was actually offset by a more classical subtitle — *Naturrecht und Staatswissenschaft* (Natural law and the science of the state) — seems above all intended to relativize law by grounding it in an extralegal — even antilegal — context of which the state, which Hegel thinks should be "venerate[d] as an earthly divinity,"[7] is the determining element. In the assertion that each stratum of objective spirit (law, morality, family, civil society, state, history) features as a "stage in the development of the Idea of freedom" and has "its distinctive right"[8] is the germ of the subordination of formal law, which becomes no more than a "subordinate moment" of this "altogether different sphere": the state, sole authentic bearer of "actual and concrete spirit."[9] Since the second half of the nineteenth century, this antilegalism and even contempt for law, which so sharply distinguishes Hegel from Kant — for whom "politics must always bend a knee"[10] to

5. Kant considers this maxim to be "a bit emphatic, but true." See *Frieden, Ak.* 8, p. 379; *PP*, p. 345. Hegel, in his early writings on the constitution of the German *Reich* transforms it ironically into *"fiat justitia, pereat Germania!"* Hegel, *W* 1, p. 470; *Hegel's Political Writings*, trans. Lawrence Dickey and Hugh Bar Nisbet (Oxford: Oxford University Press, 1964), 151.

6. See *Enzykl* 1817, § 399, *GW* 13, p. 223 (*Encyclopedia* 1817, 240). The preference for this term instead of that of *natural law* is justified by the lectures of 1817–1818: "The term 'natural right' or 'natural law' [*Naturrecht*] ought to be abandoned and replaced by the term 'philosophical doctrine of law' [*philosophische Rechtslehre*], or (as will also emerge) 'doctrine of objective spirit.'" G. W. F Hegel, *Vorlesungen über Naturrecht und Staatswissenschaft (Heidelberg 1817/18)* (Hambourg: Meiner, 1983), 6; *Hegel: Lectures on Natural Right and Political Science: The First Philosophy of Right*, trans. Michael J. Stewart and Peter C. Hodgson (Oxford: Oxford University Press, 2012), § 2A, p. 52.

7. *RPh*, § 272 Zusatz, *W* 7, p. 434 (*Elements*, 307; see *Outlines*, 258). See *Die Vernunft in der Geschichte*, 1:12; *Lectures on the Philosophy of World History*, 95: "The divine principle in the state is the Idea made manifest on earth."

8. *RPh*, § 30 Anmerkung, *GW* 14.1, p. 46 (*Elements*, 59; see *Outlines*, 47).

9. *RPh*, § 126 Anmerkung, *GW* 14.1, p. 112 (*Elements*, 154; see *Outlines*, 124).

10. Kant, *Frieden, Ak.* 8, p. 386; *PP*, p. 351. Beginning with his early writing on the German constitution, Hegel opposes Kantian legalism, where he sees a disturbing moralism; he attacks the "philanthropists and moralists" who "decry politics as a struggle and a device for seeking

law—has found a convenient explanation with several variants.[11] These run as follows: Hegel, a contemporary of the first theoreticians of the *Rechtstaat* (Robert von Mohl, Rudolf von Gneist, Lorenz von Stein) was, in fact, the precursor of ideologues of the *Machtstaat*. This, at least, was the image of him held by sycophants and detractors of state power alike, and shared by a large audience: Hegel as an enemy avant la lettre of the envelopment of the state by law, which is, it seems, characteristic of modern democracy. Since then, Hegel studies have convincingly shown that lumping Hegel in with the doctrinaires of *Realpolitik* and imperialism was overly hasty.[12] For many, however, it remains the case that he contributed to the "myth of the state," of which contemporary totalitarianism marks the ultimate development. If, as Cassirer says, Hegel contributed to this myth "more than any other philosophical system,"[13] this was through the simultaneous exaltation of politics and devalorization of law that marked his thought. Therefore, it is not surprising that the "return of law" we have witnessed over the past few years in the French philosophical scene has often targeted Hegel and his Marxist legacy.

The argument I have just summarized cannot be brushed aside: it would be unreasonable to contest the existence of Hegelian antilegalism. But it is possible to understand "antilegalism" in a variety of ways. For the sake of simplicity, let us focus on two quite distinct attitudes that term may designate: first, a hostility to law and rights that goes along with doubt about their capacity to form a specific order, and second, a hostility to legalism—that is,

---

one's own advantage at the expense of the law, as a system and work of injustice." Hegel, *W*, 1:504; *Hegel's Political Writings*, 209. The condemnation of legalism is equally strong in the mature texts: see *RPh*, § 333 Anmerkung and §337 Anmerkung, *GW* 14.1, pp. 270, 271–72 (*Elements*, 368, 370; see *Outlines*, 313, 314).

11. Two typical examples, which have had a lasting influence on the perception of Hegelianism are, in Germany, Haym, *Hegel und seine Zeit*, and in France, Charles Andler, *Les origines du socialisme d'état en Allemagne* (Paris: Alcan, 1897).

12. See in particular Bourgeois, *La pensée politique de Hegel*; d'Hondt, "La personne et le droit abstrait selon Hegel."; Franz Rosenzweig, *Hegel und der Staat (1920)*, 2 vols. (Aalen: Scientia, 1962); Eric Weil, *Hegel et l'état* (Paris: Vrin, 1994); Domenico Losurdo, *Hegel und das deutsche Erbe* (Cologne: Pahl-Rugenstein, 1989); *Hegel e la libertà dei moderni* (Rome: Editori Riuniti, 1992); Joachim Ritter, "Hegel und die französische Revolution," in *Metaphysik und Politik* (Frankfurt am Main: Suhrkamp, 2003).

13. Ernst Cassirer, *The Myth of the State* (Oxford: Oxford University Press, 1946), 248 f. Cassirer refuses to see Hegel as simply a precursor to totalitarianism, although he does claim that "no other philosophical system has done so much for the preparation of fascism and imperialism" (273).

to the absolutization of law as such. There are good arguments to be made that Hegel, at least in his mature writings, adopts the second attitude and professes what we might call a *weak antilegalism*.[14] From this perspective, it can be shown that Hegel both affirms the full autonomy of what he calls abstract law and judges necessary its relativization by the state, which is itself irreducible to any legal model. As we shall see, it is possible to understand that there is no contradiction between these two assertions only on the basis of a conception of civil society as the authentic, though conflictual, realization of the principles of the abstract legal order. But before anything else, it is important to assess the recasting of the classic concept of law performed by Hegel's thought. Only this will allow us to understand why, while proclaiming the limits of "narrow legal law," Hegel can at the same time emphatically maintain that law is "something *utterly sacred*, for the simple reason that it is the existence [*Dasein*] of the absolute concept, of self-conscious freedom."[15]

The "Philosophical Science of Law": Concept and Idea

> The subject-matter of *the philosophical science of law* is the *Idea of right*—the concept of law and its actualization.[16]

This preliminary definition of the philosophy of law is based on the distinction between concept (*Begriff*) and idea (*Idee*). The latter adds to the former (which Hegel sometimes calls "the simple concept," the "concept as such," or the "concept of the concept"[17] in order to distinguish it from the completed, fully developed concept) the dimension of realization or actualization. This

14. An example of *strong* antilegalism can be found in Carl Schmitt, who makes the sovereign political decision the founding moment of the law. See Carl Schmitt, *Political Theology*, trans. Joseph W. Bendersky (Chicago: University of Chicago Press, 2005), 10, 13, 30–32; *Politische Theologie*, trans. Joseph W. Bendersky (Berlin: Duncker und Humblot, 1990), 16, 19–20, 41–43. Strong antilegalism can also be found in the young Hegel, whose "The German Constitution" was a point of reference for Schmitt.

15. *RPh*, § 30, *GW* 14.1, p. 46 (*Elements*, 59, modified; see *Outlines*, 47).

16. *RPh*, § 1, *GW* 14.1, p. 23 (*Elements*, 25; see *Outlines*, 17).

17. See, for example, *WdL* 3, *GW* 12, p. 29 (*Science of Logic*, 526): "This is now the concept itself of the concept, but *at first only* the concept of the concept or also itself *only* concept."

distinction is presented and grounded in the *Logic*, as is the key notion of *Verwirklichung* (actualization) on which it relies.

The concept in the Hegelian sense is not to be understood as a general representation developed by a thinking subject, although it does immediately suggest this mangled and provisory meaning:

> The shape of the *immediate* concept constitutes the standpoint that makes of the concept a subjective thinking, a reflection external to the *subject matter*. This stage constitutes, therefore, *subjectivity*, or the *formal concept*.[18]

In its full meaning—that is, as it is constituted through the process that connects the three moments of the "subjective concept" (the concept as such, judgment, and syllogism)—the concept is thought itself as subject, actor, and prime mover of its development. It refers to thought's capacity to self-posit or self-produce, an autoaffection (to use Fichtean terminology) to which subjective thought, in the common sense of the term—for example, the philosopher's thought—is, so to speak, merely a spectator. The true subject of the concept, in the various senses of the term, is not a finite consciousness but rather the real in its totality, expressed in and through the concept and its fundamental articulations, which are (plural) determined concepts. Hence, "the logical forms of the concept" are not "dead . . . receptacles of representations," which would make them the objects of "a completely superfluous and dispensable *description*"; instead, they are *"the living spirit of what is actual,"*[19] the soul of the real. Thus, the subjective concept has a *necessary* relation to objectivity, a relation far more complex than that between empty form and inert content. Objectivity is not a given, closed world that faces the thinking subject; it is rather "the *real concept* that *has emerged from its inwardness* and has passed over into existence."[20] As Hegel understands it, objectivity is the realization of the concept in exteriority, "immediacy as which the concept has determined itself by the sublation of its abstraction and mediation"[21] such that the pulse of the concept, which is the soul of objectivity, seems to have

18. *WdL* 3, *GW* 12, p. 30 (*Science of Logic*, 527).
19. *Enzykl*, § 162 Anmerkung, *GW* 20, p. 178 (*Encyclopedia* 132).
20. *WdL* 3, *GW* 12, p. 30 (*Science of Logic*, 527).
21. *WdL* 3, *GW* 12, p. 130 (*Science of Logic*, 628).

disappeared within it; in reality, however, it is only the appearance of the exteriority of subjective thought with respect to the objective real that vanishes. According to the *Logic*, objectification is the decisive act by which the concept, going beyond the interiority of a privileged relationship to itself, verifies its ability to organize the objectivity of things and is experienced as an immanent structuring of the world. We must still analyze the unity of the subjective and the objective that is first given in an immediate — and thus external — manner. In the sense of speculative logic, the idea, the "subject-object,"[22] is the *process*[23] that dialectically unifies the subjective concept and objectivity without destroying their difference. Thus, the idea, in its mobility and inexhaustible vitality, is *"the adequate concept, the objectively true, or the true as such."*[24] In the Hegelian sense, an idea is entirely different from a "simple idea," if by that is meant a subjective representation devoid of any content of reality. Instead, it expresses the rational texture of the real (of objectivity), *its* thought *of itself,* "for the externality has being only as determined by the concept and as taken up into its negativity."[25] In the Hegelian sense, the idea is reason — but reason incorporated into materiality.[26] This reason thus no longer has anything to do with some subjective faculty or anthropological determination; in Hegel, reason is the philosophical name for the process by which subjectivity and objectivity, thought and worldly reality, infinitely overlap without ever being completely identical, which would be the death of all thought.[27] Thus, the idealism that Hegel claims (and doesn't he assert that "every genuine philosophy is *Idealism*"?[28]) comes down to this fundamental, two-part thesis: all reality, or rather actuality, is conceptual, and there is no concept that is not objectivized in the human and natural world. Above, I analyzed the meaning and conse-

---

22. *WdL* 3, *GW* 12, p. 176 (*Science of Logic,* 673). See also *Enzykl* 1817, § 111, *GW* 13, p. 73 (*Encyclopedia* 1817, 102) and *Enzykl,* § 162, *GW* 20, p. 177. This designation is borrowed from Schelling, who uses it both in the *System of Transcendental Idealism* (1800) and in the *Presentation of My System of Philosophy* (1801); it already existed in Fichte, in the *Attempt at a New Presentation of the* Wissenschaftslehre (1797) in *Werke* 6.

23. "The Idea is essentially *process,* because its identity is only the absolute and free identity of the Concept, because this identity is the absolute negativity" (*Enzykl,* § 215, *GW* 20, p. 218 [*Encyclopedia* 290]).

24. *WdL* 3, *GW* 12, p. 173 (*Science of Logic,* 670).

25. *WdL* 3, *GW* 12, p. 176 (*Science of Logic,* 674).

26. *WdL* 3, *GW* 12, p. 176 (*Science of Logic,* 674).

27. *Enzykl,* § 214 Anmerkung, *GW* 20, pp. 216–18 (*Encyclopedia* 288–90).

28. *Enzykl,* § 95 Anmerkung, *GW* 20, p. 134 (*Encyclopedia* 152).

quences of such a definition: we know that it expresses the conviction—which is ultimately a metaphysical and speculative conviction—that there is a fundamental coherence between the rational and the actual, between "reason that is conscious of itself" and "reason that *is*."²⁹ We must now specify the consequences of this for the conceptualization of law.

How can the above account of the logic of the concept help us understand the status of what Hegel calls the philosophical science of law and decode its definition in the *Philosophy of Right*? First of all, it allows us to give specific content to the distinction between the concept and idea of law, which Hegel describes in section 2 of the introduction:

> The science of law is *a part of philosophy*. It has therefore to develop the *Idea*, which is the reason within an object [*Gegenstand*], out of the concept; or what comes to the same thing, it must observe the proper immanent development of the thing [*Sache*] itself. As a part [of philosophy], it has a determinate *starting point*, which is the *result* and truth of what *preceded* it, and what preceded it is the so-called *proof* of that result. Hence the concept of law, so far as its *coming into being* is concerned, falls outside the science of law; its deduction is presupposed here and is to be taken as *given*.³⁰

We must first understand why Hegel writes that "the concept of law falls outside the science of law"—quite a surprising statement on the face of it. To do so, we must be attentive to the distinction between concept and idea. If for Hegel law is "freedom, as Idea,"³¹ this is because law participates in the objectivization of a principle that is initially subjective or inner—that is, freedom—which is the defining feature of spirit, or, to use a later term, of "*culture*," as distinct from "nature" and the universe of necessity, while also being essentially connected to it. Freedom is thus the *concept* that becomes objective via the successive strata of objective spirit, unfolding itself in the *idea* that is, in the totality of its determinations, the idea of the law. By thus defining the object of the *philosophical* science of law—in truth, for Hegel, there is no philosophy that is not scientific³²—he is emphasizing that law is wholly of the order of an

---

29. *Enzykl*, § 6, *GW* 20, p. 44 (*Encyclopedia* 29). See the prologue above.
30. *RPh*, § 2, *GW* 14.1, p. 23 (*Elements*, 26, modified; see *Outlines*, 18).
31. *RPh*, § 29, *GW* 14.1, p. 45 (*Elements*, 58; see *Outlines*, 46).
32. When Hegel says of the science of law that it is "a part of philosophy" (*RPh*, § 2, *GW* 14.1,

objectivization of what is initially a (merely) subjective principle, its "simple concept." This concept itself is the culmination of the process of subjective spirit,[33] a process thus akin to the philosophical deduction of law and rights. This is indeed why paragraphs 5 through 28 of the introduction to the *Philosophy of Right* recapitulate the final steps of this process.[34] The entire sphere of objective spirit (i.e., of law in the broad sense) bears the mark of this first determination. The movement included in this sphere—a movement whose phases are like the strata of the *idea* of law—is actually the negative rejoinder to the movement of subjective spirit. Whereas subjective spirit conquers its own determination (freedom) against the naturalness that initially subsumed it (under the figure of the soul), law starts off from freedom in order to constitute it as second nature. This nature is *essentially* second, since it presupposes the spirit whose concept it makes objective, and thus it is fundamentally different from "first" nature because the objective world it constitutes is "produced and to be produced" by spirit.[35] If spirit is higher than nature,[36] this is precisely due to its ability and vocation to reproduce in itself and from itself as a veritable nature *of* spirit, the nature of which it is initially, abstractly, only simple negation or going-beyond:

> The basis [*Boden*] of law is the *realm of spirit* in general and its precise location and point of departure is the *will*; the will is *free*, so that freedom constitutes its substance and destiny [*Bestimmung*] and the system of law is the realm of actualized freedom, the world of spirit produced from within itself as a second nature.[37]

---

p. 23 [*Elements*, 26; see *Outlines*, 18]), he is not speaking of positive legal science but rather of "philosophical law," i.e., natural-rational law. However, he refuses to abstractly oppose rational and positive law to one another as natural law does: see *RPh*, § 3 Anmerkung, *GW* 14.1, pp. 25–26 (*Elements*, 29; see *Outlines*, 20) and chap. 2 below.

33. The ultimate subdivision of this (§§ 481–82 in the 3rd ed.) is titled "free spirit." In the previous two editions, both sections appeared early in the doctrine of objective spirit (§§ 401–2 and 482–83, respectively), proof, if any were needed, of the essential continuity between subjective spirit and objective spirit within "finite spirit" (*Enzykl*, § 386, *GW* 20, p. 383 [*Encyclopedia* 22]).

34. See preliminary to part 1 above.

35. *Enzykl*, § 386, *GW* 20, p. 384 (*Encyclopedia* 20).

36. "Spirit, higher than nature." Hegel, *Die Vernunft in der Geschichte*, 50, margin note.

37. *RPh*, § 4, *GW* 14.1, p. 31 (*Elements*, 35, modified; see *Outlines*, 26). It is essential to Hegel to posit the *equivalence* of the concepts of will and freedom and thus not to make freedom a mere *attribute* of the will. See *RPh*, § 21, *GW* 14.1, p. 41 (*Elements*, 52; see *Outlines*, 41).

We thus see that the transposition of a merely subjective concept of freedom — a concept closed off in its own rationality — into an objectivity that is its own product is the decisive source for the movement of the *Verwirklichung* of abstract law. The doctrine of objective spirit describes the constitution of the abstract freedom of the legal person in a universe of objective determinations and the legal, social, and political institutions that give that freedom coherence and actuality. It is by developing itself within a system of objective historical configurations[38] — whose concept or principle lies in the subjectivity of spirit — that freedom reveals its properly idealized (*idéel*) character. The idea of freedom ("not the idea that [men] have of it, but the idea that they *are*"[39]) is thus objective — or rather, it is nothing other than a process of becoming-objective. However, all the figures of objective freedom must be passed through in order for its ideal (subjective-objective) nature to become manifest, a nature that is at first ensconced in the formalism of its (simple) concept.

Law is the *idea* of freedom in that it actualizes freedom's (and thus spirit's) tendency to inscribe its originally subjective and self-centered dimension in the objectivity of a world; that is to say, to express itself in the register of its other: necessity.[40] The speculative definition of objective spirit or law could thus be *freedom speaking itself in the language of necessity*. This only appears to be a paradox, for within a dialectical perspective, freedom "is not merely an independence of the Other won outside the Other"[41] — rather, it consists — a grand Hegelian theme — in being at home with oneself in the other (*Beisich-sein im Anderen*). The ground of being (subjectivity or freedom) is nothing if it does not give itself being (objectivity, necessity) and if that being does not become the *contradiction* that freedom must overcome to constitute itself.

The Stratification of Law

Freedom is not only a metaphysical property or practical determination of the subjective will: it includes a crucial dimension of objectification, of external

38. The specific nature of the determinations of objective spirit is that they are both concepts and shapes (*Gestaltungen*) historically realized "in the form of existence [*Dasein*]." See *RPh*, § 32, *GW* 14.1, p. 85 (*Elements*, 60; see *Outlines*, 49).

39. *Enzykl*, § 482 Anmerkung, *GW* 20, p. 477 (*Encyclopedia* 215).

40. See *Enzykl*, § 484, *GW* 20, p. 478 (*Encyclopedia* 217).

41. *Enzykl*, § 382 Zusatz, *GW* 10, p. 26 (*Encyclopedia* 16). Hegel adds that spirit "has the power to preserve itself in contradiction, and therefore, in pain."

realization, without which it would be illusory or pointless, not having gone through the experience of negativity. In fact, it is only after passing through abstract (private) law and subjective morality (which is subjective because it is structured by the normative expectations of a subject) and arriving at the third stratum of objective spirit, ethicality,[42] that the full scope of this conception of freedom becomes objective and is revealed, having negated itself in its first expression and thereby realized itself. Indeed, *Sittlichkeit* is "self-conscious *freedom* become nature."[43] In other words, it is the process by which the individual, in his or her claim to freedom—which is absolute, but absolutely subjective, and thus abstract—encounters freedom already realized, so to speak, in front of him or her as a world to be made his or her own. In an ethical universe made up of norms and institutions whose center of gravity is the state, the individual discovers the objective presuppositions that precede his or her attempt at normative (legal and moral) self-determination and give that attempt meaning by circumscribing it and separating it from any arbitrariness it might contain within itself. The doctrine of objective spirit can then be seen for what it is: an *institutionalism*.[44] Indeed, the doctrine states that humans only achieve true freedom—that is, ultimately, their own humanity—by recognizing the objective mediations (i.e., the political, social, familial, as well as legal institutions) that make it possible for this freedom to be part of the real and by ceasing to see these institutions as obstacles to their autonomy, instead adhering to them as the being or substance of their own aims. Statute laws, customs, and mores, says Hegel, are the "universal language" in which the "universal substance"[45] in which freedom participates is expressed. The sphere of objective spirit is thus the sphere of "institutions of meaning"[46] if by that is meant everything that contributes to anchoring subjects' aims in a normative universe that *appears* as quasi natural to them though in reality it

---

42. Hegel distinguishes "morality" (*Moralität*) from "ethicality" (*Sittlichkeit*); *RPh*, § 33 Anmerkung, *GW* 14.1, p. 49 [*Elements*, 63; see *Outlines*, 51]. Before him, common and philosophical language had more or less conflated the two. The distinction is explained by Hegel's insistence on the objectivization of freedom, which only ethicality fully honors.

43. *Enzykl*, § 513, *GW* 20, p. 318 (*Encyclopedia* 228).

44. See below, preliminary to part 4.

45. *PhG*, *GW* 9, p. 195; (*Phenomenology*, ¶ 351).

46. See Vincent Descombes, *The Institutions of Meaning* (Cambridge: Harvard University Press, 2014).

is the work of subjectivity itself—albeit a subjectivity that floats, so to speak, above empirical subjects.

We must still wonder why, beyond the speculative justification of the moment of necessary exteriorization that defines objective spirit, Hegel chose the name *law* to designate the entirety of objective spirit and not, for example, the name *Sittlichkeit* (which would be particularly fitting since ethical life or, better, "ethicality" (*Sittlichkeit*) is "the *unity* and the *truth*"[47] of abstract law and morality, which are its normative and abstract components). An initial though external reason is that this vocabulary reflects the continuity between Hegel's arguments and the still-dominant problematic of natural law—or at least, its terminology. But the metonymic usage of the term *law* is also internally justified: if it is true that legal relations are objectivity itself, then the term *law* is a fitting way of referring to the movement of self-constitution in otherness that is the general meaning of objective spirit. But this terminological choice comes at a price: a significant expansion, even *stratification*, of the concept of law.

> Law, which is to be taken comprehensively, not only as restricted juridical law, but as the embodiment of all determinations of freedom. . . . For an embodiment is a right only on the basis of the free substantial will.[48]

This multiplication is explained by the speculative decision to make law—understood as a *system* of determinations of objective spirit—the generic concept for thinking the unity of the seemingly heterogeneous field of the objective manifestations of freedom or will. Many will judge this multiplication of the concept to be arbitrary, even exorbitant, because it goes well beyond the properly legal sphere (of either private law or internal and external public law). But for Hegel, the expansion is *necessary*: law and rights, understood as the "*existence* of the *free will*,"[49] cover the entire set of processes by which freedom is objectivized, and thus cannot be restricted to the abstract (and thus not autonomous) moment of law in the legal sense, no matter how important that moment may be. Ultimately, the result of the concept of law as it is pre-

---

47. *RPh*, § 33, *GW* 14.1, p. 48 (*Elements*, 62; see *Outlines*, 50).
48. *Enzykl*, § 486, *GW* 20, p. 479 (*Encyclopedia* 218).
49. *RPh*, § 29, *GW* 14.1, p. 45 (*Elements*, 58; see *Outlines*, 46).

sented in the introduction to the *Philosophy of Right* is that law is coextensive with the entirety of objective spirit. As a consequence, not only legal rights but also the "right of the subjective will,"[50] the "right of the world spirit,"[51] morality, philosophy of history, and, of course, political theory (*Staatsrecht*, which is not the same as public law in the strictly legal sense of the term) all fall under the enlarged concept (the *idea*) of law. There is a fundamental point here for Hegel that is tightly bound up with his reformulation of natural law. If Hegel finds it necessary—and in this sense we may say that he remains deeply indebted to natural law—to propose a unitary and encompassing concept of law that overcomes the fragmentation of legal, ethical, and positive political disciplines, then his concept of law cannot be arrived at by expanding the characteristic structure of the sphere of private law, that is, the structure of property relations. While it is legitimate to reconstruct the entire sphere of private law on the basis of the legal relationship between persons and things (i.e., on the concept of property), it is equally legitimate to adopt a concept of law that is anterior to the matrix structure of abstract/private law and is foundational for it.

Thus, appearances notwithstanding, it is not arbitrary to apply the name of law to *all* forms of freedom's objectivization—though freedom is usually thought of as a property of the subjective will. Moreover, "strict" law, private law, exemplifies the process of objective spirit, because it subjects to objective norms the subjectivity of the maxims for action: it objectifies subjective claims by submitting them to procedures of formalization, thereby giving them a universal dimension. The ordinary concept of law and right also includes this double dimension of subjectivity and objectivity; we need only be a bit attentive to see this. Right is "subjective right" because it assumes a subject (the person), and, as we all know, since Hobbes, modern thought has endeavored to reconstruct the entire legal system on the basis of the individual, as a holder of rights. But it is also "objective law," because the obligations that result from the exercise of subjective rights and the procedures for (re)establishing them form an already present order, a normative system that is supposed to be complete—and we know how important the "absence of lacuna"

---

50. *RPh*, § 33, *GW* 14.1, p. 48 (*Elements*, 62; see *Outlines*, 50).
51. *RPh*, § 30 Anmerkung, *GW* 14.1, p. 46 (*Elements*, 59; see *Outlines*, 48).

was for the rise of legal positivism[52] — and on the basis of which it is possible, as the Roman jurisprudents used to say, to "give each his due." Thus, by stratifying law, Hegel is not unduly expanding the notion of law but is rather trying to emphasize that its principle coincides with his own understanding of freedom presupposing, in a circular way, its own objectification. One may or may not agree with this interpretation, but the fact remains that it determines Hegel's conception of the articulation of private law, morality, and *Sittlichkeit* in a coherent and systematic totality, one ordered by the principle of the objectivization of freedom.

The result is that the thesis of Hegelian antilegalism that I presented at the beginning of this chapter is untenable. Otherwise, how are we to explain the fact that Hegel, in spite of his acute awareness of the limits of "narrow legal law," chose that very term to metonymically designate the entire sphere of objective spirit? If there is antilegalism in Hegel, it can only be what I have called weak antilegalism — that is, a rejection of the argument that the legal order is self-sufficient; an argument that was supported by the positivists and systematized by Kelsen.[53] Furthermore, the expansion and stratification of law are strict corollaries of calling into question law as a closed system: it is because "abstract law" cannot be considered a closed system (for reasons we must still analyze) that it is possible and necessary to have an enlarged concept of law that makes it possible to formulate nonlegal (in the strict sense of the term) conditions for the efficacy of law. To better understand this weak antilegalism, we must examine the precise reasons why Hegel calls private law *abstract* law.

The Abstraction of Abstract Law

In what way is law "in the legal sense" abstract, and how does its abstraction point to an insufficiency? Indisputably, the description of private law, the law

---

52. One of the great nineteenth-century representatives of this movement stated that "the legal order can no more be lacunar than the order of nature" (Paul Laband, quoted by Carl Bergbohm, *Jurisprudenz und Rechtsphilosophie* (Leipzig: Duncker und Humboldt, 1892), 73.

53. For Kelsen, the purpose of the theory of the basic norm is to provide a theoretical basis for the positivist thesis of the closure of the normative order: "All norms whose validity can be traced back to one and the same basic norm constitute a system of norms, a normative order. . . . It is the basic norm that constitutes the unity in the multitude of norms by representing the reason for the validity of all norms that belong to this order." Kelsen, *Pure Theory of Law*, p. 195.

of jurists, as "abstract" and "formal" implies a relativization of this first objectification of freedom. But Hegel's constant reminder of this abstraction does not imply any disdain for law. Of course, Hegel rejects *legalism*, which would make law and rights the truth of objective spirit and the foundation of ethicality—but he also refuses to treat law as a mere superstructure, a deformed expression of ethical (sociopolitical) reality. Because of its very abstraction, law includes a logical and historical necessity that must be recognized. The "formal right of abstract personality," like each of the figures of objective spirit, gives a "determinate shape and existence to freedom,"[54] and this is the perspective from which the fundamental categories of formal law must be interpreted. Hegel's analysis of person, property, contracts, and forms of violation and reestablishment of law thus aim to show how these concepts, as they operate in legal reasoning, constitute outlines of the objectification of freedom—outlines that give freedom increasingly formal—and thus *in a sense* more universal—expression. Thus, legal abstraction makes it possible for freedom, as it becomes objectified in externality and nonfreedom, to lose the equally abstract subjectivity of individual consciousness. The formalism of law, which marks its limitation with respect to the concreteness of ethical-political[55] institutions, is thus far from having only negative aspects, since it allows legal reasoning to distance itself from the material singularity of a case and to access the universality of *form*. Hence, the formalities with which law accompanies elementary legal acts are what make these acts "valid before the law,"[56] and, in general, the progress of legal consciousness has kept pace with the formalization of procedures and techniques of reasoning. Whence the following statement, at first glance surprising from a philosopher quick to denounce all formalism:

> Both feeling, which remains confined to the subjective, and reflection,
> which clings to its abstract essences, reject such formalities, whereas the

---

54. *RPh*, § 30 Anmerkung, *GW* 14.1, p. 46 (*Elements*, 59; see *Outlines*, 47).

55. "Law is something *utterly sacred*, for the simple reason that it is the existence [*Dasein*] of the absolute concept, of self-conscious freedom.—But the *formalism* of law . . . arises out of the different stages in the development of the concept of freedom." *RPh*, § 30, *GW* 14.1, p. 46 (*Elements*, 59; see *Outlines*, 47).

56. *RPh*, § 217, *GW* 14.1, p. 181 (*Elements*, 249; see *Outlines*, 206).

dead understanding may for its part hold on to them in preference to the thing [*Sache*] itself and multiply them indefinitely.[57]

This is why the Hegelian definition of law deliberately distances itself from the common preconception that law implies the (reciprocal) limitation of freedoms, the mutual restriction of subjective rights. That idea found a fitting framework in modern natural law as interpreted by Hobbes: the rule of (natural and positive) law passes through a restriction of natural rights: it is established when individuals unilaterally transfer their subjective natural rights to the sovereign, who, in exchange, guarantees them the security they lack in the state of nature. This is why the transfer of rights must be total—with the significant, sole exception of inalienable rights[58]—if it is to be effective. Rousseau, adopting this perspective,[59] demonstrated that it does not necessarily imply a monarchic system, as might perhaps be feared. This classical conception of the restriction of rights by law has been adopted by thinkers who share neither Hobbes's nor Rousseau's choices. Kant, for example, sees law as implying a limitation or restriction on every individual's free choice so that law "is therefore the sum of the conditions under which the choice of one can be united with the choice of another in accordance with a universal law of freedom."[60] This postulate of reason lies at the root of "law in the strict sense" because it is the basis for any possible *constraint* being enacted on someone who, by her action, violates the universal law. For Hegel, however, such an understanding of law and rights is based on a philosophical error

57. *RPh*, § 217 Anmerkung, *GW* 14.1, p. 181 (*Elements*, 249; *Outlines*, 206).

58. "Therefore there be some rights, which no man can be understood by any words, or other signs, to have abandoned, or transferred." Thomas Hobbes, *Leviathan*, 3 vols. (Oxford: Clarendon Press, 2012), 2:202.

59. The social contract involves "the total alienation of each associate with all his rights to the whole community." Jean-Jacques Rousseau, *Oeuvres complètes* (Paris: Gallimard, 1995), 3:360; *The Social Contract and the First and Second Discourses*, trans. Susan Dunn and Gita May (New Haven, CT: Yale University Press, 2002), 1:6, 163 (*Social Contract* citations give book and chapter followed by modern translation page number). To this we must add, against the suspicion of "totalitarianism" that weighs on Rousseau, that alienation in fact corresponds only to a *conversion* of natural law into statutory law guaranteed by the political community: "instead of an abdication, they have made an advantageous exchange . . . of natural independence against freedom." *Oeuvres complètes*, 3:375; *Social Contract*, 2:4, 176.

60. Kant, *Rechtslehre: MdS*, pt. 1, Einleitung, § C, *AA* VI, p. 230; *PP*, p. 386.

since it derives the "rational will" from the "will of the single person [*des Einzelnen*] in his distinctive arbitrariness."[61] On that view, which presupposes the reciprocal externality of the universal and the singular, of law and rights, the ascendancy of the former over the latter constitutes a limitation, a constraint, whereas for Hegel, the submission of individual choice to universal law is what frees the individual from his internal limitations, which result from the fact that he is *merely* particular. At stake in this debate is the very status of law as an instance of rational universality within the order of willing. It is quite accurate to say that law, as an order objectively governed by relations between independent persons, involves a restriction of their free capacity for choice, but it is the *arbitrary*[62] aspect of the individual subjective will in its initial naturalness that is restricted, while the objective will that is the source of all legal actions is promoted. This understanding presupposes a clear distinction—already found in Kant[63]—between the free capacity for choice and will. But while Kant establishes a functional hierarchy between *Willkür* and *Wille*, Hegel makes the former a (necessary though contradictory) moment in the determination and particularization of the latter. It is precisely because law strives to go beyond the subjective, arbitrary, and structurally contradictory[64] will by subjecting it to the constraints of an objective normative order that it is not a limitation but rather an objectivization of the will on which the actuality of the will's freedom depends.

Hegel's interpretation of the notion of legal personality is indicative of his concern to make abstract law a manifestation—though no doubt an imperfect one—of freedom as it becomes objective: a freedom no longer closed in on itself but one that inscribes itself in the world and in so doing overcomes its finitude and reaches a form of universality. Significantly, Hegel's reconstruction of abstract law makes personality its *sole* principle because personality

61. *RPh*, § 29 Anmerkung, *GW* 14.1, p. 45 (*Elements*, 58; see *Outlines*, 47). Rousseau and Kant are both discussed here, which shows that Hegel's critique is a *theory* of law, not a political conception.

62. Recall that the German word *Willkür* can either mean arbitrariness (free choice) in the philosophical sense of the term or the arbitrariness that results from arbitrary misuse of it. On this point, see also the translator's note.

63. Compare *MdS*, Einleitung, *Ak*. 6, p. 226; *PP*, p. 380, and *RPh*, § 15, *GW* 14.1, p. 38 (*Elements*, 48; see *Outlines*, 37).

64. See *RPh*, § 15 Anmerkung, *GW* 14.1, pp. 38–39 (*Elements*, 48; see *Outlines*, 38).

inextricably links *law*, *rights*, and *freedom*: "law and all its determinations are based on the free personality alone, a self-determination, which is the very contrary of determination by nature."[65] But what, exactly, is personality? Here is Hegel's definition:

> It is inherent in *personality* that, as *this* person, I am completely determined in all respects (in my inner arbitrary will, drive, and desire, as well as in relation to my immediate external existence [*Dasein*]), and that I am finite, yet totally pure self-reference, and thus know myself in my finitude as *infinite*, *universal*, and *free*.[66]

A person can be defined as a pure relation of freedom to itself that is expressed as an indefinite — and in that sense, formal — relation between the person and things. The person, the starting point for the process of objective spirit, inherits the determination that characterizes free spirit, the culmination of subjective spirit: it is *"free will, which is for itself as free will."*[67] But, in the objectivized and formalized figure of the person, the will detaches itself from the context in which its concept appears, that is, finite subjectivity. Hegel is careful to point out that the *"legal* will" is not the "subjective will" but rather an "objective will,"[68] specifying that "the objective will is rational in itself, i.e. in its *concept.*"[69] The difference between these two forms of will is crucial. Whereas the subjective will exhausts itself in willing its own freedom, the objective legal will — that is, first and foremost, personality — transposes the self-relation that constitutes its freedom into an indeterminate or formal objectivity:

> The person must give himself an external *sphere of freedom* in order to have being as Idea. The person is the infinite will, the will which has being in and for itself, in this first and as yet wholly abstract determination. Consequently,

65. *Enzykl*, § 502 Anmerkung, *GW* 20, p. 488 (*Encyclopedia* 223).

66. *RPh*, § 35, *GW* 14.1, p. 51 (*Elements*, 67–68;. see *Outlines*, 53–54).

67. *Enzykl*, § 481, *GW* 20, p. 476 (*Encyclopedia* 214). See *RPh*, § 27, *GW* 14.1, p. 45 (*Elements*, 57; see *Outlines*, 46): "The abstract concept of the Idea of the will is in general *the free will which wills the free will.*"

68. *RPh*, margin note to § 104, *GW* 14.2, p. 557.

69. *RPh*, § 258 Anmerkung, *GW* 14.1, p. 203 (*Elements*, 277; see *Outlines*, 230). See *RPh*, § 13 Anmerkung, *GW* 14.1, p. 37, and § 26, *GW* 14.1, p. 44 (*Elements*, 47, 55; see *Outlines*, 36, 44).

this sphere distinct from the will, which may constitute the sphere of its freedom, is likewise determined as *immediately different* and *separable* from it.[70]

The objective will wills itself in things: it affirms itself as a capacity—in principle, unlimited—for appropriating objectivity or, in other words, as an infinite capacity for self-objectivization. The legal capacity inherent in personality is the basis for "the universal right to appropriate natural things."[71] Thus, if personality is the "(itself abstract) basis of abstract and hence *formal* right,"[72] its true expression is the formal (legal) act of appropriating things, an act empirically expressed in material possession and in even the most rudimentary symbols of possession, such as shaping and marking:

> *Personality* alone confers a right to *things*, and consequently that personal right is in essence a *right of things*—"thing" [*Sache*] being understood in its general sense as everything external to my freedom, including even my body and my life.[73]

The significance of this concept of personality can be measured by the effects it has on the common understanding of self-possession: the *res* that can be possessed include my own body and the products of my mind as well natural and artificial objects. Hegel treats personal freedom not as a natural or essentially given but rather as a particular case—one with very interesting consequences—of a person's investment in objectivity. Just as in order to be considered the legal proprietor of a thing, a person must actually appropriate it through usage and not just passively hold it;[74] she must also take possession of herself in order to be fully—physically, intellectually, and legally—sui juris:

---

70. *RPh*, § 41, *GW* 14.1, p. 55 (*Elements*, 73; see *Outlines*, 57–58).

71. *RPh*, § 52 Anmerkung, *GW* 14.1, p. 61 (*Elements*, 82; see *Outlines*, 65). § 44 notes an "absolute *right for appropriation* . . . over all things." *RPh*, § 44, *GW* 14.1, p. 57 (*Elements*, 75; see *Outlines*, 85). "Man is the master of all things in nature," notes Hegel in the margin of § 39 (*GW* 14.2, p. 391). Compare this with the Hobbesian state of nature as the war of each against all. See Thomas Hobbes, *De Cive: English Version* (Oxford: Oxford University Press, 1983), 1:10, 95–96 (*De Cive* citations give book and chapter followed by modern translation page number); *Leviathan*, 2:198.

72. *RPh*, § 36, *GW* 14.1, p. 52 (*Elements*, 69; see *Outlines*, 55).

73. *RPh*, § 40 Anmerkung, *GW* 14.1, pp. 53–54 (*Elements*, 71; see *Outlines*, 56).

74. "Through my taking possession of it, the thing [*Sache*] acquires the predicate of being

The human being, in his *immediate* concrete existence [*Existenz*] in himself, is a natural entity, external to his own concept; it is only through the *development* [*Ausbildung*] of his own body and spirit, *essentially* by means of *his self-consciousness comprehending itself as free*, that he takes possession of himself and becomes his own property as distinct from that of others. Or to put it the other way round, this taking possession of oneself consists also in translating into *actuality* what one is in terms of one's concept (as *possibility*, capacity [*Vermögen*], or predisposition). By this means, what one is in concept is posited for the first time as one's own.[75]

It is from the necessity that man take possession of his own body and mind by educating and cultivating them that Hegel deduces the legal absurdity of slavery and bondage, which can only be justified if the egalitarian formalism of law is abandoned, as is the case, for example, when legal capacity is connected to the possession of a certain social or political status. We see, then, the value of the egalitarian formalism of law. When legal capacity is based on status, the personality of humans is denied, as certain people are refused full possession of their bodies, which constitutes a negation of the principle of free personality and, thereby, is "absolutely contrary to law."[76] As Hegel declared to his students in Berlin, "Man is implicitly rational; herein lies the possibility of equality of right for all men, — the futility of a rigid distinction between races that have rights and those that have none."[77] But Hegel also objects to humanist, natural law arguments against the "so-called legal institution of slavery" as well as to historicist arguments; he objects to the former on the grounds that they invoke a problematic "human nature," for personal freedom is anything but a *natural* property or right, and to the latter on the grounds that, by reducing property to possession, they tend to justify notions such as eminent domain and thereby indirectly justify bondage.[78]

---

mine, and the will has a *positive* relationship [*Beziehung*] to it." RPh, § 59, GW 14.1, p. 66 (*Elements*, 88; see *Outlines*, 71).

75. *RPh*, § 57, GW 14.1, p. 64 (*Elements*, 86; see *Outlines*, 69).

76. *RPh*, § 57 Anmerkung, GW 14.1, pp. 64–65 (*Elements*, 87, modified; see *Outlines*, 70).

77. *Enzykl*, § 393 Zusatz, W 10, p. 57 (*Encyclopedia* 40).

78. I will not address here the broad issue of Hegel's relationship with Historical School of Law and its leader, Savigny (see chap. 2), but it is clear that the reconstruction of abstract law, especially the treatment of the relationship between possession and property, is in good part directed against his views. The work of his disciple Eduard Gans confirms the fundamental dis-

A fundamental and inalienable right, personality is a universal though indeterminate power (a "capacity") to exercise rights or, rather, the right from which all others are derived: the right to appropriate material things. Property, the completed—because legally objectified—form of possession gives expression to the primary legal relationship between person and thing from which the entire construction of law follows. Property is what allows my will and my personality to become objective and thereby truly mine. In this way, the entire sphere of abstract law can be considered to deal with real rights in the technical sense of the term: that is, with the ownership, acquisition, transfer, violation, and restitution of *res*. This is why a margin note in the *Philosophy of Right* indicates that property is the thread that runs throughout the entire examination of the sphere of abstract law,[79] and this is why Hegel rejects the traditional distinction (which goes back to Gaius's *Institutes*) between the right of persons and the right to things: "personal right is in essence a *right to things*."[80]

Of course, the choice to present the entirety of abstract law on the basis of the ownership of material goods is far from innocuous. It is intended, first and foremost, to counter Roman law, according to which the "right to have right(s)" is differentially distributed depending on a person's status—and even, according to the common teaching, on a triple status: *status libertatis, status civitatis, status familiae*:

> As for what is called the *right of persons* in Roman law, it regards a human being as a person only if he enjoys a certain *status* (see Heineccius, *Elementa iuris civilis* [1728], § 75); hence in Roman law even personality itself, as opposed to slavery, is merely an *estate* [*Stand*] or condition [*Zustand*]. . . .

---

agreement that exists on this point between historicism and the Hegelian standpoint (Eduard Gans, *Das erbrecht in weltgeschichtlicher Entwickelung*, 4 vols. [Berlin, 1824–1835]). We know that relatively early on Hegel read Savigny's *Das Recht Besitzes* (1803; repr., Goldbach, Keip., 1997), of which he owned a copy, and that he consulted his *History of Roman Law in the Middle Ages*; he was certainly aware of his programmatic or "policy" writings to which the *Philosophy of Right* alludes repeatedly (§ 3 Anmerkung, § 45, § 211 Anmerkung, § 218 Anmerkung (*Elements*, 29, 76, 241–42, 250–51; see *Outlines*, 21, 61, 199, 207).

79. *RPh*, marg. § 40, *GW* 14.2, p. 395—see the margin note: "property is what traverses [the development]."

80. *RPh*, § 40 Anmerkung, *GW* 14.1, p. 54 (*Elements*, 71; see *Outlines*, 56).

The right of persons in Roman law is therefore not the right of the person as such, but no more than the right of the *particular* person.[81]

This amounts to "discuss[ing] the right of the person in his *particular determinacy* before the universal right of personality."[82] Thus, the attention paid by the dominant legal tradition to the statutory conditions of personality is not in accordance with the objectively universal content of that concept, though the latter is at the foundation of all legal determinations. The freedom of individual private property is the concrete expression of the objectification by which personality is realized. Rosenzweig is thus right to say that the Hegelian conception of law espoused the point of view of free ownership as it is realized when the rigid structure of a society of orders is abolished and to point out that in so doing, Hegel was the first to attempt to philosophically account for "what has transpired in half of Europe since the night of August 4": the elimination of privilege, of *lex privata*, as the source and foundation of right.[83] According to Hegel, exclusive private property expresses the very essence of abstract law, which is to objectify—to the point of reifying—personal freedom. This is why the set of determinations contained in this sphere (law of contracts, forms of violating and reestablishing law) can and must be systematically ordered on the basis of personal freedom.

To summarize, the formalism of law has a positive aspect and even a certain fecundity. No doubt abstract law is the expression of a freedom that is itself still abstract, for it is situated in what is *"immediately different* and *separable* from it"[84]—but this objectifying abstraction *frees* the personality from what is *merely* subjective and particular in it. Hence, legal personality is the full, because objectified, expression of subjective personality, which it presupposes and reinforces. Abstract law of course does not give objective freedom its content (which is, ultimately, political), but it defines the abstractly universal relation between humans and material nature, concretely expressed in work, as well as the relations between people, provided that these relations are not consciously ordered by an ethical-political end that surpass it. As the

81. *RPh*, § 40 Anmerkung, *GW* 14.1, p. 54 (*Elements*, 71; see *Outlines*, 57).
82. *RPh*, § 40 Anmerkung, *GW* 14.1, p. 54 (*Elements*, 71; see *Outlines*, 57).
83. See Rosenzweig, *Hegel und der Staat* (1920), 107–11.
84. *RPh*, § 41, *GW* 14.1, p. 55 (*Elements*, 73; see *Outlines*, 58).

1802 article on natural law stated, the conversion of particularity into universality is "that by which the sphere of law is constituted."[85] Thus, the abstraction of private law guarantees the universal validity of its principles. Because it is abstract, this law belongs to no place or time (which of course does not mean that it has been honored always and everywhere). In this sense, it is insurmountable. For Hegel, there can be no freedom against law.

The Actualization of Abstract Law: Civil Society

Abstract law defines the universal form of the objectivization of freedom — but only its form. Indeed, its formalism prevents it from engendering an actual order. Hegel criticizes the "fiction of a *state of nature*"[86] but otherwise repeats Hobbes's reasoning. Hobbes emphasized this in order to demonstrate the necessity of exiting the state of nature ("exeundem e statu naturae," as the expression from *De Cive* goes): if every person has a right to every thing, then in fact no person has any power over any thing until a principle of actuality (which cannot emerge from abstract law) intervenes and converts this unlimited, though formal, right into guaranteed possession of delimited but real goods. This is no doubt a trivial point, but common legalism requires that it be emphasized: law is not realized by itself, which makes it untenable to see it as a self-sufficient normative order.

The need for there to be an operator to actualize abstract law becomes clear in the case of the equality of rights proclaimed by the Declaration of the Rights of Man and Citizen. There, equality is made an inalienable right; Hegel, on the other hand, makes it a simple analytic property of abstract law. The fact that people — all people — are legally equal is included in the concept of personhood, which is the sole inalienable and imprescriptible legal good:

> The right to such inalienable things is imprescriptible, for the act whereby
> I take possession of my personality and substantial essence and make myself
> a responsible being with moral and religious values and capable of holding

---

85. *Naturrecht, W* 2, p. 484 (*Natural Law: The Scientific Ways of Treating Natural Law, Its Place in Moral Philosophy, and Its Relation to the Positive Sciences of Law* (Philadelphia: University of Pennsylvania Press, 1975), 95.

86. *Enzykl*, § 502 Anmerkung, *GW* 20, p. 488 (*Encyclopedia* 223).

rights removes these determinations from that very externality which alone made them capable of becoming the possessions of someone else.[87]

Because personhood is a formal construction that disregards all real differences between individuals — including, first and foremost, inequalities in social position and fortune[88] — by definition, everyone has the right to it. This equality of right(s) boils down to *freedom* insofar as freedom can be reduced to a legal relation, that is, to personal freedom in the most abstract sense, as an absence of *legal* dependence on others. Thus, abstract law defines the base structure of the relations between humans when these relations are mediated by things, that is, are neither moral nor ethical relations but strictly legal. Law gives us a picture of what a society of persons who "only as owners of property ... have existence [*Dasein*] for each other"[89] would look like, but such a society is no more than an abstraction or idealization of civil society and real politics. A keen and attentive observer of England's economic and social transformations during the Industrial Revolution, Hegel is fully aware of the potentially harmful consequences of unequal implementation of formal legal equality: it is the cause of conflicts between individuals and of destitution for many. But it would be a mistake to ask law to solve a problem of which it is at most an indication and not a cause: the inequalities that formal legal equality may cover over "belong to another sphere, that of civil society."[90]

Why is it incumbent on *bürgerliche Gesellschaft* in particular to actualize abstract law? The question can be answered from two points of view. First, from a *systematic* point of view, it is explained by the position of civil society within the economy of *Sittlichkeit*. Ethicality guarantees the connection — or rather, the mutual copenetration — of the subjective and objective poles of freedom, hitherto abstractly separated from one another, as are formal-objective law and the "right of *subjective freedom*."[91] Of course, the ethical reconciliation of objectivity and subjectivity is not their completed reconciliation: it remains

---

87. *RPh*, § 66 Anmerkung, *GW* 14.1, p. 71 (*Elements*, 96; see *Outlines*, 78).

88. "The equality of abstract persons as such" must of course be distinguished from "equality in the distribution of ground or even wealth" (*RPh*, § 49 Anmerkung, *GW* 14.1, p. 60 [*Elements*, 80; see *Outlines*, 64]).

89. *RPh*, § 40, *GW* 14.1, p. 53 (*Elements*, 70; see *Outlines*, 56).

90. *RPh*, § 49 Anmerkung, *GW* 14.1, p. 60 (*Elements*, 80; see *Outlines*, 64).

91. *RPh*, § 124 Anmerkung, *GW* 14.1, p. 110 (*Elements*, 151; see *Outlines*, 122).

but an *objective* reconciliation of the two dimensions of spirit, which still appear distinct within it, whereas, according to its speculative concept, they come from an internal division within a single totality that, as idea, is only thinkable as subject-object. But in any case, spirit becomes truly objective as an ethical totality in the sense that objectivity ceases to be a formal predicate of spirit, as it is in the sphere of law, and is revealed to be its true — because mediated or second — nature and is thereby verified: "Ethicality is duty, substantial law, second nature (as it has rightly been called); for man's first nature is his immediate animal existence."[92] Hence, ethicality implies the actualization of the abstract concept of law and ensures that its formalism is surpassed. But of the three spheres that ethicality includes, the task of actualization falls to *civil society* in particular. The family, which corresponds to the moment of immediate naturalness within the ethical sphere, is essentially located at a "sub-legal" level; as we know, Hegel condemns the "infamy" of Kant's "legalization" of marriage, which according to Hegel obliterates the specific determination of the natural moment of ethical life.[93] The state, for its part, is superlegal, at least if one sticks to the narrow understanding of the concept of law. Civil society, the middle term between the family and the state, is the space where abstract (private) law is actually realized. Conversely, abstract private law must be considered a working draft or formal framework of civil society.

Second, from a *historical* point of view, we know that for Hegel, the (relatively) autonomous constitution of civil society is a distinctive property of modern ethicality:

> Civil society is the [stage of] difference which intervenes between the family and the state, even if its full development occurs later than that of the state; for as difference, it presupposes the state, which it must have before it as a self-sufficient entity in order to subsist itself. Besides, the creation of civil society belongs to the modern world, which for the first time allows all determinations of the Idea to attain their rights.[94]

92. Hegel, *Die Vernunft in der Geschichte*, 115–16; *Lectures on the Philosophy of World History*, 97. See the analogous formulations in *RPh*, § 142, and 151, *GW* 14.1, pp. 137, 141 (*Elements*, 189; see *Outlines*, 154, 159) and *Enzykl*, § 513, *GW* 20, pp. 494–95 (*Encyclopedia* 228).

93. See *RPh*, § 75 A. and 163 Anmerkung, *GW* 14.1, pp. 78, 146 (*Elements*, 105–6, 203; see *Outlines*, 85, 165).

94. *RPh*, § 182 Zusatz, *W* 7, p. 339 (*Elements*, 220; see *Outlines*, 181). See also *RPh*, § 256

Hegel here gives expression to a still-diffuse consciousness of the irreducibility of the social bond to its political forms and profoundly transforms the term *civil society*, which previously had been synonymous with *political society*.[95] Hegel's wholly intentional innovation is meant to correspond to the creation of a space of production, exchanges, and social interactions that is to a large degree independent from political authority properly speaking, which, in Hegelian terms, is charged with the universal. In a pure market society, interdependencies and the objective coordination of individuals' needs, activities, and self-interested projects would render concerted actions by a public power useless, even harmful. But civil society in the Hegelian sense is not reducible to the spontaneous order of the market. It is thus both conceptually and actually inseparable from the modern (constitutional) state as well as from a certain configuration of law. Indeed, if the existence of civil society presupposes in general *a* state, only the *rational* state is strong enough to let the moment of social life develop freely for itself. The rational state, and only the rational state, offers an "actuality" and a "guarantee" of the "*prevailing principles of* [*law in force*]," that is, the rights of "freedom of property and also of personal freedom, the principles of civil society, of its industry and of the communities, and of the regulated performance of the particular authorities subject to the [statute-]laws."[96] This explains why civil society, in its complex connection to the postrevolutionary state, is the authentic—that is to say, *nonpolitical*—realization of the equally modern demand (which materialized with the French Revolution) for the rule of law.[97] Thus, the actual realization of law in itself—which in itself is not historic—is only accomplished late in history and bears a constitutive relation to the problematic of legal equality and personal freedom of which the Declarations of Rights are the manifesto.

In what sense does civil society—in its concept—presuppose an abstract legal order? To find out, we must examine civil society in its economic reality: that is, we must consider it—following Hegel's conceptualization in his Jena writings—as a system of needs. The economic subsystem perfectly illustrates the definition of civil society as "the system of ethicality, lost in its

---

Anmerkung, *GW* 14.1, pp. 199–200 (*Elements*, 273–74; see *Outlines*, 227–28), and Hegel, *Vorlesungen über Rechtsphilosophie*, 3:565.

95. See below, preliminary to part 2.

96. *Enzykl*, § 544 Anmerkung, *GW* 20, p. 518 (*Encyclopedia* 242–43).

97. See chapter 5 below.

extremes,"[98] split between the particularity of the egotistical aims of individuals and a universality that, because it remains separate from the particular, is merely formal:

> The determination of *particularity* ... is related to *universality*, but in such a way that the latter is its basis — though still only its *inner* basis; consequently, this universality is present only as a formal *shining* in the particular.[99]

This formal-universal takes the shape — as we have known since Adam Smith's *Wealth of Nations* — of an "invisible hand," by which is meant economic regulations that ensure if not the harmony then at least the adjustment of particular ends within a "system of multilateral dependence" such that "the subsistence and welfare of the individual and his legal existence [*Dasein*] are interwoven with, and grounded on, the subsistence, welfare, and right of all."[100] But the "blind necessity"[101] of self-regulation — which cannot, on its own, guarantee the harmonious functioning of the system — is not, and cannot be, the only mode of universality's presence within civil society. Production and exchange, the appropriation of nature to satisfy needs that the system multiplies (thus freeing economic actors from their servility to supposed "natural needs"[102]), the aleatory interaction of particular ends: all this also requires the existence of a homogenous space whose formative rules are defined by the law, that is, a formal space in the image of the economic composition of particular goals.

Modern work takes the form of an abstract activity intended to satisfy needs incompletely, needs that themselves become ever more abstract because the logic of production and exchange deprives them of any semblance of naturalness. It presupposes the existence of a legal order that makes it possible to determine what belongs to whom on the basis of formalized procedures.

> In the state of affairs in which this standpoint of mediation is realized, immediate seizure (§ 488) of external objects as means to satisfaction no longer occurs, or very rarely; the objects are property. Their acquisition is,

98. *RPh*, § 184, *GW* 14.1, p. 160 (*Elements*, 221; see *Outlines*, 182).

99. *RPh*, § 181, *GW* 14.1, p. 159 (*Elements*, 219, modified; see *Outlines*, 180).

100. *RPh*, § 183, *GW* 14.1, p. 160 (*Elements*, 221; see *Outlines*, 181).

101. *Enzykl*, § 532, *GW* 20, p. 505 (*Encyclopedia* 235).

102. On the transformation of natural need into social need and its liberating effects, see *RPh*, § 194, *GW* 14.1, p. 167 (*Elements*, 230; see *Outlines*, p. 189).

on the one hand, conditioned and mediated by the will of their possessors, which, as particular will, has as its aim the satisfaction of variously determined needs, just as, on the other hand, it is conditioned and mediated by the ever renewed production of exchangeable means by one's own labour, this mediation of satisfaction by the labour of all constitutes the general resources.[103]

In other words, the formal-universal condition for the social satisfaction of needs is that every thing has an identifiable owner and an order of private law based on personal property is in place. In bourgeois civil society, there can be no res nullius, things without master, immediately appropriable. Private ownership of the means of production and exchange is the *formal*-universal condition for the collective satisfaction of particular needs.[104] *Homo oeconomicus*, who is simply man tout court, a being of needs and work, is thus the concrete historical figure of the abstract legal person.[105] The existence of a social space of production and exchange — that is, the system of needs — creates the conditions for the actualization of the abstract principles of the legal order. Conversely, abstract law, because it is abstract, is the general condition of production and exchange in their modern, capitalist form. The production, exchange, and consumption of commodities at the scale of a "great society," to use Adam Smith's expression, presupposes the homogenous basis of a universally applicable law: there is no market society without commodities and thus without a universal definition of property and the conditions of its transfer.

Civil society is thus structurally congruent with private law. First, it *presupposes* private law as the formal condition of its own operation: without an abstract legal order, concrete social life would be impossible. Second, civil society *actualizes* the law because the relations between individuals and social groups offer concrete material for the formal determinations of right. As we know, Hegel thinks that civil society preserves within itself the "remnants of the state of nature."[106] But only the remnants; the universal is not absent from civil society as it is from a pure state of nature, which, as Hobbes proved, can only be conceived as lawless. The interaction between right and economic regulations

103. *Enzykl*, § 524, *GW* 20, p. 499 (*Encyclopedia* 230–31).
104. See *RPh*, § 46, *GW* 14.1, pp. 57–58 (*Elements*, 77; see *Outlines*, 61).
105. *RPh*, § 190 Anmerkung, *GW* 14.1, p. 166 (*Elements*, 228; see *Outlines*, 188).
106. *RPh*, § 200 Anmerkung, *GW* 14.1, p. 170 (*Elements*, 234; see *Outlines*, 192).

within the space of exchange is precisely what demonstrates the difference between this space and a state of nature: right—the formalism of which makes a positive contribution at this level—makes possible an economic and social space that functions *relatively* independently from the state and its own specific modes of action. It allows for a *civil*, rather than *civic*, society. However, the actuality of legal formalism and "formal" economic regulations must not be overestimated, for the system of needs and a civil society administered according to law do not contain within themselves the resources that would allow them to be *absolutely* self-regulated, as in the liberal dream of a pure market society. Unlike liberals, Hegel is convinced that it is necessary for the state to regulate—that is, intervene in—the economic and social sphere:

> The differing interests . . . may come into collision with each other, and even if, *on the whole*, their correct relationship re-establishes itself automatically, its adjustment also needs to be consciously regulated by an agency which stands above both sides.[107]

The need for the state to correct the negative effects of the spontaneous workings of the system of needs through good policing (within certain limits that we must take into account, just as we must not forget that the term *police* had a much broader meaning in the administrative language of Hegel's time than it does today[108]) demonstrates the limits of a purely formal (economic and legal) actualization of the universal in a social world that would be doomed to perish in the frozen waters of egotistical calculation (as Marx would say) if there were not above it a real, *political* actualization of that universal. I have said that for Hegel, there is no freedom against the law—but nor can freedom be acquired by law alone, for there can be no formal surpassing of formalism.

Private Law, Social Conflict, and Political "Union"

We must now turn to the question of the relationship between the state and the law in the narrow sense of abstract/private law. At first glance, Hegel's texts seem to suggest an ambiguous, if not contradictory, relationship:

---

107. *RPh*, § 236, *GW* 14.1, p. 190 (*Elements*, 261–262; see *Outlines*, 217).

108. On this subject see Hans Maier, *Die ältere deutsche Staats und Verwaltungslehre* (Munich: DTV, 1986).

In relation to the spheres of civil law and private welfare, the spheres of the family and civil society, the state is on the one hand an *external* necessity and a higher power to whose nature their laws and interests are subordinate and on which they depend. But on the other hand, it is their *immanent* end, and its strength consists in the unity of its universal and ultimate end with the particular interest of individuals, in the fact that they have *duties* towards the state to the same extent as they also have rights.[109]

If this is not mere rhetoric, how are we to understand the declared reciprocity between individuals' rights and their obligations to the state (obligations that imply a relativization of individuals' rights) once we know that this reciprocity is characteristic of the sphere of ethicality and thereby goes beyond the double formalism of abstract (legal) right and abstract (moral) obligation? How can the task of the state be to "make *law* a necessary actuality" — a strong claim — if the state must at the same time bring the law — and along with it the private property that individuals aim for in exercising their rights — "into the life of the universal substance," which may "curtail these subordinate spheres?"[110] In other words, how can the affirmation of the autonomy of abstract law be reconciled with the relativization of abstract law by a more concrete authority, and in what way is that authority more concrete? The key to the problem, or paradox, lies in what I have called the stratification of law. Once it has been asserted that everything that contributes to the objectivization of freedom is part of the law in the broad sense, each successive figure of this objectivization is both verified and relativized by the figures that follow it:

> Each stage in the development of the idea of freedom has its distinctive right, because it is the existence of freedom in one of its own determinations. ... They can come into *collision* only in so far as they are all in equal measure rights. ... But a collision also contains this further moment: it imposes a limitation whereby one stage is subordinated to another.[111]

This is not only the case in the relationship between the state and law. For example, obeying the moral norm might require violating strict law. Unlike

---

109. *RPh*, § 261, *GW* 14.1, p. 208 (*Elements*, 283; see *Outlines*, 235–36).
110. *Enzykl*, § 537, *GW* 20, p. 508 (*Encyclopedia* 236).
111. *RPh*, § 30 Anmerkung, *GW* 14.1, p. 46 (*Elements*, 59, modified; see *Outlines*, 47–48). See also *Enzykl*, § 380, *GW* 20, p. 381 (*Encyclopedia* 8).

Kant, for whom, "there could be no necessity that would make what is wrong conform with law,"[112] but like Fichte,[113] Hegel—reviving a certain theological tradition—recognizes the existence of a right of necessity or distress (*jus necessitatis, Notrecht*), which allows for the possibility of a violation of that which nevertheless lies at the very base of private law: the moral point of view that makes it necessary to affirm the *legal* superiority of life—the deprivation of which is an "infinite violation" of personhood—over property, which is merely the "particular" trace of the person:

> *In extreme danger* and in collision with the legal property of someone else, this life may claim (not in equity but as a right) a *right of necessity*; for the alternatives are an infinite injury to existence with total loss of rights, and an injury only to an individual and limited existence of freedom.[114]

However, Hegel does not grant individuals an absolute right to life, and even less does he make the preservation of life the foundation of the whole legal system. Indeed, to give unlimited value to the principle of individual self-preservation would imply that the state itself must be subject to this principle, which would amount to making it a mere tool in the service of "life, liberty, and property" and would thus deprive it of its own ethical dignity. This kind of Lockean understanding of the relation between the state and life—which in a certain sense is also Hobbesian—rests on a confusion between the state and civil society and would, in the name of law, lead to the ruin of law's own political condition of actuality. If the ultimate end of the state institution were to protect the life and property of individuals, then it could not possibly legitimately require individuals to sacrifice life or property to it and would in this way abandon its essential predicate, sovereignty:

> It is a grave miscalculation if the state, when it requires this sacrifice [of life], is simply equated with civil society, and if its ultimate end is seen merely as the *security of the life and property* of individuals. For this security cannot be achieved by the sacrifice of what is supposed to be *secured*—on the contrary.[115]

---

112. See the introduction to Kant, *Rechtslehre: MdS*, Einleitung, *Ak.* 6, p. 236; *PP*, p. 392.

113. See Fichte, *Naturrecht, Werke*, 3:252.

114. *RPh*, § 127, *GW* 14.1, p. 112 (*Elements*, 154; see *Outlines*, 125).

115. *RPh*, § 324 Anmerkung, *GW* 14.1, p. 265 (*Elements*, 361; see *Outlines*, 306).

Military service, war, and taxes are in principle only acceptable if the state is recognized as having a "higher nature"[116] with respect to its citizen-subjects and to particular social interests, and thus, there is a supremacy over abstract law that proclaims the inviolability of person and property. In short, it is the very concept of objective spirit, or law in the broad sense, that justifies in its principle the theory of a legal (political) limitation of subjective rights, a theory that breaks with the individualist perspective of modern natural law according to which any restriction of rights can be justified only by the requirement to safeguard natural subjective rights.

However, Hegel does not only seek to establish the state's superiority over abstract law: the mission of the state is also to work to realize this law that reaches its limit in the state, to "make law a necessary actuality." The point here is not the trivial one that the state plays a role in administering civil and penal justice. Moreover, as we have seen, it is fundamentally the role of civil society itself to manage the law, though it does so under government control and via the intermediary of state functionaries.[117] If the state is the condition of the actuality of the law and rights, this is not because it oversees the application of norms that exist by themselves. Hegel's point is rather to show that the state's intervention in the field of abstract law is required by the very conditions of the social actualization of abstract law. Indeed, civil society actualizes abstract law, but this actualization is conflictual to the point of endangering the very existence of a society that in certain respects recalls the state of nature as Hobbes understood it, and this conflict threatens the legal order itself. The risk is inherent in the way social life constitutes the universal in and through the clash of individual and particular interests. In an overt allusion to Hobbes's *bellum omnium contra omnes,* Hegel writes that civil society is "the field of conflict in which the private interest of each individual comes up against that of everyone else."[118] For this reason, social conflict cannot be resolved socially. Here is not the place to present this aspect of the doctrine of civil society, which is quite well known thanks to Marx's use and development of it. But the conclusion of this doctrine gives us an answer to the questions I have raised

---

116. *RPh,* § 75 Anmerkung, *GW* 14.1, p. 78 (*Elements,* 106; see *Outlines,* 85), and *RPh,* § 100 Anmerkung, *GW* 14.1, pp. 92–93 (*Elements,* 126; see *Outlines,* 191). On the justification of taxes, see *RPh,* § 299 and Anmerkung, *GW* 14.1, p. 247 (*Elements,* 337–38; see *Outlines,* 285–86).

117. See *RPh,* § 287, *GW* 14.1, p. 241 (*Elements,* 328–29; see *Outlines,* 277–78).

118. *RPh,* § 289 Anmerkung, *GW* 14.1, p. 241 (*Elements,* 329; see *Outlines,* 278).

here: the structurally conflictual nature of the actualization of abstract law in bourgeois civil society establishes the need for a political authority outside of social particularity that can infringe on legal principles in order to ensure their actual, effective validity. The best example of this doctrine can be found in infringements on private property by a public power. This was a burning issue in the nineteenth century, when the requirements of legal security expressed by the problematic of the *Rechtstaat* intersected with imperatives linked to administrative organization and to the state's participation in economic and social transformations. Strictly speaking, such infringements are violations of private law and property, but they become legitimate when the implementation of the general principles of the law—personal freedom, the right of each individual to property and enterprise—risks being impeded by the particular assertion of certain rights or interests. Thus, the state may have to expropriate in the name of public utility or take control over certain activities (e.g., public services or even business in situations of monopoly) when the actual exercise of individual rights—and consequently the very existence of a civil society based on free enterprise—are compromised:

> [But those] determinations which concern private property may have to be subordinated to higher spheres of law, such as a community or the state. ... Nevertheless, such exceptions cannot be grounded in contingency, private arbitrariness, or private utility, but only in the rational organism of the state.[119]

The state's supremacy over law and rights is a result of the fact that it is impossible for the law to be spontaneously and coherently actualized in real civil society. The *social* actualization of the formal, legal universal is endangered by the particular material interests with which it must come into contact in order to be realized; it must therefore be reinforced by a *political* actualization.

The state—at least, the rational, postrevolutionary, constitutional state—is present in civil society in multiple forms because of the latter's structural inability to conform to its own principle and the tendency of the "system of atomism"[120] to endanger the atoms themselves—that is, social individuals in-

---

119. *RPh*, § 46 Anmerkung, *GW* 14.1, p. 58 (*Elements*, 77, see *Outlines*, 61).
120. *Enzykl*, § 523, *GW* 20, p. 498 (*Encyclopedia* 230).

sofar as they are "bourgeois" rather than "citizens."[121] Thus, contrary to the liberal view, the state is the condition of actualization of civil society itself rather than an appendix to it or the manager of its dysfunctions. The state has a social mission: to ensure that the universal exerts its influence over the particular. But its proper, political mission is to promote the unity of the particular and the universal *within the element of universality*. Just as the state encourages the flourishing of individuals and the always-particular (social) exercise of their rights, it must also lead individuals back "*to substantial unity*" and subordinate them to "the interest of the universal."[122] Initially, it is only the state (along with the philosopher) that knows that the state is also the "immanent end" of particular interests.[123] Consequently, if it is true that "freedom enters into its highest right" in the state, "an absolute and unmoved end in itself,"[124] then the right in question can no longer be identified with the right that jurists speak of. Thus, the actualization of formal law—first social, then political—culminates in a relativization of its principle: realizing its content (individual freedom) means going beyond what Hegel calls "law in a form that is lawful."[125] Of course, the state is not the negation of law—or rather, of the *rights* of individuals and social groups—but is on the contrary the ultimate condition of its actuality. But this task is far from exhausting its concept, and Hegel constantly works to denounce the error that consists in making the state a mere guarantor of the operations of private law and the night watchman of civil society.

It is necessary to rigorously separate the spheres and modes of action of abstract/private law from those of the state in order to prevent the risk of weakening the political fabric (as in the case of feudalism and the *Ständestaat*, blighted by the "privatization" of political relations) as well as the risk of politics taking on the attributes of law and ignoring its own limits (which can lead to a reign of terror). Hence, the specific nature of the political bond as well as the articulation of civil society and the state requires the political relativization of abstract law, but this relativization corresponds to precise conditions. Though Hegel does contest the ideology of the rights of man because it cloaks

---

121. See chapter 4 below.

122. *RPh*, § 260, *GW* 14.1, p. 208 (*Elements*, 282; see *Outlines*, 235).

123. *RPh*, § 261, *GW* 14.1, p. 208 (*Elements*, 283; see *Outlines*, 236).

124. *RPh*, § 258, *GW* 14.1, p. 201 (*Elements*, 275; see *Outlines*, 228).

125. *RPh*, § 220, *GW* 14.1, p. 183 (*Elements*, 252, modified; see *Outlines*, 209).

an absolute politics that seems dangerous to him, he does consider personal freedom and the legal forms that express it to be the intangible core of "eternal human rights."[126] Consequently, a temporary infringement of property may be necessary to save the principle of personal freedom, but in order not to destroy that very principle in the process, the infringement must not be made solely in the name of legal values that are more or less arbitrarily invoked against positive law. If the state can, without contradiction, be the guarantor of the legal order while also committing violations of its principles, this is precisely because it itself is not a construction that arises from abstract law. Thus, the goal of refusing to give the state a legal underpinning is not only to distinguish between public and private law; it is also to authorize the state, understood as the political realization of objective freedom, to be the *external*, fully legitimate guarantor of the law and its actualizations. What might at first glance appear to be an ambiguous or contradictory position—the state must simultaneously promote and relativize (and thus contradict) the law—is in fact the expression of a coherent theoretical choice: it is because the essence of the state is not legal and because its "right" is a higher form of freedom than private law that it is able to see to it that private law is actualized in civil society.

But this is only the case if the state conforms to its concept, if it truly is the institutionalization of a community of individuals whose "destiny" is, thanks to the state, to "lead a universal life"[127] rather than a machine subjecting individuals to an arbitrary and oppressive law. The goal of the distinction between state and civil society is not to oppose the rights of the latter to the former but rather to constantly affirm that which connects "the external state"[128]—in truth it is first external to itself—to the "rational life of self-conscious freedom"[129] as it unfolds in the public space. The state, says Hegel, is "*union* as such";[130] it unites a city that everything else condemns to division and conflicts of interests, especially after the distinction between the political and the social has been made. Moreover, this inevitable conflict enriches a community that lives on its differences and tensions if it is overcome otherwise than through violence (in which case civil society would truly become

126. *Enzykl*, § 433 Zusatz, *W* 10, p. 224 (*Encyclopedia* 160).

127. *RPh*, § 258 Anmerkung, *GW* 14.1, pp. 201–2 (*Elements*, 275; see *Outlines*, 229).

128. *RPh*, *GW* 14.1, § 157, 183, *GW* 14.1, pp. 143, 160 (*Elements*, 198, 221; see *Outlines*, 162, 181); *Enzykl*, § 523, *GW* 20, p. 498 (*Encyclopedia* 230).

129. *RPh*, § 270 Anmerkung, *GW* 14.1, p. 218 (*Elements*, 297; see *Outlines*, 248).

130. *RPh*, § 258 Anmerkung, *GW* 14.1, p. 213 (*Elements*, 276; see *Outlines*, 229).

the state of nature whose trace it preserves). The path to achieving this enrichment is open when there exists a state in the emphatic sense, an instance of the universal on which the affirmation of particularity in its relative right depends but which has become concretely actual through this instance. For Hegel, the state's supremacy is the condition of law's actuality, for there is no individual freedom that is not supported and circumscribed by a freedom that is combined with the universal.

Law below and beyond Law

The arena in which the law is actualized — that is, where law's abstract concept becomes concretely objective — is civil society, the full development of which is itself only possible within and under the hegemony of the rational state. Thus, the full actualization of the law is very recent. We know that for Hegel, the French Revolution represents the explosive and terrible ascent of law and rights as such to the rank of principle of the social and political order:

> The conception, the idea of Law asserted its authority *all at once,* and the old framework of injustice could offer no resistance to its onslaught. A constitution, therefore, was established in harmony with the idea of Law, and on this foundation all future legislation was to be based.[131]

The corruption of this principle (e.g., the Terror) does not result from its abstraction, which in itself is neither good nor bad, but rather from the attempt to make it the foundation of a state. That attempt is the concrete culmination of the theoretical errors of natural law doctrines: the very structure of that kind of reasoning, the full consequences of which Rousseau developed, could not but encourage the project of razing the existing state of things and undertaking the refounding of the state on purely rational bases, at least in the sense of reason as mere understanding (*Verstand*).[132] On the other hand, the historical achievement of the Revolution was to have encouraged and even imposed the institution of an order of private law and the development of a civil, bourgeois society, which translates the relative but real positivity of the legal

131. *Geschichte, W* 12, p. 529 / 466 (modified). See also *Wurtemberg, W* 4, p. 507; *Proceedings,* in *Hegel's Political Writings,* 282.

132. See *RPh,* § 258 Anmerkung, *GW* 14.1, p. 202 (*Elements,* 276–77; see *Outlines,* 229–30).

principle of social abstraction. The articulation of law, economy, and politics that Hegel presents in the *Philosophy of Right* can only have actuality in the postrevolutionary world. I will retain just one point from this analysis of the French Revolution as a revolution of the law (and rights): the actualization of law, which in itself is essentially nonhistorical, maintains a noncontingent relation with history, the actualizing act of reason in its totality. The actualization of abstract law is an integral part of the universal process by which Spirit reaches its concrete truth. But what about law at the margins of world history?

For Hegel, there is no history other than political and state history. Strictly speaking, what happened before the appearance of the city must be considered prehistoric. That situation corresponds to what is traditionally called a *state of nature*, though this term has most often been understood erroneously, or more precisely, fictively. But the term does designate — inadequately, no doubt — a situation that must be considered: it is a fiction, but a necessary fiction, one that constitutes "the crudest contradiction."[133] The state of nature according to Hobbes, who "takes this state [of nature] in its true sense,"[134] is a "state governed entirely by force," against which "the Idea sets up a *right of heroes*."[135] We know how important the figure of Theseus was in the young Hegel's political writings,[136] but the figure of the mythical city's founder also appears in his mature work, where it plays a key role. The hero is the one who through violence brings an end to the violence of the state of nature. His right — which in truth is proclaimed by no one but himself and in the language of force alone — is based solely on that which it brings to an end, and the only legitimacy that can be retroactively recognized in the hero is to have factually opened the space of history and political reason. Such right is prelegal, because it is exercised before "the actual beginning of history,"[137] whereas all true right is part of a historical process of institutionalization; such right is even *anti*legal, because although violence can be and actually is "the external beginning" or the "beginning as it appears" of law, it cannot constitute its "substantial principle"

---

133. *Naturrecht, W* 2, p. 445 (*Natural Law*, 63).

134. *W* 20, p. 227.

135. *RPh*, § 93 Anmerkung, *GW* 14.1, p. 88 (*Elements*, 120; see *Outlines*, 98). Hegel specifies that this is "a right of heroes to establish states" (*RPh*, § 350, *GW* 14.1, p. 277 [*Elements*, 376; see *Outlines*, 319).

136. See "Verfassung," *W* 1, p. 579 ("German Constitution," in *Hegel's Political Writings*, 241) and *GW* 8, p. 258.

137. *RPh*, § 349 Anmerkung, *GW* 14.1, p. 277 (*Elements*, 375; see *Outlines*, 318).

or "foundation."[138] In certain respects, the right of heroes is an absolute right: it symbolically designates the original decision that ensures passage from the state of nature to the legal and political order. This mythological representation replaces the idea of social contract, which Hegel explicitly rejects on the grounds that it generates theoretical illusions[139]; and in effect, this representation has the twofold advantage first of not reducing public law to private law even implicitly and second of avoiding the normativist fiction of a closed, self-founding legal order. But the mythical figure of the hero also takes on the role of Plato's lawgiver: with this figure, Hegel consciously chooses to link the originary act with that which precedes it—the blind violence of the war of all against all—and not with what comes after it—the history and objective development of ethical and legal rationality. The first negation of nonright, the "right" of heroes remains on the side of nonright or violence. It is absolute, but it is not a right, because, like the master's right over the slave or the conqueror's over the conquered, it is exercised within a milieu that, compared to "the *concept* of the human being as spirit," is "absolutely contrary to right."[140]

There is nothing coincidental about the similarity between the "right" of heroes and the master's power over the slave. Like the master's power, the hero's is a *Herrenschaft*, a brutal domination, rather than a *Herrschaft*, a legitimate subordination:

> The alleged justification of *slavery* . . . as well as the justification of the *master's status* as simple lordship in general . . . depend on regarding the human being simply as a *natural being* whose *concrete existence* [*Existenz*] . . . is not in conformity with his concept.[141]

Discussing the figure of "lordship and bondage" from the *Phenomenology of Spirit*, Hegel indicates that it involves the "relationship of lordship [*Herrenschaft*] and servitude [*Knechtschaft*]."[142] Similarly, at the beginning of the lectures on history, he says, regarding the creation of the state, "during this first phase in its evolution, the state is imperious [*herrisch*] and ruled by instinct."[143]

---

138. *Enzykl*, § 433 Anmerkung, *GW* 20, p. 431 (*Encyclopedia* 160).
139. See chapter 3 below.
140. *RPh*, § 57 Anmerkung, *GW* 14.1, p. 65 (*Elements*, 86–87; see *Outlines*, 69–70).
141. *RPh*, § 57 Anmerkung, *GW* 14.1, p. 65 (*Elements*, 86–87; see *Outlines*, 69–70).
142. *RPh*, § 57 Anmerkung, *GW* 14.1, p. 64 (*Elements*, 87, modified; *Outlines*, 70).
143. Hegel, *Die Vernunft in der Geschichte*, 146; *Lectures on the Philosophy of World History*.

It thus seems clear that in Hegel's mature writings, the term *Herrschaft*, distinguished from *Herrenschaft*, refers exclusively to the specifically political act of governing (*herrschen* in the sense of "to govern") and not to any prepolitical form of brute dominance. This is demonstrated a contrario by what Napoleon, one of the few modern heroes, said to the Germans he had defeated: "I am not your prince, I am your master." However, unlike the master's "right" over the slave, which is null because it claims to be a right, the (non)right of the hero has absolute—though temporary—legitimacy because it does not invoke a right in order to institute it. In this respect, it is similar to the absolutely absolute right of the world spirit.

If the right of heroes is not yet right, the right of absolute spirit lies beyond right. Hegel repeatedly says that this right of the *Weltgeist* is the only "absolute"[144] right, but it is clear that this right, like the right of the hero, has only a distant relation to right in the legal sense of the term. In that case, why keep using the name *right*? A first answer lies in the definition of *right* given in the *Philosophy of Right*, which states that "each stage in the development of the Idea of freedom has its distinctive right."[145] It is somewhat difficult, however, to apply this definition to the world spirit which, though it is the ultimate figure of objective spirit, does not in its full sense belong to that sphere, nor, consequently, does it exhibit its type of freedom, *objective* freedom. We may find proof of this in Hegel's use of Schiller's expression, "die Weltgeschichte ist das Weltgericht."[146] This expression, so often cited, actually contains a double meaning—and far from signaling some ambiguity of Hegel's argument, the double meaning translates the complexity of the process of objective spirit, whose ultimate sense is created within history, while also going beyond history's (merely) objective dimension.

In the first place, the world spirit's judgment cannot be appealed: it is always a death sentence, and it applies to each of the nations [*Volk*] that have, in turn, been the "agents of its actualization" and "witnesses and ornaments of its splendour."[147] It is true that unlike the nation that "dominates" an epoch,

144. *RPh*, § 30 Anmerkung, *GW* 14.1, p. 46 (*Elements*, 59; see also *Outlines*, 48). See also § 33, 340.

145. *RPh*, § 30 Anmerkung, *GW* 14.1, p. 46 (*Elements*, 59; see *Outlines*, 47).

146. See *RPh*, § 340, 342, *GW* 14.1, pp. 272, 274 (*Elements*, 371–72; see *Outlines*, 315–16) and *Enzykl*, § 548, *GW* 20, p. 523 (*Encyclopedia* 246).

147. *RPh*, § 352, *GW* 14.1, p. 278 (*Elements*, 376; see *Outlines*, 319).

"the spirits of other nations are without rights";[148] but it is true, too, that every nation, once its task has been accomplished, must step aside in favor of a higher principle that first appears as "simply the negative of its own."[149] However depressing this process might appear at first glance, it must not be confused with "the abstract and irrational necessity of a blind fate":[150] the history of the world is and remains the work of rational freedom becoming objective in history through combat with its own negativity; it is "the actualization of the universal spirit" in the successive negations of its particular figures.

The figure of a tribunal here takes on a second, final meaning: the world spirit's judgment not only refers to one of its particular, successive expressions; it is the judgment the world spirit pronounces on the totality that it is, revealing itself in this act as *absolute* spirit. *Weltgericht* in the ordinary sense of the term refers to the Last Judgment: in it, the world itself in the totality of its historical figures is judged—in other words, objective spirit, insofar as in its very concreteness it is still only the abstract form of spirit's absolute presence to itself:

> But the thinking spirit of world history, when it sheds these limitations of the particular national spirits as well as its own worldliness, grasps its concrete universality and ascends to *awareness of the absolute spirit*, as the eternally actual truth in which rational awareness is free for itself, and necessity, nature and history are only servants of its revelation and vessels of its honour.[151]

Absolute spirit's presence to itself—of which philosophy is the reflected expression—of course can only be achieved when objective spirit has arrived at its ultimate ethical-political expression, when spirit's reconciliation with itself has "become objective" through the "rationality of right and law" and insofar as the state has been revealed as "the image and actuality of reason."[152] But this self-presence cannot possibly be exhausted in *objective* reconciliation.

---

148. *RPh*, § 347, *GW* 14.1, p. 506 (*Elements*, 374; see *Outlines*, 317).
149. *RPh*, § 347 Anmerkung, *GW* 14.1, p. 276 (*Elements*, 374; see *Outlines*, 318).
150. *RPh*, § 342, *GW* 14.1, p. 504; *PPD*, p. 431 (*Elements*, 372; see *Outlines*, 316).
151. *Enzykl*, § 552, *GW* 20, p. 530 (*Encyclopedia* 250).
152. *RPh*, § 360, *GW* 14.1, p. 512 (*Elements*, 380; see *Outlines*, 323).

Once law has reached the end of the historical process of its realization, it is left behind once and for all along with the sphere of objective spirit in its entirety, whose backbone is composed of the various figures of the law. It is indicative of the system's speculative ambition that the ultimate and absolute realization of law is strictly speaking no longer of the order of law and that full freedom is no longer *objective* freedom but rather is reflected in itself as freedom of the concept: as the act of philosophizing. This is perhaps why our own epoch—if it is indeed the epoch of "postmetaphysical thought"—must necessarily find it difficult to endorse a philosophy ordered around the "relativization" of right, law, and politics through "metaphysical" speculation.

2

Between Nature and History

The Law

In studying modern legal-political theories, it is descriptively useful to contrast, as Leo Strauss did,[1] natural law and historicism. One can then show that these doctrinal currents (the first of which, according to Strauss, is actually a double current, because modern natural law is in many respects a renunciation of the principles of classical natural law) are based on opposite theoretical premises: in one case, the basis is the existence of a universal, atemporal reason that can form the foundation of practical philosophy and the positive disciplines it governs, the law first and foremost; in the other case, the premise is that law, like any other cultural configuration, is part of a unique tradition (national, cultural, scientific) that presupposes an interpretative work intended to elucidate the always original configurations of meaning that constitute it. In addition, in historical-chronological terms, it is common to distinguish the age of natural law (the seventeenth to eighteenth centuries) from the century of history (the nineteenth century), which was also the century that saw the rise of the various currents that can be grouped under the general name of *historicism*.[2] However, this double distinction—thematic and dy-

1. See the first chapter of Leo Strauss, *Natural Right and History* (Chicago: University of Chicago Press, 1965).

2. On this, see the classic works of Ernst Troeltsch, *Der Historismus und seine Probleme*, vol. 3

namic—quickly reaches its limit when it comes to studying specific examples. In chronological terms, natural law as a structure of thought and as a program of teaching and research long outlived its supposed end.[3] In theoretical terms, it is sometimes difficult to separate the natural law elements from the historicist elements of a given theory: thus, today's research on the works of Friedrich Carl von Savigny, the spokesperson for legal historicism, emphasizes the massive presence of elements of natural law in his work due to the influence of Kant in particular.[4]

Like Savigny, his colleague in Berlin and his theoretical adversary Hegel lived through a time of transition during which the natural law constructions that had dominated theoretical production began to give way as historicism temporarily imposed itself. This in part explains why assessments of Hegel's work contain some striking contradictions. Despite the subtitle to the *Philosophy of Right, Naturrecht und Staatswissenschaft im Grundrisse* (Natural law and the science of the state)—which is more traditional than the primary title—many commentators saw the work as a break with the metaphysical and anthropological presuppositions of modern natural law and a return to the holistic, or at least nonindividualist, perspective of ancient natural law. Joachim Ritter, for example, interprets the theory of ethicality as a rejection of the individualist assumptions and contractualist constructions of modern political theories. Without contesting the crucial consequences that abandoning references to the model of the *polis* had on the formation of the Hegelian system, Ritter sees the concept of *Sittlichkeit* as a kind of rehabilitation of the Aristotelian concept of nature and therefore of *nomos*.[5] Inversely, Manfred Riedel and Norberto Bobbio see in Hegel both the culmination and the criti-

of *Gesammelte Schriften* (Tübingen: Mohr, 1922), and Friedrich Meinecke, *Die Entstehung der Historismus*, vol. 3 of Friedrich Meinecke, *Werke* (Munich: Oldenbourg, 1959).

3. On this point, see Jan Schröder and Ines Pielemeier, "Naturrecht als Lehrfach an den deutschen Universitäten des 18. und 19. Jahrhunderts," in *Naturrecht, Spätaufklärung, Revolution*, ed. Otto Dann and Diethelm Klippel (Hambourg: Meiner, 1995), pp. 255–92, and Diethelm Klippel, "Die Historisierung Des Naturrechts," in *Recht zwischen Natur und Geschichte*, ed. Heinz Mohnhaupt and Jean-François Kervégan (Frankfurt: Klostermann, 1997), 103–24.

4. See in particular Dieter Nörr, *Savignys philosophische Lehrjahre: Ein Versuch* (Frankfurt: Klostermann, 1994); Joachim Rückert, *Idealismus, Jurisprudenz und Politik bei F. C. von Savigny* (Ebelsbach: Gremer, 1984); Walter Wilhelm, "Savignys überpositiv Systematik," in *Philosophie und Rechtswissenschaft. Zum Problem ihrer Beziehung im 19. Jahrhundert*, ed. Jürgen Blühdorn and Joachim Ritter (Frankfurt: Klostermann, 1969), 123–36.

5. See Joachim Ritter, "Moralität Und Sittlichkeit. Zu Hegels Auseinandersetzung mit der

cal dissolution of modern natural law.[6] Riedel, in particular, emphasizes that the distinction between civil society and the state has come to replace natural law's separation between the state of nature and the state of society and in a sense continues it by maintaining this dual structure. In an entirely different perspective, Karl Löwith sees Hegel as promoting the historicist point of view that seized hold of modern thought as soon as it tried to renounce the assumptions of historical theology. Because Hegel conceives history as well as nature itself on the basis of the concept of spirit, he secularizes the Christian (Augustinian) understanding of history as an eschatological expectation of the fulfillment of a promise of meaning.[7] Read in such a light, Hegel breaks both with the political thought of antiquity and with the Christian theology of redemption. The transformation of salvation (*Heilgeschehen*) into the course of world history (*Weltgeschehen*), of the Last Judgment into the tribunal of history, and of Providence into the cunning of reason is, according to this view, the result of substitutions whose general gist is that humanity is the privileged vector of spirit.[8] On this point, Löwith agrees with Leo Strauss, for whom Hegel and Marx completed the turn to historicism and humanism that had been gradually underway in modern thought since Machiavelli and Hobbes. However, for Strauss, the decisive factor in this development was Hegel's break with ancient practical philosophy and thus, in a sense, with natural law (Aristotle, the Stoics).[9] How can we make sense of such differences of interpretation? We could of course explain them through the Hegelian "ambiguity" that has been so often decried since the time of Rudolf Haym.[10] But we might also con-

---

Kantischen Ethik," in *Metaphysik und Politik: Studien zu Aristoteles und Hegel* (Frankfurt: Suhrkamp, 1969. Reprint, 2003), 203–309.

6. See Manfred Riedel, "Hegels Kritik des Naturrechts," in *Zwischen tradition und Revolution: Studien zu Hegels Rechtsphilosophie*, ed. Manfred Riedel (Stuttgart: Klett-Cotta, 1982), 170–203. Norberto Bobbio's argument is similar: "With regard to the tradition of natural law, Hegel's legal philosophy is both a dissolution and a fulfillment." See Norberto Bobbio, *Studi Hegeliani* (Turin: Einaudi, 1981), 3.

7. See Karl Löwith, *Meaning in History: The Theological Implications of the Philosophy of History* (Chicago: University of Chicago Press, 1949), 52–59.

8. See Löwith, "Mensch und Geschichte" and "Hegels Aufhebung der christlichen Religion," in *Sämtliche Schriften* (Stuttgart: J. B. Metzler, 1988), 2:364–68 and 116–66, respectively.

9. See Leo Strauss, *What Is Political Philosophy? And Other Studies* (Chicago: University of Chicago Press, 1988), 53–54, 88.

10. See Haym, *Hegel und Seine Zeit*, 368–71. In general the discussion between Haym and Karl Rosenkranz ("Hegel und seine Zeit, 1844"; "Apologie Hegels gegen Dr. Haym, 1858"; "Hegel

sider that all these assessments of Hegel accept, perhaps too easily, the *topos* of modern thought wherein nature and history are opposed. We may then wonder whether one of the original features of Hegel's legal-political thought, as well as its richness, comes precisely from rejecting this opposition, or at least, inscribing it within a theoretical context that transforms its meaning.

The Critique of Modern Natural Law: The Historical Emphasis

Hegel's critique of modern natural law, which he began in his 1802 article "Scientific Ways of Treating Natural Law," remained consistent and stable down to his last Berlin writings, although his philosophy at large underwent considerable transformations. Certainly the critique of the two major currents Hegel identifies in modern natural law—the "empiricist" natural law of Grotius, Hobbes, Pufendorf, and Locke[11] and the "formalist" view of Kant and Fichte—is principally carried out from the point of view of Schelling's philosophy of identity as presented in the latter's *System of Transcendental Idealism* and the *Presentation of My System of Philosophy*. It is also, however, based on an understanding of the ethics of the *polis* that rests on a very free use of certain texts by Plato and Aristotle, and the coordination of these two lines of argumentation does pose some problems. Through his critique of certain major concepts in the theory of natural law (mainly, the state of nature and the social contract), Hegel condemns modernity itself insofar as it creates a scission between the political and the legal-economic, between citizen and burgher, to the exclusive benefit of the latter. As Rousseau writes, "The real meaning of this word ['city'] has been almost completely erased among the moderns; most people take a town for a city, and a bourgeois for a citizen. They do not know that houses make the town, and that citizens make the city."[12] In the 1802

---

als deutscher Nationalphilosoph, 1870") established the terms of the debate over the meaning of the entirety of Hegelianism in a remarkably enduring manner. See Henning Ottmann, *Individuum und Gemeinschaft: Hegel im Spiegel der Interpretationen* (Berlin: Walter de Gruyter, 1977), 74–85.

11. The case of Rousseau is more complex. On one hand, he clearly fits into the conceptual framework of modern natural law; on the other hand, the young Hegel (and this is still true in the 1802 article) based his thought on Rousseau's in order to denounce the modern perversion of ethics, where the point of view of the "bourgeois" has supplanted that of the citizen. See below, chapter 4.

12. Rousseau, *Oeuvres complètes*, 3:361; *Social Contract*, 1:6, 164.

article as well as in the fragment known as the "System of Ethicality" (*System der Sittlichkeit*), the critique of modernity through modernity's own thought of itself is made by explicit reference to the idea of an ethic of the *polis* or citizenship. Modern humans abandon "what the Greeks called *politeuein*, which mean[t] living in and with and for one's people, leading a general life wholly devoted to the public interest."[13] Absolute ethicality (*Sittlichkeit*—civic) is a rejection of the privatization of existence embodied by relative ethicality (*Sittlichkeit*—bourgeois), to which modern natural law gives theoretical form.

As we know, Hegel quickly abandoned the model or ideal of the *polis*, which guided his argument in the article on natural law. This abandonment was in part linked to his disillusion following the tragic course of the French Revolution, which represented a revitalization of the *polis* and in part to the constitution of his definitive philosophy, first expressed in the *Phenomenology of Spirit*. The transformation can be seen in the later Jena writings. Thus, the 1805–1806 *Philosophy of Spirit* sanctions the crisis addressed by the model of the "beautiful ethical totality," which the article on natural law and the *System der Sittlichkeit* still valorized against the modern world. On one hand, individuals' immediate belonging to the political universal—the principle of ancient *Sittlichkeit*—is still presented as an ideal "that was and remains so envied."[14] But, precisely, it is nothing more than an *ideal* that the modern world has rejected, which is not necessarily a bad thing. Hegel contrasts ancient *Sittlichkeit* with the "highest principle of modern times, which Plato and the Ancients did not know. . . . By this principle, actual external freedom is effectively lost in individuals' immediate existence, but inner freedom, freedom of thought, is obtained."[15] Hegel became more and more clearly aware of this principle as he moved from the *Phenomenology of Spirit* to the *Philosophy of Right* and the *Encyclopedia*: the superiority of modernity derives from the fact that under certain legal and political conditions the affirmation of the particular individual is not incompatible with the primacy of the universal, outside of which the very existence of an *ethical*-political community is impossible. As we know, this "union with time"[16] (i.e., with modernity) undertaken by Hegel beginning in

13. *Naturrecht, W* 2, p. 489 (*Natural Law*, 100).

14. Hegel speaks of the "beautiful happy freedom of the Greeks," *GW* 8, p. 262. See also *PhG, GW* 20, pp. 194–96; *Phenomenology of Spirit*, trans. A. V. Miller (Oxford: Oxford University Press, 2015), ¶¶ 349–53.

15. *GW* 8, pp. 263–64.

16. *Systemfragment, W* 1, p. 427.

his Frankfurt period and culminating during his stay in Jena (1802–1807) owed a great deal to his discovery of Anglo-Saxon political-economic thought.[17]

This transformation of the very bases of Hegel's ethical-political thought had a twofold effect on his reiterated critique of modern natural law.

1. First of all, Hegel maintained and deepened his criticism of the *conceptual tools* of the doctrine of natural law: "the fiction of the state of nature" and the social contract. I will discuss only the former here, as the next chapter deals with contracts. Hegel's argument about the state of nature remained essentially the same as in the 1802 article on natural law. The state of nature is a fiction, but it is a necessary fiction if the individualist premises of modern natural law are accepted. Moreover, if such a perspective is adopted, Hobbes's view must be emphasized, for it is the most rigorous and the most probable — and above all, it is the only one capable of supporting the argument for the unconditional necessity of the political order.[18] Hegel uses the *exeundum e statu naturae* (go forth from a state of nature) of *De Cive*, though he erroneously attributes it to Spinoza,[19] but he gives it a new scope. In reality, if the notion of the state of nature still has (relative) relevance, it is because it provides an image of the very negation of all legal relations. The state of nature can only be conceived or imagined (*erdichtet* is the word used in the article on natural law) as the inverse, or more precisely, the negative of *Rechtzustand*, the "condition of law" constituted by society and state:

> But in fact law and all its determinations are based on the free personality alone, a self determination, which is the very contrary of determination by nature. The law of nature is therefore the embodiment of strength and the assertion of force, and a state of nature is a state of violence and wrong, of which nothing truer can be said than that one ought to depart from it.[20]

17. See below, the preliminary to part 2.

18. For the relationship between Hegel and Hobbes, see Victor Goldschmidt, "État de nature et pacte de soumission chez Hegel," *Revue Philosophique de la France et de l'Étranger* 89 (1964): 45–65; Ludwig Siep, "Der Kampf um Anerkennung. Hegels Auseinandersetzung mit Hobbes" *Hegel-Studien* 9 (1974): 155–207; Jacques Taminiaux, "Commentaire," in *Naissance de la philosophie Hégélienne de l'état: Commentaire et traduction de la Realphilosophie d'Iéna (1805–1806)* (Paris: Payot, 1984), 133 ff.

19. Hegel, *Die Vernunft in der Geschichte*, 117; *Lectures on the Philosophy of World History*, 98.

20. *Enzykl*, § 502 Anmerkung, *GW* 20, p. 488 (*Encyclopedia* 223). This passage is the only Berlin text in which *Gesellschaft* is used in the traditional sense of *societas civilis* (= *politica*), not the new meaning it acquired in Hegel from 1817 on. This is explained by the fact that the text was

Consequently, if the state of nature is something other than a negation in thought of the actual political-legal order, if it has de facto existence,[21] it constitutes *violence* against the possibility of ethicality. In any case, the state of nature cannot take on any *normative* signification because it is that by which all normativity is rendered impossible by principle. At most, the notion has descriptive utility insofar as it reveals, by antithesis, the distinctive characteristics of sociopolitical actuality. Hegel always uses the state of nature in this way, but in fact Rousseau did the same, writing that "the researches, in which we may engage on this occasion, are not to be taken for historical truths, but merely as hypothetical and conditional reasonings, fitter to illustrate the nature of things, than to show their true origin."[22] It thus seems established, at least on the basis of this example, that Hegel's critique of the foundational *concepts* of modern natural law does not imply that he rejects the *project* of natural — or, more accurately, rational — law.

2. But Hegel does not limit himself to critiquing the conceptual tools of the modern theory of natural law; he also seems to critique its very intention, as in the Remark to section 502 of the *Encyclopedia*:

> The expression natural law, which has been customary for philosophical jurisprudence, involves ambiguity: it may mean that law is present in an immediately natural way, or it may mean that law is determined by the nature of the thing, i.e. by the concept.[23]

This passage is generally understood as a radical critique of the problematic of natural law. In reality, it is only the *vocabulary* of natural law that is called into question here because of the fallacious representations to which it can give rise. The 1817–1818 Heidelberg course (which was the first draft for the *Philosophy of Right*) is much clearer on this point:

---

written earlier: it was used in a very similar form in the 1809 Nuremberg Gymnasium course, which still opposed, as Aristotle did, *Staatgesellschaft* to *natürliche Gesellschaft*, the family. See *Propädeutik, W* 4, pp. 245–46.

21. This question of the factual or solely conceptual character of the state of nature is a stumbling block for even the most rigorous natural law theories; see Hobbes, *Leviathan*, 2:194–96; Rousseau, *Oeuvres complètes*, 3:123 and 32–33.

22. Rousseau, *Oeuvres complètes*, 3:132–33; *Social Contract*, 88.

23. *Enzykl*, § 502 Anmerkung, *GW* 20, p. 488 (*Encyclopedia* 223).

The term "natural law" [*Naturrecht*] ought to be abandoned and replaced by the term "philosophical doctrine of law" [*philosophische Rechtslehre*], or (as will also emerge) "doctrine of objective spirit." The expression "nature" [*Natur*] contains the ambiguity that by it we understand [(1)] the essence [*Wesen*] and concept [*Begriff*] of something, (2) unconscious, immediate nature as such.[24]

We see here that though he distances himself from the term *natural law*, Hegel does indeed validate modern natural law's intention to ground law in reason. However, the theoretical uncertainties of this doctrinal current, revealed by notions such as the state of nature, are not coincidental.

In reality, Hegel's fundamental reproach to modern natural law has less to do with its terminology—if that were the case it would be enough to replace the word *nature* with the word *reason* to give it full and complete validity—and more with the insufficiency of its concept of rationality. It is the reduction of reason to a capacity for calculation—a reduction Hobbes made with great consequence[25]—that, in turn, caused natural law theory to hold erroneous views about the foundation of law and led to fallacious conclusions about the state. But if it is true that the fatal flaw in the theory of natural/rational law is that it uses an impoverished version of reason, it is only fitting—and this seems to be Hegel's implicit argument—to *reconstruct this theory on the basis of a different concept of rationality*, the very one developed by speculative philosophy, especially in the *Science of Logic*. As we saw in the last chapter, this led Hegel to articulate, from the very first paragraph of the *Philosophy of Right*, a distinction between the *concept* and the *idea* of law, which profoundly changes the meaning and scope of the term.

Therefore, the rationality of law—axiomatic in theories of natural law—is no longer known solely by the subtle deductive constructions of the understanding; it is also, and even more importantly, measured by the ability of legal abstraction to be embodied in a set of concrete historical configurations, *Gestaltungen*.[26] Thus we can already see that, on Hegel's view, philosophy of

---

24. Hegel, *Lectures on Natural Right and Political Science: The First Philosophy of Right*, trans. Michael J. Stewart and Peter C. Hodgson (Oxford: Oxford University Press, 2012), § 2, p. 52; *Vorlesungen über Naturrecht und Staatswissenschaft*, 6.

25. See chapter 5 in Hobbes, *Leviathan*, 2:64.

26. See *RPh*, § 32, *GW* 14.1, 47 (*Elements*, 60; see *Outlines*, 49).

law must necessarily be connected to and used within a *political philosophy* and a *philosophy of history* as well as a moral philosophy. This cannot but have consequences for his attitude toward natural law. Of course, Kant and Fichte also connect law, morality, politics, and history, but only Hegel conceives the process of world history as the field in which the abstract principles of law in the broad sense are actualized. Consequently, his thinking about law includes a shift in emphasis from *nature* to *history*.

The Historical and the Rational: The Normativity of the Concept

This way of understanding rational law implies a new articulation between rational and positive law in which the *historicity* not solely of law itself but also of its actualization in objective configurations (e.g., in the family or in civil society) plays a determining role. The historical achievement of the determinations of law that are in themselves ahistorical (e.g., the freeing of private property from all the hindrances imposed by the feudal and postfeudal orders) shows that these determinations, which are isolated and made absolute by the constructions of natural law theorists, are in truth a "dependent moment within *one* totality, in the context of all the other determinations which constitute the character of a nation and age."[27] The fact that in presenting the connection between natural or philosophical law and the "historical element of positive law" Hegel refers to Montesquieu is indicative of the changes he intends to make to natural law without thereby trying to reject its fundamental intention. The argument he makes against historicism in the same context shows this clearly.

The "true historical view" that Hegel, following Montesquieu, advocates in this same passage opposes the *isolation of law*[28] that legal historicism operates. In this regard, legal historicism is similar to natural law theory, though its aims and routes are entirely different. Hegel responds to the representatives of rigid natural law—as embodied by Christian Wolff, whom Hegel mocks on several occasions for his claim to demonstrate empirical, contingent provisions as if they were geometry theorems[29]—by emphasizing the unsurpass-

27. *RPh*, § 3 Anmerkung, *GW* 14.1, p. 26 (*Elements*, 29; see *Outlines*, 20).

28. See Yan Thomas, "Mommsen et l'*Isolierung* du droit," in Théodore Mommsen, *Le droit public romain* (Paris: De Boccard, 1992), 1:1–48.

29. Wolff "extended this application to every kind of bits of knowledge that he dragged into

able "limit" of "philosophical law," which allows him to "rule out any possible idea [*Vorstellung*], let alone expectation, that [philosophical law's] systematic development should give rise to a positive code of laws such as is required by an actual state."[30] It is absurd to want to deduce a civil or penal code from the requirements of reason or scientific understanding alone. Moreover, authentic, speculative reason knows that historically concrete actual law includes an irreducibly contingent, nonscientific element. However, to the "historian" adversaries of natural or philosophical law (Hegel somewhat unfairly has Gustav Hugo representing this school, although in fact Savigny is the implicit target of the polemic in § 3 of the *Philosophy of Right*), Hegel points out that "philosophical law" and "positive law" are of course different but not nessarily opposite or contradictory: the relation between them is instead "like that between Institutes and Pandects."[31] The comparison is no doubt a clumsy one and shows the limits of Hegel's information about Roman and scholarly notions of law — limits that Gustav Hugo did not hesitate to point out in his review of the *Philosophy of Right*.[32] But the point is to emphasize that the inevitable discordances between the historical-positive and the rational — discordances whose causes Hegel lays out in his very definition of the positivity of law — do not and cannot affect their unity of principle:

> Law is in general *positive* (a) through its *form* of having validity within a [particular] state; and this legal authority is the principle which underlies knowledge [*Kenntnis*] of law, i.e. *the positive science of law*. (b) In terms of *content*, this law acquires a positive element (α) through the particular *national character* of a people, its stage of *historical* development, and the whole context of relations governed by *natural necessity*, (β) through the

---

philosophy and mathematics — cognitions which were partly of a wholly analytical nature, and partly also devoted to practical matters of an incidental kind." See *WdL* 3, *GW* 12, p. 228 (*Science of Logic*, 726). This desire to rationalize (in this case, to geometrize) the empirical results in a "barbarism of pedantry" that is also a "pedantry of barbarism." Hegel, *Werke*, 20:263; *Lectures on the History of Philosophy*, 356.

30. *RPh*, § 3 Anmerkung, *GW* 14.1, p. 25 (*Elements*, 28–29; see *Outlines*, 20).

31. *RPh*, § 3 Anmerkung, *GW* 14.1, p. 25 (*Elements*, 28–29; see *Outlines*, 20).

32. "The author of the review assures you that twenty-two years ago, when he wrote this [the passage on philosophers' ignorance, which Hegel criticized], he was not thinking of Professor Hegel; but he now admits that in his humble opinion, Hegel too is really not able to understand positive law." See Hugo, Review of the *Grundlinien*, in *Göttinger Gelehrten Anzeigen* 61 (1821), reprinted in Hegel, *Vorlesungen über Rechtsphilosophie*, 1:381.

necessity whereby a system of legal law must contain the *application* of
the universal concept to the particular and *externally* given characteristics
of objects [*Gegenstände*] and instances — an application which is no longer
[a matter of] speculative thought and the development of the concept, but
[of] subsumption by the understanding; (γ) through the *final* determinations required for *making decisions* in actuality.[33]

The reference to the "universal concept" in the proper definition of positive
law is important, for it suggests that the relationship between the rational and
the positive or historical element of law is to be thought of as a historical process of the rational incorporation of positivity, as a dialectic of the immanent
norm and its partial and gradual realizations. It is inherent to the abstract and
ahistorical essence of rational law that it produces and so to speak exteriorizes
the successive expressions of its rationality, which, though historically determined, are nonetheless necessary in their very contingency. But such unity
of the positive and the rational can only be established if the rational point of
view is adopted — that is, the point of view of a *philosophy* of law. Followers of
historicism and of legal positivism have remained blind to this point.

It is thus quite clear that by taking the historical and positive dimensions
of the actualization of law into consideration (in other words, its passage from
simple concept to idea), Hegel in no way subscribes to the historical school of
law as presented by Savigny in his 1814–1815 writings.[34] The *Philosophy of Right*
and, even more, the Heidelberg and Berlin lectures, are full of critical allusions
to Savigny. In this way, Hegel participates in the debate over the codification
of law that took place in Germany following the defeat of the Napoleonic army
(a moment that was also the occasion for historicism to constitute itself as a
doctrine). Hegel clearly favors the argument by his old friend from Heidelberg, the jurist Thibaut, that the German states, free from foreign occupation
but aware of the merits of the Napoleonic Code, must give themselves a common civil code that would outline the future political unification of the coun-

---

33. *RPh*, § 3, *GW* 14.1, p. 25 (*Elements*, 28; see *Outlines*, 19–20).

34. F. C. von Savigny, *Vom Beruf unserer Zeit für Gesetzgebung und Rechtswissenschaft* (1814)
and "Über den Zweck dieser Zeitschrift," *Zeitschrift für geschichtliche Rechtswissenschaft* 1 (1815):
1–12. These texts are reprinted, with other pieces from the debate surrounding codification,
in Hans Hattenhauer and Anton Friedrich Justus Thibaut, eds., *Thibaut und Savigny: Ihre programmatischen Schriften* (Munich: Vahlen, 1973).

try.[35] This went against Savigny's position that codification can only occur within conditions defined by the national character (*Volksgeist*) of a country and by the present state of legal science—conditions that, in Savigny's eyes, the Germany of 1814 did not fulfill. Hegel responds to Savigny—who contests the German people's "vocation" (*Beruf*) for providing itself with a unified and unifying civil code,[36] as France did through the intermediary of Bonaparte— by saying, in direct line with Thibaut's arguments, that "to deny a civilized nation, or the legal profession within it, the ability to draw up a legal code would be among the greatest insults one could offer to either."[37] In addition, to reject codification on the grounds that a legal culture is not mature enough has harmful consequences in the practical domain. It amounts to giving judges the task of legislating, as in common-law countries:

> The *law of the land* (or common law) *of England* is contained, as everyone knows, in *statutes* (formal laws) and in so-called *unwritten law*; this unwritten law, incidentally, is likewise recorded in writing and knowledge of it can and must be acquired solely through reading (of the many quarto volumes which it fills). . . . Since this unwritten law is contained in the verdicts of courts of laws and judges, the judges constantly act as *legislators*.[38]

As for the argument that codification would hinder the development of law, it is rejected by means of a distinction between principles, which must be inviolably fixed, and specific clauses, which can and must evolve with civil society. Codification presents no obstacle to this; it merely obliges legislators—

35. See Thibaut, "Über die Notwendigkeit eines allgemeinen bürgerlichen Rechts für Deutschland" (1814), in Hattenhauer and Thibaut, *Thibaut und Savigny*, 67,73.

36. See Savigny, *Vom Beruf unserer Zeit für Gesetzgebung und Rechtswissenschaft* (1814) in Hattenhauer and Thibaut, *Thibaut und Savigny*, 112, 25, 88.

37. *RPh*, § 211 Anmerkung, *GW* 14.1, p. 177 (*Elements*, 242; see *Outlines*, 200). The attacks on Savigny are more cutting in 1819/1820: "A large part of those who have written and screamed against Napoleon's Code knew very well what the danger of it was for them. Napoleon's Code contains those great principles of freedom of property and the elimination of all that stems from the feudal period." Hegel, *Philosophie des Rechts*, 172–73.

38. *RPh*, § 211 Anmerkung, *GW* 14.1, pp. 176–77 (*Elements*, 242; see *Outlines*, 199). On this point, the lectures of 1817–1818 contain formulations that contrast with the *Philosophy of Right* and subsequent formulations. For example, "for freedom and citizens' rights, good organization of the courts is more necessary than a new code of laws" (Hegel, *Philosophie des Rechts*, § 115, p. 152), a sentence Savigny would have willingly penned.

not the apocryphal legislators that judges all too often are—to gradually re-fine it:

> A code, it is thought, will never be complete, because there will always be
> new cases. But the provisions added are nothing new; they are simply the
> particular details of general provisions. So there is nothing new, merely
> minor details of little importance. So if a good Code is created, many sub-
> sequent cases will be added, but it [will not be a matter of] adding anything
> that, according to the [nature of the] Thing, goes against principles, but
> only of adding further particularizations. And the principle of decision for
> these new particularities must already be included in the existing principles.
> ... A large old tree branches out without thereby becoming a new tree, and
> it would be foolish not to want to plant any trees because of new [future]
> branches.[39]

Law is undoubtedly part of a historical movement, and this implies constant refining and adaptation of its positive provisions. But this is not an argument against codifying its principles, which is desirable in all respects; nor is it a rele-vant objection to the natural law thesis of the rationality of the fundamental principles of law.

Indeed, beyond the question of codification and its opportuneness, Hegel's polemic against legal historicism also has a major theoretical goal con-cerning the relationship of rational ("natural") law to positive law and the way in which science (legal or philosophical) must act with regard to each. Just before launching into his polemic against Gustav Hugo (which of course is aimed at Savigny as well), Hegel draws a distinction between "development on the basis of historiographical reasons" (*die Entwicklung aus historischen Gründen*) and "development on the basis of the concept" ([*die*] *Entwicklung aus dem Begriff*).[40] Of course, historical inquiry is "meritorious and praise-worthy within its own sphere."[41] But when it comes to legal institutions and other configurations that participate in the objectivization of freedom, his-torical inquiry cannot take the place of rational legitimation—or, to use the vocabulary of Kant and Fichte, deduction. If this legitimation or deduction is

---

39. Hegel, *Vorlesungen über Rechtsphilosophie*, 3:657–58.
40. *RPh*, § 3 Anmerkung, *GW* 14.1, p. 26 (*Elements*, 29; see *Outlines*, 21).
41. *RPh*, § 3 Anmerkung, *GW* 14.1, p. 26 (*Elements*, 29; see *Outlines*, 21).

to proceed from the *concept* of law, it is solely the affair of the "philosophical approach," the only approach that can provide "justification which is *valid in and for itself*."[42] We see that despite his harsh criticism elsewhere of the abstractions of natural law, here Hegel adopts a form of reasoning typical of natural or rational law, though he uses a different vocabulary. A clause of positive law can be perfectly explained by studying the historical conditions of its appearance, and yet it can nevertheless be "irrational in and for itself"; this is the case, in particular, with "numerous determinations of Roman civil law [*Privatrecht*] that followed quite consciously from institutions such as Roman paternal authority and Roman matrimony"[43] yet constitute insults to reason and, hence, to law and right. Such judgments raise the question—which partisans of the "historical approach" did not fail to raise—of the criteria used to decide whether a certain "legal construct" (*Rechtsinstitut*, to use Savigny's word) is or is not rational and therefore does or does not comply with law. It would seem that to define these criteria requires a *normative*, not factual or descriptive, concept of law. And this is precisely what the introduction to the *Philosophy of Right* develops. As we have seen, it shows that freedom, initially confined to the abstract space of subjectivity, aims to become objective for itself, "both in the sense that it becomes the rational system of the spirit itself, and in the sense that this system becomes immediate actuality,"[44] from which follows this *normative* definition of legal right:

> *Right* is any existence [*Dasein*] in general which is the *existence* of the *free will*. Right is therefore in general freedom, as Idea.[45]

This normative definition is presupposed by many critical arguments developed in the *Philosophy of Right*, in particular regarding those clauses of positive law that Hegel rejects (e.g., restrictions on the status of personality,[46] or the types of property in Roman law, or the distinction between *domaine eminente*

42. *RPh*, § 3 Anmerkung, *GW* 14.1, p. 26 (*Elements*, 29; see *Outlines*, 21).

43. *RPh*, § 3 Anmerkung, *GW* 14.1, p. 26 (*Elements*, 29; see *Outlines*, 21).

44. *RPh*, § 27, *GW* 14.1, p. 44 (*Elements*, 57. See *Outlines*, 46). See above, the preliminary to part 1.

45. See *RPh*, § 29, *GW* 14.1, p. 45 (*Elements*, 58; see *Outlines*, 46).

46. See *RPh*, § 40 Anmerkung, *GW* 14.1, p. 54 (*Elements*, 71; see *Outlines*, 57).

and *domain utile* in feudal law)[47] or regarding philosophical constructions (Kant's revision of the traditional classification of the species of rights;[48] Fichte's interpretation of contractual obligation).[49] Certainly, Hegel's philosophy rejects usual forms of normativism. However, analysis also shows that for Hegel there is a proper use of normativity, as we can see by looking at the practical idea in the *Science of Logic*[50] and moral subjectivity in the *Philosophy of Right*.[51] But it is important that the relationship between subjects and norms — which is constitutive of the being of practical duty — never be separated from the terrain of actuality or from the institutionally realized normativity that the actualization of norms presupposes. This is why "the objective system of these principles and duties [moral norms; but the same goes for legal norms as well], and the union of subjective knowledge with this system are present only when the ethical point of view has been reached."[52] To put it differently, legal and moral norms are objectively founded as norms only if they are converted into established norms that are recognized within a community.

However, there are some problems with a normative definition of law as the objective and institutionalized actualization of freedom. The first — which I will only mention here — has to do with Hegel's repeated condemnation of theories of duty or the "ought," the prototype for which can be found in Kantian or Fichtean practical philosophy. What are we to make of this critique, which is more or less constant from the *Phenomenology of Spirit* onward, given that Hegel's own philosophy includes manifestly prescriptive arguments — for example, regarding slavery or private property? Thus, it is absolutely true that "the human being in and for himself [is ineligible for] slavery," but this must not be thought of "merely as something which *ought to be*."[53] In other words,

47. See *RPh*, § 62 Anmerkung, *GW* 14.1, pp. 67–68 (*Elements*, 90–92; see *Outlines*, 73–74).

48. *RPh*, § 40 Anmerkung, *GW* 14.1, pp. 53–54 (*Elements*, 70–71; see *Outlines*, 56–57). See Kant, *Rechtslehre: MdS*, § 10, Ak. 6, pp. 259–60; *PP*, pp. 411–14.

49. See *RPh*, § 79 Anmerkung, *GW* 14.1, pp. 80–81 (*Elements*, 109–10; see *Outlines*, 89). The young Fichte argued that a contractual obligation only becomes binding when the other party begins to perform it. See *Beitrag zur Berechtigung der Urtheile des Publicums über die französische Revolution, Werke*, 6:114–15.

50. See *WdL* 3, *GW* 12, pp. 231–35 (*Science of Logic*, 729–34).

51. See below, chapter 10.

52. *RPh*, § 137, *GW* 14.1, p. 119 (*Elements*, 164; see *Outlines*, 132).

53. *RPh*, § 57 Anmerkung, *GW* 14.1, p. 65 (*Elements*, 87–88; see *Outlines*, 70).

though Hegel considers both the rejection of slavery on the sole grounds that humans are "free by nature" and usual justifications of slavery as belonging to "formal thought," he clearly opts for the first position, which, unlike "all historical views on the right of slavery and lordship" has "the advantage that it contains the absolute *starting point*—though only the starting point—on the way to truth."[54] This affirmation is as unambiguous as what Hegel says about property: "Since my will, as personal and hence as the will of an individual, becomes objective in property, the latter takes on the character of *private property*."[55] This normative definition of property on the basis of the concept of the person makes it possible to symmetrically refute the point of view that rules out the principle of private property.[56] Here, as with the issue of slavery, Hegel refutes contradicting *arguments* en bloc, but not the *theses* that they serve (albeit poorly). If we do not suspect him of grossly contradicting himself, we must accept that in the domain of law as in the domain of morality, Hegel distinguishes the concrete normativity of the concept from the abstract normativity of the understanding or sentiment. In this sense, there is an *immanent* normativity, one where the universal concept of law is the rule of its positive historical realizations. This is a normative order that does not belong to the abstract normativity of philosophies of "ought" (*Sollen*), which is abstract because it is *transcendent* to historical-positive material. But we must acknowledge that this approach is open to suspicion of being based on arbitrary decisions, as in fact it often was.

A second problem: if it is true that every embodiment of free will belongs to law, what is the order of the difference between this broad understanding of law, which is a synonym of what Hegel calls objective spirit, and what he calls "narrow legal law," that is, private law, or, as we shall see, its rational basis? The following passage provides a clue:

> This reality in general, as embodiment of the free will, is right, which is to be taken comprehensively, not only as restricted juridical right, but as the embodiment of all determinations of freedom.[57]

---

54. *RPh*, § 57 Anmerkung, *GW* 14.1, p. 65 (*Elements*, 87; see *Outlines*, 70).

55. *RPh*, § 46, *GW* 14.1, p. 57 (*Elements*, 77; see *Outlines*, 61).

56. *RPh*, § 46 Anmerkung, *GW* 14.1, p. 58 (*Elements*, 77; see *Outlines*, 61).

57. *Enzykl*, § 486, *GW* 20, p. 479 (*Encyclopedia* 218). See also *RPh*, § 29, *GW* 14.1, p. 45 (*Elements*, 58; see *Outlines*, 46).

No matter what answers are given to the question I have raised — and several options are possible — there is clearly a difference in normative status between the right to property, which is the backbone of abstract law, and the right of the subjective moral will, the right of ethical institutions, and, finally, the "right of the world spirit," which alone is "absolute in an unlimited sense."[58] This brings us back to the issue of the "stratification of right" discussed in the previous chapter. From Hegel's point of view, it is important to maintain both the specificity of "law in the legal sense"[59] of abstract law (and we have seen that this abstraction has positive aspects) and to include the common legal-philosophical understanding of the term *law* within a metaconcept: the concept of objective spirit as the relatively unified field of the manifestation of subjectivity in the order of objectivity.

The third problem directly concerns our current subject, the articulation of law, nature, and history. For Hegel, history is the still-external field of universality in which the abstract concept of law is ultimately actualized, that is, ethically and politically objectivized. It is through history that the actuality of the rational is gradually and laboriously — but not yet definitively — revealed. Here is the place to recall — against the common misconception that Hegel's final word amounts to a trivial understanding of the philosophy of history and of the end of history — that the *Weltgeist* is only an "externally *universal* spirit";[60] in other words, it is no more than the expression, externalized in time (time that is the being-there of the concept, but *merely* its being-there),[61] of absolute spirit. Beyond the time of history, there is the time of the concept, that of the *Aufhebung* of time into the absolute self-presence of thought as absolute knowledge. Nothing illustrates the "seriousness, the suffering, the patience, and the labor of the negative" evoked in the preface to the *Phenomenology of Spirit* better than the history of the world,[62] precisely insofar as it can be considered the history of (the objectivization of) freedom. But how

---

58. *RPh*, § 30 Anmerkung, *GW* 14.1, p. 46 (*Elements*, 59; see *Outlines*, 48).

59. Hegel speaks of a "definition of legal and rightful property." *RPh*, § 43 Anmerkung, *GW* 14.1, p. 57 (*Elements*, 75; see *Outlines*, 60).

60. *Enzykl*, § 549, *GW* 20, p. 524 (*Encyclopedia* 246).

61. "*Time* is the *concept* itself that *exists there* and is represented to consciousness as empty intuition. Consequently, spirit necessarily appears in time, and it appears in time as long as it does not *grasp* its pure concept, which is to say, as long as it does not annul time" (*PhG*, *GW* 9, p. 429 [*Phenomenology*, ¶ 801]).

62. *PhG*, *GW* 9, p. 18 (*Phenomenology*, ¶ 19).

are we able to distinguish, within the "thick" course of history, between what reflects the direction of the concept, if I dare say, and what expresses the resistance of the empirical to spirit, or, quite simply, the fact that the empirical has a *tempo* of its own? How, within the unity of the historical process, are we to establish a nonarbitrary distinction between the actual and the contingent, between the rational and the nonrational? After all, from the philosopher's point of view, there is only *one* history, the *history of the world* as the history of humanity's arrival at itself and at what within it pushes it beyond itself and toward the absolute timelessness of spirit. In other words, is it possible to distinguish *philosophically* between what is historical and rational and what is historical without being rational? What is the nature of a reason that allows that which seems destined to prevent or slow its arrival at itself to be realized only to dissociate itself from it? We see now that Hegel's point of view supposes not only a normative definition of law but also a normative definition of *history*.

It is possible that the Hegelian answer—which one may choose not to accept, once one knows it for it what it is—to these questions regarding the status of a nonabstract natural law involved in actual history is partly contained in Hegel's conceptualization of what he sometimes calls abstract law, sometimes formal law, sometimes strict law, and finally, sometimes law tout court.[63]

Hegel's Natural Law: The Normative Foundations of Private Law

Up to this point, we have tacitly accepted, as Hegel himself seems to invite us to do, that the philosophical science of law (*philosophische Rechtswissenschaft*) corresponds to what is classically termed *natural law*, which it is preferable to rebaptize *rational law*. Of course, Hegel's "philosophy of law" is not just a new name for natural law, for as we have seen, it rejects the principal conceptual tools of natural law theory. Rather, like Hegelian logic with respect to traditional metaphysics, this philosophy of law comes to occupy the territory of natural law, to fill in for it, taking its place and at the same time taking over for it.

63. See in particular *RPh*, § 33, *GW* 14.1, p. 48, and § 94 Anmerkung, *GW* 14.1, p. 89 (*Elements*, 62, 121; see *Outlines*, 50, 98); *Enzykl* 1817, § 401, *GW* 13, p. 224 (*Encyclopedia* 1817, 241); *Enzykl*, § 487, *GW* 20, p. 481 (*Encyclopedia* 219). See also the lecture course of 1824–1825: "This is the sphere of formal law, it is abstract, i.e., formal because the content that I give to myself, although mine, is at the same time only here an external object, not free according to its content. Therefore, it is still abstract law, only a form." Hegel, *Vorlesungen über Rechtsphilosophie*, 4:164.

To explain the double title of Hegel's 1820 work, the 1824–1825 course reiterates that "the name 'natural law' is the usual name for our science."[64] Next,
repeating his critique of the naturalist assumptions of natural law—in particular, the thesis of natural sociability—Hegel emphasizes that "natural law"
and the "philosophy of law" have an analogous relationship to positive law;
a relation of both coordination and supraordination. Basing himself on the
description of positivity given in section 3 of the *Philosophy of Right*, Hegel
also specifies what separates natural, "empiricist" law (to use the terminology
from the article on natural law) and the philosophy of law from positive law:
they reject the decisionist step that being instituted by authority implies for
the latter, and in spite of their differences, are both based on principles of self-
determination and universality.

> Although [natural law] proceeds empirically, though it places natural incli-
> nations and needs at the foundation [of law], fully or partially, it has in com-
> mon with the philosophy of law the fact that the source from which law is
> drawn is that which is specific and inherent to every human. . . . Regardless
> of their differences, philosophy of law and natural law have in common the
> fact that their source must be something internal. . . . The positive science of
> law has to do with legal authority, and law must become positive. . . . Rights
> and law, the statute-laws of civil society and the political laws of the state,
> must become positive, though the positive is generally considered to be
> opposed to the concept of thinking, intelligence, conviction, and the will. . . .
> But laws must be positive, for laws and constitutions are determinations of
> the state, of the actual world, and must therefore take the shape of laws of
> nature.[65]

In the same introduction to the 1824–1825 course, Hegel also notes that
there is a difference between natural law in the usual sense and the philosophy of law as he conceives it, despite their similar aims. This difference has to
do not only with theoretical style but also with scope: the philosophy of law
covers a larger field than natural law, which "did not contain the science of the
state," which was "discussed on its own."[66] Whence the second (though actu-

64. Hegel, *Vorlesungen über Rechtsphilosophie*, 4:75.
65. Ibid., 4:81–82.
66. Ibid., 4:75.

ally chronologically first) title to the *Grundlinien der Philosophie des Rechts*: *Naturrecht und Staatswissenschaft* (Natural Law *and* the Science of the State). The difference is not a mere nuance or quantitative difference. In abandoning the science of the state to other disciplines (history, *Statistik*, and *positives Staatsrecht*),[67] the modern doctrine of natural law—and it is clear that Hegel has the German version of this doctrine (in particular, Wolff's) in mind—gives credit to the idea, which certain of its representatives explicitly defend, that the state is an institution of pure convention with no basis in natural law properly speaking. Thus, the antistatist bias transmitted by trivial interpretations of Rousseau, the flat positivism of political science (called "science of the police" or "cameralism" in Germany), and the naturalist assumptions of the dominant theory of natural law conspire to separate the field of private law, the only one governed by the principles of natural law, from the field of public law, which is abandoned to the contingencies of history and the arbitrariness of power.

We see, then, that the expressions "philosophy of law" and "philosophical law" can have two meanings in Hegel. The first meaning, which has a broader scope, covers the entirety of the sphere of objective spirit; in other words, it includes all the figures in which freedom is made objective (legal, moral, social, ethical-political, historical). The other meaning, more restricted in scope, corresponds to what is generally understood by "natural law" in modern thought: a set of metapositive legal principles, discoverable by rational deduction (the concept of reason used here varies) on the basis of certain anthropological premises, that are themselves variable—thus, one may or may not choose to count the "social impulse" (*Gesellschaftstrieb* or *socialitas*) among these premises. It is therefore desirable to prevent ambiguity by distinguishing, more systematically than Hegel himself did, between the "philosophy of law" in the broad sense of the doctrine of objective spirit and "natural law," properly speaking. This distinction makes it possible to understand the "philosophy of law" in its full scope not only as "an exemplary *Aufhebung* of natural law de-

---

67. Hegel is known to have flipped through the *Neues Teutsches Staatsrecht* by Johan Jacob Moser (1766–1782) as he drafted the manuscript on the constitution of the German Empire. Moser's work is a massive compilation that served as one of Hegel's sources as he prepared for his courses in Heidelberg and Berlin. See Hegel, *Vorlesungen über Naturrecht und Staatswissenschaft*, § 125A, 75; *Lectures on Natural Right*, 225. In regard to *Statistik* or *Staatenkunde*, the German ancestor of political science, itself a branch of *Polizeiwissenschaft*, see Michael Stolleis, *Geschichte des öffentlichen Rechts in Deutschland* (Munich: Beck, 1988), 1:372.

veloped by the modern period"[68] but also as the *Aufhebung* of natural law in the narrow sense.

My argument is that within the architecture of the doctrine of objective spirit (i.e., of the "philosophy of law and right"), the theory of abstract or formal law (the first level of that ensemble) is homologous to natural law in the sense that modern thought understands it: it defines the abstract — that is, among other things, atemporal — presuppositions of a reasonable *social* order. However, Hegel's "natural law" (understood as the doctrine of abstract law) cannot be the basis for a *political* order, and this is why Hegel repeats throughout his discussions of the determinations of abstract law that these determinations either do not apply or apply only indirectly to that which, within objective spirit, belongs to the state.[69] This problematic, which on the one hand accepts the legacy of natural law constructions and on the other goes beyond or rejects them, implies a new type of connection between the natural and the historical, a connection that natural law has not been able to theorize precisely.

What of abstract law in this regard? By its content (the rights of personhood and property, contract law, laws of action, and penal law), it corresponds to the sphere of private law, whose general principles it exposes on the basis of its unique philosophical foundation: the concept of the person as the universalized form of free will. Even if Hegel sometimes goes into technical considerations (for example regarding the classification of contracts, though there he simply follows Kant),[70] his argument belongs entirely to natural law in the usual sense. There are two clear indications of this.

The first indication, which I have already discussed, has to do with the meaning and value of the abstraction of abstract law.[71] Abstract law presents

68. Bernard Bourgeois, "Sur le droit naturel de Hegel (1802–1803)," in *Études Hégéliennes* (Paris: Presses Universitaires de France, 1992), 178–79.

69. See, for example, *RPh*, § 46 Anmerkung, *GW* 14.1, p. 58 (*Elements*, 77; see *Outlines*, 61) on political limits of private property; *RPh*, § 57 Anmerkung, *GW* 14.1, pp. 64–65 (*Elements*, 86–87; see *Outlines*, 70) on refutation of enslavement as the original figure of the political; *RPh*, § 75 Anmerkung, *GW* 14.1, p. 78 (*Elements*, 105; see *Outlines*, 85) on refusal of the application of the template of a contract to the state.

70. See *RPh*, § 80, *GW* 14.1, pp. 81–83 (*Elements*, 110–12; see *Outlines*, 90–92). Though Hegel is following Kant here, whose legal concepts he nevertheless strongly criticizes, it is primarily because Kant's classification of contracts appears to Hegel to be rational and adequate to its object, especially when opposed to the "routine" of Romanists.

71. See above, chapter 1.

the most general form, the schema, of the objectification of freedom through the foundational relationship of a person's appropriation of a thing in general (*Sache*). Personality is the universal and formal expression of free subjectivity, as it emerges at the end of the doctrine of subjective spirit;[72] it is the objectivized shape of free subjectivity, which explains the privileged position of the shape of law among the various dimensions included in free subjectivity. Personhood in Hegel's sense is *primarily* legal personhood even if it is not only that. In fact, its characteristic determination is legal ability; that is, the fact of being able to be and act as a subject of rights. Personhood must itself be understood as the formal requisite of a power, in principle indefinite, to appropriate a "nature it encounters before it" (the world of things) by a will that, through this activity, "gives itself reality."[73] This could be taken as the Hegelian definition of subjective right. Thus, it appears that the *power to appropriate*, precisely because it is defined in purely formal and ahistorical terms, is the base structure of natural law in Hegel's sense. The appropriation of things is the act by which a person is constituted as a concrete abstraction, so to speak. The explicit return to Hobbes's understanding of natural right as expanded into a *jus in omnia* shows to what extent Hegel's argument resonates with natural law.[74] Furthermore, as in Hobbes, the refusal to posit *legal* limits to the exercise of the fundamental subjective right to appropriate in no way implies that such limits do not exist; it is just that they are not formal, but real; not legal, but social and political. This is why the abstraction of "abstract law" is not only negative or pejorative. Indeed, if this abstraction implies that law on its own cannot be the principle of any concrete political and social order—a conclusion that goes against legalism and most natural law doctrines—it also implies that there are legal principles whose validity is unconditional, independent of any determinate historical circumstance or context. In short, the abstraction of abstract law is what allows it to have *normative value*.

The second sign of the natural law streak in Hegel's argument was mentioned earlier: despite Hegel's repeated attacks against normativism (mostly Kantian), the Hegelian theory of abstract law abounds in normative proposi-

---

72. See *RPh*, § 35, *GW* 14.1, pp. 51–52 (*Elements*, 67–68; see *Outlines*, 53–54).

73. *RPh*, § 39, *GW* 14.1, p. 53 (*Elements*, 70; see *Outlines*, 55–56).

74. *RPh*, § 44, *GW* 14.1, p. 57 (*Elements*, 75; see *Outlines*, 60): "A person has the right to place his will in any thing. The thing thereby becomes mine . . . the absolute *right of appropriation* which human beings have over all things."

tions, that is, in propositions that function as critical measures of the empirical. This is obvious in the case of property, as we have already observed. When Hegel states that "in relation to external things, the *rational* aspect is that I possess property,"[75] he grants normative power to rationality. Even clearer are his statements about personal freedom, which is presented as the base element of *any* legal order but at the same time must be considered as the result of a work of self-appropriation to which Hegel gives the general name of "culture" (*Bildung*). This means that law's empire, which is in itself abstract and timeless, can also be considered the result of the historical work of freedom's self-constitution at both the ontogenetic and phylogenetic level:

> The human being, in his *immediate* concrete existence [*Existenz*] in himself, is a natural entity, external to his concept; it is only through the *culture* [*Ausbildung*] of his own body and spirit, *essentially* by means of *his self-consciousness comprehending itself as free*, that he takes possession of himself and becomes his own property as distinct from that of others.[76]

The remark that follows this paragraph shows that the argument here concerns not only the culture or development of the individual but also of the human species (an acculturation that Hegel sees as essentially happening through work as the objective and concrete constitution of universality).[77] The subject of this remark is slavery, and it is the occasion for Hegel to once again settle the score with what he calls in section 3 the historical view of things. He rejects back-to-back the "historical" (which here means factual) justification of slavery and domination, as elaborated by Grotius,[78] for example, and natural law's refutation of slavery, which is based on the ahistorical claim that humanity is by nature free. Each of these is in fact an equally one-sided aspect

75. *RPh*, § 49, *GW* 14.1, p. 60 (*Elements*, 79; see *Outlines*, 63). The normative content of the argument is even clearer in the 1817–1818 course: "it follows that property ought to be private." Hegel, *Vorlesungen über Naturrecht und Staatswissenschaft*, § 26, 29; *Lectures on Natural Right*, 75.

76. *RPh*, § 57, *GW* 14.1, p. 64 (*Elements*, 86, modified; see *Outlines*, 69).

77. See *RPh*, § 187 Anmerkung, *GW* 14.1, pp. 162–64 (*Elements*, 224–26; see *Outlines*, 184–86).

78. See Hugo Grotius, *De jure belli ac pacis* (Aalen: Scientia, 1993), 1:3, §8: "Any man might surrender to another as a slave" (101); "as there are men who, according to Aristotle, are naturally slaves" (103). The opposite point of view (that man is free by nature) is perfectly represented by Rousseau; see Rousseau, *Oeuvres complètes*, 3:355–58; *Social Contract*, 1:4, 158–62.

of an antinomy that emerges from "formal thought," that is, the opposition between nature and freedom. But the equivalence between these two theses is quickly rejected in favor of the second:

> The point of view of the free will, with which law and the science of law begin, is already beyond that untrue point of view whereby the human being exists only in itself, and is therefore capable of enslavement.[79]

Whereas the historicizing justification of slavery, and consequently of the absolute domination that results from it, is a crude reduction of right to fact, as the *Social Contract* emphasized,[80] the natural law point of view offers the "advantage that it contains the absolute *starting point*—though only the starting point—on the way to truth."[81] What justifies Hegel's choice of one side of the antinomy over the other? The answer lies in an implicit opposition between the *state of nature* and the *state of law*. Indeed, slavery "emerges from a *situation before law*."[82] That situation corresponds to what classical natural law terms the *state of nature*, which Hegel agrees with Hobbes must be left behind at all cost.[83] An addition to the *Encyclopedia* clearly indicates that this is precisely the goal of one of the most famous passages of the *Phenomenology of Spirit*, the struggle for recognition:

> The fight for recognition in the extreme form here indicated can only occur in the state of nature, where men live only as individuals; by contrast it is absent from civil society and the political state because what constitutes the result of this combat, namely recognition, is already present there.[84]

---

79. *RPh*, § 57 Anmerkung, *GW* 14.1, p. 65 (*Elements*, 87, modified; see *Outlines*, 70).

80. "His [Grotius's] steady line of reasoning is to establish right by fact. A more consistent method might be used, but none more favorable to tyrants." See Rousseau, *Oeuvres complètes*, 3:353; *Social Contract*, 1:2, 157.

81. *RPh*, § 57 Anmerkung, *GW* 14.1, p. 65 (*Elements*, 87; see *Outlines*, 70).

82. *RPh*, § 57 margin note, *GW* 14.2, p. 431. See also Hegel, *Vorlesungen über Rechtsphilosophie*, 3:226–27.

83. Hegel, *Vorlesungen über Rechtsphilosophie*, 4:209. See Thomas Hobbes, *Hobbes: On the Citizen* (Cambridge: Cambridge University Press, 1998), 30, 1:13: "And so it comes about that we are driven by mutual fear to believe that we must emerge from such a state."

84. *Enzykl*, § 432 Zusatz, *W* 10, p. 221 (*Encyclopedia* 159). See the so-called master/slave dialectic in *PhG*, *GW* 9, p. 109–116 (*Phenomenology*, ¶¶ 178–96).

There is something paradoxical in Hegel's argument against the "right of slavery": in order to challenge the absolutization of what he considers a "necessary and legitimate moment"[85] in the passage from nonright to right—that is, the violence that orchestrates the struggle for recognition—he turns to a conceptuality that he nevertheless rejects both because of its philosophical assumption (the representation of humans as "naturally free") and because of the view of history to which it leads. The explanation of this paradox lies in the unique status of what Hegel calls abstract law and that I have been calling his "natural law." By its principle, law is ahistorical, and this is why its concept—only certain dimensions of which have been discussed here—can act as a measure of historical reality: on the basis of this concept, which goes along with the concept of humans as (constituting themselves as) free beings, it is possible to claim, along with Rousseau, that slavery is an "absolute denial of law"[86] in all times and places. We may thus say that the Hegelian doctrine of abstract law contains the foundations for a *nonnaturalist* view of human rights and a *critical* theory of the state of law (*Rechtsstaat*).[87] However, the *actualization* of these abstract legal principles has a history, which is History itself. It also has a *prehistory* that corresponds to a time before time, to the "struggle for recognition," the original dialectic of violence, the exit from which is *symbolically* presupposed by law, the state, and history, that is, the self-surpassing of nature into culture and of the pure violence of domination (*Herrenschaft*) into political subordination (*Herrschaft*):

> The actual beginning of history is preceded on the one hand by dull innocence which lacks all interest, and on the other hand by the valour of the formal struggle for recognition and revenge.[88]

Indeed, if history is the story of humanity's coming to consciousness of its freedom—that is, in the broadest sense of the term, of its *right*—everything that is absolutely incompatible with this definition must be rejected from

---

85. *Enzykl*, § 433 Anmerkung, *GW* 20, p. 431 (*Encyclopedia* 160).

86. *RPh*, § 57 Anmerkung, *GW* 14.1, p. 64 (*Elements*, 87; see *Outlines*, 70).

87. See chapter 5 below.

88. *RPh*, § 349 Anmerkung, *GW* 14.1, p. 277 (*Elements*, 375; see *Outlines*, 318). See also esp. *RPh*, § 57 Anmerkung, *GW* 14.1, pp. 64–65 (*Elements*, 86–88; see *Outlines*, 69–71).

actual history into a "state of nature" that is the negative of any legal status (*Rechtzustand*). And I do mean everything that is *absolutely* incompatible with the normative definition of history and law. Because, of course, violence and injustice, which are the concrete figures of negativity, cannot be absent from history: we know how harsh Hegel is toward the Enlightenment's representation of harmoniously linear historical progress. But though historical violence is ubiquitous, it cannot be thought of as irreconcilable, as an absolute negative, for the starting point of history—its transcendental condition, in non-Hegelian language—is humans' recognition of the humanity of other humans. This does not mean that domination disappears, but it does offer the constant possibility of contesting it.

Thus, we see that the normative function of law, which is the positive side of its abstraction and formalism, comes from its unique position *between nature and history*. According to Hegel, law is neither within history nor outside of it. Law is history's immanent norm of intelligibility and rationality: history is the history of freedom, that is, the history of the actualization of the necessarily abstract principles of law. In relation to history as spirit's coming to consciousness of its freedom and as the constitution of this freedom in sociopolitical *nature*,[89] law is a form of nature. But this nature itself has a history: the history of humanity's struggle with its own naturalness, that is, its cultivation of naturalness by which humanity arrives at a true expression of itself, which is political. If the *concept* of law is independent from the concept of the state, the *idea* of law—which is just the *history* of its realization—is the concrete record of the normative actuality of this concept.

89. See *RPh*, §§ 342–43, *GW* 14.1, p. 274 (*Elements*, 372; see *Outlines*, 316).

3

Contract

The Legal Conditions of the Social

Whereas much of Hegel's doctrine of abstract right and law has given rise to a substantial body of literature, his theory of contract, which is central to that doctrine, has been more or less neglected, especially in comparison to the thousands of pages dedicated to his theory of the state or civil society. Of course, aspects of Hegel's theory of contract are often discussed, but only negatively, in order to point out what contracts are not and in which domains they cannot serve as models: neither marriage nor the political bond, both of which belong to the ethical sphere, can, according to Hegel, be subsumed under the legal framework of contract.[1] These aspects of contract are of course important, especially for situating Hegel with respect to the school of natural law, but they do not indicate—or at least not directly—what contracts are in the properly legal sense. Only a few works deal with contracts as relations constitutive of the sphere of private law. Of these we must mention Julius Binder's lecture on obligatory contracts,[2] an excellent text though one burdened by the questionable (racializing) overtones of Weimar-era neo-Hegelianism. We should also cite the legal historian Peter Landau's precise study of Hegel's jus-

---

1. See *RPh*, § 75 Anmerkung, *GW* 14.1, pp. 157–58 (*Elements*, 105–6; see *Outlines*, 85).

2. Julius Binder, "Der obligatorische Vertrag im System der Hegelschen Rechtsphilosophie," in *Verhandlungen des dritten Hegel-Kongresses*, ed. B. Wigersma (Tübingen: Mohr, 1934), 37–59.

tification of contractual law. Though this study focuses less on the internal architecture of Hegel's argument and more on its relation to the legal culture of the nineteenth century,[3] it has the great merit of emphasizing the decisive role of the concept of value within this theory of contract.

Commentators' general lack of interest in the Hegelian theory of contract stems from the fact that it appears to lack originality. For the most part, Hegel limits himself to essentially repeating the main features of imperial Roman law—*obligationes ex contractu*—as presented in the manuals written by Heineccius and G. Hugo from which he drew his information.[4] In a way, Hegel himself emphasizes this lack of originality by indicating, for example, that his classification of contracts "coincides on the whole with that of Kant's," which, in contrast to certain classical divisions within Roman law (real, consensual, named, and unnamed contracts), Hegel considers a "rational classification."[5] This praise is surprising given that elsewhere Hegel severely criticizes Kant's *Rechtslehre* as well as classical Roman law for having introduced into the sphere of private law elements belonging to other spheres— in this case, the sphere of *Sittlichkeit*. His reproach is particularly directed at Kant's three-part classification of rights:

> The chief characteristic of this division [into the law of persons, things, and actions] is the confused way in which it jumbles together rights which presuppose substantial relations, such as family and state, with those which refer only to abstract personality. Kant's division of rights, which has since found favour with others, into the *right to things* and the *right of persons*, and *personal right of a real* [*dinglich*] *kind* is an example of this confusion.[6]

---

3. Peter Landau, "Hegels Begründung Des Vertragsrechts," *ARSP: Archiv für Rechts-und Sozialphilosophie/Archives for Philosophy of Law and Social Philosophy* 59 (1973): 117–38.

4. Heineccius was the author of several very popular books in the late eighteenth century. Hegel uses the tenth edition of his *Antiquitatum romanarum jurisprudentiam illustrantum syntagma secundum ordinem institutionum justiniani digestum* (Frankfurt, 1771), *Elementa juris civilis secundum ordinem institutionum* (Berlin, 1765), and the fifth edition of *Elementa juris civilis secundum ordinem pandectarum* (Frankfurt, 1747). With Hugo, with whom he has a debate in the note of section 3 of the *Philosophy of Right*, Hegel uses the sixth edition of the *Lehrbuch der Geschichte des römischen Rechts bis auf Justinian* (Berlin, 1818), the third of seven volumes of *Lehrbuch eines civilistischen Cursus*.

5. *RPh*, § 80, *GW* 14.1, p. 82 (*Elements*, 111; see *Outlines*, 90).

6. *RPh*, § 40 Anmerkung, *GW* 14.1, p. 53 (*Elements*, 71, modified; see *Outlines*, 56).

Regardless of the validity of this statement, it points us in the direction of what is undoubtedly most remarkable and specific about Hegel's doctrine of contract: it attempts both to identify the properly legal element of contract — that is, to establish why and how they belong to the sphere of *abstract* law — and to elucidate in what way this abstractness of the contractual relation requires a principle of actualization or realization that must be sought in the ethical sphere, for the function of that sphere is, in general, to actualize the two abstractions of law and morality. More specifically, this principle of actualization is to be found at the heart of the ethical sphere, where its most modern and conflictual aspects are concentrated: in civil society. In contrast to reductive interpretations that would see Hegel's theory of contract as merely indicating the internal limitations of a conception of private law that ignores its own social and ethical-political conditions, we will see that in Hegel's perspective, contracts have uncontestable richness both in themselves — because of their function within the economy of abstract law — and in relation to what appears to be their true realm of actualization, civil society.

The Objectivization of Recognition

Insofar as contracts belong to abstract law (and we now know that the qualification "abstract" must not be understood in a solely negative manner) and, in general, emerge from a speculative idea of law, they must be understood not as limitations or restrictions but rather as objective manifestations, *Verwirklichungen*, of freedom. This effort to think of law, even abstract law, as a realization rather than a restriction of freedom explains the fact that unlike theories of positive law, Hegel's theory of contract does not leave room for the specifically legal obligations that arise *ex contractu*[7] — or, at least, he does not pay much attention to the question, essential to jurists, of the "actions" to be taken if one party does not respect his or her contractual obligations. The explanation for this lack of attention lies in the fact that for Hegel, such actions do not concern "the nature of contract itself."[8] But then what is this nature?

We have seen that the property relation provides the structure of abstract law. At that level, a person relates exclusively to the thing she appropriates and

7. Binder, "Der Obligatorische Vertrag," 45.
8. *RPh*, § 77 Anmerkung, *GW* 14.1, p. 79 (*Elements*, 108; see *Outlines*, 87).

merges with it in a kind of objectification of freedom that leaves no remainder: "Subjective will is only actual will insofar as it is [the will of] an owner."[9] This reification of the person is a perfect, adequate expression of "abstract will *in general*," that is, legal will.[10] The person, a "perfectly abstract self,"[11] only has actuality for herself and other persons by being materially inscribed in the things whose legally guaranteed possession she has secured. So then what about contracts, and how does Hegel's analysis of them affect his concept of law? The paragraph in the *Philosophy of Right* that presents the transition from property to contracts indicates that the essential contribution of the latter is to introduce the mediation of another will into the relationship between a will and an object:

> As the existence of the *will*, [property's] existence for another can only be *for the will* of another person. This mediation whereby I no longer own property merely by means of a thing and my subjective will, but also by means of another will, and hence within the context of a common will, constitutes the sphere of *contract*. [12]

It is a truism to say that a contract implies a relationship between the wills of the contracting parties, but this obvious truth contains something more profound if we take into account what results from the theory of subjective spirit: a will is not immediately or naturally itself, that is, a free will; it is so only in the mediation it establishes between self and self, or in wanting its own freedom. The doctrine of abstract law shows that the subject's will for his or her own freedom, if it is not to remain mere beatific contemplation of the self, implies mediation first by the world of things, where the self indefinitely inscribes its *animus domini* (this is the constitutive moment of the legal, the objectification of willing), and second and above all by mediation through other wills that recognize this will and posit it as free. Recognition—that is, each person's assumption of the other's humanity and only thereby of one's own humanity—requires that consciousness break with the singularity and immediacy of desire and satisfaction. In *The Phenomenology of Spirit*, this occurs

9. *RPh*, margin note to § 46, *GW* 14.2, p. 411.

10. *RPh*, § 40, *GW* 14.1, p. 53 (*Elements*, 70; see *Outlines*, 56).

11. *RPh*, § 35 Anmerkung, *GW* 14.1, p. 51 (*Elements*, 68; see *Outlines*, 54).

12. *RPh*, § 71, *GW* 14.1, p. 76 (*Elements*, 102; see *Outlines*, 83).

through the painful experience of negativity, the loss of self that submission to a master represents for servile consciousness. But we know that beyond the fight to the death and subordination, it is work, "desire held in check" that plays the decisive role in this process, allowing self-consciousness to accede to universality:

> Although the fear of the lord is indeed the beginning of wisdom, consciousness is not therein aware that it is a being-for-self. However, by means of work this servile consciousness comes round to itself. . . . Work is desire *held in check*, it is vanishing *staved off*, that is, work *cultivates and educates*.[13]

All else being equal, the universal is similarly constituted in and through the confrontation of particular wills that occurs in the transition from property to contract. It has not been sufficiently emphasized that contract — in a less explosive but just as fertile a manner as the fight to the death between two consciousnesses — sheds light on the crucial role of *recognition* in constituting freedom:

> Contract presupposes that the contracting parties *recognize* each other as persons and owners of property; and since it is a relationship of objective spirit, the moment of recognition is already contained and presupposed within it.[14]

Indeed, the conclusion and execution of a contract confirm that mutual recognition of persons — recognition that cannot be coerced once a political and social order is in place[15] — is the *presupposition* of, and in a sense the milieu for, any legal relation. It seems that once humanity has left the state of nature and reached its true place — which is political, familial, and social — recognition

---

13. *PhG, GGW* 20, p. 114 (*Phenomenology*, ¶ 195). See *Enzykl*, § 435, *GW* 20, p. 224 (*Encyclopedia* 161): "The bondsman, works off his individual will and self-will in the service of the master, sublates the inner immediacy of desire and in this alienation and in the fear of the master he makes a beginning of wisdom — the transition to universal self-consciousness."

14. *RPh*, § 71 Anmerkung, *GW* 14.1, p. 76 (*Elements*, 103; see *Outlines*, 83–84).

15. *RPh*, § 57 Anmerkung, *GW* 14.1, pp. 64–65 (*Elements*, 87; see *Outlines*, 70): "The point of view of the free will, with which law and the science of law begin, is already beyond that false point of view whereby the human being exists as a natural being and as a concept which has being only in itself, and is therefore capable of enslavement."

by contract takes the place of recognition by combat[16]; in this respect, a contract is a remarkable manifestation of rational freedom in the process of its objectivization.

In general, any process of recognition is oriented toward the creation of a space of universality that, in retrospect, confers meaning on that process: this is the space of "universal self-consciousness" in the *Phenomenology*, and *Sittlichkeit* and the state as the genuine foundation (if not the empirical origin) of law in the broad sense within the economy of objective spirit. Here, thanks to contract, property is "posited in general as an abstract, *universal* thing"[17] because legal persons mutually recognize one another as such. This formulation also suggests that the recognition at work from the very first dialectics of abstract law remains incomplete in that sphere: fully *ethical* recognition of humans by humans cannot function with the resources of abstract law alone and on the limited terrain of legal personhood. The 1824–1825 lectures, while underscoring the universality of contract, also point to its limitations:

> In the contract, there is a common will; such a will is universal, although not yet true universality but rather a universality that still contains contingency. Moreover, the universal as such, the law itself is this; the will is bound by contract — it can only be so bound by the concept of law, not by its own contingency or by another will. In contract, the moment of being bound, that is the law as law, is present.[18]

A contract generates obligation ("the moment of being bound," Hegel says) because it is a vector of universality, but this universality is not "true" because it is still tainted by contingency.

The Legal Significance of Contract

Why is it that the law is present "as law" in contracts but not yet in the relationship between persons and things? The answer, according to another passage from the 1824–1825 lectures, is that the contractual relationship creates "an ex-

16. See *RPh*, § 349 Anmerkung, *GW* 14.1, p. 277 (*Elements*, 375; see *Outlines*, 318); *Enzykl*, § 433 Anmerkung, *GW* 20, p. 431 (*Encyclopedia* 160).

17. *Enzykl*, § 494, *GW* 20, p. 484 (*Encyclopedia* 221).

18. Hegel, *Vorlesungen über Rechtsphilosophie*, 4:263.

tension of my immediate will" and even an extension "to the universal."[19] The act of contracting, by instituting a relationship between one will and another, between one person and another, reveals a potential for universality within objective legal willing that it at first appears to lack when, as the will of *one* person, it is totally invested in indeterminate externality and atomized into particular things. From the moment I enter into a contract, and despite the fact that the object of the contract is always a particular thing—the reason why the "relation of will to will is the true distinctive ground in which freedom has its *existence*"—I am no longer only the owner of a given object; I become for others, and thus for myself, a legal person or owner *in general*.[20] This is not a change of ground but rather a kind of strengthening of the determinations of objective spirit as they are manifested in the sphere of abstract law: even more than the person-thing relation, contract disassociates will "as such" from the empirical subject of willing and, in so doing, reveals the objectivity of the will. With contracts, the will is no longer essentially the will of one, two, or several persons; it is a *formally* universal, and thus legal, will. Three dimensions of the analysis of contract emphasize this legalization of the will, which in this way is sundered from the subjective and particular figure of its immediate expression.

First, in contracts, the legal relationship between persons and things is always mediated by legally formalized acts of will. In other words, right always presupposes law, since, for there to be contracts, each *res in commercio* must have an identifiable owner, and this requires a constituted, stable order of property. The fundamental structure of property (the appropriation of things by persons) could lend credence to the idea that the legal sphere is rooted in the contingency of empirical acts of appropriation, as if having always resulted from an original act of taking that would then form the structure of law. We can find an example of this point of view, which is based on a radicalization of the Hobbesian thematic of *jus in omnia*, in the work of Carl Schmitt, who argues that of the "three meanings" of the word *nomos* (to take, to divide, and to produce), the first is the original, definitive meaning: all legal order presupposes a *Landnahme*, a "taking," a first appropriation of territory and resources.[21] This

---

19. Ibid., 179.

20. *RPh*, § 71, *GW* 14.1, p. 76 (*Elements*, 102; see *Outlines*, 83).

21. Carl Schmitt, "Nehmen, Teilen, Weiden: Ein Versuch der Grundfrage jeder Sozial-und Wirtschaftsordnung vom Nomos her richtig zu Stellen," in *Verfassungsrechtliche Aufsätze aus den*

is not Hegel's position; for Hegel, original appropriation arises out of what has been called "pre-law"[22] and thus must be considered as a sort of nonlegal prerequisite to the establishment of the legal order. But this marginal condition is far from insignificant: if it is not met, there is no legal *order*, for the regularity of transactions can only be guaranteed if it is in principle possible to identify the legitimate owner of any alienable good. Of course, within a constituted legal order and the social order that rests on it as well as the political-state order, the fiction of a state of nature in which everything is up for grabs no longer applies. To the contrary, the cohesiveness of this order supposes that the process of primitive legal accumulation through immediate appropriation of res nullius be considered complete, finished (insofar as this process has any historical or protohistorical reality, but that is not the question here):

> In the state of affairs in which this standpoint of mediation is realized, immediate seizure (§488) of external objects as means to satisfaction no longer occurs, or very rarely; the objects are property.[23]

Nevertheless, there is some plausibility to this fiction if we consider property on its own, in isolation from its complex social and historical actualizations:

> That a thing [*Sache*] belongs to the person who *happens to be the first* to take possession of it is an immediately self-evident and superfluous determination, because a second party cannot take possession of what is already the property of someone else.[24]

Indeed, if we accept that appropriation is not one phenomenon among others that could illustrate the nature of the property relation but rather the prelegal condition of property, we must then consider that the *jus in omnia* expresses the fundamental or original structure of all legal relations:

Jahren 1924–1954: Materialien zu einer Verfassungslehre (Berlin: Duncker und Humbolt, 1953), 489–504.

22. Louis Gernet, "Droit et société dans la Grèce ancienne," in *Droit et institutions en Grèce antique* (Paris: Champs Flammarion, 1982), 7–119.

23. *Enzykl*, § 524, *GW* 20, p. 499 (*Encyclopedia* 230–31).

24. *RPh*, § 50, *GW* 14.1, p. 61 (*Elements*, 81; see *Outlines*, 65).

A person has the right to place his will in any thing [*Sache*]. The thing thereby becomes *mine* and acquires my will as its substantial end (since it has no such end within itself), its determination, and its soul—the absolute *right of appropriation* which human beings have over all things [*Sachen*].[25]

However, for two reasons this structure of *occupatio primaeva* cannot be the last word. First, even if we restrict ourselves to the register of property alone, abstract law cannot be reduced to the figure of immediate appropriation. This is why in listing the criteria of ownership Hegel gives less value to possession than to usage and, within the former, valorizes "giving form to" and, to a lesser extent "marking" property rather than mere "immediate *corporeal seizure*," for these procedures are already a step removed from the immediacy of the original act of appropriation. Thus, because when I give form to something "its determinate character as mine receives *an independently* [*für sich*] existing [*bestehende*] externality and ceases to be limited to my presence in *this* time and space and to my present knowledge and volition," this is "the mode of taking possession most in keeping with the Idea, inasmuch as it combines the subjective and the objective."[26] Second, and above all, the contractual transfer of property, insofar as it is a relationship between persons who "only as owners of property ... have existence [*Dasein*] for each other,"[27] shows that there is a circularity of the law, or more precisely, a structure of self-presupposition. Thus, law cannot be conceived according to the decisionist model of the emergence of order out of "normative nothingness" and "concrete disorder"[28] but rather must be understood as a contradictory process in which the transfer of a good is the objective verification—even the establishment—of the rights of its (former) owner. Legally, I possess at the moment when I cease possessing, and I can only cede insofar as I am an owner. It is by relinquishing my property or by acquiring it through an act of will *carried out in common* with another person—an act that has objective legal existence—that

---

25. *RPh*, § 44, *GW* 14.1, p. 57 (*Elements*, 75; see *Outlines*, 60).

26. *RPh*, § 56 and Anmerkung, *GW* 14.1, 64 (*Elements*, 85–86; see *Outlines*, 68–69).

27. *RPh*, § 40, *GW* 14.1, p. 53 (*Elements*, 70; see *Outlines*, 56).

28. Carl Schmitt illustrated what distinguishes "decisionist thinking" from "normativism" and "concrete-order thinking." See Carl Schmitt, *On the Three Types of Juristic Thought*, trans. Joseph W. Bendersky (Westport: Praeger, 2004), 43 ff. The claim that Hobbes represents the "purest type" of this thought obviously faces strong objections.

I am effectively an owner both for others and for myself. Thus, contract exposes a "contradiction . . . I *am* and *remain* an owner of property, having being for myself and excluding the will of another, only in so far as, in identifying my will with that of another, I *cease* to be an owner of property."[29]

A second dimension in the analysis of contract shows the objectivization and (formal) universalization of the will proper to it: this is the role played by *value*. Within contracts properly speaking—for Hegel, this means "real" or synallagmatic contracts whose goal, unlike "formal" or unilateral contracts, is the exchange of good or services (buying/selling, renting, salary contracts)[30]—what is at stake is less the thing in its unique, particular identity (such and such material good, a certain type of work) and more the element of abstract universality by which qualitatively diverse things find common measure: value, which "is their *universal*."[31] However, the value in question here is not the labor-value conceptualized by classical economists, in particular Ricardo (which is somewhat surprising given Hegel's constant attention to political economy, the "interesting science that makes an honor out of finding laws in a mass of contingencies"[32]); it is, rather, the universalized expression of the specific need to which it corresponds and thus the abstract measure of its "specific utility."[33] Peter Landau rightly emphasizes that the concept of value used here is Aristotelian[34] and thus stands in contrast to the Ricardian doctrine according to which although the condition for the "exchangeable value" of objects is some form of utility, that value ultimately "depends on the rela-

---

29. *RPh*, § 72, *GW* 14.1, p. 77 (*Elements*, 104; see *Outlines*, 84).

30. The Hegelian typology of contracts (wrongly) treats as overlapping two distinctions that are on different levels: one between formal and real contracts and the other between unilateral and bilateral contracts. Classical Roman law distinguishes formal contracts (which involve the fulfillment of certain formalities; they are the oldest and most rigid) and actual contracts (*mutuum* [deposit], *commodatum* [pledge]), which assume, "in addition to the formal element, convention, a material element, the *res*, the delivery of a tangible thing." See Paul Frédéric Girard, *Manuel élémentaire de droit romain* (Paris: A. Rousseau, 1929), 538. Unilateral contracts, which include most formal contracts but also *mutuum*, produce obligations for only one party. On the other hand, synallagmatic or bilateral contracts entail reciprocal obligations: in sales or rentals, each party is both creditor and debtor. See Girard, *Manuel*, 468–69. That is why here they take on paradigmatic value.

31. *RPh*, § 77, *GW* 14.1, p. 79 (*Elements*, 107; see *Outlines*, 86).

32. Hegel, *Vorlesungen über Rechtsphilosophie*, 4:487.

33. *RPh*, § 63, *GW* 14.1, p. 69 (*Elements*, 92; see *Outlines*, 74).

34. Landau, "Hegels Begründung des Vertragsrechts," 182.

tive quantity of labour which is necessary for its production."[35] According to Aristotle, monetary value "has become, by agreement, a kind of exchangeable representation of need."[36] A handwritten note in the *Philosophy of Right* indicates that value is the "possibility to satisfy a need."[37] Perhaps Hegel, the first philosopher to have registered the profound changes that political economy implies for social philosophy, ignores the Ricardian theory of value here because according to him this theory applies only to modern civil society, whose reality is historically situated and cannot have any direct effect on the atemporal terrain of abstract legal relations. In this sense, labor-value is the particular form taken by value within the context of the conditions of production and the commercial exchange of goods created by the system of needs — this is certainly not Ricardo's point of view, but it presages Marx's critiques of the "Robinsonades" of political economy:

> Each individual's production is dependent of the production of all others; and the transformation of his product into the necessaries of his own life is [similarly] dependent on the consumption of all others. Prices are old; exchange also; but the increasing determination of the former by costs of production, as well as the increasing dominance of the latter over all relations of production, only develop fully, and continue to develop ever more completely, in bourgeois society, the society of free competition. What Adam Smith, in the true eighteenth-century manner, puts in the prehistoric period, is rather a product of history.
>
> This reciprocal dependence is expressed in the constant necessity for exchange, and in exchange value as the all-sided mediation. . . . The reciprocal and all-sided dependence of individuals who are indifferent to one another forms their social connection. This social bond is expressed in *exchange value*, by means of which alone each individual's own activity or his product becomes an activity and a product for him; he must produce a general product, *exchange value*, or, the latter isolated for itself and individualized, *money*.[38]

35. David Ricardo, *On the Principles of Political Economy and Taxation* (London: Penguin, 1971), 55.

36. Aristotle, *Aristotle's Nicomachean Ethics*, trans. Robert C. Bartlett and Susan D. Collins (Chicago: University of Chicago Press, 2011), 5.1133a28.

37. *RPh*, margin note to § 63, *GW* 14.2, p. 455.

38. Karl Marx, *Grundrisse: Foundations of the Critique of Political Economy (Rough Draft)*,

The fact that in his analysis of contract, Hegel considers value not the expression of a particular need but rather a measure of "need in general"[39] illustrates the universalizing function of legal actions in the very abstraction of their structure. It is here, even more so than in the study of the formal characteristics of property, that the true fecundity of abstract law is revealed: abstract law outlines the formal schemata presupposed by any society of exchange, especially (bourgeois) modern civil society, which is both subject to the rule of the law of value and exposed to all forms of "commodity fetishism."

The third and final element of Hegel's study of contract that I would like to focus on here is the place it gives to procedures of stipulation, which Hegel says contain "the aspect of will, and hence the *substantial* legal element in a contract."[40] We may wonder why Hegel gives so much space (two of the ten paragraphs in the section on contract) to a specific, archaic procedure from Roman law that "serves to make all manner of agreements obligatory through a simple ceremony" involving uttering set questions and answers.[41] The reason is that stipulation, as a symbolic and codified procedure, is a remarkable example of the use of the performative function in legal language. In his own personal copy of *The Philosophy of Right*, Hegel noted that "such words [those that contracting parties pronounce following an intangible procedure] are deeds and actions."[42] Hegel's focus in describing this ceremony is the fact that words — more specifically, the *exchange* of ritualized phrases — is the unique vector of the objective legal value of an action independent of the physical object of the agreement and the reality of its execution:

> The *existence* which the *will* has in the formality of gesture or in language which is determinate for itself is already the complete existence of the will, as intellectual [*intellektuellen*] will, and the performance [of the agreement] is merely its selfless consequence.[43]

---

trans. Martin Nicolaus (London: Penguin, 1973), 156–57. I quote this passage rather than the corresponding one in *Capital* (bk. I, chap. 1, § 1) because its very expressions evoke phrasing from the *Philosophy of Right*, as for example, when Hegel calls civil society "a system of all-round interdependence." See *RPh*, § 183, *GW* 14.1, p. 160 (*Elements*, 221; see *Outlines*, 181).

39. *RPh*, § 63, *GW* 14.1, p. 69 (*Elements*, 92; see *Outlines*, 75).

40. *RPh*, § 79, *GW* 14.1, p. 80 (*Elements*, 109, modified; see *Outlines*, 88).

41. Girard, *Manuel*, 515.

42. *RPh*, marginal note to § 79, *GW* 14.2, p. 497.

43. *RPh*, § 79 Anmerkung, *GW* 14.1, p. 81 (*Elements*, 110; see *Outlines*, 89).

This illocutionary aspect of legal formalism sheds light on two fundamental dimensions of contract, which have already been alluded to here though in a general way. First, it emphasizes the "intentional" nature of contracts, which in legal terms are nothing more than agreements between objective wills, that is, wills embodied in procedures. Unlike Fichte, who claimed that a pact only becomes mutually binding from the moment of its execution,[44] Hegel emphasizes that the formalities of law (here, stipulation) give body to the "decision of my will" in such a way that the property I commit to ceding to another "has *now* ceased to be my property" and "I already recognize it as the property of the other party,"[45] which implies "recognition [of the other party] not only because they possess [some property], but recognition of their will as such."[46] Second, stipulation highlights the universalizing vocation of legal formalism; just as language allows subjective representations to become both objective and universal,[47] stipulation separates the legal action from its empirical particularity (this person, owner of this good, gives it to this other person on such and such conditions), giving it a high degree of generality. As the *Philosophy of Right* emphasizes regarding stipulation, language is "the most appropriate medium of intellectual representation";[48] thanks to language, the common will that is established in the contractual act is truly an "intellectual will."[49] In stipulation, it becomes clear that abstract law has a formal power to universalize, a power comparable in certain respects to that of the "hard sciences" in their richest aspects.

The contractual relationship takes the fundamental structure of abstract law (the property relation) into the domain that is truly its own: the domain of universality. Thanks to this transfer, objective freedom, which is first expressed in the mode of abstract singularity (*a* person is the owner of *a* thing), finds its true dimension. But the universality of personality as it is manifested in the contractual relations between persons, has certain limits: these are, in

44. This claim is part of an argumentative strategy that aims to legitimize the people's right to rise up when a sovereign violates the social compact. See Fichte, *Beitrag, Werke*, 6:112–15.

45. *RPh*, § 79 Anmerkung, *GW* 14.1, p. 80 (*Elements*, 109; see *Outlines*, 88).

46. *RPh*, margin note to § 81, *GW* 14.1, p. 511.

47. *Enzykl*, § 459 Anmerkung, *GW* 20, p. 454 (*Encyclopedia* 195): "But the *formal* element of language is the work of the intellect which impresses its categories on language; this logical instinct gives rise to the grammar of language."

48. *RPh*, § 78, *GW* 14.1, p. 80 (*Elements*, 108; see *Outlines*, 88).

49. *RPh*, § 79 Anmerkung, *GW* 14.1, p. 81 (*Outlines*, 89; *Elements*, 110).

general, the limits of *abstract* universality. They are revealed in the fact that the objective will posited by contracts and symbolized in formalities remains "a *common* will, not a will which is universal in and for itself."[50] In Hegel's presentation, contracts, which are shared elements of particular wills that remain attached to their particularity at the same time that they overcome it objectively, have a structure akin to Rousseau's "will of all."[51] The will of all is an approximation of the general will and can become an illusion if it is conflated with the general will, which is characterized by the double universality of its essence and its object.[52] Similarly, in Hegel, the egalitarian formalism of law, which is illustrated by contractual procedures, provides an abstract harbinger of the ethical-political realization of the universal. But in both cases, the approximation is imperfect and creates confusion, since it gives the universal (the general will in Rousseau, the state in Hegel) a derivative, secondary position in relation to the particular, whereas—at least in Hegel—the universal is the condition of actuality of the particular. In contract, the "inner universality" of law is but a "*common factor* in the arbitrariness and particular wills of those concerned":[53] this is the limit of the kind of universality that is built on the ground of abstract law. Confirmation of this limitation can be found in (unsuccessful) attempts to export the contractual schema out of its sphere of origin, the sphere of private law.

The State without Contract

Hegel repeatedly reaffirms that the state, in particular the modern state, is not the result of a "social" contract (which in certain German translations of Rousseau is rendered *Staatsvertrag!*). His constant critique of contractualism, beginning with the 1802 article on natural law, resulted in his being generally categorized as an adversary of natural law. But, as we saw in the previous chapter, it is the *expression* "natural law" that Hegel contests on the grounds of its ambiguous reference to nature, not the theoretical project behind it. Let us

---

50. *RPh*, § 75, *GW* 14.1, p. 78 (*Elements*, 105; see *Outlines*, 85).

51. See Rousseau, *Oeuvres complètes*, 3:371; *Social Contract* 2:2, 172. "There is often a great deal of difference between the will of all and the general will; the latter regards only the common interest, while the former has regard to private interests, and is merely a sum of particular wills."

52. See Rousseau, *Oeuvres complètes*, 3:306. "The general will, to be truly such, must be general in its object and essence."

53. *RPh*, § 82, *GW* 14.1, p. 85 (*Elements*, 115; see *Outlines*, 93).

simply recall that the second title of the text known as *Elements of the Philosophy of Right* is *Natural Law* (*Recht*) *and Political Science,* and that Hegel himself sometimes speaks of "natural law."[54] However, he takes every opportunity to remind us that he subscribes (while rethinking its terms) to the problematic of *rational* law hidden beneath that unfortunate expression; it is just that the type of rationality mobilized by natural law (the rationality of the understanding) cannot meet its own requirements. A striking illustration of Hegel's fidelity to natural law can be found in his article on the Diet of Württemberg, where he contrasts "good old law" with "the eternal law of reason,"[55] going so far as to enthusiastically approve of the 1789 revolutionary expression of it. We may note in passing, and with a grain of salt, how strange it is to attribute the notion that "all that is real is rational" to a thinker who incessantly criticized the conservative argument that "good old law" is good because it is old.

What specific reasons explain Hegel's refusal of social and political contractualism? As we know, Hegel rejects all attempts to apply the model of the contract to the ethical institutions of the family and the state:

> Marriage is not a contractual relationship as far as its essential basis is concerned. For the precise nature of marriage is to begin from the point of view of contract—i.e. that of individual personality as a self-sufficient unit—*in order to supersede it* [*ihn aufzuheben*].[56]

> Rousseau considered the will only in the determinate form of the *individual* [*einzelnen*] will (as Fichte subsequently also did) and regarded the universal will not as the will's rationality in and for itself, but only as the *common element* arising out of this individual [*einzelnen*] will *as a conscious will.* The union of individuals [*der Einzelnen*] within the state thus becomes a *contract,* which is accordingly based on their arbitrary will and opinions, and on their express consent given at their own discretion.[57]

54. See Hegel's letter to Niethammer dated March 26, 1819, in Hegel, *The Letters,* 441–44; Hoffmeister, *Briefe von und an Hegel,* 2:262. See also the letter to Daub from May 9, 1821, in Hegel, *The Letters,* 460; Hoffmeister, *Briefe von und an Hegel,* 2:213. On the same page, Hegel writes of "my philosophy of law."

55. *Wurtemberg, W* 4, p. 496; *Proceedings,* in *Hegel's Political Writings,* 274.

56. *RPh,* § 163 Anmerkung, *GW* 14.1, p. 146 (*Elements,* 203; see *Outlines,* 165).

57. *RPh,* § 258 Anmerkung, *GW* 14.1, p. 202 (*Elements,* 277; see *Outlines,* 230). See *RPh,* § 75 Anmerkung, *GW* 14.1, p. 78 (*Elements,* 105; see *Outlines,* 85): "the nature of the *state* has just as

The fundamental reason for this assessment is the same in both cases: the nature of contracts, which are actions of private law as it has just been analyzed, makes them unsuitable to account for the constitution of an *ethical* relationship such as matrimonial union or political union; they are unfit for thinking "union as such."[58] Hence, contracts reduce the universal will to common will, or, in Rousseau's terms, the general will to the will of all, and they maintain wills in their individuality and separation. Marriage and the state, on the other hand, set into motion a type of universality that, far from hypostatizing a particular will, rectifies it and carries it beyond itself—in different ways in the two cases of marriage and the state. The concrete universality of the ethical sphere cannot be reduced to the abstract universality of legal relations, which makes any transposition of legal schemata into it inoperative. However, though the contract model cannot account for the ethical within ethicality, it does adequately apply to what is nonethical within it: we will see that it plays an important role in Hegel's conceptualization of civil society, where ethicality risks its downfall.

The argument takes on particular depth when applied to the state. Let us turn to the 1817 article, whose general aim is to denounce the resistance of the "states" (*Stände*) convoked by the King of Württemberg after Napoleon's fall to the creation of a constitutional system similar to the French code. In the article, Hegel does not only criticize, as he does in the *Philosophy of Right*, "the intrusion of this [contractual] relationship, and of relationships concerning private property in general" into "a sphere of a totally different and higher nature."[59] He goes further, indicating the reason why applying this concept of private law to the state is fundamentally erroneous. It is worth citing a passage from the article at length:

> It should be added that the qualitative difference between a fief and a state entails a radical alteration in the precise form of the relation between prince and vassals in the former. Since prince and country, as property-owners and possessors of special prerogatives, confronted one another as privileged *indi-*

---

little to do with the relationship of contract, whether it is assumed that the state is contract of all with all, or a contract of all with the sovereign and the government."

58. *RPh*, § 258 Anmerkung, *GW* 14.1, p. 201 (*Elements*, 276; see *Outlines*, 229). Similarly, marriage is above all "consent to *constitute a single person*" (*RPh*, § 162, *GW* 14.1, p. 145 [*Elements*, 201; see *Outlines*, 164]).

59. *RPh*, § 75 Anmerkung, *GW* 14.1, p. 78 (*Elements*, 106; see *Outlines*, 85).

viduals and so stood under a third party, the power of Emperor and Empire, they were subject to a Praetor, and this made it possible for them to conclude contracts with one another and have relations with one another on the footing of *private* law. Even in more recent times, when truer concepts have taken the place of the old idea, adopted thoughtlessly and irrationally, that governments and princes had a divine authority, the expression "contract of the state" appeared to contain even yet the false thought that the concept of contract was applicable in the *state* to the relation of prince and subjects, government and people, and that the legal specifications of private law, which flow from the nature of a contract, could and even should find their employment in this context. It takes only a little reflection to realize that the connection of prince and subject, government and people, has an original and substantial *unity* as its very basis, while in a contract almost the opposite is the case, since it proceeds from the mutual independence and indifference of the two parties. An association which they enter in relation to some matter is a casual tie arising from the subjective need and choice of the parties. A contract of that kind is essentially distinct from a political bond which is a tie objective, necessary, and independent of choice or whim.[60]

A contract is an agreement between legal persons, that is, "a casual tie arising from the subjective need and choice of the parties." The political bond, on the other hand, is "a tie objective, necessary and independent of choice or whim"; it presupposes "an original and substantial *unity*" that is at the foundation of both the unequal relation between rulers and the ruled (*Herrschaft*) and the relation between the ruled themselves, which is a relation of equality in subordination not to any person or group of persons but rather to the state as the *idea* of a shared life, of a living together. In this regard, modern contractualism represents a regression with respect to classical political philosophy, which maintained the ethical dimension of the political bond, as the article on natural law reiterates:

Of late, however, in the internal economy of natural law, this external justice (infinity reflected in the persistent finite, and for this reason formal infinity) that constitutes the principle of civil law has secured a special predominance over constitutional and international law. The form of such an inferior rela-

60. *Wurtemberg, W* 4, pp. 504–5; *Proceedings,* in *Hegel's Political Writings,* 280–81, modified.

tion as the contractual one has forced its way into the absolute majesty of the ethical totality . . . and by relations of this kind which are wholly in the sphere of the finite, the Idea and the absolute majesty of the ethical totality are destroyed.[61]

Thus, the major flaw of contractualism is that it makes the political bond contingent—according to Locke, the consequences of this are, for example, that it is possible to proclaim a right of secession or emigration[62]—thereby depriving the state of its own necessity and politics of its intrinsic dignity. From the Hegelian point of view, there is thus no contradiction between rejecting the doctrine of the social contract—which is generally considered to have reached its culmination with the principles of 1789[63]—and adhering to the "elementary catechism"[64] those principles express. For "the famous *Droits de l'homme et du citoyen*" cannot possibly stand in place of a political constitution: at the very most, they are "stable regulators" of the state's operation.[65] On this point Hegel is less radical than the American constitutionalists, who refused to preface the United States Constitution with a Declaration of Rights on the grounds that "the constitution is itself, in every rational sense, and to every useful purpose, a Bill of Rights."[66] For Hegel, the value of a Declaration like the French one is that it solemnly proclaims the raison d'être of the *social* order—that is, individual rights, principles that are eternal because they are based on reason or at least on understanding. But even if such a declaration were to be a "preamble," it could not possibly act as a foundation for public law (*Staatsrecht*). The principles of the political order cannot be reduced to those of the legal order, which is the abstract underpinning of civil society.

But Hegel does not reject contractualism on principle alone. Behind the theoretical attempt to derive the principles of public law from those of private law he senses the risk of the public sphere being subordinated to private

61. *Naturrecht, W* 2, p. 518 (*Natural Law,* 123–24).

62. See chapter 8, section 121 of John Locke, *The Second Treatise of Government* (London: J. M. Dent, 1993), 177.

63. Ernst Bloch, *Natural Law and Human Dignity* (Cambridge, MA: MIT Press, 1986), 120–30; Jürgen Habermas, "Natural Law and Revolution," in *Theory and Practice* (Boston: Beacon, 1973).

64. *Wurtemberg, W* 4, p. 492; *Proceedings,* in *Hegel's Political Writings,* 270.

65. *Wurtemberg, W* 4, p. 492; *Proceedings,* in *Hegel's Political Writings,* 270.

66. *The Federalist Papers* (London: Oxford University Press, 2008), no. 84, p. 422.

interests. The requirement of a strong state, the trademark of Hegelianism, is rooted in his observation of the powerlessness of the imperial state, a powerlessness that had been established in the name of princes and cities, that is, in the name of the law tout court. The 1817 article sees the invocation of "good old law" by the *Stände* deputies as the specter of anarchy, legalized in the name of respect of rights and freedoms. These freedoms are not individual liberties but rather exemptions and privileges accorded to various corporations (i.e., to *Zünfte*, the traditional "guilds" and "confraternities," not the modern *Korporationen* Hegel calls for). These bodies see the strength of a modern state as a danger to their independence, which is why Hegel denounces their "guild mind" (*Zunftgeist*).[67] In short, the Diet's distrust of "French" institutions — that is, those based on a strict distinction between the public sphere and private law — expresses the neofeudal temptation of a society that is not yet a "civil society" and that does not want to be a political society.

This battle for the state and what Hegel calls "rational public law," both of which are exposed to the risk of the hegemony of private law, shows that of the two major constructions that emerged from the contractualist problematic, the contract of submission is the most revealing and most dangerous. The contract of association, understood in Hobbes's or Rousseau's sense, implies "the total alienation to the whole community of each associate with all his rights"[68] and consequently maintains the supremacy of the public sphere; on the other hand, the pact of submission (which may be combined with the pact of association as in Pufendorf)[69] leads to limiting sovereignty on prin-

---

67. See *Wurtemberg, W* 4, p. 483; *Proceedings*, in *Hegel's Political Writings*, 263. The theme of this piece is the denunciation of the "estates'" desire to restrict public law (which for Hegel was born in 1791) to "good old law" and to privileges.

68. Rousseau, *Oeuvres complètes*, 3:360; *Social Contract*, 1:6, 163.

69. On the "double contract" see VII/2, section 7–8, in Samuel von Pufendorf, *De jure naturae et gentium libri octo vol. 2: The Translation of the Edition of 1688*, trans. C. A. Oldfather (Oxford: Oxford University Press, 1934), 974–77. In the abridged version of the treatise, *De officio hominis et civis juxta legem naturalem*, he summarizes "that any Society may grow together after a regular Manner, there are required Two Covenants, and One Decree, or Constitution." According to the first covenant, the social compact, "of all those many, who are supposed to be in a Natural Liberty, when they are joined together for the forming and constituting any Civil Society, every Person enters into Covenant with each other, That they are willing to come into one and the same lasting Alliance and Fellowship." The constitution determines "what Form of Government is to be pitched upon." The second covenant establishes the respective rights and duties of rulers and the ruled: "when he or they are nominated and constituted upon whom the Gov-

ciple and reserving certain rights or privileges for certain individuals or social groups. A paradox appears: neofeudalism (*Ständestaat*[70] is the German expression) is a correct consequence of the contractualist view, which is usually associated with the Enlightenment and the Revolution, for it completes the privatization of the public sphere that results from the total juridification of the state. The postfeudal structuring of the political bond through *Herrschafts-verträge* ("contracts of domination") rests on a view of the political orders that is not essentially different from the one presupposed by liberal, revolution-inspired contract theories. In both, the private contract, as an agreement between preexisting individual wills, is the model, casting doubt on the modernity of modern natural law. Thus, we should not be surprised to find that in the *Philosophy of Right*, Hegel's critique of Karl Ludwig von Haller's retrograde views comes immediately after his critique of Rousseau's contractualism and its revolutionary consequences. Each of these views reduces *power* to *property*, thus showing a fundamental misunderstanding of the specificity of the political bond. Hegel emphasizes the theoretical proximity of these politically opposed options:

> Just as in earlier times [but this also applies to Hegel's contemporary Haller] political rights and duties were regarded as, and declared to be, the immediate private property of particular individuals in opposition to the rights of the sovereign and the state, so also in more recent times have the rights of sovereign and the state been regarded as objects of contract and based on a contract. . . . However different these two points of view may be in one respect, they do have this in common: they have transferred the determinations of private property to a sphere of a totally different and higher nature.[71]

---

ernment of this Rising Society is conferr'd; by which Covenant the Persons that are to govern, do oblige themselves to take Care of the Common Safety, and the other Members do in like manner oblige themselves to yield Obedience to them" (Samuel von Pufendorf, *The Whole Duty of Man According to the Law of Nature*, trans. Andrew Tooke [Indianapolis: Liberty Fund, 2003], 195).

70. This expression refers to the Holy Roman Empire of the German Nation where, between the sixteenth and the end of the eighteenth century, imperial power, which had always been limited, gradually lost all substance as the major *Stände*, such as Prussia and Bavaria, constituted themselves as sovereign states.

71. *RPh*, § 75 Anmerkung, *GW* 14.1, p. 78 (*Elements*, 105–6; see *Outlines*, 85).

From the moment the general will is considered to *derive* from the particular will or to be logically secondary to it, one is inevitably, though perhaps
unwillingly, led to subordinate public law to private law, the universal to the
particular, rational concepts to arbitrary opinions. The immense contribution
of the French Revolution was to have established the autonomy of the principles of public law: "One must regard the start of the French Revolution as
the struggle of rational constitutional law against the mass of positive law and
privileges by which it had been stifled."[72] The mistake its actors made was not
to have drawn all the consequences and to have maintained an inadequate
perspective by believing that an abstract definition of freedom—the definition that corresponds to the program of the rights of man—could provide a
foundation for the public sphere. The article on the English Reform Bill repeats this criticism of the politics of human rights: it states that "For *men of
principles*, national legislation is in essence more or less exhausted by the *droits
de l'homme et du citoyen*, framed by La Fayette [*sic*] and the model for the
earlier French constitutions."[73] Hegel's conviction is precisely that one does
not govern with legal principles, for otherwise one will fall into the dangerous
abstraction of revolutionary utopia and the "fury of destruction"'; this is what
happened in France. The Terror was of course not the consequence of the law
but of a *politics of law* (and of "natural and inalienable" rights)—a politics that
reinforces the constitutive abstraction of the law. And contractualism is what
makes this derivation theoretically possible.

The Contractualization of the Social

The positivity of contracts (they are the first objectivization of a legal person's particular will in relation to another particular will) and their limits
(their universality remains tributary to the particularity of the wills they bring
together)—in short, the *contradictory* nature of the act of contracting—
explains the function and situation specific to it no longer within abstract law
itself but within the architecture of *Sittlichkeit*. Indeed, one cannot stop at a
radical critique of political contractualism: the critique of the abstraction of
abstract law on the one hand and of contractualist representations of the political bond on the other hand leads most commentators to maintain that for

72. *Wurtemberg, W* 4, pp. 506–7; *Proceedings*, in *Hegel's Political Writings*, 282.
73. *Reformbill, W* 11, p. 127; *Reform Bill*, in *Hegel's Political Writings*, 329.

Hegel the contractual scheme has no value outside the narrow sphere of relations of private law. Though Hegel does refuse to base the state on contracts for the reasons that I have just pointed out, contracts are not absent from the sphere of *Sittlichkeit*. Quite to the contrary, they play a fundamental role in structuring its median moment, which Hegel initially analyzes as the negative moment of the externalization of ethical essence,[74] that is, civil society (*bürgerliche Gesellschaft*).

Indeed, Hegelian civil society is not a pure market society; it is also a legal society: "The substantial basis for all of this is the right to ownership. The system of needs and its intricacy cannot exist without law."[75] The existence of a legal order is even the presupposition not only of civil society in general but also of its most dynamic and modern component:

> When you make industry the purpose, and law the means, one can say [too] there is an industry in a state only when law is there. Law is the absolute means; there can be no industry, and no trade . . . if administration of justice varies arbitrarily, is bad, slow; the more powerful the trade, the swifter the administration of justice must be.[76]

The actualization of the universal in the competitive play between particular interests cannot merely be the result of the invisible hand; the relationship between these interests must be "consciously regulated"[77] both legally and administratively. Or rather, because civil society is a market society based in large part on the self-regulation of the system of needs, its proper functioning presupposes what Hegel calls a *"legal constitution [Rechtsverfassung]"*[78] of civil society, which he examines in a passage titled "The Administration of Justice" (*die Rechtspflege*). The location of this passage, between the analysis of the economic and social structures of civil society (the system of needs) and the analysis of its institutional configurations (police and corporations), in-

---

74. "This relation of reflection accordingly represents in the first instance the loss of ethicality; or, since the latter, as the essence, necessarily *appears*, this relation constitutes the *world of appearance* of the ethical, i.e., *civil society"* (*RPh*, § 181, *GW* 14.1, p. 159; *Elements*, 219; see *Outlines*, 180).

75. Hegel, *Philosophie des Rechts*, 168.

76. Hegel, *Vorlesungen über Rechtsphilosophie*, 4:528–29.

77. *RPh*, § 236, *GW* 14.1, p. 190 (*Elements*, 262; see *Outlines*, 217).

78. *RPh*, § 157, *GW* 14.1, p. 143 (*Elements*, 198; see *Outlines*, 162).

dicates that what is discussed here is something more and in part something other than the legal organization of procedures. Moreover, the fact that this analysis has no place in either the study of abstract law or the study of the state (although the administration of justice is clearly part of what Hegel calls governmental power)[79] indicates that the expression of the law plays a specific role in the complex workings of civil society. In a word, the market, (private) law, and the institutional nodes represented by "corporations" are the three levels from which the complexity of the modern social world in its differences from the political-state sphere is organized (in part spontaneously and in part following regulated procedures).

The model of the contract, which Hegel constantly reminds us is unsuitable for conceptualizing the state, plays a crucial role in constituting civil society in accordance with legal relations. Civil society, as a market society—and this is one of the reasons why its development was necessarily historically belated—presupposes what I have called a primitive legal accumulation. In other words, commercial society presupposes a legal order and a distribution of property that conforms to it. Thus, within civil society, unlike in the domain of abstract law understood ahistorically, *property does not precede contract but instead results from it*: what is mine is what I have acquired in conformity with the prescriptions of current legislation:

> Just as law *in itself* becomes statute-law in civil society, so too does my individual [*einzelne*] right, whose existence [*Dasein*] was previously *immediate* and *abstract*, acquire a new significance when its existence is recognized as a part of the existent [*existierenden*] universal will and knowledge. Acquisitions of property and transactions relating to it must therefore be undertaken and expressed in the *form* which that existence gives to them. Property is accordingly based on *contract* and on those *formalities* which make it capable of proof and confer upon it legal validity.
>
> The original, i.e. immediate, modes of acquisition and titles (see §§54 ff.) are in fact abandoned in civil society, and occur only as individual accidents or limited moments.[80]

---

79. See *RPh*, § 287, *GW* 14.1, p. 241 (*Elements*, 328–29; see *Outlines*, 278): "the powers of the *judiciary* and the *police* . . . have more immediate reference to the particular affairs of civil society, and they assert the universal interest within these [particular] ends."

80. *RPh*, § 217 and Anmerkung, *GW* 14.1, p. 181 (*Elements*, 249, modified; see *Outlines*, 206).

The proclamation that within civil society (as a society of commercial production and exchange) "property is based on contract" (and not on the exercise of *jus in omnia*) can seem trivial in certain respects. However, from another point of view, the remark is far from inconsequential. It indicates that contracts, the central figure of abstract law, find their specific effectiveness and function only with the constitution of a "civil" society (specific to modernity) that is distinct from the state, though still subordinate to it, with modes of structuration and regulation that are not political: the market, the administration of civil and penal law, and (also) the intervention of the administration (the police).

However, it cannot be said that bourgeois civil society (instead of the state as construed by natural law) is based on contracts in the sense that they are its origin and foundation; if this were the case, Hegel would have done no more than shift the field of application of the contractual scheme from the political sphere toward the economic and social sphere. Instead, we must understand that civil society, which as a market society is "structurally depoliticized," as Jürgen Habermas put it,[81] can only function properly if there is a seamless legal order, an order whose coherence is based on a generalization of the contractual relation. From this point of view, one must observe the irreversible march of civil society "from status to contract"[82] and recognize that in the very abstraction of their determinations, contracts are the legal condition of the social, and to this extent they represent a pillar of "the freedom of the Moderns." However, if the contractualization of the social bond is an essential component in constituting a market society, it cannot on its own structure it sufficiently: the market needs not just a legal basis but also institutional and dispositional conditions (*habitus*) that are studied in the third moment of the analysis of civil society: police and corporations. This is why, ultimately, Hegelian civil society is no more a purely contractual society than it is a pure market society, though it is both of those things.

81. Jürgen Habermas, *Legitimation Crisis* (London: Heinemann, 1976), 37; *Legitimationsprobleme im Spätkapitalismus* (Frankfurt am Main: Suhrkamp, 1973), 55.

82. Henry S. Maine presented the history of legal culture as an evolution "from Status to Contract": see Henry S. Maine, *The Ancient Law* (Boston: Beacon, 1963), 172–74. Max Weber objected to this analysis on the grounds that contracts are present in ancient legal forms; he proposes that it would be better to speak of an evolution of the contractual form itself from "status-contract" to the "function-contract" (*Zweckkontrakt*) of market societies. See Max Weber, *Economy and Society: An Outline of Interpretive Sociology* (Berkeley: University of California Press, 1978), 672.

PART II

The Vitality and Flaws of the Social

The Hegelian conception of civil society (or civil-bourgeois society, or bourgeois society; the choice of translation is not insignificant here) as distinct from the state but subordinate to it completed the profound change in understandings of the political that had been underway since the seventeenth century. Hegel emphasizes that it is essential not to confuse the state (political society) with civil society if one wishes to understand either of them. One may therefore consider that the guiding principle of the doctrine of objective spirit (recognition of the rights of the nonpolitical while simultaneously maintaining the supremacy of the objective political state) is the culmination of efforts made by modern thought to break from the classical model of κοινωνία πολιτική. Hobbes's philosophy, which consciously breaks with the theological and legal-political tradition to which the concept of *societas civilis* belongs, brings up, as if it were its negative, the problem that Hegel's social and political philosophy seeks to resolve. That problem, stated schematically, is the existence and status of a bundle of relations that cannot be understood in purely political terms within a community that is and must be politically defined. Carl Schmitt claimed that the Hobbesian opposition between the state of nature and society is the matrix for all modern political thought, down through

Hegel and Marx.[1] The analyses that follow will test the validity and limits of that claim.

It is practically a banality to say that the study of civil society is the most innovative, if not revolutionary, part of Hegel's doctrine of objective spirit. This of course has to do with how Marx, exploiting the polysemy of the adjective *bürgerlich*, appropriated the concept and turned it into a critical tool, a "theoretical missile" against the bourgeoisie. Many commentators, following Lukács and Marcuse, have fruitfully explored this topic to the point that it has become difficult to read Hegel's claims—in particular those dealing with the formation of the "rabble" (*Pöbel*) and the inability of civil society (and the state) to deal with it—without thinking of the powerful extension given to these arguments by Marxism. However, I will take a different path here. Within the perspective of a history of concepts, my first goal will be to show that the distinction between bourgeois and citizen (which Hegel certainly did not invent) in a way condenses an analysis of the necessarily contradictory relations between the social and the political in the modern world (chap. 4). I will then describe the theory of civil society as an anticipation—a critical one—of the liberal doctrine of the *Rechtsstaat*, which spread during the decades following Hegel's death. What is remarkable is that this analysis attributes to *society* properties and functions that liberal jurists would later describe as belonging to the *state* of law (chap. 5). Finally, I will study the formation and reworking of the concept of *Sittlichkeit*; it will become clear that analysis of civil society, including its aporetic aspects, is the focal point for understanding what is specifically modern in civil society (chap. 6).

---

1. See Carl Schmitt, *The Nomos of the Earth* (New York: Telos, 2003); *Der Nomos der Erde* (Berlin: Duncker und Humboldt, 1988).

→ Preliminary ←

The Archeology of Society

Near the end of the eighteenth century, the classical concept of civil or political society (κοινωνία πολιτική, *societas civilis, civil society, bürgerliche Gesellschaft*)[1] underwent a profound transformation leading relatively quickly to a new concept of civil society as distinct from and opposed to the state; this transformation would ultimately yield a representation of the "social" as opposed to the political that would become sociology's object of study.[2] We could debate at length the conditions and reasons for this semantic change, as well where it occurred: was it already present in English Scottish thinking — in Adam Smith's "great society"[3] — or in French thought, among the physiocrats,

1. See Manfred Riedel, "Gesellschaft, bürgerliche," in *Geschichtliche Grundbegriffe*, 8 vols., ed. Otto Brunner, Werner Conze, and Reinhart Koselleck (Stuttgart: Klett-Cotta, 1974–1997), 2:719.

2. At around the same time as Auguste Comte in France, Lorenz von Stein forged this new term to denote the scientific study of society, although he speaks instead of *Gesellschaftslehre*. See Lorenz Von Stein, *Der Begriff der Gesellschaft, in Geschichte der sozialen Bewegung in Frankreich, von 1789 bis auf unsere Tage*, 8 vols. (Leipzig, 1850).

3. "[The man of system] seems to imagine that he can arrange the different members of a great society with as much ease as the hand arranges the different pieces upon a chess-board. He does not consider that the pieces upon the chess-board have no other principle of motion besides that which the hand impresses upon them; but that, in the great chess-board of human society, every single piece has a principle of motion of its own, altogether different from that which

for example? Regardless, one thing is certain: Hegel's work was the first explicit example of this change. He proposed a global interpretation of the structure of civil society as the result of a self-differentiation of the political or state sphere—an interpretation that would go on to have considerable influence: one need only think of Marx's use of the concept. In Marx's unfinished commentary on the *Philosophy of Right*, the concept of *bürgerliche Gesellschaft* is used to set up a radical "critique of politics"[4] that bears on civil *and* bourgeois society, as well on the state (also bourgeois), which is its "superstructure."[5] The scope of the lexical and theoretical change that occurred was considerable, namely, a notion that in ancient and medieval philosophy as well as in modern natural law designated *political* existence and made the *polis, societas,* or state the specific site of humans' humanity, came to denote what is fundamentally *not* political or *not immediately* political about human existence, without reducing it to the properties of singular individuality. It is the bourgeois, in Rousseau's sense, who are members of civil society: *private persons* who by their interests and modes of being are absolutely distinct from citizens (*Staatsbürger*), which they may also be or aspire to become.[6] Indeed, for the social individual—whom Hegel identifies with the human as such[7]—the universal, which is the horizon of all rational politics, is not an end, much less a supreme end; rather, it is at most a means to be used in the service of the individual's particular interest.[8] At the same time, this interest can only be satisfied through cooperative interaction with other interests, all equally bound to their own particularity.

The very structure of the doctrine of *Sittlichkeit*—family, civil society, state—makes it clear that in Hegel, the distinction between the state and

---

the legislature might choose to impress upon it." Adam Smith, *The Theory of Moral Sentiments* (Oxford: Oxford University Press, 1976), 234.

4. Marx, *Critique of Hegel's "Philosophy of Right,"* 132.

5. See Karl Marx, *A Contribution to the Critique of Political Economy*, trans. N. I. Stone (Chicago: Charles and Kerr, 1904), 12.

6. See chapter 4 below.

7. See *RPh*, § 190 Anmerkung, *GW* 14.1, p. 166 (*Elements*, 228, modified; see *Outlines*, 188): "In law, the object is the *person*; at level of morality, it is the *subject*, in the family the *family-member*, and in civil society in general, the *citizen* (in the sense of *bourgeois*). Here, at the level of the needs, it is that concretum of *representational thought* which we call the *human being*; this is the first, and in fact the only occasion on which we shall refer to the *human being* in this sense."

8. As "citizens" of the *external* state, that is, civil society, individuals are merely "private persons" (*RPh*, § 187, *GW* 14.1, p. 162 [*Elements*, 224; see *Outlines*, 184])

civil society, between the "properly political" state and the "external state," replaces the very old distinction between the *oikos* and the *polis* as conceptualized in particular in book 1 of Aristotle's *Politics*. In Aristotle's view[9] — one that would prove to be astonishingly durable, outlasting the decomposition of the Greek city, since echoes of it can be found in the feudal world and in the postfeudal estate-based society (*ständische Gesellschaft*) — the *oikos*, that is, the family or rather the household, represents the "private," nonpolitical part of human life in opposition to the city. The *oikos* is not only the place of the physical and moral reproduction of the species but also the site of "economic" activities (the etymology of *oiko-nomia* reminds us that it was originally linked to the domestic side of existence), in particular the legitimate, "natural" part of these activities. The distinction between the legitimate and illegitimate arts of acquisition, between (domestic) economy and chrematistics, is based precisely on criteria of self-sufficiency and self-limitation that are supposed to be guaranteed by restricting the arts of production to the circle of the household.[10] In short, the activities located in the closed world of the *oikos* maintain the simple life, the production and reproduction of the infraethical conditions of individual and community existence; in contrast, political praxis is geared entirely toward the supreme — or perhaps sole — ethical and political end: the good or happy life, the *eu zên*.

Within the modern theory of natural law, this distinction is replaced by another binary structure that, all else being equal, plays a comparable role: the distinction between the state of nature and civil society. Thus, the opposition between the state of nature and the civil/political state takes over for the opposition between *polis* and *oikos* without any change in the partition or hierarchy between the political and the nonpolitical (or prepolitical) dimensions of humanness. This substitution corresponded to a fundamental change in the way the political order was perceived: political society was no longer considered humanity's natural end but rather a means — in fact, the only means — of allowing individuals to pursue their own ends by resolving from above, so to speak, the problem of their coexistence. It is, Hobbes writes, the *artifice*[11] humans invented to solve the problem of coexistence, a problem that

9. See Aristotle, *Politics*, 1.2.1242b27.
10. See Aristotle, *Politics*, 1.8.1256a
11. "For by art is created that great Leviathan called a Common-Wealth or a State (in Latin, *Civitas*) which is but an artificial Man." Hobbes, *Leviathan*, 2:16.

remains insoluble in a hypothetical state of nature. To use a different lexicon, the constitution of the state, which is conventionally represented as an act of origination, allows individuals, who are by their nature engaged in unending quests for independence, well-being, or dominance, to freely enjoy—that is, independently of any external constraint—their "natural and imprescriptible" rights: life, liberty, and property, to use Locke's triad,[12] or liberty, property, and security, in the terms of the 1789 Declaration.[13]

It is surprising that in such conditions the expression "civil society" continued to designate the political community when this latter was no longer in a position to maintain the emphatic significance it had in Aristotle and in Aristotelian thought. The reason for this persistence—which was incongruous, since modern political theories see the city as a derivative and conventional reality, while the individual is accorded the rank of an ontologically primary reality— is undoubtedly the fact that when the modern theory of natural law emerged in the first half of the seventeenth century,[14] it would have been impossible to discern, let alone conceptualize, the profound effect that the commercial and industrial revolutions and the establishment of an economy of profit would have on representations of human relations and politics. It was only during the eighteenth century that, thanks to English Scottish thought, awareness of the fact that social institutions are "the result of human action but not the execution of any human design"[15] was born. At the source of this new vision of the political and the social—terms that would then have to be distinguished—lies the conviction, hammered out by liberal thinkers, that "trade [is] older than the State"[16] and that consequently it is illusory to believe that *politics* can

12. "Man . . . hath by nature a power to preserve his property, that is, his life, liberty, and estate." Locke, *Second Treatise of Government*, chap. 7, § 87. See also chap. 9, § 123, and chap. 15, § 173.

13. "The aim of all political association is the preservation of the natural and imprescriptible rights of man. These rights are liberty, property, security, and resistance to oppression" (Declaration of the Rights of Man: 1789, art. 2; cited from http://avalon.law.yale.edu/18th_century /rightsof.asp).

14. Grotius's *De jure belli ac pacis* dates from 1625; Hobbes's *Elements of Law*, *De Cive*, and *Leviathan* were published in 1640, 1642, and 1651, respectively.

15. Adam Ferguson, *Ferguson: An Essay on the History of Civil Society* (Cambridge: Cambridge University Press, 1995), 119. Hayek chose this phrase as the slogan for liberal political philosophy; see Friedrich August Hayek, *Law, Legislation and Liberty: A New Statement of the Liberal Principles of Justice and Political Economy* (London: Routledge, 1977), 1:23.

16. See Hayek, *Fatal Conceit*, 43. Regarding the birth of this topic, see John Greville Agard

hold the key to the *social* problem of human coexistence. While that view may have had some validity in ancient societies, feudal societies, or the German *Ständestaat*, all of which defined themselves and the relations within them in primarily political terms, it was not suitable to a commercial society, where the flexible space open to individuals' actions was no longer determined by their intangible *status* as it was in Rome. Thus, the specific characteristic of modern "trading nations," to use Benjamin Constant's vocabulary, is that they gradually erase all traces of purely political determinations of social being as they existed in the older "conquering nations."[17] Though Hegel's analysis of the effects of commerce is far more dialectical than Ferguson's or Constant's, he too notes that in civil society (in the sense the term has in his philosophy) *"a human being counts as such because he is a human being"*[18] — that is, in his quality as a private person and not as a function of the place he occupies in the segmented space of religious belonging or the hierarchical universe of state functions. The fact that the *social* constitution of the bourgeois does not allow one to dispense with the political constitution of the citizen has no bearing on the matter: for Hegel, as for liberal thinkers, modernity has put to rest any *immediately* political definition of humanity.

Three initially independent elements shaped the new understanding of civil society that came into being during the second half of the eighteenth century. First was the awareness that the family could no longer be considered the natural and principal site of activities of production. The *oikos* was no longer the seat of economy, and it became appropriate to substitute political economy for the old domestic economy with its techniques for managing the "household." Second, the eighteenth century discovered that civil society, far from constituting the normative horizon along which the political animal has always evolved, itself has a history, and not just a prehistory identified with humanity's state of nature. Thenceforth, the oppositions that structured mod-

---

Pocock, *Virtue, Commerce, and History: Essays on Political Thought and History, Chiefly in the Eighteenth Century* (Cambridge: Cambridge University Press, 1985), and *The Machiavellian Moment* (Princeton, NJ: Princeton University Press, 1975), chap. 14, 462 ff.

17. See Benjamin Constant, *Constant: Political Writings* (Cambridge: Cambridge University Press, 1988), 119. The political is here thought of on the model of war, and the social is defined through an economic paradigm: "War then comes before commerce. The former is all savage impulse, the latter civilized calculation. It is clear that the more the commercial tendency prevails, the weaker must the tendency to war become" (ibid., 53).

18. *RPh*, § 209 Anmerkung, *GW* 14.1, p. 175 (*Elements*, 240; see *Outlines*, 198).

ern political thought (between the natural and the artificial in Hobbes, or between nature and history) became less clear, as the following passage from Ferguson shows:

> If we are asked therefore, Where the state of nature is to be found? we may answer, It is here. . . . While this active being is in the train of employing his talents, and of operating on the subjects around him, all situations are equally natural. . . . If the palace be unnatural, the cottage is so no less; and the highest refinements of political and moral apprehension, are not more artificial in their kind, than the first operations of sentiment and reason.[19]

This will lead me to examine the "civilizing process," to use Norbert Elias's term[20] — in other words, the history by which, without planning, humanity reaches what retrospectively appears to be its very nature: civilization or culture.

The third trait of the new concept of society is less apparent. While modern political philosophy formally maintained the traditional (in short, Aristotelian) notion of civil society, it also contributed to subtly destabilizing it. No matter the form of government, κοινωνία πολιτική is composed of individuals who are free and alike (if not truly equal) if only because they all obey the same law; let us recall that the first name for what would retrospectively be labeled, often with pejorative connotation, democracy, was *isonomia*.[21] On the contrary, the modern concept of civil society as elaborated by Hobbes includes the idea of a necessary relation of subordination: the essential problem then becomes that of *sovereignty*, the institution of which is not an effect of the constitution of civil society but rather its very meaning. This is because political society is based on a structurally unequal relation of power and not, as in Aristotle, on an always-reversible relation between *archein* and *archesthai*. Therefore — and this is what made it necessary to recast the concept of society — problems that do not arise from the hierarchical structure of political space (e.g., those having to do with economic or social relations between

19. Ferguson, *Ferguson: An Essay*, 14.

20. See Norbert Elias, *The Civilizing Process* (Oxford: Blackwell, 1982).

21. See Gregory Vlastos, "Isonomia," *American Journal of Philology* 74, no. 4 (1953): 337–66. See also Christian Meier, *The Greek Discovery of Politics* (Cambridge, MA: Harvard University Press, 1990).

subjects or classes of subjects) must be dealt with in a different framework. In short, the new content that the notion of civil society took on beginning in the nineteenth century was already implied (in negative form) in the way that modern philosophy had, since the seventeenth century, understood the political bond. [22]

The various elements I have just evoked disrupted the traditional notion of civil/political society. Anglo-Saxon thought was at the forefront of this change: the distinction between "society" and "government" was quickly accepted as a given. Here, we may think of Adam Smith's "big society," a market and society of exchange ordered by a "clear and simple system of natural freedom," whose dynamic exceeds the boundaries of political society or at least restricts its scope and means of acting.[23] We may also think of the opening of Thomas Paine's *Common Sense*, published in the same year as *The Wealth of Nations*: "Society in every state is a blessing, but government even in its best state is but a necessary evil, in its worst state an intolerable one."[24]

In German territories, things were more complex and even confused, in particular because of Germany's economic and political lag behind both England and France. Near the end of the eighteenth century, we can observe a kind of blurring and an initial obscuring of the notion of *bürgerliche Gesellschaft*.[25] Thus, in 1793 the economist Jung-Stilling distinguished three levels of social life: the family, *bürgerliche Gesellschaft*, and *Staatsgesellschaft*. The state was thus a *societas civilis cum imperio*, which implies that at least de jure the concept of civil society is independent from that of political power. Similarly, in 1790 the jurist Hufeland claimed that there is a difference between civil society and the state; he attributes this difference to the privatization of social existence that is an indirect consequence of political absolutism. Kant too was aware that a change in the concept of society was underway. Of course, for the

---

22. See on this subject Jean-François Kervégan, "Société civile et droit privé: Entre Hobbes et Hegel," in *Architectures de la raison: Mélanges Alexandre Matheron*, ed. Pierre-François Moreau (Lyons: ENS Editions, 1996), 145–64.

23. See Adam Smith, *An Inquiry into the Nature and Causes of the Wealth of Nations* (Oxford: Oxford University Press, 1976), bk. 4, chap. 9, 687–88. The chapter ends with a discussion of the "Great Society."

24. Paine, *Common Sense*, in Thomas Paine, *Rights of Man: Common Sense, and Other Essential Writings* (Oxford: Oxford University Press, 1998), 5.

25. Examples given by M. Riedel; see "Gesellschaft, bürgerliche," in Brunner, Conze, and Koselleck, *Geschichtliche Grundbegriffe*, 2:753.

most part he maintains the traditional equivalence between civil society and political society. But he also notes that "The *civil union (unio civilis)* cannot itself be called a *society*, for between the *commander (imperans)* and the *subject (subditus)* there is no partnership. They are not fellow-members: one is *subordinated to*, not *coordinated with* the other."[26] This leads to a new distinction, though Kant did not draw out all its implications, between the *social (gesellschaftlich)* state, which is not opposed to the state of nature—for there is sociality in a state of nature—and the *civil (bürgerlich)* state, or in other words, the political state: "there can certainly be society in a state of nature, but no *civil* society (which secures what is mine or yours by public laws)."[27] On the other hand, the young Fichte explicitly differentiated between state and society in his *Contribution to the Rectification of the Public's Judgment of the French Revolution* (1793) and *Some Lectures Concerning the Scholar's Vocation* (1794). The first work emphasizes that the word *Gesellschaft* can apply to any kind of contractual association, not only to the particular form of association based on the *Bürgervertrag*, the social contract—that is, *civil* (political) society.[28] In addition, not every society (*Gesellschaft*) is based on a contract. It might simply be a form of physical coexistence between individuals, nonintentional and above all lacking any legal nature; in this sense, society is not incompatible with the state of nature, that is, with the lack of legal bond that characterizes the *bürgerlicher Zustand*—the civil condition. Fichte saw the Revolution as an insurrection of society against the state. But his economic ideas, which certainly were not liberal (as we see in *The Closed Commercial State*), and his vision of an educating state working toward its own abolition prevented him from accepting the idea of even partial autonomy of the social from the political.

It was clearly with Hegel that for the first time (and not only in Germany) a precise conceptual distinction was drawn between the *bürgerliche Gesellschaft* and the *Staat*, between the social and the political.[29] There has been a great deal of discussion about when in his intellectual development Hegel became aware of the issue: was it an innovation of the *Philosophy of Right* or was it already present de facto in his Jena writings (1802–1807)? For some, Hegel

26. Kant, *Rechtslehre: MdS*, § 41, *Ak.* 6, p. 306; *PP*, p. 451.

27. Kant, *Rechtslehre: MdS*, *Ak.* 6, p. 242 (see also p. 306); *PP*, pp. 397, 451.

28. See Fichte, *Beitrag, Werke*, 6:130.

29. See Ernst Böckenförde, ed., *Staat und Gesellschaft* (Darmstadt: Wissenschaftliche Buchgesellschaft, 1976).

became aware of what he would name civil society in the course of composing the 1820 work.[30] I myself share the position of other commentators[31] who hold that it was the Jena writings, in particular the two versions of the *Philosophy of Spirit* and the *System of Ethicality*, that laid the groundwork for the distinction between state and civil society, integrating into political philosophy themes drawn from political economy,[32] that "science of opposition" (opposition to the police state, to political totality), as it was sometimes called. The analysis of tools, of the division of labor, and in certain respects, of language in the "first System," and of social estates (*Stände*) and the mentalities (*Gesinnungen*) proper to them in the "second philosophy of Spirit" and in the *System of Ethicality* are all premises that would be systematically revisited and would lead to the distinction between the state and civil society[33] once Hegel realized that the understanding of society that emerged from these analyses was incompatible with the ideal of the *polis* he still upheld in the Jena writings. A famous passage from the *Phenomenology of Spirit* also illustrates this ideal.[34] However, immediately after emphatically describing the "happiness" that results from the fusion of particular individuality with the living, ethical totality of the people, Hegel adds, "reason *must depart* from this *happy fortune*, for the life of a free people is merely *in itself* or *immediately* a *real ethicality*."[35] The second *Philosophy of Spirit* (1805) glorifies the "*beautiful* public life" of the Ancients, which guaranteed "the immediate unity of the universal and the particular" but opposes to it "the *superior principle of modern times*,"[36] which is expressed in the functional differentiation between the moments of the ethi-

---

30. See Manfred Riedel, "Der Begriff der bürgerlichen Gesellschaft und das Problem seines geschichtlichen Ursprungs," in *Zwischen Tradition und Revolution: Studien zu Hegels Rechtsphilosophie*, ed. Manfred Riedel (Stuttgart: Klett-Cotta, 1982), 139–69.

31. See Rolf-Peter Horstmann, "Über die Rolle der bürgerlichen Gesellschaft in Hegels Politischer Philosophie," *Hegel-Studien* 9 (1974): 209–40. See also Norberto Bobbio, "Sulla nozione di società civile," in *Studi Hegeliani* (Turin: Einaudi, 1981); Bernard Bourgeois, *Le droit naturel de Hegel* (Paris: Vrin, 1986), 638–39; Norbert Waszek, *The Scottish Enlightenment and Hegel's Account of "Civil Society"* (Dordrecht: Kluwer, 2012).

32. See "Die Rezeption der Nationalökonomie," in Riedel, *Zwischen Tradition und Revolution*, 116–39.

33. See "Philosophie des Geistes"' (1803–1804) in *GW* 6, pp. 277–79, 88–94, 97–300, 17–26. See also "Philosophie des Geistes" (1805–1806) in *GW* 8, pp. 242–45, 70–77.

34. See *PhG*, *GW* 9, p. 194–195 (*Phenomenology*, ¶¶ 350–54).

35. *PhG*, *GW* 9, p. 195 (modified; *Phenomenology*, ¶ 354).

36. *GW* 8, p. 263.

cal totality. We also know with certainty, thanks to the publication of a *Nachschrift* from the 1817–1818 Heidelberg course on "Natural Law and Science of the State," that it was then that the distinction between state and civil society formally appeared. We also see that in this text, the distinction is explicitly connected to the theoretical advances of *Staatsökonomie*.[37] As was already the case in 1805, here the conceptual distinction is illustrated by the opposition between "bourgeois" and "citizen."[38] The significance of this innovation can be measured by its conspicuous absence from the first edition of the *Encyclopedia*, which appeared in the same year, where the differentiation between estates is still based, as it was in the Jena writings, on their ethical properties (their "virtues") rather than on their objective economic-social properties.[39] Similarly, Hegel's courses at the Nuremberg Gymnasium between 1808 and 1811, edited under the title *Philosophical Propadeutic*, juxtaposed in a very classical manner—Aristotelian, even—family, which is a "natural society" based on ethical feelings ("love, trust, obedience"), and *Staatsgesellschaft*, which is the "society of men subjected to legal relations."[40]

The "discovery" of *bürgerliche Gesellschaft* was part of Hegel's process of "reconciliation with the [present] time," during which the strong criticism of the "bourgeois" that typified his early writings softened. Beginning with the 1817–1818 course, *civil society*, distinguished from the state and from the family, became the mediating term making it possible to escape from the dualist topoi that modern theories of natural law had inherited from the Aristotelian contraposition of *oikos* and *polis*. The mediation is one of exteriority: civil society is an "external state."[41] But this exteriority, far from being a mere deficiency, is what gives the social moment its fecundity. The social negation of the closed world of the family—for doesn't the individual become a *"son of civil society"*[42] and no longer merely of his progenitors or ancestors?—is certainly a purveyor of alienation, and civil society first appears as "the system

37. See Hegel, *Vorlesungen über Naturrecht und Staatswissenschaft*, 89; *Lectures on Natural Right*, § 72, 137.
38. See chapter 4 below.
39. See *Enzykl* 1817, § 433, *GW* 13, p. 234 (*Encyclopedia 1817*, 251).
40. *Propädeutik, W* 4, pp. 245–46.
41. *RPh*, § 157, *GW* 14.1, p. 143 (*Elements*, 198; see *Outlines*, 162).
42. *RPh*, § 238, *GW* 14.1, p. 192 (*Elements*, 263; see *Outlines*, 218).

of ethicality, lost in its extremes,"[43] but this disintegration of the *immediate* unity of the ethical sphere is also what makes humanity's political reconciliation with itself mediately possible; it is what makes it possible to go beyond the split existence of *homo oeconomicus* within the rational state.

Civil society, as it is presented in the *Philosophy of Right*, has four distinct characteristics:

(1) It is a society of *labor*, one based on diverse needs — needs that it itself creates, replacing a lost nature — and on the complementarity of work activities. The system of needs, in keeping with the (reinterpreted) teachings of the nascent field of political economy, consists of an interaction between social needs and social production and also has a certain number of traits that distinguish civil society from traditional forms of socialization: the technical and social division of labor, the limitlessness of need, alienation (which Hegel analyzes in terms that directly prefigure Marx's), and the functional stratification of the social body into *Berufstände*, institutionalized yet open socioprofessional groups (replacing the stratification by status that characterized estate-based societies).[44]

(2) Civil society is a milieu of *culture* not only for the individual but also for the community itself.[45] Indeed, the process of untangling the political from the social is the very same as the process of civilization in the sense given to the term by Enlightenment thinkers. Civil society is no doubt a product of modern history,[46] but it contains within itself all of history as the process of humanity's constitution of itself. Let us be clear: the "human being" is a product of society and not vice versa, and it would be fallacious to use society to define the human according to some vague concept of naturalness.[47]

---

43. *RPh*, § 184, *GW* 14.1, p. 160 (*Elements*, 221; see *Outlines*, 182). See chapter 6 below.

44. "The question of which particular estate the *individual* will belongs to is influenced by his natural disposition, birth, and circumstances, although the ultimate and essential determinant is *subjective opinion* and the particular *arbitrary will*." See *RPh*, § 206, *GW* 14.1, p. 172 (*Elements*, 237; see *Outlines*, 195.)

45. See *RPh*, § 187, *GW* 14.1, pp. 162–64 (*Elements*, 224–26; see *Outlines*, 184–86).

46. See in particular Hegel, *Werke*, 19:227; *Vorlesungen über Rechtsphilosophie*, 3:565.

47. *RPh*, § 190 Anmerkung, *GW* 14.1, p. 166 (*Elements*, 228; see *Outlines*, 188).

(3) Civil society is neither a pure market society operating through "catallactics" (as Hayek called it) nor is it a simple milieu of civilization, as a culturalist perspective would claim; it is a *Rechtsgesellschaft*, a society structured by a "legal constitution."[48] It is thus civil society and not the state properly speaking that gives actuality to the abstract principles formulated by the theory of natural subjective rights and the theory of human rights. Thus, civil society is the condition of existence of what would soon come to be called the state of law (*Rechtsstaat*). It is instructive to note that it was Hegel, a supposed apologist of the power state (*Machtstaat*), who formulated this doctrine.

(4) Finally, civil society is a society of classes — or at least its logic seems to make it tend toward becoming one. We may look here to the famous passages in the *Philosophy of Right* where Hegel studies pauperization, the polarization of classes between the "poorest" and the "richest," and colonialism as a way of smoothing out internal social contractions. Thus, Hegel writes,

On the one hand, as the association [*Zusammenhang*] of human beings through their needs is *universalized*, and with it the ways in which means of satisfying these needs are devised and made available, the *accumulation of wealth* increases; for the greatest profit is derived from this twofold universality. But on the other hand, the *specialization* [*Vereinzelung*] and *limitation* of particular work also increase, as do likewise the *dependence* and *want* of the class which is tied to such work; this in turn leads to an inability to feel and enjoy the wider freedoms, and particularly the spiritual advantages, of civil society.[49]

It is not insignificant that the Hegelian conception of civil society (which for Hegel himself culminates in principle in a political-statist *Aufhebung* of social contradictions[50]) gave rise to a philosophy infinitely more radical than the *Rechtsstaat* theoreticians' and that turned the critical potential of Hegel's analysis against the state and against society itself (understood as bourgeois

48. RPh, § 157, GW 14.1, p. 143 (*Elements*, 198; see *Outlines*, 16).
49. RPh, § 243, GW 14.1, p. 193 (*Elements*, 266; see *Outlines*, 220–21).
50. But see chapter 6 below.

society): that is, Marx's philosophy. Indeed, without overinterpreting Hegel's text, we can discern in it the critique that Marx would go on to develop of alienation as the result of the selfish conditions that civil-bourgeois society imposes on humanity. Nothing better summarizes the young Marx's point of view than the following passage from "On the Jewish Question":

> Man is far from being considered, in the rights of man, as a species-being; on the contrary, species-life itself—society—appears as a system which is external to the individual and as a limitation of his original independence. ... The citizen is declared to be the servant of egoistic "man," that the sphere in which man functions as a species-being is degraded to a level below the sphere where he functions as a partial being, and externally that it is man as a bourgeois and not man as a citizen who is considered the true and authentic man.[51]

There is no doubt that Hegel's argument did not have the revolutionary aims of Marx's writings; the Young Hegelians castigated him for his political tepidness and conservative leanings. But the *dialectical* manner in which he conceived the concept of *bürgerliche Gesellschaft* makes the Marxian critique of that society—understood as *bourgeois* rather than *civil* society—theoretically possible and, simultaneously, allows the invention of a revolutionary politics that seeks to overcome the reduction of the political to the state, all of which culminates precisely with Hegel. For it was Hegel's creation of a nonpolitical (in the classical sense of the term) concept of the social that allowed Marx in a single movement to radically critique politics and to conceptualize the alienating aspects of (only) bourgeois society—which is nothing other than Hegelian civil society brought back to its truth—in the name of a strong, metapolitical concept of *society*. Thenceforth, human emancipation, which necessarily occurs by means of *social* revolution, must be understood as the *Aufhebung* of the separation between the social and the political; it passes through a repoliticization of civil-bourgeois society that the merely political

---

51. Karl Marx, "On the Jewish Question," in *The Marx-Engels Reader*, ed. Robert C. Tucker (New York: Norton, 1978), 43. Cf. also the remarks in *Critique of Hegel's "Philosophy of Right"* and the *Economic and Philosophic Manuscripts of 1844*, trans. Martin Milligan (Amherst, NY: Prometheus Books, 1988).

revolution of 1789 thought it had succeeded in depoliticizing.[52] Conversely, human emancipation supposes that the state as a tool of domination in general be abolished, not just one class's domination of another. We may then be right to wonder whether, consciously or not, the goal of the Marxian vision of society is not after all the *Aufhebung* of politics itself. But that is another story.

52. See Marx, "On the Jewish Question," p. 45.

4

"Citoyen" versus "Bourgeois"?

The Quest for the "Spirit of the Whole"

When Hegel and Kant, following Rousseau, sought to draw the opposition between *bourgeois* and *citoyen* (citizen) they turned to French terminology, highlighting a difficulty in German legal and political language. Hegel himself expressed this difficulty in a commentary on the Aristotelian conception of the *polis*: "we do not have two words for 'bourgeois' and 'citoyen.'"[1] The term *Bürger* refers both to a bourgeois in the first sense, that of a city resident (*Stadtbürger*), and to a member of the political community, the citizen (*Staatsbürger*); in the nineteenth century the French word (*bourgeois*) was added to German scientific terminology to designate the economic and cultural properties of a particular social class.[2] But the reasons for this difficulty are not solely linguistic, for they stem from the particularities of Germany's political history. The structures of the *Ständestaat* (a term that is itself nearly impossible to translate into French and is most commonly rendered in English as "corporate state") make it impossible to conceive of a political community whose members could — even if only in certain respects — be legally equal. In short, the lack of distinction between *bourgeois* and *citoyen* that exists

1. *GdP, W* 19, p. 228.
2. See the title of Werner Sombart, *Der Bourgeois* (1913).

at the level of vocabulary expresses the chasm that separates the idea of citizenship—whether in the ancient or revolutionary sense—from the political structures of a divided Germany, where the idea of equality was more or less void of meaning.

The difficulty persisted even after the French Revolution reactivated the ethos of citizenship. The Revolution was born with the Declaration of the Rights of Man and [it is sometimes forgotten] Citizen, and the first constitutions attempted to provide a legal definition of citizenship.[3] German philosophers then appropriated the new vocabulary. Fichte, for example, wrote in 1793,

> But what does a caste that appropriates the exclusive right to certain professions do? . . . Such a privilege does not only make the nobility a state within a state, with its own interest separate from that of other citizens [*Bürger*]; it entirely eliminates other classes of the people from the list of citizens [*Staatsbürger*] and suppresses their right to citizenship [*Bürgerrecht*], turning them into slaves subjected to obstinate domination.[4]

However, when Fichte and Kant brought the vocabulary of citizenship to Germany, they faced not only the hostility of the Revolution's enemies, such as Gentz or Rehberg,[5] but also the sarcasm of some of its partisans. Thus, Klopstock—an honorary citizen of the French Republic!—exclaimed in 1793, after becoming aware of Kant's opuscule *Theory and Practice*, "If we are to speak of a *Staatsbürger*, why not a *Wasserfisch* (water fish)?"[6] implying that Kant's distinction was mere verbal caprice. Therefore, if we want to determine what was new in Hegel's use of the distinction between bourgeois and citizen, we must situate it within the tradition of German legal and political language.

3. French Constitution of 1791, Title 2, Article 2; French Constitution of 1793, Articles 4–6 and especially Article 7: "The French people is the whole of its citizens."

4. Fichte, *Beitrag*, *Werke*, 6:235.

5. Rehberg wrote in 1793, "To introduce the new system, which was to build on the universal equality of all citizens, we should abolish the prerogatives of certain states and destroy these states themselves." August Wilhelm Rehberg, *Untersuchungen über die Französische Revolution* (Hannover: Ritscher, 1793), 1:177.

6. See M. Riedel, "Bürger, Staatsbürger, Bürgertum" in Brunner, Conze, and Koselleck, *Geschichtliche Grundbegriffe*, 1:692.

Retrospective

The words *bourgeois* and *citoyen* first appeared in French during the twelfth and thirteenth centuries, respectively. In the language of jurists, the first term designated the privileged status of certain residents of a city who had the right to hold office within the city's corporate structures and communal administration. Thus, the bourgeois is distinguished, both by his place of residence and by the nature of his rights, from the nobility and clergy on the one hand and from nonfree men (serfs and servants) on the other. As for the term *citoyen*/ citizen (*civis*), it does not have much meaning in a social order where the individual's place is determined by the particularities (i.e., the privileges) of his estate. However, the term appears or reappears with the creation of the modern state, where it takes a decisive new direction.

Jean Bodin, who first defined sovereignty as "the absolute and perpetual power of a Republic"[7] and made it an essential attribute of the state, was also the first to distinguish between bourgeois, citizen, and subject in a discussion of the Aristotelian concept of the *polis*. Aristotle, said Bodin "does not differentiate between Republic and city [*cité*]," though he does clearly perceive the difference between town (*ville*), which is merely a geographical place, and city (*cité*), which "is a word of law."[8] The resident of a town, insofar as he bears certain privileges, is titled to the right of the bourgeoisie. The citizen, however, is a member of the city (*la cité*). But—and here is Bodin's innovation with respect to traditional political language—the citizen, although sui juris, is also a member of the Republic, and therefore a subject. Indeed, to distinguish the citizen from the bourgeois, Bodin specifies that "it is not privileges that make the citizen but rather the mutual obligation between sovereign and subject."[9] Thus, the traditional idea of citizenship should be reinscribed into the relation of protection and obedience specific to the state (or the "Republic.") Hence, the following definition, which occurs no less than three times in Bodin's work: a

7. See I/8 in Jean Bodin, *Les six livres de la république* (Paris: Fayard, 1986), 1:179. For more on Bodin's theory of sovereignty, see Olivier Beaud, *La puissance de l'état* (Paris: Presses Universitaires de France, 1994), 53ff; J. H. Franklin, *Jean Bodin and the Rise of Absolutist Theory* (Cambridge: Cambridge University Press, 1973).

8. Bodin, *Les Six Livres*, I/6, 1:118–19.

9. Ibid., 131.

citizen is "a free subject, dependent on the sovereignty of another."[10] And he specifies:

> It is the free subject's recognition of and obedience to his sovereign prince and the prince's protection, justice, and defense toward the subject that makes the latter a citizen; this is the essential difference between a bourgeois and a foreigner.[11]

The theory of natural law systematized this new understanding of the citizen-subject, which was clearly suited to the reality of what would be termed *absolutism*. One of Hobbes's works is titled *The Citizen* (*De Cive*), but for him the word means nothing more than subject:

> Each of the citizens, and every subordinate civil person is called a subject of him who holds the sovereign power.[12]

Pufendorf's theory of the double contract gave this equation definitive grounding: from then on, the requisite complement to the contract of association was a contract of submission: the citizen essentially became subject, and his first duty was obedience.

For the most part, the identification of citizen with subject remained intact until the French Revolution. However, Enlightenment thinkers shortened its life span. Over the course of the eighteenth century, the discussion of citizen and bourgeois took a turn, thanks to the popularization of a third term that encompassed the other two: *man*. The short-term result was to obscure the question, resulting in a vagueness that infects the articles "Bourgeois" and "Citoyen" in the *Encyclopédie*, both written by Diderot — to say nothing of the articles "Société" and "Société civile" by Jaucourt, which are truly confused. The distinction between bourgeois and citizen seems to have become astonishingly slippery:

> A bourgeois is someone whose regular residence is a town [*une ville*]; the citizen is a bourgeois considered in relation to the society of which he is a

10. Ibid., 113.
11. Ibid., 141.
12. Hobbes, *De Cive: English Version*, 5:11, 134.

member. . . . Residency pre-supposes a place, the bourgeois pre-supposes a city, and citizenship implies a society whose affairs all individuals are familiar with and whose good they love.[13]

Of course, Diderot was writing against Hobbes, who "makes no distinction between subject and citizen," and he proclaimed that "the name *citizen* is suitable neither for those who are subjugated nor for those who are isolated."[14] But Diderot does not at all specify what separates the two notions, saying merely that "the citizen has rights that never leave him."[15] As for the difference between bourgeois and citizen, he seems to have considered it merely a difference of degree.

Rousseau was certainly thinking of these (frequent) approximations when in a note to the *Social Contract* he observed that

> The real meaning of this word [*cité*] has been almost completely erased among the moderns; most people take a town for a city, and a bourgeois for a citizen. They do not know that houses make the town, and that citizens make the city.[16]

Proof that Rousseau was thinking here of Diderot's articles lies in the fact that he adds that besides d'Alembert, the author of the "Genève" article in the *Encyclopédie*, "no other French author . . . has understood the real meaning of the word *citizen*."[17] Although Rousseau refers to Bodin, he strongly differs from him, and no matter what he says, he is not content to reestablish a traditional concept of the citizen, from which "moderns" have unfortunately strayed. According to the *Social Contract*, the specific quality of a citizen is not simply that he is a member of the Republic as a "free subject": it is that he participates in "sovereign power."[18] As Kant would later say, a citizen is essentially a "colegislator," and not merely a "cosubject"[19]: the citizen is different from

---

13. *Encyclopédie; ou, Dictionnaire raisonné des sciences, des arts et des métiers* (1777), s.v. "Bourgeois."

14. Ibid., s.v. "Citoyen."

15. Ibid..

16. Rousseau, *Oeuvres complètes*, 3:361; *Social Contract* 1:6, 164, modified.

17. Rousseau, *Oeuvres complètes*, 3:362; *Social Contract*, 1:6, 164.

18. Rousseau, *Oeuvres complètes*, 3:362; *Social Contract*, 1:6, 164.

19. Kant, *Gemeinspruch*, Ak. 8, pp. 292–94; *PP*, pp. 292–94.

the bourgeois not quantitatively but qualitatively on the basis of the specific political quality that his participation in sovereignty grants him. Thus, while pretending to restore a classical concept, Rousseau introduces a fundamental innovation: he adjusts the concepts of *cité* and *citoyen* to modern conditions of political sovereignty, whereas Bodin had merely juxtaposed them. This reinterpretation involves a new relationship between bourgeois and citizen: no longer simply hierarchical, but antithetical. In *Emile*, bourgeois and citizen appear as the two truly contradictory types of civil man, who is himself the result of the denaturation of natural man—a denaturing process that must be total in order to succeed. And this double distinction gives rise to a highly pessimistic diagnosis of modernity:

> He who in the civil order wants to preserve the primacy of the sentiments of nature does not know what he wants. Always in contradiction with himself, always floating between his inclinations and his duties, he will never be either man or citizen. He will be good neither for himself nor for others. He will be one of these men of our days; a Frenchman, an Englishman, a Bourgeois. He will be nothing. . . . Public instruction no longer exists and can no longer exist, because where there is no longer fatherland, there can no longer be citizens. These two words, fatherland and citizen, should be effaced from modern languages.[20]

For Kant, on the other hand—and in this respect he prefigures nineteenth-century liberal thought—the truly important contrast is no longer between citizen and bourgeois, though he does maintain the distinction; instead, it is between the citizen properly speaking, who enjoys legal and economic independence, and the *Schutzgenosse* ("passive citizen" in Sieyès's words), who benefits only from rights pertaining to his quality as a man. Human beings, as such, have the right to civil liberty and to public freedoms: this is the fundamental meaning of the 1789 declaration. But a division arises between those who, politically, are merely subjects and those who are both subjects and citizens—that is, colegislators.[21] This would appear to be a simple repetition of

20. Rousseau, *Oeuvres complètes*, 4:249–50; *Emile; or, On Education*, trans. Christopher Kelly and Alan Bloom (Lebanon, NH: University Press of New England, 2002), 164–65.
21. Kant, *Gemeinspruch*, Ak. 8, pp. 292–94; *Frieden*, Ak. 8, pp. 349–50; *Rechtslehre: MdS*, § 46, Ak. 6, p. 314; *PP*, pp. 292–94, 322–23, 457.

antiquity's distinctions between, for example, Athenian citizens and metics or between *cives, clientes,* and *peregrini* in Rome. But in fact Kant was on the trail of the distinction between civil society and the state. What is important in his eyes is not so much political inequality as *civil* equality—in other words, the constitution of a unified space of (private) law and the limitation on political authority that results from it. This is precisely the meaning of the exclusion of the principle of public happiness, which was at the center of the doctrine of absolute sovereignty:

> The public well-being . . . is precisely that lawful constitution that secures everyone his freedom by laws, whereby each remains at liberty to seek his happiness in whatever way seems best to him provided he does not infringe on that universal freedom.[22]

Kant's distinction between the conditions of political citizenship and the social legal order incontestably makes him—before Hegel—one of the precursors of the *Rechtsstaat.*

Whereas in Germany, the most clairvoyant thinkers—Kant, Fichte, Rehberg—immediately realized that the French Revolution implied a redefinition of the concept of the *Bürger* and of citizenship, one cannot help but notice that in the legal literature of the time, the issue was far from clear. Let us take a few examples.[23] In a work cited by Fichte three times in his *Contribution to the Rectification of the Public's Judgment of the French Revolution* (1793/1794), Theodor von Schmalz, a colleague of Kant's at Königsberg, attempts to include the new notion of citizenship in Pufendorf's problematic of the double contract in such a way that the citizen is also a subject: "citizens can be called associates [*Mitgenossen*] in relation to a contract of association and subjects

---

22. Kant, *Gemeinspruch, Ak.* 8, p. 298; *PP,* p. 297. This brings to mind a sentence from Benjamin Constant: "Let us ask the authorities to keep within their limits. Let them confine themselves to being just. We shall assume the responsibility of being happy for ourselves." Constant, *Political Writings,* 326.

23. I rely on Manfred Riedel, "Bürger, Staatsbürger, Bürgertum"; Hans-Peter Schneider, "Der Bürger zwischen Stadt und Staat im 19. Jahrhundert," *Der Staat* 8 (1988): 143–78; Michael Stolleis, "Untertan-Bürger-Staatsbürger: Bemerkungen zur juristischen Terminologie im späten 18. Jahrhundert," in *Bürger und Bürgerlichkeit im Zeitalter der Aufklärung,* ed. Rudolf Vierhaus (Heidelberg: Schneider, 1981): 65–99; Paul-Ludwig Weinacht, "Staatsbürger: Zur Geschichte und Kritik eines politischen Begriffs," *Der Staat* 8, no. 1 (1969): 41–63.

in relation to a contract of obedience."[24] During this same period, Karl Heinrich Heydenreich made citizen and subject identical to one another, pure and simple. Going against what was about to become the leading doctrine of the time, he refused to consider the sovereign (*Oberherr*) a *Bürger*. Indeed, "members of the state, amid the people broadly, are called citizens (*Bürger*) as equal participants in sovereignty, and subjects (*Untertanen*) as subordinates to the state."[25] These were not marginal or merely retrograde positions: Heydenreich and Schmalz were among the best-known *Naturrechtler* of the late eighteenth century. Their conflation of citizen and subject simply corresponded to the political reality of the German Empire: the expression *Bürger und Untertanen*, where the "and" means "that is," was a common stock expression in administrative and constitutional documents of the time. As for the equally common confusion between *Bürger* and bourgeois, it is explained by the fact that most noncity dwellers were serfs, or at least were not sui juris. Hence, the terms *Bürger* (in its two meanings) and *Untertan* were often used interchangeably. Heinrich Gottfried Scheidemantel, for example, declared that there was "a significant difference" between citizen and subject:

> There are subjects that are not citizens, for example, servants. . . . However, there are citizens who are not subjects, such as the monarch.[26]

This "significant difference," however, does not mean that one is not normally both subject and citizen! While the general sense of *Bürger* (the subject-citizen) must be distinguished from the particular sense ("someone who enjoys advantages specific to the constitution of a town [*ville*])," the term may also refer both to "members of the state" or *subditi primarii* and to those who participate in "the economy and administration of a town [*ville*]."[27]

---

24. Theodor Anton Heinrich Schmalz, *Das natürliche Staatsrecht* (Königsberg: Friedrich Nicolovius, 1794), §§ 49, 39. See also Schmalz and Friedrich Nicolovius, *Das reine Naturrecht* (Königsberg: Friedrich Nicolovius, 1792), §§ 141–77.

25. Karl Heinrich Heydenreich, *Grundsätze des natürlichen Staatsrechts und seiner Anwendung nebst einem Anhange staatsrechtlicher Abhandlungen* (Leipzig: Weygandsche Buchhandlung, 1795), 178.

26. See the article "Bürger" in Heinrich Gottfried Scheidemantel, *Repertorium des teutschen Staats- und Lehnsrechts* (Munich: Bayerische Staatsbibliothek, 1782), 1:439.

27. Scheidemantel, *Das Staatsrecht nach der Vernunft und den Sitten der vornehmsten Völker Betrachtet* (Cröcker, 1773), 3:174, 179, 242–43.

These authors had at least more or less accepted the ideals of the *Aufklä-rung*. If we look to authors such as Johann Jacob Moser or Johann Stephan Pütter, writers from whom Hegel drew the information included in "The German Constitution," we find much more traditional understandings of the political and social order. Moser, the most illustrious of the *Staatsrechtler*, whom the young Hegel evoked pitilessly, completely conformed to the outmoded structures of the German Empire: he is above all interested in the relations between the empire and the *Stände*, that is, the territories that made up the empire: principalities, church lands, free towns, and so forth. When he uses the term *Bürger*, it is to refer to some or all residents of a town, but it does not have unequivocal meaning. For Moser also writes that the word *civis* "in Latin means the same thing as *subditus* (subject)"[28] and therefore must be translated using the German word *Untertan*!

To summarize: when Hegel began his philosophical career, the meaning of terms such as *bourgeois* and *citizen* were still relatively fluid in German legal language. In giving precise and in some respects entirely new meaning to these notions, he illustrated a fundamental and *new* aspect of modern reality. This can be seen by comparing the Bern and Frankfurt writings with those from Jena, Heidelberg, and Berlin, for between the two groups of texts there was a break that casts light on his later discovery of civil society.

From Bern to Frankfurt

Hegel's writings from Bern and Frankfurt (1794–1800) express his powerful support for the ethical and political (ethical *because* political) ideal of the *polis*. We find this enthusiasm intact in certain fragments transmitted by Rosen-kranz under the titles *Politische Studien* and *Historische Studien*.[29] These texts develop a vision of the city (*cité*) and the citizen that the French Revolution appeared to have realized (at least originally; Hegel very quickly distanced

28. Johann Jacob Moser, *Neues Teutsches Staatsrecht: Von der Landeshoheit in Steuer-Sachen* (Metzler, 1773), 17:1–2; see also pp. 460–61.

29. See Karl Rosenkranz, *Hegels Leben* (Berlin: Duncker und Humblot, 1844), 59–61, 85–94. The texts published in the appendix of this biography were collected with some others and published in Johannes Hoffmeister, ed., *Dokumente zu Hegels Entwicklung* (Stuttgart: Fromann-Holzboog, 1974), 257–82. In current editions, see Hegel, *Werke*, 1:427–48. For problems of dating, see Gisela Schüler, "Zur Chronologie von Hegels Jugendschriften," *Hegel-Studien* 2 (1963): 111–15.

himself from the Jacobin radicalization of the 1789 reformist project).[30] A fragment written in French exalting the "joys of freedom,"[31] which Hegel may have written himself or simply copied, illustrates this. The characteristic quality of the ethic of the *polis* is the total subordination of the private sphere, the activities belonging to it—first and foremost economic practices—and "solicitude for [property]"[32] to the public-political sphere and the values that emanate from it; private existence is almost reabsorbed into public existence. Because "in a Republic, one lives for an idea,"[33] everything that does not help realize this idea—the idea of freedom, the idea of the city—is harmful and must be proscribed. This is the source of measures written into constitutions from antiquity dissuading citizens from being overly attached to their property, for "the disproportionate wealth of some citizens is able to endanger the freest form of constitution and [thereby] destroy freedom itself."[34]

A fragment written between May and August of 1796, shortly after the text on the positivity of the Christian religion, expresses this republican ideal most forcefully. Hegel reminds the reader that for the Greek or Roman citizen, "the idea of his country, of his state [was] . . . the final goal of the world, or the final goal of his world." Not only did he sacrifice his property and life to it, his whole being was in it, for he had being only through this "supreme order of things" and "before this idea, his individuality disappeared."[35] The city demands the citizen's unlimited identification with what Hegel calls the "spirit of the whole" in contrast to an esprit de corps:

> But when a class—of leaders, priests, or both—loses this spirit of unity that founded and animated its laws and orders, not only is the loss irreparable, but oppression, dishonor, and forfeiture of the people are then insured (that is why the fact that these classes are isolated is already a threat to freedom, because it can result in an esprit de corps that soon opposes the spirit of the whole).[36]

30. The letter to Schelling from December 24, 1794, already condemned "the shame of Robespierrists." See Hoffmeister, *Briefe von und an Hegel*, 1:12.

31. Hoffmeister, *Dokumente zu Hegels Entwicklung*, 276.

32. *W* 1, p. 126; on the same topic, see also pp. 204–5, 206, 213–14, and esp. 439.

33. *W* 1, p. 207n60.

34. *W* 1, p. 439.

35. *W* 1, p. 205.

36. *W* 1, p. 57.

This means going so far as to rule out all personal faith: only a civic religion, a *Volksreligion*, can be compatible with the ethic of the state or city. For the republican citizen as for the modern Christian, "the soul is immortal," but this soul, *his* soul, is the Republic itself:

> The republic . . . outlived the republican, and the latter came to realize that the former, his soul, is something eternal.[37]

If Cato the Younger dived into his reading of the *Phaedo* on his deathbed, it was in a sense as a last resort, since his true soul, that is the spirit of the Roman Republic, was already dead. In short, if, as Carl Schmitt said, the article on natural law offers "the first polemically political definition of *bourgeois*," the texts from Bern purely and simply deny the existence of any such thing if by "*bourgeois* is meant an individual who does not want to leave the apolitical riskless private sphere."[38] The very existence of a sphere of private values — even those having to do with love[39] — compromises the ethical totality, which exists only if it exists without remainder. For the citizen, the "I" is always a "We," and "before it [the assembly of the people] and from its mouth 'we' have complete truth."[40]

There are two noteworthy effects, at two different levels, of such absolutization of the political totality and the *ethos* of citizenship. The first effect has to do with vocabulary. With one exception — a stock expression from traditional legal language, *die Bürger und Bauern*[41] — the terms *Bürger* and *bürgerlich* always refer to the political order, to *societas civilis* in the classical sense, in particular in the expressions *bürgerliche Gesellschaft*, *bürgerliche Rechte*, *bürgerliche Gesetze*, *bürgerliche Verfassung*. Thus, citizens (*Staatsbürgern*) of the civil state (*bürgerlicher Staat*) as such possess civil-political rights (*bürgerliche Rechte*).[42] From this point of view, the idea of civil and private law distinct from public

---

37. *W* 1, p. 206.

38. Carl Schmitt, *Der Begriff des Politischen* (Berlin: Duncker und Humboldt, 1979), 62; *The Concept of the Political* (Chicago: University of Chicago Press, 1996), 62.

39. See the diatribe by Aristide, who fancifully rails against the language of courtly love, indignant that one would devote "all this luxury of feelings, acts, enthusiasm" to something other than the city. *W* 1, p. 437.

40. *W* 1, p. 433.

41. *W* 1, p. 167.

42. *W* 1, p. 171.

law is inconceivable. There is but one legal order, and it is political: "it lies in the nature of political society (*bürgerliche Gesellschaft*) and in the rights of its sovereigns and legislators, that individual rights have become rights that the state is obliged to assert and to protect."[43] Clearly, the distinction between private and public law is far from being established here. But Hegel's writings from Bern and Frankfurt quite simply exclude any such distinction. True, "civil laws [concern] the safety of the life and property of every citizen,"[44] but they do not constitute their own autonomous legal space. This is not only because they presuppose the state's sanction—which nobody contests—but above all because the privatization of human existence that would result from an autonomous legal-civic space would compromise the law of the city (in the sense of *polis*). However, Hegel has one important reservation regarding this principle: freedom of conscience, the only right he calls an inalienable human right (*Menschenrecht*) and which he sees as a "fundamental article of the social contract"[45] must be upheld. On this last point, Hegel, who had just read Lessing, Mendelssohn, and Kant's *Religion within the Boundaries of Mere Reason*, is (in spite of himself) more *Aufklärer* than Greek or Roman.

The second effect is that the ethic of the *polis* implies condemning what Hegel, echoing the *Social Contract*, calls "small societies," those "partial societ[ies]" which stand in opposition to "great civil society" and whose "private laws" threaten public institutions and the spirit of citizenship.[46] This theme is greatly expanded in the Bern essay on positivity, which explains the purely positive fate of Christian confession—that is, its sclerosis—by the fact that "the church went from private society to state." [47] What was once a sect whose rules and commandments only applied to members *in foro interno* became a clerical state, a *kirchlicher Staat* that first stood against the political state and then ultimately identified with it, arrogating some of its essential rights. Thus, the church and the state along with it forgot that "for faith, there is strictly speaking no social contract":[48] we may believe, we may want to be-

43. *W* 1, p. 160.
44. *W* 1, p. 149.
45. *W* 1, p. 170.
46. *W* 1, pp. 63 and 66. Compare with Rousseau: "partial associations are formed to the detriment of the whole society." See Rousseau, *Social Contract*, 173; *Oeuvres complètes*, 3:371–72.
47. *W* 1, p. 179.
48. *W* 1, p. 166.

lieve, but we cannot commit to believing. This is not the place to examine why Hegel argues for a strict separation between the churches and the state—a separation he would later consider unrealizable—nor to analyze the connection between these considerations and the idea of a *Volksreligion* (which is not a religion *in* the state but rather a religion *of* the state). Another aspect will be emphasized here, for it directly concerns the subject of this chapter: the argument he lays out regarding the relations between the *bürgerlicher* and *kirchlicher Staat* in the "The Positivity of the Christian Religion" has the same structure as his analysis in "The German Constitution" of the relations between the "fictive state in idea" (*Gedankenstaat*)[49] that the German Empire had become and the partial societies comprising it, that is, essentially, the territorial principalities. However, whereas the 1795–1796 text does not establish a difference between the two *Gesellschaften* of church and state, the 1799–1802 texts attribute the decline of the empire to the contamination of public law by private law and the language of privilege:

> There is always an in and for itself contradiction in supposing that relationships bearing directly on the state, and not property only, are to have the form of private rights.[50]

This clear distinction between public law and private law allows Hegel in "The German Constitution" to recognize, as "The Positivity of the Christian Religion" had not, a specific domain of validity in which the principles of public law are absolutely legitimate. On the other hand, the text on the constitution of the German Empire, while affirming more strongly than ever the specificity of *Staatsrecht* and the political necessity of a strong state, clearly proclaims the existence of nonpolitical, or not directly political, aspects within the political community:

> This is no place to argue at length that the centre, as the public authority, i.e., the government, must leave to the freedom of the citizens whatever is not necessary for its appointed function of organizing and maintaining authority

49. "Verfassung," *W* 1, p. 507–8; "German Constitution," in *Hegel's Political Writings*, 180.
50. "Verfassung," *W* 1, p. 538; "German Constitution," in *Hegel's Political Writings*, 207, modified.

and thus for its security at home and abroad. Nothing should be so sacrosanct to the government as facilitating and protecting the free activity of the citizens in matters other than this. This is true regardless of utility, because the freedom of the citizens is inherently sacrosanct.[51]

By insisting in this way on the difference between the public and the private, this passage already—though this is not its main intention—relativizes the "heroic understanding of freedom" (to use Hyppolite's expression) that was still prevalent in the article on natural law but that would later be replaced by the idea that an individual is *both* bourgeois and citizen. From the critique of the spiritual state in the Bern text to the distinction between the public and the private in the Jena text we see the outlines of what the *Philosophy of Right* will clearly formulate: the existence of a depoliticized legal and social space.

In the Bern text, the condemnation of partial societies goes along with discussion of a topic that also closely concerns the later concept of civil society: the harmful effects that the separation of classes (*Stände*) has on the city and on the spirit of citizenship. In a standard panegyric to the simplicity of the ways of antiquity, Hegel writes,

> But when a class — of the leaders, priests, or both—loses this spirit of unity that founded and animated its laws and orders, not only is the loss irreparable, but oppression, dishonor, and forfeiture of the people are then insured (that is why the fact that these classes are isolated is already a threat to freedom, because it can result in a feeling of pride that soon opposes the spirit of the whole). . . . [Thus] it is no longer a community that comes together, unanimously, before the altar of the gods.[52]

On its own, there is nothing particularly original about this observation; it repeats the classical idea that political equality, the foundation of democracy, requires a high level of homogeneity among a people and cannot accommodate strong inequality. Among the moderns, Rousseau expressed this idea most forcefully, writing that unequal conditions are perilous for the state:

---

51. "Verfassung," *W* 1, p. 482; "German Constitution," in *Hegel's Political Writings*, 161–62.
52. *W* 1, p. 57. Similarly, p. 94. And with respect to corporations and guilds, see *W* 1, p. 150.

If, then, you wish to give stability to the State, bring the two extremes as near together as possible; tolerate neither rich people nor beggars. These two conditions, naturally inseparable, are equally fatal to the general welfare.[53]

Especially in a democracy, there must be "considerable equality in class and fortune, without which equality in rights and authority could not long survive."[54] It is less the content of the young Hegel's text that is remarkable than the fact that its author would later go against this analysis and make esprit de corps the principle means of upholding the "spirit of the whole." The understanding of patriotism, or the *politische Gesinnung* developed in the *Philosophy of Right*, consciously breaks with the heroism of freedom praised by the young Hegel, who found it alive and well among the soldier-citizens of the year II, the new Hellenes.[55] In 1795, Hegel's position was exactly the opposite:

> It is in a manner similar to the church that corporations relate to the state vis-à-vis their rights to it. They also form a corporation in the state. . . . Here, the state has renounced the rights of its citizens.[56]

The difference is even more striking when we read the 1817–1818 lectures in parallel with the 1794 fragment that contrasts the *esprit de corps* with the *esprit du tout*: the later text uses the same terms but emphasizes the ethical and indirectly political vocation of the corporate institution and the subjective dispositions it creates:

> A universal spirit of patriotism is formed by the fact that universal freedom comes about through particularization. There must be universal patriotism, but it must come about through *esprit de corps*.[57]

Here we can see what separates the young Hegel's purely political conception of ethicality from a differentiated ethical totality whose political moment,

---

53. Rousseau, *Oeuvres complètes*, 3:392; *Social Contract*, 2:11, 189.
54. Rousseau, *Oeuvres complètes*, 3:405; *Social Contract*, 3:4, 201.
55. See chapter 11 below.
56. *W* 1, pp. 150–51.
57. Hegel, *Vorlesungen über Naturrecht und Staatswissenschaft*, § 132A, 86; *Lectures on Natural Right*.

while it encompasses and relativizes two other moments, is only truly universal and rational because those moments (the family and civil society) are each organized according to their own principles. Between the Bern texts and the mature writings lies a major discovery implying new appreciation for the figure of the bourgeois: the discovery of the modern significance of civil society.

Hegel's works from Frankfurt, very few of which have been published, played a decisive role in forming Hegelian thought. His encounter with Kant's practical philosophy, his return to thinking about the "destiny" of Christianity, and his discovery of the specific traits of modern reality through his studies of history and economy all contributed to the change of scale that marks the Jena writings, though at the time, Hegel did not conceive of their unity. Let us examine what paved the way for this major change. There seems to be little or no difference between the Frankfurt and Bern texts regarding the bourgeois-citizen relationship. Several fragments provided by Rosenkranz — some of which date back to Hegel's time in Bern — reaffirm the Greek ideal of citizenship, contrasting it to the "bourgeois" spirit of modern institutions. The characteristic property of what the article on natural law calls "the class of the property owners [*die erwerbende Klasse*; i.e., the bourgeoisie]"[58] — that is, its valorization of the economy and law — is once again contrasted with the political *ethos* of the citizen of antiquity. First, Hegel questions economism:

> In *modern states, security of property* is the pivot around which all legislation turns, and it is connected to the most citizen rights. In some free republics of antiquity, strict property rights . . . the pride of our states, were wronged simply because of the state constitution. In the Spartan constitution, security of property and industry almost never came into consideration. . . . One has perhaps not done justice to the system of *sansculotism* in France if one sees its source in rapacity alone rather than in an aspiration to the greatest equality of property.[59]

Thus, at the moment this passage was written, Hegel still admired the classical ethical-political idea and the Revolution's effort to restore it even in its "terror-

58. *Naturrecht, W* 2, p. 490 (*Natural Law*, 100).
59. *W* 1, p. 439.

ist" form. It is presented with surprising enthusiasm given Hegel's later assessments of the harmful effects of "absolute freedom."

Juridism, a corollary of *economism*, is also judged severely. Reading Hume's *History of England*, Hegel makes the following observation:

> The object of his [Hume's] history is a state of the modern era, whose internal relationships are not only legally determined, as with the ancients, but that owes its consistency more to legal form than to the free, unconscious life at the heart of it. The legal, which is consciousness of universality and also of its opposition, particularity, assigns the various estates to their place, but the people [within] do not act as a whole people from an *idea* that animates all.[60]

Subjected to the double alienation of legal formalism and economic necessity, modern man is a *bourgeois*—in the sense of *Emile*—who has become incapable of immediately and unreservedly supporting the "spirit of the whole." In his eyes, this whole is no longer his true being or essence: it "exerts on [him] a domination."[61] "Torn and separated," the life of modern peoples has lost, the *Systemfragment* says, the "most perfect wholeness" that "happy peoples" enjoy, or rather used to enjoy.[62]

However, without Hegel necessarily realizing it clearly, the break with the ideal of classical citizenship was being prepared. It would take three paths. In Bern, Hegel had begun reading history (Hume, Gibbon, etc.) and discovered Montesquieu. During his time in Frankfurt, these readings, along with his study of the history and legal structures of the German Empire, brought him to what would soon become a certainty: the irreducible originality of modern ethical-political reality and, consequently, the outmodedness of ideals that did not take this reality into account. Hegel's interest in England—which he no longer denied—played a determining role in this regard: he read Hume's historical works, he followed parliamentary debates, and he reflected on Montesquieu's famous chapter on the English Constitution. His concern for historical particularities and details, his attention to the actual conditions in which

60. *W* 1, p. 446.
61. *W* 1, p. 433.
62. *W* 1, p. 426.

general principles were implemented—what would later be called Hegelian "realism"—are reflected in his annotated translation of Jean-Jacques Cart's *Lettres confidentielles* and in what remains of the 1798 text lampooning the political situation in Württemberg.

The first of these two texts contains an observation that does not agree with the previously cited extracts: Hegel deplores the fact that "security of property" had in many respects been "compromised" by Pitt's policies, that "personal freedom" had been limited "because of the fact of the suspension of fundamental law" and that civil rights (*staatsbürgerliche Rechte*) as well were "under the effect of positive laws."[63] Rosenzweig would later write that the "revolutionary will and inventive future" had not disappeared from the 1798 texts and that at that moment Hegel was not yet the philosopher who would task himself with "conceiving what is"[64] and thus, in a sense, justifying it. Nevertheless, passages such as this one do not agree either with the condemnation of the bourgeois ethics of property or with the refusal to grant absolute value to personal freedom.

As for the text on the political situation in Württemberg, the concern expressed therein for the concrete, immediate consequences of decisions made on principle incontestably prefigures the lucid realism of "The German Constitution", the 1817 *Ständeschrift*, and the article titled "On the English Reform Bill." Certainly Hegel eloquently calls on individuals and social groups to "rise above their petty interests and reach justice."[65] But the crux of the text—the need for elected political representation—is connected, if we are to believe "The German Constitution," to the entirely modern existence of a "bourgeois estate [*Stand*]."[66] However, this claim is not advanced without restriction: it is certainly in conformity with justice but will be politically effective only under certain conditions (first and foremost, the existence of a common mind [*Gemeingeist*], a truly unifying political culture) in the absence of which the claim, though just, could be harmful. Thus, Hoffmeister was correct to emphasize that in his translation of Cart, "Hegel's teacher was not Rousseau

63. *W* 1, pp. 257–58.
64. See Rosenzweig, *Hegel und der Staat*, 1:50.
65. *W* 1, p. 270.
66. "Verfassung," *W* 1, p. 536 ("German Constitution," in *Hegel's Political Writings*, 206): "Representation is so deeply interwoven with the essence of the feudal constitution in its development along with the rise of the bourgeois that we may call it the silliest of notions to suppose it an invention of the most recent times."

but rather Montesquieu."[67] Undoubtedly, Hegel was already on the path that would eventually lead him to condemn abstract ideals to which, at the time, he still subscribed. At the beginning of his address to the people of Württemberg, he wrote,

> The image of a better, more just time has come alive in the souls of men, and a longing, a sigh for a purer, freer state has moved all hearts and separated them from reality.[68]

This assessment concerns the attitude of some of Hegel's compatriots at the time. But it also seems to refute a certain fragment from Bern denouncing the corrupting influence of withdrawal to the private sphere by a people "lacking civic virtue." There we read

> Only a nation of the highest depravity . . . could make blind obedience to the wicked whims of despicable men into a maxim. Only time and complete forgetting of a better situation could have led to this point.[69]

Isn't it clear that in this sort of self-criticism lies the sign of a reconciliation with the times, with concrete historical actuality?

This brings me to the second path that this reconciliation took. As we know, it was at Frankfurt that Hegel discovered political economy, crucial to his development of the concept of civil society. Hegel would later say that this new discipline was "one of the sciences which have originated in the modern age as their element."[70] We know from Rosenkranz that "between February 19 and May 16 of 1799"—so, in Frankfurt—Hegel wrote a "commentary in the form of annotations" of the German translation (by Garve, a colleague of Kant's at Königsberg) of J. Steuart's *Inquiry into the Principles of Political Oeconomy* (1767).[71] However, this piece, which was decisive in shaping Hegel's economic thought, has disappeared. In any case, some of the characteristics of Hegel's thought that are considered retrograde with respect to

---

67. Hoffmeister, *Dokumente zu Hegels Entwicklung*, 464.

68. *W* 1, pp. 268–69.

69. *W* 1, p. 100.

70. *RPh*, § 189 Anmerkung, *GW* 14.1, p. 165 (*Elements*, 227; see *Outlines*, 187).

71. Rosenkranz, *Hegels Leben*, 86.

what would become the dominant classical doctrines (Smith's, Ricardo's) can be explained by Steuart's long-lasting influence on him. Marx, for his part, emphasized that Steuart offered a "rational expression of the monetary and mercantile system" and in contrast to Smith "is much more concerned with the genesis of the process of capital," thus, with its *history*.[72] This study was undoubtedly at the source of certain themes that would be developed in Jena: reflection on the beneficial effects of luxury commerce, the doctrine of social estates (*Stände*) developed in the *System of Ethicality* and later in the *Philosophy of Spirit* of 1805, the figure of the administrator (*Geschäftsmann*),[73] perhaps related to the figure of the legislator in Steuart, and, in general, Hegel's understanding of the relations between the state and the system of needs were some of the lasting effects of this reading. But there is more: it was undoubtedly in Steuart (and in Smith of course) that Hegel first encountered the idea that the common good — at least if it is reduced to what he would later call formal universality — results from the interaction of selfish pursuits; in fact, an interest in the common good need not be consciously pursued by social actors and indeed even excludes all concerted aims. At the beginning of the second volume of the translation of Steuart's text used by Hegel, we find the following remark:

> If, instead of private interest, love of country should be the motive for the actions of the members of a well-ordered state, everything would be corrupted. Patriotism among the governed must be as superfluous as it ought to be in powerful statesman.[74]

No doubt this is a subject that since Swift and Mandeville has become almost banal within Anglo-Saxon thought: "private vices, public benefits," to quote the subtitle of Mandeville's *The Fable of the Bees*. In any case, the young Hegel encountered the topic through Steuart. That author's remarks, which

72. Karl Marx, *Theorien über den Mehrwert* (Berlin: Dietz, 1965), 1:11.

73. See *GW* 8, p. 273.

74. Sir James Steuart, *Untersuchungen über die Grundsätze von der Staatswissenschaft* (Hamburg, 1796), 2:4. Hoffmeister emphasizes the importance of this passage to the future doctrine of ethics. But it is a simplification to think that Hegel later opposes these "capitalist principles" to a "proclamation of the reign of the state in the economy"; even in the Berlin writings, the state does not have any vocation to govern the system of needs. Hoffmeister, *Dokumente zu Hegels Entwicklung*, 467.

directly contradict the ancient *ethos* of citizenship, certainly contributed to Hegel's later reevaluation of the figure of the bourgeois and to his raising civil society to the status of a necessary component—in its relative right of course—of an ethical totality that can no longer be immediately or exclusively political. It is likely that Hegel at first rebelled against a doctrine that went counter to what was still his ethical and political ideal at the time. A fragment from his time at Frankfurt (written on the basis of his reading of Hume) offers an echo of this probable reaction. Whereas Steuart uses the image of the individual as a cog in the economic machine, Hegel regrets the fact that most actors within the historical record "present themselves as no more than cogs in a machine."[75]

One last element should be mentioned. Why didn't the reconciliation of bourgeois and citizen occur as soon as Hegel became definitively aware of the irreducibility of the modern world to the model of the beautiful totality? It is probably because he was still lacking the speculative means for thinking the *identity* of ethicality in its *difference* from its familial, social, and political moments. It was at Frankfurt that he found those means. However, the discovery occurred in a context that does not yet allow it to be applied to the issue in question here, the emergence of the positive figure of the bourgeois: this context was in fact Hegel's reflection on the fate of Christianity. It was in this connection that Hegel, at the same time (or nearly the same time) as he was reading Steuart and beginning to become interested in current forms of political life, developed concepts (that at the time he wanted to be nonconceptual, "inconceivable," as a reaction against Kantianism) that would lead him, at Jena, to the explicit program for a speculative—that is, also dialectic—rationality. The statement from the *Systemfragment* that "life is the linking of the linking and the nonlinking"[76] undoubtedly marks the moment when Hegelian philosophy came into its own. It led Hegel down a path, and he himself did not know where it would take him. It was by following this path that, at the end of his stay in Jena, he came to reconsider the ideas he had hitherto supported in the ethical-political domain.

75. *W* 1, p. 446. See also "Das älteste Systemprogramm des deutschen Idealismus," *W* 1, pp. 234–35.

76. *W* 1, p. 422.

From Jena to Berlin

The opposition between bourgeois and citizen appears in the Jena texts. It occurs explicitly for the first time in the 1805 *Philosophy of Spirit* but is also perceptible in the article on natural law and in the *System of Ethicality*. However, it cannot be found in any of the earlier writings, though it is prefigured in them in multiple ways. The reason for this is clear: such a distinction could only become relevant with the abandonment, or at least the relativization, of the ethical ideal of the beautiful Greek totality, which lay at the heart of the Bern and Frankfurt writings. Hegel's return to a distinction he found in Rousseau and then in Kant is tightly connected, as we will see, to his acknowledgment of the existence of nonpolitical or not immediately political forms of ethicality, which beginning in 1817 would correspond to what he would call *bürgerliche Gesellschaft*.

In the Jena writings, the distinction between citizen and bourgeois has a critical content that it would maintain, albeit in attenuated form: following in Rousseau's footsteps, Hegel underscores the dangers of the modern reduction of the individual to a legal person and economic actor. The bourgeois point of view is based on a belief in the self-sufficiency of the private sphere and its supremacy over the political sphere. The article on natural law develops this critique polemically: the opposition it draws between "those who are free" and "those who are not free" in fact measures the distance separating the "general life"[77] of the *politeuein* and the "universal private life,"[78] condemned to "political nullity" of the "*Bürger* in the sense of bourgeois."[79] To support this polemical characterization, Hegel cites a passage from Gibbon, but we may wonder whether he did not have in mind the passage from *Emile* cited above, where Rousseau says precisely that the bourgeois is "nothing."

In the other Jena texts, the tone of the argument is less polemical. The *System of Ethicality* defines the bourgeois as someone who, because of his "sinking into possession and particularity,"[80] "is not capable of virtue or bravery";[81] the bourgeois is a man of work and profit, and he seeks to abstract himself

---

77. *Naturrecht,* W 2, p. 489 (*Natural Law,* 100).
78. *Naturrecht,* W 2, p. 492 (*Natural Law,* 102).
79. *Naturrecht,* W 2, p. 494 (*Natural Law,* 103).
80. *SS, GW* 5, p. 336.
81. *SS, GW* 5, p. 338.

from the universal, for he only knows and recognizes its abstract form: money. However, the doctrine of social estates and ethical dispositions (*Gesinnungen*) developed in this text hints at a new direction. Indeed, the autonomy Hegel recognizes at various levels—which are of course hierarchically organized—in fact points to the way the ethical whole enriches the differences that exist within it.

> In the absolute real totality of ethicality, the three forms of ethicality must be equally real. Each one must organize for itself, be an individual, and have a shape, for their mixing is the absence of form of what is naturally ethical, the absence of wisdom.[82]

We see here that Hegel's recognition of the (entirely relative) right of the bourgeois goes along with his questioning of a naturalist vision of ethicality that no doubt corresponds for the most part to the older paradigm of the beautiful totality.

The 1805 *Philosophy of Spirit* also maintains a strict hierarchy between the estate of universality—the public estate dedicated to carrying out the state's administrative and warring functions—and the estates of the peasantry, the merchant class, and the bourgeoisie, which are confined to the lesser tasks of producing, distributing, and consuming commodities. But the work also brings about a turn, essentially prefiguring the later significance of the doctrine of civil society.[83] It states that the objective attitudes and practices designated by the terms *citizen* and *bourgeois* correspond to different though connected aspects of modern reality. No doubt these attitudes oppose one another, but this opposition is an internal cleavage within modern man, divided between contradictory "vocations" (in the complex sense of the German world *Beruf*) rather than a Platonic "division of labor":

> The same person takes care of himself and his family, works, concludes contracts, and so forth, but this person also works for the universal, driven by one goal; the first aspect is known as "bourgeois," and the second as "citizen."[84]

82. *SS*, *GW* 5, p. 333.
83. See the preliminary to part 2, "The Archaeology of Society."
84. *GW* 8, p. 261.

At the very moment that he makes this point, Hegel introduces a connection to the analyses contained in "The German Constitution": "Bourgeois [*Spieß-bürger*] and citizen of the empire, each is as much a formal bourgeois as the other." In a state-in-idea, there is neither state nor civil society, neither bourgeois nor citizen. This insight represents a break and certainly owes a great deal to Hegel's readings in economics.[85] Earlier I discussed Steuart's influence on Hegel. As for Adam Smith, the Jena manuscripts show that Hegel's reading of *The Wealth of Nations* made a decisive contribution to his analysis of work and consequently of the "cunning of reason" as well as of "recognition."[86] The result of this appropriation of economic knowledge is the realization that the ideal of the *polis* and the ethics of citizenship cannot be transposed as such into modern conditions, for modern conditions have superior *ethical* resources. True, the 1805 manuscript still evokes "the beautiful and happy freedom of the Greeks, which was and remains envied,"[87] but the immediate identification of the individual with the ethical substance already appears too simple, too abstract. The modern world allows subjectivity to affirm itself as an autonomous ethical figure thanks to both the appearance of a subjective moral authority and the creation of a nonpolitical or indirectly political-social space: "By this principle, external freedom is lost, effectively, by individuals in their immediate concrete existence, but obtained is inner freedom, freedom of thought."[88] In fact, Hegel would never go back to such a judgment, decreeing the end of "nostalgia for Greece," that is, the ethics of the *polis*.

It was in Heidelberg and Berlin that Hegel, giving definitive shape to the doctrine of civil society, completed his reflection on the bourgeois-citizen relationship. The term *bürgerliche Gesellschaft* appears in its truly Hegelian sense in the 1817–1818 lectures at Heidelberg on "Natural Law and Science of the

85. For a clear analysis of the Hegelian "reception" of political economy and of the Scottish Enlightenment more broadly, see Waszek, *Scottish Enlightenment*, 60–65, 112–34. See also Waszek, "Hegels Lehre von der 'Bürgerlichen Gesellschaft' und die politische Ökonomie ser schottischen Aufklärung," *Dialektik* 3 (1995): 35–50. There are also the classic articles by Manfred Riedel: "Die Rezeption der Nationalökonomie" and "Hegels Begriff der bürgerlichen Gesellschaft und das Problem seines geschichtlichen Ursprungs," in Riedel, *Zwischen Tradition und Revolution*, 116–38 and 139–69, respectively.

86. See "Philosophie des Geistes" (1803–1804), *GW* 6, pp. 321–24; "Philosophie des Geistes" (1805–1806), *GW* 8, pp. 223–25.

87. *GW* 8, p. 262.

88. *GW* 8, pp. 263–64. Compare with *RPh*, § 124 Anmerkung, *GW* 14.1, p. 110 (*Elements*, 151; see *Outlines*, 122–23).

State." Here, Hegel says in defining civil society that "members of the state are bourgeois, not citizens,"[89] which means before (eventually) dedicating themselves to the political service of the universal, they are legal persons and economic actors who seek to satisfy their selfish goals and are caught in a system of needs. The *Philosophy of Right* and the *Encyclopedia* present civil society as the "external State."[90] This description highlights two opposing or complementary aspects. First—this is the principal aspect—civil society is, or is merely, "the state of necessity and of the understanding."[91] Hegel here uses the Fichtean motif of the *Notstaat*, though not in regard to the state strictly speaking but rather to civil society: it is civil society insofar as it is the external reflection or "phenomenon" of the political coming together of citizens that must be qualified as *Notstaat*. Based on the mechanical operation of the system of needs, this social *Notstaat* is governed by necessity, which distinguishes it entirely from the state strictly speaking (which is political). If the universal is present in civil society, it is so only in the external form of unconscious and abstract regulations of the economy and in the formal dictates of private law. The competition between particular ends evokes, though from afar, the war of each against all: civil society "[contains] remnants of the state of nature."[92] This is why the state, because of its particular political task and its conscious orientation toward the principles of objective freedom and concrete universality, must be clearly distinguished from the space of abstraction that is civil society. Thus Hegel's repeated denunciation of the liberal tendency to "confuse the state with civil society." Anyone who sees the state's vocation as the "protection of personal property and liberty" does not understand that the state's true vocation is to guarantee *"union as such,"*[93] and by failing to recognize this, thereby lowers the citizen to the rank of bourgeois.

However, civil society is the outside *of* the state, *its* other, *its* mediation. The being-outside of itself of the ethical totality is the moment of negativity

89. Hegel, *Vorlesungen über Naturrecht und Staatswissenschaft*, § 89, 112; *Lectures on Natural Right*. See also Hegel, *Vorlesungen über Naturrecht und Staatswissenschaft*, § 72, 89.

90. *RPh*, §§ 157, 183, *GW* 14.1, pp. 143, 160 (*Elements*, 198, 221; see *Outlines*, 162, 181). See *Enzykl*, §§ 523, 534, *GW* 20, pp. 498, 506–7 (*Encyclopedia* 230–31).

91. *RPh*, § 183, *GW* 14.1, p. 160 (*Elements*, 221; see *Outlines*, 181).

92. *RPh*, § 200 Anmerkung, *GW* 14.1, p. 170 (*Elements*, 234; see *Outlines*, 192). Only remnants; civil society is not, according to Hegel, a state of nature precisely because it is not limited at any moment to a system of the needs (a point of view that separates Hegel from Marx).

93. *RPh*, § 258 Anmerkung, *GW* 14.1, p. 201 (*Elements*, 276, see *Outlines*, 229).

through which it achieves its political being-at-home. Thus, living adhesion to the universal and the seemingly immediate trust the citizen feels for the state as an institution are not obtained by reprimanding the egoism of the bourgeois, "private persons who have their own interests as their end,"[94] but instead by leaning on it. For, as the *Logic* establishes, freedom is not the opposite of necessity, its abstract other, but rather its truth, which means that it includes necessity within itself structurally as its own moment of negativity. Within Hegelianism, the bourgeois and the citizen, like society and state, are as identical as they are different. Rousseau saw them as two antithetical figures. Hegel, on the contrary, arrived at the idea that modern civil society, by reducing the individual to the abstract properties of *homo oeconomicus*, for the first time gave concrete content to the idea of humanity. For the bourgeois is man himself, man in general, abstract man engaged in abstract work and in this very abstraction possesses distinct existence.[95] As for the citizen, he is true confirmed man who has arrived at the concrete expression of his effective universality. Without the reality that modernity gives to the abstract existence of the bourgeois, the very old idea of citizenship itself remains an abstraction.

The difficulty Hegel faced once he was no longer content to contrast antiquity's ethics of citizenship with the negation of ethicality implied by being rooted in particularity lay in establishing mediations that would make it possible to think the necessary conjunction of contradictory realities and attitudes. The Frankfurt reflections on Christianity and the "nonconceptual" tools it provides—life, love, destiny—are the first theoretical sketches of this later task because they attempt to conceptualize the identity of the identical and the nonidentical. Hegel's intense reflection in Frankfurt and then in Jena on ethical-political questions allowed him to develop the core of the solution to the problem facing him. But this problem, illustrated by the difficult articulation of the "esprit de corps" and the "spirit of the whole" would only find its *philosophical* conclusion thanks to the vast undertaking of the *Logic*. To fully think politics and its modern limitations, Hegel needed all the resources of speculative philosophy, even metaphysics. That does not mean that one must accept those resources in order to draw on his sociopolitical views.

---

94. *RPh*, § 187, *GW* 14.1, p. 162 (*Elements*, 224; see *Outlines*, 184).

95. See *RPh*, § 190 Anmerkung, *GW* 14.1, p. 166 (*Elements*, 228; see *Outlines*, 188). On this point, see Riedel, "Bürger, Staatsbürger, Bürgertum," 706–9. See also Bernard Bourgeois, "L'homme hégélien," in *Etudes Hégéliennes: Raison et décision*, 181–205.

5

The State of Law

Civil Society

It may perhaps seem surprising to look to German idealism, and Hegel in particular, for the premises underlying the problematic of the *Rechtsstaat* (state of law), which was developed during the first half of the nineteenth century by liberal jurists. Indeed, if it is true that the *Rechtsstaat* was a polemical response to the *Polizeistaat*—absolutism's police state—and an alternative to the *Machtstaat* glorified by the historian Heinrich von Treitschke,[1] then there are good reasons to class Hegel among its adversaries, for isn't his system "the scientific residue of the spirit of Prussian restoration?"[2] Furthermore, it would seem that the roots of this characteristically German doctrine should be sought instead in constitutionalism, both Anglo-Saxon (Locke, Burke) and French (Montesquieu). However, Kant and the post-Kantians forged intellectual tools that *Rechtsstaat* theoreticians would later translate into legal and political demands. This is the case of the distinction between the state and civil society. But we may also think of a whole set of themes no doubt inherited from English and French thought to which German philosophers turned their

---

1. "The essence of the state is first power, secondly, power, and third, still power." Heinrich von Treitschke, *Historische und politische Aufsätze* (Leipzig, 1886), 152. See Catherine Colliot-Thélène, "Les origines de la théorie du *Machtstaat*," *Philosophie*, no. 20 (1988): 24–47.

2. Haym, *Hegel und Seine Zeit*, 359.

speculative creativity: the rights of man, the separation of powers, political representation, constitutional review, and so on. Here, classical German philosophy prepared the way for the doctrine of the *Rechtsstaat*. It is thus relevant to "analyze the meaning of constitutionalism . . . *starting from* German idealism."[3] In this chapter, I will make a simple argument: Hegel can be considered an intellectual precursor of the theory of the *Rechtsstaat* if it is true that this is less a theory of the state than a vision of how it must take into account, in its practices and institutional configuration, the new autonomy of the social. But Hegel was also the first critic of the theoretical grounds of this doctrine even before it found its classical expression.

From the Kantian "Republic" to the Liberal *Rechtsstaat*

In the French lexicon, the notion of the state of law has a shifting, even contradictory, meaning.[4] The ambiguity of the word *état* (state) contributes to this, for it can refer both to the political institution of the state (*der Staat* in German) and to the situation or "status" of a thing or person (*der Zustand*; *status* in Latin). Thus, the *Rechtsstaat* is not the same thing as a state of law. "State of law" means that "law" rules, as in the English expression "rule of law"; it is in contrast to rule by force and to the representation of a lawless state of nature. On a strictly legal level, a *Rechtsstaat* is a state whose activity is defined and limited by explicit norms: essentially, fundamental rights (either in the form of "rights of man" or constitutionally guaranteed public freedoms) and the constitutional organization of powers, implying their separation. The two notions are thus distinct. The notion of a state of law expresses the idea of an organization of the political community that is based on law, but nothing in the concept specifies the content, scope, formal characteristics, or principle of actuality of that kind of law. One could even argue that every human group constitutes a state of law if it follows rules, even implicit ones, and includes a body that can, if necessary, compel them to be observed—for right is distinguished from mere convention by the existence of a mechanism of con-

---

3. Olivier Jouanjan, "État de droit, forme de gouvernement et représentation: A partir d'un passage de Kant," *Annales de la Faculté de Droit de Strasbourg* 2 (1998): 280. See also Jouanjan, ed., *Figures de l'État de droit* (Strasbourg: Presses Universitaires de Strasbourg, 2001).

4. See Michel Troper, "Le concept d'état de droit," in *La théorie du droit, le droit, l'état* (Paris: Presses Universitaires de France, 2001), 267–81.

straint.[5] The state of law is a *Rechtsgenossenschaft*, a community organized according to formal or customary legal rules: essentially, the notion expresses the political bond insofar as it creates obligations; it designates human belonging to a shared world structured by a *nomos*.

The notion of *Rechtsstaat* is more technical: it means first and foremost that the state's actions must be subjected to the principle of *legality*. Unlike a despotic state, a *Rechtsstaat*'s power is instituted and defined by a body of formalized principles. This corresponds to the type of state — liberal, democratic, or bourgeois — that was established in the United States and then in France and the rest of Europe beginning in the late nineteenth century. But though the *Rechtstaat* became a widespread notion, within the German tradition it has much greater density than anywhere else: it is "a German lexical form that has no equivalent in the languages of other nations."[6] We must thus specify what German public law has understood by *Rechtsstaat* since the nineteenth century. The history of the concept sheds light on its meaning. Surprisingly, one of the first to use it was Adam Müller, a conservative political thinker with ties to the romantic school, who exalted "the true state of organic law" in his courses at the court of Berlin.[7] But there is no question that it was the heralds of constitutionalism from the south of Germany who, after 1815, as the country was entering a period of restoration, popularized the expression and made it the watchword for liberal demands. Rotteck's and Welcker's *Staats-Lexikon*, reedited many times after 1834, introduced the concept to the public domain and popularized "principles that truly reflect the rational idea of the state, i.e., the idea of the *Rechtsstaat*."[8] Beginning in 1830, the *Rechtsstaat* became a crucial component of liberal legal constructions, and various significant works referred to it in their titles.[9] But as a result of political conditions,

5. See Max Weber, "Basic Sociological Terms," in Weber, *Economy and Society*, 3–63.

6. Klaus Stern, *Der Rechtstaat* (Krefeld: Scherpe, 1971). From among the large body of literature on the subject, let us cite "Entstehung und Wandel des Rechtsstaatsbegriffs," in *Recht, Staat, Freiheit* (Frankfurt am Main: Suhrkamp, 1992), 143–69; "Rechtsstaat," in *Historisches Wörterbuch der Philosophie*, vol. 8, ed. Ritter et al. (Basel: Schwabe, 1992), 332; Olivier Jouanjan, "Présentation," in *Figures de L'état de droit* (Strasbourg: Presses Universitaires de Strasbourg, 1998); Katharina Sobota, *Das Prinzip Rechtsstaat* (Tübingen: Mohr, 1997); Michael Stolleis, "Rechtsstaat," in *Handwörterbuch der deutschen Rechtsgeschichte* (Berlin: Schmidt, 1990), 4:367.

7. See Adam Heinrich Müller, *Die Elemente der Staatskunst* (Jena: Fischer, 1809), 1:199–200.

8. K. von Rotteck, cited by Jouanjan, "Présentation," 19.

9. Robert von Mohl, *Die Polizeiwissenschaft nach den Grundsätzen des Rechtsstaats* (1832);

the notion underwent some important developments. Liberals, most of whom rallied to the empire and became national liberals in the wake of Bismarck and who feared the rising power of socialism, nuanced their project of subjecting the state's actions to law and shifted their hopes to developing forms of legal control over the administration. The *Rechtsstaat*, wrote a specialist in administrative law at the end of the nineteenth century, is "the State of well-ordered administrative law."[10] This is far from the demands of the first liberals.

But we must go back to Kant to discover the premises of the concept of *Rechtsstaat*—on this point at least, partisans and adversaries of the doctrine agree.[11] Kant's writings from the 1790s, marked by the experience of the French Revolution, define what *Perpetual Peace* would dub the "republican constitution."[12] The principles of the Kantian State of Law are "not so much laws given by a state already established as rather principles in accordance with which alone the establishment of a state is possible."[13] They are thus the universal conditions of a political institution that conforms to human law and rights (*Menschenrecht*), and they outline the traits of the "state according to idea," or the *respublica noumenon*, "eternal norms for any political [*bürgerliche*] constitution in general,"[14] which is "one and identical," while the *respublica phaenomenon* takes many forms, corresponding to the classical types of constitutions. The following are the principles of the republic constitution:[15]

Otto Bähr, *Der Rechtsstaat: Eine publizistische Studie* (1864); Rudolf Gneist, *Der Rechtsstaat und die Verwaltungsgerichte in Deutschland* (1879).

10. Otto Mayer, *Das deutsche Verwaltungsrecht* (1895), cited in Böckenförde, "Entstehung und Wandel des Rechtsstaatsbegriffs," 148.

11. According to Mohl, Kant made an "essential advance" in the theory of the state of law. See Robert Von Mohl, *Die Geschichte und Literatur der Staatswissenschaften* (Erlangen: F. Enke, 1856), 1:241. For Schmitt, "Kant . . . is already a typical advocate of bourgeois Rechtsstaat thinking." See Carl Schmitt, *Constitutional Theory*, trans. Joseph W. Bendersky (Durham, NC: Duke University Press, 2008), 249; *Verfassungslehre*, trans. Joseph W. Bendersky (Berlin: Duncker und Humboldt, 2003), 217.

12. See Kant, *Frieden*, Ak. 8, pp. 349–50; *PP*, p. 322.

13. Kant, *Gemeinspruch*, Ak. 8, p. 290; *PP*, p. 291.

14. Kant, Reflexion 8077, Ak. 19, pp. 609–10. See also *Der Streit der Fakultäten*, Ak. 7, p. 91. The *Rechtslehre* speaks of a state "in idea,": *Rechtslehre: MdS*, § 45, Ak. 6, p. 313; *PP*, p. 457.

15. Kant, *Rechtslehre: MdS*, § 46, Ak. 6, p. 314; *PP*, pp. 457–58. Other presentations, which differ from the one in the *Doctrine of Law*, can be found in *Theorie und Praxis*, Ak. 8, pp. 390–96; *PP*, pp. 290–96, and in *Zum ewigen Frieden*, Ak. 8, pp. 349–50; *PP*, pp. 322–23.

(a) the "freedom to obey no other law than that to which consent was
given";

(b) "civil equality," which implies the elimination of all unilateral obligations.
Perpetual Peace puts it more precisely: the equality of members of society
as *citizens*;

(c) "civil *independence*." Here, Kant goes back to Sieyès's distinction
between active and passive citizenship.[16] Does it contravene the principles of freedom and equality to accept such a distinction between citizens? No, because passive citizens are *free* (they have legal personhood:
no slavery, servitude, or *capitis deminutio*—at least not for adult male
individuals of sound mind), and they are *equal* before the law. However, they are not "colegislators";[17] only those who enjoy an independence that is not only legal but also social and economic, guaranteeing
the independence of their judgment and vote, can participate in making
the law (by electing representatives). This argument would go on to have
great success among nineteenth-century liberals; it clearly indicates the
"bourgeois" perspective (*Bildung und Besitz!*) of *Rechtsstaat* theories.

By virtue of these principles, the state is normatively subjected to the law,
which is its foundation, and in return it guarantees that the law is administered properly. However, these are not mere "abstract" principles of natural
law, for they can only be satisfied if legal persons constitute a political society:
"whereas it can be said of a *rightful* condition that all human beings who could
(even involuntarily) come into legal relations with one another *ought* to enter
this condition."[18] Belonging to a political society is a legal imperative, and the
principles of liberty, equality, and independence are the metanorm that society must observe to be in conformity with the law—that is, to be a republic.

In the first definitive article of *Perpetual Peace*, Kant specifies the constitutional measures that make it possible to satisfy these three principles.[19] He

---

16. See Sieyès, "Reconnaissance et exposition raisonnée des droits de l'homme et du
citoyen" (July 1789), in *Écrits politiques*, ed. Roberto Zapperi (Paris: Éditions des Archives Comtemporaines, 1985), 199. This distinction was included in the Thermidorian Constitution of the
Year III (1795).

17. Kant, *Gemeinspruch, Ak.* 8, p. 294; *PP*, p. 294. The "passive citizens" are *Schutzgenossen*.

18. Kant, *Rechtslehre: MdS*, § 41, *Ak.* 6, p. 306; *PP*, p. 451.

19. Kant, *Frieden, Ak.* 8, pp. 351–53; *PP*, pp. 324–25.

spells out two criteria for a republican constitution. First, for its "form of governance," which Kant distinguishes from its "form of *Herrschaft*," that is, its political regime, the criterion is the *separation of powers*, and more precisely separation of the executive and legislative branches. For Kant, as for Locke, only the legislator is sovereign, and this sovereign "can belong only to the united will of the people,"[20] whereas the "regent" (the chief of the state), as a "moral person," is only the leader of the executive branch.[21] The second criterion of Kantian republicanism is the *representative* nature of the exercise of both executive and—though this is not clear—legislative powers. Whence the argument, "any form of government that is not *representative* is, strictly speaking, *without form*."[22] However, even more important than these two criteria is the statement, made as if in passing, that the mode of government (*Regierungsart*) is, for the people (i.e., for the subjects), "incomparably" more important than the regime (*Staatsform*).[23] Here we see one of the axes of the *Rechtstaat* doctrine: it does not define a politics, it establishes a restrictive framework for all politics. If, for the governed, the manner of governing is more decisive than the identity of the governors, it would seem to lead to relativizing the issue of regime. Kant's firm rejection of any revolutionary perspective[24] took the same direction as the prudent reformism of liberal Germans during the *Vormärz*.

Several points in Kant's political philosophy prefigure the concept of the *Rechtsstaat*; I will focus on three. First is the ideal of the juridification of politics: for Kant, as later for Kelsen, the state is identical to the legal order; it is nothing other than the *rechtlicher Zustand*. Conversely, the characteristic feature of the state of nature is not "injustice" but the "absence of law," for there is no public administration by a "judge [who is] competent."[25] The Kantian approach to politics tends to reduce it to its juridical dimension. We therefore must not be lured into a summary interpretation of the statement, "true politics can therefore not take a step without having already paid homage to

---

20. Kant, *Rechtslehre: MdS*, § 47, *Ak*. 6, p. 313; *PP*, p. 457.

21. Kant, *Rechtslehre: MdS*, § 49, *Ak*. 8, p. 316; *PP*, p. 460.

22. Kant, *Frieden*, *Ak*. 8, p. 352; *PP*, p. 324. The nonrepublican form of government is a "nonform" (*Unform*).

23. Kant, *Frieden*, *Ak*. 8, p. 353; *PP*, p. 325.

24. See in particular point A in "On the effects with regard to rights that follow from the nature of the civil union" in Kant, *Rechtslehre MdS*, *Ak*. 6, pp. 318–23; *PP*, pp. 461–66.

25. Kant, *Rechtslehre: MdS,*, § 44, *Ak*. 6, p. 312; *PP*, p. 456.

morals," for this is morality "regarded as a doctrine of law."[26] In Kant's vocabulary, morality is the genus and law and ethics are its species.[27] Thus, Kant does not propose *moralizing* politics but rather *juridifying* it: "The law must be held sacred for human beings, however great a sacrifice this may cost the ruling power."[28] Second, the emphasis is on formal rather than material legal principles. The two distinctive traits of the republican mode of government—the separation of powers and political representation—belong, in the terms of nineteenth-century jurists, to the "formal constitution" and not to a "material constitution." The absence of any positive determination of the state's goals and concrete organization implies relativizing a question hitherto considered central in political philosophy: what is the best form of government? It is true that the formal criteria of the Kantian State of Law lead to rejecting democracy on the grounds that it would "necessarily [be a] despotism."[29] Democracy, however, is not rejected for its substantive characteristics but rather because of the consequences it has on the mode of exercising power, explicitly at least; in fact democracy (of course, here this means "pure" democracy, distinct from the republic, as *The Federalist*[30] emphasizes) harms the principles of the separation of powers and of representation. Third, Kant proclaims that the state must be self-limiting. This is the positive meaning of the proscription on all right to resist the chief of the executive (regent) or the sovereign legislator. No one besides the constituted sovereign has the right to set limits to the action of the government, but this limiting is inherent to the very conditions of political society, in particular because it results directly from its first principle: the freedom of all.

Nineteenth-century liberal jurists developed the doctrine of the *Rechtsstaat* in the technical sense of the term. This development went along with that of bourgeois civil society in a context of strong resistance by the political

26. Kant, *Frieden*, Ak. 8, pp. 380, 383; *PP*, pp. 347, 349.

27. In the "Division of the Metaphysics of Morals," *Recht* and *Ethik* are presented as the two branches of morality (*Rechtslehre: MdS*, Ak. 6, p. 242; *PP*, p. 397). The table included in these editions is erroneous and located in the wrong place, as B. Ludwig has shown. Ludwig corrects it and puts it back in the General Introduction to *Metaphysik der Sitten*: see Immanuel Kant, *Metaphysische Anfangsgründe der Rechtslehre*, ed. Bernd Ludwig (Hamburg: Felix Meiner, 1986), 34.

28. Kant, *Frieden*, Ak. 8, p. 380; *PP*, p. 347.

29. Kant, *Frieden*, Ak. 8, p. 352; *PP*, p. 324.

30. *The Federalist Papers* (Oxford: Oxford University Press, 2008), nos. 10, 14.

system of *Obrigkeit* to timid liberal and democratic demands. Inversely, during and after the Weimar Republic, the crisis of the parliamentary system led either to questioning the *Rechtsstaat* model or to transforming it. The first was the response of doctrinaires of the "Total State," with Carl Schmitt at their head. During the 1920s, Schmitt developed a critique of the State of Law that emphasized the difficulty of combining the liberal logic of a State of Law with the political logic of democracy.[31] In 1935, after having rallied to the Nazi cause, Schmitt launched a "surrealist discussion" with Olivier Jouanjan on the subject: must the national-socialist state be defined as a State of Law?[32] The other possibility, developed during the Weimar regime by social-democratic leaning jurists such as H. Heller, O. Kirchheimer, and F. Neumann, led to the definition of the social State of Law in the Fundamental Law of the Federal Republic of Germany. This gave rise to a vast debate: to what extent is assigning social goals to the state — which implies an "interventionist" politics in administering and redistributing the social product — compatible with the non-interventionist principles of the State of Law? This was the subject of much discussion during the 1950s in Germany.[33] But regardless of their position on the concept, jurists more or less agree on the criteria that determine the *Rechtsstaat*. According to a disciple of Carl Schmitt, these are as follows:

(1) the principle of the *division of powers*, with separation of legislative, judicial, and executive powers; (2) the principle of the *independence of the courts*: procedures and judgments are exempt from any influence from above or below; (3) the principle of the *legality of the administration*, which excludes any administrative act that lacks legal basis; (4) the principle of *judicial protection of rights*, which guarantees that in the event of any unlawful adminis-

31. See Schmitt, *Constitutional Theory*, 167–252; "The Rechtsstaat component of the modern constitution," *Verfassungslehre*, 123–220. That same year, Schmitt published a text that was much more polemical and which, regarding the problem of "the integration of the proletariat in the new state," ended with an observation of "the inadequate methods of the state of bourgeois law." See "Der bürgerliche Rechtsstaat," in *Staat, Grossraum, Nomos: Arbeiten aus den Jahren 1916–1969* (Berlin: Duncker und Humboldt, 1995), 44–50.

32. In 1935 Schmitt published the chapter titled "Der Rechtsstaat" in the *Nationalsozialistisches Handbuch für Recht und Gesetzgebung*, edited by Hans Frank, as well as an article "Was bedeutet der Streit um den 'Rechtsstaat'?" These can be found in Schmitt, *Staat, Grossraum, Nomos*, 108–17 and 21–31.

33. See the texts collected in Ernst Forsthoff, ed., *Rechtsstaatlichkeit und Sozialstaatlichkeit* (Darmstadt: Wissenschaftliche Buchgesellschaft, 1968).

trative intervention, there can be an appeal to an independent court; (5) the principle of the *indemnification of public law*, which as a general rule guarantees compensation for any intervention, legal or illegal, by the administration in the sphere of personal property.[34]

We can arrive at a minimal description of the State of Law by reducing these criteria down to three. First, the criterion emphasized by Kant and the first liberals: *legality*, or the supremacy of the law. Any administrative measure, any government action, any intervention in the public sphere, must be based on a legal provision. Legality, understood as conformity with a rule promulgated according to a codified procedure, is thus the sole principle of the legitimacy of acts of state. This principle of legality is all the more limiting because it goes along with a restrictive definition of statute law and its field of application, a point I will return to later. Second, the criterion that every state act, including those originating with legislators, must be able to be legally assessed and controlled. This implies the existence of a norm superior to ordinary law even if the latter is the expression of the general will. The constitution alone is sovereign in a State of Law, which is a clear limitation of the democratic logic of the sovereignty of the people. Third, the criterion that states the independence of the judiciary, or rather its dependence on the law—and on it alone.[35] In a word, the State of Law is a *legal* state, a *constitutional* state, and a *judicial* state.

The theory of the *Rechtsstaat* institutes a new conception of the law, breaking with Hobbes's idea of the law as the sovereign's commandment.[36] In a State of Law, the law is a *general and formal norm* bearing a manifest rationality that is regularly expressed and collectively accepted. Thus, not every act by a legislator is eo ipso a statute law; it is so only if its object itself is general, "when the whole people decree concerning the whole people."[37] One must therefore distinguish *decrees*, which have particular objects and are local in application and temporary in their validity, from *statute laws*, which are char-

---

34. E. R. Huber, "Rechtsstaat und Sozialstaat in der modernen Industriegesellschaft," in ibid., 593.

35. According to Schmitt, the *Rechtsstaat* culminates in the ideal of "conformity of the entire state life to general judicial forms" (*Constitutional Theory*, 176). But he objects that "the state is not merely a judicial organization."

36. "And first it is manifest, that Law in generall, is not Counsell, but Command." Hobbes, *Leviathan*, 2:414.

37. Rousseau, *Oeuvres complètes*, 3:379; *Social Contract*, 2:6, 179.

acterized by their generality and indefinite duration. Without this distinction, the rule of law inevitably becomes the rule of the legislator, and thus, a form of tyranny.[38] Moreover, the essential principle of the State of Law, equality before the law, requires that this law be a general, formal, and rational norm (in the sense of what Weber calls "instrumental rationality" [*Zwecksrationalität*], not "value rationality" [*Wertrationalität*]).[39] Such an understanding of the law determines what the State of Law's mode of action can be: it cannot enact "social laws"; only administrative measures can, if needed, guarantee certain categories of the population specific benefits. The sole role of the legal norm is to guarantee the protection of the fundamental rights of each and all, the rights of man, and to define inviolable zones of freedom. Current forms of legislation fall quite far from this conception of the state's acts. The structural transformations of the state over the course of the twentieth century weakened the "hard core" of the *Rechtsstaat*. The contemporary state is no longer the liberal State of Law of the nineteenth century but rather a provider of services, a *social* and administrative state.[40]

The State of Law makes the state's acts subordinate to the requirements of personal freedom guaranteed by the constitution. At the heart of this construct are the fundamental rights (*Grundrechte*) that preserve an absolute space of freedom for the individual. These inalienable fundamental rights are above all freedom rights (*Freiheitsrechte*) that can be enforced against the state. The list of these freedoms was more or less established in the middle of the nineteenth century. Personal freedom (servitude and slavery are banned), free private property, the inviolability of the domicile, and freedom of conscience, of opinion, of expression, of association, of assembly, and of the press: in short, these plural freedoms are the expression of freedom. As for the conditions of political *equality*, they are guaranteed by the rights of citizenship: equality before the law, equal right to the vote ("one man, one vote"), equal ac-

---

38. Aristotle distinguishes democracies where the *nomos* rules from those where, under the impulse of "demagogues," the *psephismata* of the "mass" are sovereign, making the people a "monarch" (*Politics* 1.4.1292a5–11).

39. See Weber, *Economy and Society*, 26. We know that according to Weber, rationalization—of which the formalization of law is an important aspect—accompanies the triumph of the legal and bureaucratic type of *Herrschaft* politics in the modern world.

40. See E. Forsthoff, "Begriff und Wesen des sozialen Rechtsstaats," in *Rechtsstaatlichkeit Und Sozialstaatlichkeit*, 41.

cess to public employment, and the right to petition. Finally, social rights provide means for social *fraternity*, which, however, is subordinate to the absolute primacy of individual freedoms. In its own way, the *Rechtsstaat* actualizes the tripartite motto of the framers of the 1791 Constitution, but in the *Rechtsstaat* only freedom is honored unconditionally. Well before the antistate radicalism of neoliberals or libertarians (von Mises, Hayek, Nozick, Rothbard, etc.), the State of Law already tended to restrict the state's power of intervention to a social sphere understood to be fundamentally nonpolitical.

Even before it was legally formulated, the State of Law was a political demand. In the two decades leading up to the 1848 Revolution (the period known as the *Vormärz*), conservatives in Germany endeavored to restore the *Obrigkeitstaat* and rejected the "revolutionary" idea of organizing the state constitutionally.[41] The word *Rechtsstaat* summed up the aspirations of a social and economic world seeking to ensure its autonomy. The demand for a State of Law, issued from the new reality designated by the term *civil society*,[42] accompanied the rise in power of the "estate of commerce" (*Stand des Gewerbes*),[43] whose activity required autonomous structures of production and an independent market and thus spelled the end of the police state. The *Rechtsstaat* and the political values it institutes correspond closely to the development of a capitalist market economy, which Hegel was one of the first to perceive could imply surpassing the national form of the state.[44] The State of Law is modern society's weapon against a state perceived as an obstacle to its free development.

41. Karl-Ludwig von Haller's enormous treatise *Restauration der Staatswissenschaft*, 6 vols. (1820–1825; Aalen: Scientia, 1964), illustrates these trends to the point of caricature, contrasting patrimonial royalty with the "chimera of the social contract" and "artificial civil society." Hegel is harsh toward Haller's assessments; see *RPh*, § 219 A and § 258 Anmerkung, *GW* 14.1, pp. 182, 204–7 (*Elements*, 252, 278–80; see *Outlines*, 208, 231–33).

42. "The concept of civil society was a controversial concept. Similarly, the concept of the bourgeois State of Law (*bürgerlicher Rechtsstaat*), which was organized according to the objective of civil society, was a controversial political concept when it appeared." E. R. Huber, "Rechtsstaat und Sozialstaat in der modernen Industriegesellschaft," in Forsthoff, *Rechtsstaatlichkeit und Sozialstaatlichkeit*, 591.

43. *RPh*, § 204, *GW* 14.1, p. 172 (*Elements*, 236; see *Outlines*, 195).

44. *RPh*, § 246, *GW* 14.1, p. 195 (*Elements*, 267–68; see *Outlines*, 222). Weber emphasizes that rationalization and state control of the law are, as the development of a mode of domination, connected to modern transformations of the economy. Weber, *Economy and Society*, 904 ff.

Let us draw three lessons from this historical study of the concept of *Rechtsstaat*. First, at the political level, as the whole history of the nineteenth century confirms, the problematic of the State of Law objectively tended toward maintaining the social status quo; it became a tool used by the wealthy to defend against demands calling into question the "spontaneous order of the market." Beginning at end of the nineteenth century, the rise of such demands put the State of Law into crisis. Second, the principles of the State of Law imply a hegemony of private law over public law: it is the private person, whose primary attribute is property, who is the true subject of fundamental rights rather than the citizen. The absoluteness of private property is the touchstone of the State of Law, and it determines the limitations imposed on politics. The State of Law is first and foremost the State of Private Law. Third, the doctrine of the State of Law establishes a barrier between law and politics, a division unacceptable for classical philosophy. It does not aim to prescribe ends or give meaning to the state's actions but rather to erect barriers to them. It is, at bottom, a denegation of politics.

That fact that the State of Law had Kantian ancestry is clear. But can the Hegelian state—the terrestrial divine![45]—claim to be a State of Law? The question seems absurd if we hew to the image of Hegelianism codified by Rudolf Haym.[46] In addition, the *Phenomenology of Spirit* develops a merciless analysis of what Hegel calls *der Rechtzustand*, the "state of law" whose description matches certain traits of the Roman Empire. This is characterized, on the one hand, by the hegemony of formalist, meticulous private law—Roman imperial law "codified" by Justinian—in determining the relations between persons[47] and, on the other hand, by the violent domination of the "lord of the world," that "monstrous self-consciousness who knows himself as an actual

45. "We should therefore venerate the state as an earthly divinity." Hegel, *Vorlesungen Über Rechtsphilosophie*, 3:744. *RPh*, § 272 Zusatz, *W* 7, p. 434 (*Elements*, 307; see *Outlines*, 258). In the *Philosophy of Right*, it is the *constitution* that "should be regarded as divine and enduring" (*RPh*, § 273 Anmerkung, *GW* 14.1, p. 229 [*Elements*, 312; see *Outlines*, 262]).

46. See in particular Haym, *Hegel und seine Zeit*, 357 ff. Rosenzweig, an attentive reader, seems to accept that in Hegel "the intuition of the state as power" contrasts with "the Kantian doctrine of the state of law." Rosenzweig, *Hegel Und Der Staat*, 138. For an opposing view, see Steven B. Smith, *Hegel's Critique of Liberalism: Rights in Context* (Chicago: University of Chicago Press, 1991), 132 ff.

47. See *PhG*, *GW* 9, pp. 260–61 (*Phenomenology*, ¶ 476).

God."[48] In other words, the rule of egalitarian legal formalism is in no way incompatible with the most brutal of tyrannies, and the state of law may well clothe a "destructive violence." But this analysis just shows the limits of abstract law when it is not part of a framework suitable for actualizing it in a reasonable manner: this is the framework of the modern state and (especially) civil society. Hegel's legal *and social* philosophy, while it does not belong to the logic of the *Rechtsstaat*, whose theoretical grounds it rejects, nevertheless anticipates its concrete demands while giving them a different foundation than those most often invoked. We will see this by turning to various aspects not of the *Rechtsstaat* in the technical sense of term—which would not emerge until the end of the Hegel's life—but rather the principal themes it articulates: human rights and the rule of law.

The Rights of Man: Freedoms

The question of fundamental rights, or, in more political language, the rights of man and citizen, is at the heart of the *Rechtsstaat* doctrine. It demonstrates its antiabsolutist, even antistate orientation: only a restriction of the state's powers (by an appropriate mechanism) allows individuals to fully enjoy these rights, which are considered to be original and independent of the state. Hegel notes the guarantee of these rights by the liberal and republican traditions, but he transforms the problematic that implicitly guided their construction. At the same time, he does not treat the rights of man uniformly. Following Sieyès, who "had a great reputation for deep insights into the organization of free constitutions,"[49] Hegel differentiates between these rights and uncovers the tensions that run through the seemingly compact block they form. Since Sieyès, it has become common to divide the rights of man into "freedoms" and "claims" (*créances*). The freedoms are "rights to," for example, the right

48. *PhG, GW* 9, p. 263 (*Phenomenology*, ¶ 480).

49. *Reformbill, W* 11, p. 117; *Reform Bill,* in *Hegel's Political Writings,* 322. This is Hegel's only explicit reference to Sieyès. But we may conjecture that he was familiar with his writings, many of which were translated into German. The first translation of Sieyès, by C. F. Cramer, appeared in 1794 under the title *Sieyès Schriften: Versuch über die Vorrechte und Was ist der Bürgerstand?* A second translation in 1796, by J. G. Ebel, included most of what was available at the time under the title *Sieyès: Politische Schriften.* Finally, also in 1796, Cramer published a volume titled *Collection des écrits d'Emmanuel Sieyès* in French with a short preface in German.

to property, to free movement, to enterprise, to express one's opinions, and so forth—freedoms that are based in the very nature of humans. Claims, or social rights, are "rights to the common benefits that may arise from the state of society,"[50] such as the right to public aid or to education. One of Sieyès's favorite images is of claims as checks that can be drawn on the "public establishment" or "the great social enterprise" in which individuals are all to some degree shareholders;[51] thus they presuppose the existence of a constituted political society. Various twentieth-century authors[52] would emphasize that there is not only a difference but also a possible contradiction between freedoms and claims; in a way, Hegel was ahead of them.

Hegel's texts do not give a detailed analysis of the *freedom rights* in Sieyès's sense, which are the rights of man properly speaking since they guarantee the independence of individual and social life with respect to the state. But Hegel does consistently reiterate the full validity of their principle and the ethical and political—not moral—imperative to respect them:

> The *legal principles* in force . . . have their actuality and guarantee in the state power. These principles are those developed in earlier spheres, the principles of freedom of property and also of personal freedom, the principles of civil society, of its industry and of the communities, and of the regulated performance of the particular authorities subject to the laws.[53]

Here, Hegel advances two points regarding freedom rights. First, they find in the state "their actuality and their guarantee," and the public space is their domain of exercise. Thus, for example, freedom of opinion and expression contribute, for better or worse, to the necessary regulation of public life through controversy,[54] which is why "public opinion deserves to be respected as well

50. Sieyès, "Reconnaissance et exposition raisonnée des droits de l'homme et du citoyen," 204.

51. Ibid., 199.

52. See Schmitt, *Verfassungslehre*, 168; *Constitutional Theory*, 207. See also Hayek, *Law, Legislation and Liberty*, 2:85–86, 101–6.

53. *Enzykl*, § 544 Anmerkung, *GW* 20, p. 518 (*Encyclopedia* 242–43, modified).

54. "Everything that is stimulating in a debate stems from the fact that men gather together to affirm, prove, refute, persuade, in a hand to hand confrontation with the living presence of spirit" (*Wurtemberg, W* 4, p. 516; not translated in *Hegel's Political Writings*). See also *RPh*, §§ 316–319, *GW* 14.1, pp. 258–261.

as despised . . . despised for its concrete consciousness and expression, and respected for its essential basis."[55] Of course, Hegel does not subscribe to the principle of religious freedom without restriction, but this is precisely because in his eyes religious freedom does not belong solely to the domain of individual rights of conscience, rights that he, contrary to Catholicism, forcefully reaffirms. When religion is organized into a church or churches, it becomes a political force whose full autonomy would mean the state's dependence on it—something of which history offers many examples. This is why it is important that the state control not consciences but rather the institutional forms of communication within the religious space insofar as it interferes (as it necessarily does) with the public space.[56]

However, freedom rights—those proclaimed in Article 2 of the Declaration of the Rights of Man and Citizen—are above all nonpolitical rights and, insofar as they are rights of man *in his universality*, their field of actualization is *civil society*: "property and personality have legal recognition and validity in civil society."[57] Of course, within the ethical totality, civil society is "the degree of *difference*":[58] it separates individuals from one another as it indefinitely diversifies their needs and aspirations; between the abstract universality of the familial bond and the concrete universality of the political bond, civil society appears as the terrain of exploded particularity, as "the system of atomization."[59] But it is precisely because modern civil society—and civil society is, essentially, modern—is a powerful creator of differentiation between individuals and human groups that it requires the principle of *equal freedom*, which is the basis for human rights. Civil society both requires the principle of equal freedom and gives it eminently concrete meaning.[60] It strips the individual, confined to the functions of a legal person and economic actor, of any status-based predicates assigned by a society of orders (and privileges), and it reduces the individual to a being of need and work, thus giving concrete

55. *RPh*, § 318, *GW* 14.1, p. 260 (*Elements*, 355; see *Outlines*, 301).

56. See *RPh*, § 270 Anmerkung, *GW* 14.1, pp. 213–23 (*Elements*, 291–302; see *Outlines*, 242–53), and *Enzykl*, § 552 Anmerkung, *GW* 20, pp. 531–41 (*Encyclopedia* 250–56).

57. *RPh*, § 218, *GW* 14.1, p. 181 (*Elements*, 250; see *Outlines*, 207).

58. *RPh*, § 181, *GW* 14.1, p. 159 (*Elements*, 219; see *Outlines*, 180).

59. *Enzykl*, § 523, *GW* 20, p. 498 (*Encyclopedia* 230).

60. Balibar demonstrates the architectonic nature of the "proposition of equaliberty" for the rights of man. See Étienne Balibar, *Equaliberty: Political Essays* (Durham, NC: Duke University Press, 2014); "Les Universels," in *La crainte des masses* (Paris: Galilée, 1997), 441 ff.

content to egalitarian legal formalism. The human being, that "concretum of representation,"[61] is the social—or more exactly, economic—concretization of the abstract legal person and the actual bearer of fundamental rights, which are thus (in a very different sense than "claims") *social rights*.

The core of freedom rights are two abstractions that, as the first part of the *Philosophy of Right* demonstrates, are the matrix of abstract law: *personality*, expressed by legal capacity, and *property*, which objectifies that capacity in the context of a civil society freed from the hindrances of feudalism. Person and property are thus central concepts in a rigorous conceptualization of human right and law, whence the cardinal position of personal freedom and the right to property among the freedom rights. "Man" is first a person free in his body and mind (neither serf nor slave); he must make himself so through the work of self-appropriation and physical and intellectual acculturation that give him "possession of himself."[62] The person that every human must be able to become is defined by the legal capacity to appropriate outside goods.[63] The right to property (in the broad sense used by Locke, which includes life, liberty, and property[64]) is thus the basis for all freedoms, in particular freedom of action and enterprise. It is with full awareness of the implications for the rights of man that Hegel declares at the beginning of his analysis of the system of needs that "this is the first, and in fact the only occasion on which we shall refer to *the human being*."[65]

Freedom rights, the rights of man in their liberal sense, are thus connected—though undoubtedly in a complex manner—to the existence and operation of a (bourgeois) civil society detached from the state by the process of differentiation that is constitutive of modernity. The true holder of these rights is neither the citizen nor the moral subject nor merely the person in the sense of abstract law; rather, it is the "burgher in the sense of a bourgeois"[66]: *homo oeconomicus* or *homo socialis*. Though freedom rights have a political component (those rights having to do with citizenship), they are

61. *RPh*, § 190 Anmerkung, *GW* 14.1, p. 166 (*Elements*, 228; see *Outlines*, 188).

62. *RPh*, § 57, *GW* 14.1, p. 64 (*Elements*, 86, see *Outlines*, 69).

63. *RPh*, § 36, *GW* 14.1, p. 52 (*Elements*, 69, modified see *Outlines*, 55): "Personality contains in general the legal capacity and constitutes the concept and the (itself abstract) basis of abstract and hence *formal* law."

64. Locke, *Second Treatise of Government*, chap. 5, §87, and chap. 9, §123, p. 57–58, 78.

65. *RPh*, § 190 Anmerkung, *GW* 14.1, p. 166 (*Elements*, 228; see *Outlines*, 188).

66. *Naturrecht*, *W* 2, p. 494 (*Natural Law*, 103).

above all *nonpolitical* rights; this is why they appear as "natural" rights. Hegel thus *seems* to embrace the natural law perspective: fundamental rights are rights that derive from human nature. But for Hegel, the human is the *social* human, the human of *civil society*, a perspective entirely different from that of natural law or *Rechtsstaat* theoreticians. It is in the modern organization of production and exchange, in the system of needs, that individuals find their common nature as beings of need and work: they no longer have a status that determines their rights and duties without regard for their aptitudes or aspirations as they did in old estate societies. The abstract human, like abstract work, is a product of modern forms of socialization and must be recognized as the "abstract" bearer of rights that are not linked to his or her particular being— are not *privileges*:

> The human being . . . shows his universality, first by *multiplying* his needs and means [of satisfying them], and secondly by *dividing* and *differentiating* the concrete need into individual parts and aspects which then become different needs, *particularized* and hence *more abstract*. . . . That abstraction which becomes a quality of both needs and means (see §191) also becomes a determination of the mutual relations [*Beziehung*] between individuals.[67]

But for Hegel, the social redefinition of man's natural rights must be accompanied by their *political* relativization. Two points prove this. First, the state may be led to occasionally intervene in the realm of private property, sacred to liberals:

> Those determinations which concern private property may have to be subordinated to higher legal spheres, such as a community or the state. . . . Nevertheless, such exceptions cannot be grounded in contingency, private arbitrariness, or private utility, but only in the rational organism of the state.[68]

Here we find the principle of expropriation for public utility (resulting in compensation); this principle is accepted by states today, but it contradicts the inviolability of private property as represented by the liberals of Hegel's time. But we can also imagine that the state may be led, exceptionally, to nationalize

---

67. *RPh*, § 190 and 192, *GW* 14.1, p. 166 (*Elements*, 228–29; see *Outlines*, 187–89).
68. *RPh*, § 46 Anmerkung, *GW* 14.1, p. 58 (*Elements*, 77; see *Outlines*, 61).

private wealth when the concentration of property is contrary to the general interest of society and the state itself.

Second, Hegel rejects the representation of freedom used in the common thematic of the rights of man. That representation makes freedom a native attribute[69] of the subjective will, unlimited in principle, that can only be hindered by the external authority that is the state. However, this representation is both insufficient and contradictory. It is insufficient because it makes freedom into a fortress perpetually besieged by the objectivity of the natural and human world. It is contradictory because this prepolitical (*natural* in the various senses of the word) freedom needs to be achieved through political avenues: according to the 1789 Declaration, "the aim of all political association is the preservation of the natural and imprescriptible rights of man" (Article 2), and for them to be effectively respected, a "social guarantee" is required. For Hegel, to the contrary, it is because there is nothing natural about freedom (and the rights through which it is expressed) that it must be legally, socially, and politically *instituted*:

> Freedom as the ideal condition of what is as yet purely immediate and natural does not itself possess an immediate and natural existence. It still has to be earned and won through the endless mediation of discipline acting upon the powers of cognition and will.[70]

Freedom rights (and consequently the rights of man in general) thus do not have the same status in Hegel as in the *Rechtsstaat* of the liberals. Of course, the Hegelian state recognizes these rights and guarantees individuals that they will enjoy them; it even "mak[es] right a necessary actuality,"[71] but at the same time, it deprives them of their character as absolute principles. Rights and right owe their actuality to the state, for merely proclaiming them, no matter how solemnly and systematically, is not enough to carry them out as effective freedom. Without the state, the fundamental legal principles would remain abstract, even illusory. Only the *rational* state gives actuality to the

---

69. According to Kant, of the natural subjective rights, only freedom is "native" or "innate" rather than "acquired." (*Rechtslehre: MdS, Ak.* 6, p. 237; *PP*, pp. 392–93).

70. Hegel, *Die Vernunft in der Geschichte*, 117; *Lectures on the Philosophy of World History*, 98–99.

71. *Enzykl*, § 537, *GW* 20, p. 508 (*Encyclopedia* 236).

rights of man by letting civil society organize itself independently—at least to the point where it is threatened by its own contradictions and it becomes necessary to overcome politically social particularity. The state turns civil society and its abstract legal principles into components of its own universality. But it thereby takes from them their claim to be the foundation of human living together, that is, of political being.

The Rights of Man: "Claims"

Social rights are clearly identified and recognized in Hegel, and in this he diverges from *Rechtsstaat* doctrines, which are primarily concerned with keeping the space of personal freedom free from state intervention. Of course, he was not the first one to do this: the French Revolution recognized and proclaimed "rights to relief," but with hesitation; the 1789 Declaration did not acknowledge them, although the idea had appeared in certain draft versions. It was the 1793 Declaration that, following Robespierre and Condorcet,[72] affirmed that "public relief is a sacred debt," specifying that "society owes maintenance to unfortunate citizens, either in procuring work for them or in providing the means of existence for those who are unable to labor" (Article 21); it also stipulates that society must "put education within reach of every citizen" and defines the "social guarantee" as "the action of all to secure to each the enjoyment and the maintenance of his rights" (Article 23). But Hegel proposes a particular interpretation of social rights, one based on his understanding of the relations between the state and civil society. He is also more attentive than the French revolutionaries to the imbalances that the different structures of freedom rights and social rights can introduce into the complex edifice of human rights.

Hegel makes social policy an important aspect of the state's activity. Central and local administrative authorities are to actively intervene in civil society to correct imbalances in the commercial economy that are dangerous for individuals and for society itself: they provide economic oversight (control and regulation of production and prices) and social protection to the impoverished. But the fact that there is a social *policy* does not necessarily mean

---

72. In Robespierre, this principle means redistribution: "essential relief to those who are without necessities" (Article 9 of the draft of the *Déclaration des droits* presented in the speech of April 24, 1793).

that there are social *rights*: the monarchies of the ancien régime justified their interventions in economics and monetary flows with paternalistic arguments without their subjects having any "rights" to lay claim to. Kant denounces such a paternalist view of society, which is the view of the police state: "A government established on the principle of benevolence toward the people . . . that is, a *paternalistic government* . . . is the greatest *despotism* thinkable."[73] In Hegel, on the other hand, the vision of a relatively autonomous civil society and the understanding of humans as the product of modern processes of production lead to recognizing the existence of a right to "particular well-being [*Wohl*]":

> In the *system of needs*, the livelihood and welfare of each individual [*jedes Einzelnen*] are a *possibility* whose actualization is conditioned by the individual's own arbitrary will and particular nature, as well as by the objective system of needs. . . . But the right *which is actually present in particularity* means not only that *contingencies* which interfere with this or that end should be *cancelled* [*aufgehoben*] and that the *undisturbed security* of *persons* and *property* should be guaranteed, but also that the livelihood and welfare of individuals should be *secured* — i.e. that *particular welfare* should be *treated as a right* and duly *actualized*.[74]

The task of making right actual in particularity — that is, carrying out a social *policy* — is analyzed in the section on civil society under the headings "police" and "corporation." The *state* administration, charged with "universal provision and direction" in the domain of economic affairs implements this policy by arbitrating, most notably, in conflicts of interest between producers and consumers and between "large branches of industry";[75] in today's terms, it is in charge of economic and social policy. But to this end, the state cooperates with the *social* institution of the corporation. Just as Hegel's *Stände* do not correspond to the ancien régime's "estates," the corporation is not the equivalent of traditional guilds or confraternities: the 1817 *Ständeschrift* explicitly distinguishes the old corporations (*Zünfte*), which were animated by "the guild spirit" (*Zunftgeist*) and restricted themselves to defending their privileges, from modern professional corporations, which are necessary for regulating

---

73. Kant, *Gemeinspruch*, Ak. 8, pp. 290–91; *PP*, pp. 290–91.

74. *RPh*, § 230, *GW* 14.1, p. 189 (*Elements*, 259–60; see *Outlines*, 215).

75. *RPh*, § 236, *GW* 14.1, p. 191 (*Elements*, 262; see *Outlines*, 217).

the blind operation of the market.[76] In the context of diversification and the capitalist competition of interests, the corporation is an organized social interest. But it also has a political vocation because it contributes to representing the social world in legislative bodies; this is why the government exercises a right of oversight on its operations.[77] Thus, the administration and corporations work together to promote "the universal interest as such" and the "conservation of particular interests."[78]

Economic and social policing by the state and the actions of corporations are all activities that work toward private happiness and go beyond the limits of a State of Law understood in the liberal sense. The Hegelian state is a *social state* before its time because, as an instance of the universal, it must ensure a balance between particular interests, which the market and social institutions could never establish on their own. No doubt civil society has its own instance of universality: civil and penal justice. But the formal guarantee of respect of the law does not allow for adequate administration of the approximation of the state of nature that is civil society. There must therefore be a *political* administration of social particularity. Of course, social policy is but one of the state's tasks. As we saw in the last chapter, making social policy its raison d'être would amount to making the state an external state (external to its own universality), an institution of need (*Notstaat*): this is precisely the liberal night watchman state. It would be to confound the state with civil society by giving it no other end than "*the interest of individuals* [*der Einzelnen*] *as such.*"[79] But to underestimate this function would be to forget that the state's mission is also to fill the gap that constantly threatens to open between universality and particularity, between the political and the social. This is confirmed by Hegel's attentive and nuanced treatment of the "social question" in paragraphs 236 and following in the *Philosophy of Right,* where he studies the harmful con-

---

76. *Wurtemberg, W* 4, p. 483; *Proceedings,* in *Hegel's Political Writings,* 263. In addition, the *Philosophy of Right* specifies that "the corporation in and for itself is not an enclosed guild" (*RPh,* § 255 Zusatz, *W* 7, p. 396 [*Elements,* 273; see *Outlines,* 227]).

77. *RPh,* §§ 308, 311, *GW* 14.1, pp. 254, 256 (*Elements,* 346–47, 350; see *Outlines,* 294, 296–97). On the "supervision of the public authority," see *RPh,* § 252, *GW* 14.1, p. 197 and § 255 Zusatz, *W* 7, pp. 396–97 (*Elements,* 270, 273; see *Outlines,* 224, 227).

78. *RPh,* § 270, *GW* 14.1, p. 212 (*Elements,* 290; see *Outlines,* 242).

79. *RPh,* § 258 Anmerkung, *GW* 14.1, p. 201 (*Elements,* 276; see *Outlines,* 228). See also *RPh,* § 270 Anmerkung, *GW* 14.1, p. 219 and § 324 Anmerkung, *GW* 14.1, p. 265 (*Elements,* 298, 361; see *Outlines,* 249, 306).

sequences of the English Industrial Revolution: the creation of a "rabble" (*Pöbel*), impoverished and above all desocialized, and the destabilization of civil society itself, whose normal modes of regulation (economic, legal, and social) no longer seem capable of functioning effectively. The following chapter will return to this crucial detail. I will limit myself here to what this implies for "claims," emphasizing two points.

First of all, while social rights obviously presuppose concerted intervention by public powers, their authentic field of exercise is indeed civil society: it is in the individual's quality as a "*son of civil society*" that he has "rights" in relation to it.[80] The "rights to social relief," as Sieyès said,[81] thus belong more properly to the bourgeois than to the citizen. And thus the mission of corporations becomes clear: by establishing an institutional network within civil society, they prevent it from becoming a pure and simple market society and guarantee individuals that their "particular well-being" will be considered a "right."[82] Therefore, it is above all thanks to *social* institutions (the police are also a social institution, at least by virtue of their field of action) that civil society can be *more than* the grounds of a war of each against all.[83]

In the second place, there is a latent contradiction between freedom rights and social rights, between "rights of" and "rights to" that demands *political* resolution. To the degree that the rights of man are in their very principles nonpolitical (but this statement has a totally different meaning than it would in a natural law perspective, since for Hegel the idea of original or natural rights is confused or contradictory), the tensions that trouble the block they supposedly form (they reflect those that affect civil society in a socially insurmountable way) must be borne by the state. Only the moment (*instance*) of the *real* universal, which must be political (for the universality guaranteed by the law and the universality that economic laws uncover in the contradictory play of particular interests are *formal*), is capable of guaranteeing individuals and social groups actual enjoyment of particular and competing rights and can make the decisions necessary for resolving the contradictions that might crack the block of the rights of man. Thus, when it comes to the conflict of

---

80. *RPh*, § 238, *GW* 14.1, p. 192 (*Elements*, 263; see *Outlines*, 218).

81. Sieyès, "Second projet de déclaration des droits de l'Homme et du Citoyen," art. 27, in Stéphane Rials, ed., *La déclaration des droits de l'homme et du citoyen* (Paris: Hachette, 1988), 619.

82. *RPh*, § 255, *GW* 14.1, p. 199 (*Elements*, 273; see *Outlines*, 226).

83. See *RPh*, § 289 Anmerkung, *GW* 14.1, p. 242 (*Elements*, 329; see *Outlines*, 278).

interest between producers and consumers, Hegel considers that they ultimately must be "consciously regulated by an agency which stands above both [interests]."[84] According to Hegel, who in this regard is more "liberal" than often thought, these decisions by the state tend toward *freedom* rather than *equality*; they are freedom rights rather than social rights. But if Hegel's choice appears to be the same as that of liberals (the modern world has chosen social freedom to the detriment of political equality), the *concept* of freedom that underlies his choice is profoundly different from that of the liberals.[85] Here Hegel shows, as he so often does, that one can accept a solution while rejecting the way the problem it solves has been posed.

What, in the end, is the position of the rights of man within the Hegelian state? The Hegelian rational state, an institutional expression of political freedom, recognizes and guarantees (as do revolutionary constitutions) "eternal human rights";[86] thus, the Declaration of these rights is an "elementary catechism"[87] that lays out the bases—but only the bases—of the constitutional edifice. However, because of their abstraction, the rights of man—especially freedom rights—cannot form the content of an actual politics. Or, if they did, they would lead to an *abstract* politics as conceived and carried out not by "statesmen" but by "men of principle"[88] driven by an ethics of conviction; this would be a *dogmatic* politics, a politics of virtue whose forms and effects (here of course one thinks of the Terror) are necessarily disquieting. Robespierre declared that "the French Revolution is the first that was based on the theory of the rights of man and the principles of justice,"[89] but he also thought, with consequences we all know, that "kings, aristocrats, tyrants, whoever they are, are slaves who have revolted against the ruler of the land and the legislator of the universe, the former being the human race and the latter,

---

84. *RPh*, § 236, *GW* 14.1, p. 190 (*Elements*, 262; see *Outlines*, 217).

85. On the liberal conception of freedom, see Lucien Jaume, *La liberté et la loi: Les origines philosophiques du libéralisme* (Paris: Fayard, 2000). The conceptions of freedom that underlie the debates leading up to the adoption of the 1789 Declaration are analyzed by Marcel Gauchet in *La révolution des droits de l'homme* (Paris: Gallimard, 1989).

86. "[In Rome] the slaves tried to free themselves, to obtain recognition of their eternal human rights" (*Enzykl*, § 433 Zusatz, *W* 10, p. 224 [*Encyclopedia* 160]).

87. *Wurtemberg*, *W* 4, p. 492; *Proceedings*, in *Hegel's Political Writings*, 270.

88. *Reformbill*, *W* 11, p. 122; *Reform Bill*, in *Hegel's Political Writings*, 325.

89. Robespierre, Last speech (July 26, 1794), *Oeuvres* (Paris: Presses Universitaires de France, 1967), 10:544.

nature."[90] Hegel rejects this abstract politics of the rights of man. But unlike counterrevolutionaries, who consider that such a politics is based on "an error of theory,"[91] he thinks of it as the practical corruption of an idea that is true in itself, whose grounds must simply be made explicit. The rights of man do not need to be claimed in opposition to the state; to the contrary, they are actualized by it, though outside it. Thus, Hegel's position, far from being determined by political or moral considerations, is entirely driven by his innovative way of thinking the relation between the state and civil society, between the political and the legal-economic in the conditions of modernity, that is, in the world issued from the Protestant Reform, the French political revolution, and the English economic revolution. This relation is dialectical. Hegel's conviction, which Marx would later take up in his own way, that the solution to the contradictions of modern civil society must necessarily be political, led him to adopt a position that certainly does not coincide with the liberal though not "social" perspective of *Rechtsstaat* theoreticians. Because the rights of man—whether freedoms or claims—are attached to civil society, which is a sphere of relativity, their scope and value are *relative*.

The Order of Statute Laws: Civil Society as "State of Law"

It is not only in the *Phenomenology of Spirit* that Hegel uses the term *state of law*; in his mature work it designates the rule of abstract law with the reservations that this requires on his part. The fact that this "state of law" only corresponds to a small part of his expanded concept of the law can be seen in his assessment of Fichte's conception of the state: in Fichte, "right is the supreme principle, the state is not conceived in its essence, but only as rule of law [*Rechtszustand*], that is to say, precisely as an external relation of finite beings to finite beings."[92] According to Hegel, Fichte made the state into a *Notstaat*, an "emergency state,"[93] because like liberals (whom he would appear to oppose), he thinks of the state as an extension of civil society and private law, thereby making him incapable of conceptualizing its properly political

---

90. Speech by Robespierre, *Archives parlementaires*, ser. 1, vol. 63, p. 198.

91. Joseph de Maistre, *Considérations sur la France* (Paris: Garnier, 1980), 64–65.

92. *GdP, W* 20, p. 412 (*Lectures on the History of Philosophy*, 503, modified).

93. Fichte, *Naturrecht, Werke*, 3:302; *Sittenlehre, Werke*, 4:238. Hegel, it has been said, applies this denomination to civil society (*RPh*, § 183, *GW* 14.1, p. 160; *Elements*, 221; see *Outlines*, 181).

vocation. To adequately define this vocation, one must examine the limits of the "state of law" where civil society is under certain conditions. In Hegel, the notion of *Rechtszustand* corresponds more or less to that of *gesetzlicher Zustand* (legal state) and that of *Rechtsverfassung* (legal constitution), a term that appears in the description of civil society and is contraposed with the term *Staatsverfassung* (political constitution).[94] These expressions indicate that in civil society, abstract law is actualized in the form of a rule of law guaranteed by legal institutions. This "state of law" is an important moment in the presentation of civil society because it returns to the universal a society that would seem to be condemned to particularity by the logic of the system of needs:

> In the administration of justice, civil society, in which the Idea has lost itself in particularity and split into the division between inward and outward, returns to its *concept*, to the unity of the universal which has being in itself.[95]

The passage titled "The Administration of Law" (*die Rechtspflege*) deals with positive statute laws as an expression of abstract law and poses the problem (at the time, a burning political question) of its systematization in a civil code. Hegel then moves on to studying the conditions of social life organized according to the law, leading him to consider legal institutions and procedures. At first, the location of these analyses seems surprising: why is the administration of law part of the analysis of civil society, and why does it come between the study of modern structures of production (the system of needs) and that of the administrative and institutional regulation of social life (police and corporations)? We might have expected the issue to be discussed in the section on abstract law, but Hegel separates the study of the (legal) administration of the legal norm from that of abstract/private law, integrating the former into a speculative discussion of the statute law (*das Gesetz*) as the being-posited (*Gesetzsein*) of law. Even if we accept this dissociation of abstract law from the modality of its expression and application within in the framework of a positive legal order, why aren't these topics studied within the framework of the state, since the administration of law, just like the police, falls under the juris-

94. See *RPh*, § 157, *GW* 14.1, p. 143 (*Elements*, 198; see *Outlines*, 162). The 1817 article on Württemberg does indeed mention a "legal constitution of the state" (*W* 4, p. 494; *Proceedings*, in *Hegel's Political Writings*, 272), but this is a quote.

95. *RPh*, § 229, *GW* 14.1, p. 188 (*Elements*, 259; see *Outlines*, 214–15).

diction of the government administration[96] and thus "should be regarded both as a duty and as a right on the part of the public authority"?[97] Why does Hegel make the administration of law a *social* question and not a legal or political one? The answer lies in his definition of a law:

> When what is law *in itself* is *posited* in its objective existence [*Dasein*] — i.e. determined by thought for consciousness and *known* [*bekannt*] as what is law and valid — it becomes *statute law*, and through this determination, law becomes *positive* in general. . . . In this identity of *being in itself* and *being posited*, only what is *statute law* has binding force as *law*.[98]

Two aspects of this analysis of the statutes laws or acts should be pointed out: first, the law is characterized as the objective and positive existence of abstract law; second, a connection is made, which is more than a play on words, between the statute law (*das Gesetz*) and the logical function of "positing" (*setzen*).

Positive law is characterized above all by its *statute form*. In Hegel's terminology, abstract law, made explicit by the statutes in effect in a state, is *posited*. Far from implying a lack of rationality, the positivity of the statute law is the condition of the *actuality* of law, but it does not, of course, exhaust its possible rationality. In his last political text, Hegel writes,

> It is true that every right and its corresponding law is in *form* something positive, ordained, and instituted by the supreme power in the state, something to which obedience must be given just because it is a statute. But at no time more than the present has the general intelligence been led to distinguish between whether rights are purely positive in their material *content* or whether they are also *inherently* right and rational.[99]

Let us focus on the first sentence. Legal form converts the formal right of the legal person into the social actor's concrete exercise of rights within civil so-

---

96. See *RPh*, § 287, *GW* 14.1, p. 241 (*Elements*, 328; see *Outlines*, 278).

97. *RPh*, § 219 Anmerkung, *GW* 14.1, p. 183 (*Elements*, 252; see *Outlines*, 208–9).

98. *RPh*, §§ 211, 212, *GW* 14.1, pp. 175, 177 (*Elements*, 241, 243, modified; see *Outlines*, 198, 201).

99. *Reformbill*, *W* 11, p. 88; *Reform Bill*, in *Hegel's Political Writings*, 299.

ciety. For example, the abstract and unlimited right to own things (Hobbes's *jus in omnia*) is realized as the socially established appropriation (property) of a *certain* thing:

> Just as right *in itself* becomes statute in civil society, so too does my individual [*einzelne*] right, whose existence [*Dasein*] was previously *immediate* and *abstract*, acquire a new significance when its existence is recognized as part of the existent [*existierend*] universal will and knowledge.[100]

Abstract subjective right (*my* right), as statute, and even more so as a codified system of civil and penal statutes, acquires actuality. This means, first of all, that law (objective law, the system of statute laws) must be known by all: "for the law to have binding force, it is necessary . . . that the statute laws should be made *universally known*."[101] Next, it means that a legal institution protects this law and the rights that flow from it and reestablishes them when they have been violated, thus raising them to a sort of universality. Far from being a mere indication of contingency, the statute law's positivity is what makes it such that a right, ceasing to be a singular claim, is posited as universal: "Only when it becomes statute law does what is lawful take on both the *form* of its universality and its true determinacy."[102] The statute law is law actualized and *thought* in its universality. This is why "those rulers who have given their peoples a collection of statutes—if only a formless collection like that of Justinian . . . did . . . a great *act of justice*."[103]

Let us retain two facts from this analysis. First—and this explains the location of the passage on the administration of law—civil society is the space of the concretization and universalization of abstract law: it is its terrain of actuality. In a way, the institutionalized social world is the true milieu of law—even if the point of imputation of rights (to use Kelsen's expression) is the particular person, an abstraction. Which means, conversely, that in the absence of civil society (and thus in the absence of a partially self-regulated market and the institutions it requires), abstract law is likely to remain an

---

100. *RPh*, § 217, *GW* 14.1, p. 181 (*Elements*, 249; see *Outlines*, 206).

101. *RPh*, § 215, *GW* 14.1, p. 179 (*Elements*, 246; see *Outlines*, 203).

102. *RPh*, § 211 Anmerkung, *GW* 14.1, pp. 175–76 (*Elements*, 241, modified; see *Outlines*, 198–99).

103. *RPh*, § 215 Anmerkung, *GW* 14.1, p. 179 (*Elements*, 247; see *Outlines*, 204).

ideality, law "in itself." Second, when Hegel comes out in favor of adopting a civil code, he is not just intervening in the legal and political debates of Germany in the 1810s and 1820s and supporting a more Napoleonic model (the Civil Code) over the Frederickan one (the Allgemeines Landrecht für die preussischen Staaten). It is also and above all a *choice of rationality*: a code, no matter how imperfect its realization (certainly the case of the Prussian code), expresses "the principles of law in their *universality*, and hence in their determinacy."[104] In so doing, the law expressly and adequately states the type of universality—a universality of the understanding, and not of reason[105]— that social life is capable of. The rule of law (the state of law) is for Hegel what raises civil society to the level of thought and thus shows that it is not merely the moment of scission of the ethical idea but also the formal anticipation of its true reconciliation.

But in order to grasp the full scope of this theory of statute laws, we must be attentive to the logical concepts it deploys. The statute law (*das Gesetz*) is the being-in-itself (*Ansichsein*) of abstract law in a relation of positing (*Setzen*). Positing is one of the processual modalities of essence. Each sphere of the *Logic* (being, essence, concept) is characterized not so much by the specificity of its object—in a way, the object of Hegelian logic is always the same: being in the movement of its rational becoming-explicit, its becoming-concept— as by the processual mode in which this object is apprehended. The logic of being is entirely a logic of passing (*Übergehen*), in which it is always the relation to a given alterity that determines the constitution of categories and their *Aufhebung*. In the sphere of the concept, the process is the free development (*Entwicklung*) of the concept in its moments.[106] The median sphere of essence uses the process of the reflection of the negative within itself: "The negativity of essence is *reflection*, and the determinations are *reflected*—posited by the

104. *RPh*, § 211 Anmerkung, *GW* 14.1, p. 177 (*Elements*, 242; see *Outlines*, 199). Regarding the argument between Thibaut and Savigny over codification and Hegel's support of the former, see chapter 2 above.

105. See *RPh*, § 216 Anmerkung, *GW* 14.1, p. 180 (*Elements*, 248; see *Outlines*, 205): It is a "misapprehension of the difference between the universal of reason and the universal of the understanding" that leads some (Savigny and the Historical School) to refuse the codification of the law on the pretext that it might be imperfect.

106. See *Enzykl*, § 161, *GW* 20, p. 177 (*Encyclopedia* 237): "The progression of the Concept is no longer either passing-over or shining into another, but development."

essence itself in which they remain as sublated."[107] Essence designates being's noncoincidence with self insofar as it makes discourse on being possible. Its determinations help think the inner contradiction by which each thing is what it is, that is, mediately becomes what it immediately is. For Hegel, essence, "*truth of being*,"[108] is something altogether different than a background, an immobile *Hintergrund* that would provide a stable internal foundation for phenomenality, the superficial existence of things. Essence is, and is only, the reflection of being, that is, negativity. The two correlative modalities of this reflexivity are positing (*Setzen*) and presupposing (*Voraussetzen*); essential reflection is simultaneously "positing" and "presupposing":

> The movement, as forward movement, turns immediately around into itself and so is only self-movement — a movement which comes from itself in so far as *positing* reflection is *presupposing* reflection, yet, as *presupposing* reflection, is simply *positing* reflection.[109]

Reflection posits determinateness, categories used in every activity of thought: identity, difference, contradiction, and foundation. But if there is reflection, it is because essence itself "*finds* an immediate *before it* which it transcends and from which it is the turning back."[110] As a result, positing reflection and outside reflection (presupposing) correlate. In the same movement essence posits being as being (thus it is its foundation) and presupposes it as what is to be surpassed (it is its truth or *eidos*). Thenceforth, *being-posited (das Gesetztsein)* designates the properly essential structure of determination, the fact that there is no determinacy, no matter how immediate it might appear, that is not in reality mediated or posited: "In the *sphere of essence, positedness* is what corresponds to existence."[111] But since what posits this being-posited is not a positive movement, like the passage from one determination to another in the sphere of being, but rather pure negativity (the essential reflection of being), the determination of reflection is not a relation to something else but

107. *WdL* 2, *GW* 11, p. 243 (*Science of Logic*, 339).
108. *WdL* 2, *GW* 11, p. 241 (*Science of Logic*, 337).
109. *WdL* 2, *GW* 11, p. 252 (*Science of Logic*, 348).
110. *WdL* 2, *GW* 11, p. 252 (*Science of Logic*, 348).
111. *WdL* 2, *GW* 11, p. 255 (*Science of Logic*, 351).

rather a "negation . . . [equal] with itself"; it "is, therefore, positedness, negation, but as reflection into itself it is at the same time the sublatedness of this
positedness, infinite reference to itself."[112] Of course, outside of the context of
logic, these concepts have a less technical meaning, which does not mean that
they signify less; nevertheless, the status of *Setzen* in the process of essence is
the speculative basis for the argument in the *Philosophy of Right* regarding the
law. Abstract law (in classical terms, natural law) is "the essence" of the statute
law; the statute law is its being-posited, its being-there, or better yet, its phenomenon. But the essence that is abstract law is not a background, an order of
truth hanging in the heavenly realm of ideas that would act as an intelligible
norm for positive legal measures, which are empirically and historically situated. Law, strictly speaking, *is* not; or rather, it only is by adopting the reflexive
(posited) figure of the statute law.

"Posited" as positive statute law, law is no longer a body of general prescriptions regarding property, contracts, and compensation for infractions
in general but rather a concretely universal norm with which complex social
relations, infinitely diverse and always at risk of degenerating into violence,
must comply. In this form, law is the universalizing mode of regulating the
disagreements that run through civil society. Of course, there are several ways
of activating the general interest in the sphere of particular interests: market
regulations, the order guaranteed by the police, the work of corporations. But
what is specific to the statute law is that its work, solemnly *spoken* by a tribunal, gives expression to "the ideas [*Vorstellung*] and consciousness of civil
society."[113] Conversely, positive statute law is not sufficient in itself: it requires
the abstract foundation of the law "in itself" as a general norm of objective
spirit. Thus, it is not, or not just, because a law has been adopted in appropriate
forms that it is valid; it must also conform to what today we would call general legal principles. Does Hegel here share a normativist conception, analogous to the one illustrated by natural law constructions? No, because this "law
in itself" that legal measures express is nothing other than the rational kernel
of positive civil law. The relationship between positive law and abstract rational law thus illustrates the argument made at the beginning of the *Philosophy
of Right*: "Natural law or philosophical law is different from positive law, but
it would be a grave misunderstanding to distort this difference into an oppo-

---

112. *WdL* 2, *GW* 11, p. 257 (*Science of Logic*, 353).
113. *RPh*, § 218 Anmerkung, *GW* 14.1, p. 182 (*Elements*, 250, modified; see *Outlines*, 207).

sition or antagonism."[114] The statute law converts legal abstraction into the actual structuration of the social world. Thus, it constitutes civil society as a *"relative totality"*[115] with specific rules of operation and (partial) independence from the state: that is, as a *state of law.*

In certain respects this understanding of the statute law is close to liberal theories of the *Rechtsstaat.* Unlike the political conception of the statute law illustrated by the maxim "auctoritas, non veritas facit legem,"[116] it emphasizes that legal norms are "universal principles," *"simple* and universal determinations."[117] This universality should be preserved, and the task of applying these laws to particular cases should be left to jurisprudence rather than the statute law trying to foresee everything. In addition, the Hegelian definition of the domain of legislation is similar to that found in *Rechtsstaat* theories: positive statute law establishes rules in the field of private law, and its essential component is the civil and penal code. However, Hegel incorporates family law (inheritances, spousal relations), as well as certain aspects of the life of the state and the organization of legal institutions and procedures into civil law.[118] The domain of legislation thus exceeds private law. Nevertheless, the ultimate goal of statute laws is to ensure that "property and personality have legal recognition and validity in civil society."[119] Hence, the rule of law is nothing other than the lawful constitution (*Rechtsverfassung*) of civil society.

There is, however, a major difference between Hegel's position and that of the *Rechtsstaat* doctrine: according to Hegel, the state has the right to enact social legislation to allow civil society to function according to its own rules — that is, to *actually* be a society of markets and free exchange. This perspective deviates from the liberal program of the *Rechtsstaat* and approaches the later idea of the social state (*Sozialstaat*). The objects of legislative power include setting taxes and establishing "benefits which the state enables [individuals] to enjoy," meaning "the statutes of civil law [*die privatrechtlichen Gesetze*] in general, the rights of communities and corporations, all arrangements of a wholly universal character,"[120] which precisely means social legislation, albeit

114. *RPh,* § 3 Anmerkung, *GW* 14.1, pp. 25–26 (*Elements,* 29; see *Outlines,* 20).

115. *RPh,* § 184, *GW* 14.1, p. 160 (*Elements,* 221; see *Outlines,* 182).

116. Hobbes, *Leviathan,* 2:431 (Latin).

117. *RPh,* § 216, *GW* 14.1, p. 180 (*Elements,* 247; see *Outlines,* 204).

118. See *RPh,* § 213, *GW* 14.1, p. 178 (*Elements,* 244; see *Outlines,* 201–2).

119. *RPh,* § 218, *GW* 14.1, p. 181 (*Elements,* 250; see *Outlines,* 207).

120. *RPh,* § 299, *GW* 14.1, p. 247 (*Elements,* 337; see *Outlines,* 285).

a very rudimentary one in comparison to what, much later, would come with the welfare state. The existence (or possibility) of social *legislation* is surprising at first glance. Indeed, Hegel, who agrees on this point with *Rechtsstaat* theoreticians, considers that legislators need only legislate on "internal concerns of the state whose content is wholly universal";[121] on the other hand, administrative bodies and the government are responsible for "the particular and the ways and means whereby measures are *implemented*."[122] There are two observations to be made here. First, the boundary between legislation and the work of the administration is not drawn precisely. Legislators, in establishing an explicit social law that is "annexed to the law of the state," do no more, says Gurvitch, than sanction a "pure and independent"[123] social law that emerges from social institutions themselves (the rules and operation of corporations); they establish the formal framework of social policy, which is carried out by the administration. Only the most general directions of social policy and decisions relating to principle belong to the field of legislation; Hegel, for example, would have approved of a law making child labor illegal. However, it is the administration that enacts this policy in the form of measures that apply to certain groups. But it is the whole state, and not just a specialized bureaucracy, that must handle the dysfunctions of social and economic life. One example: if colonial expansion is primarily the result of a process that pushes civil society "beyond itself" (a double movement to seize raw materials, labor power, and markets and at the same time to get a handle on the impoverishment of the working classes), it nevertheless takes the form of a state policy.[124] Second observation: legislators themselves are in part emanations of social estates and institutions such as communities and corporations.[125] Because of this social grounding, assemblies are "*mediating* organ[s]" (though in a different sense than government authorities) and provide[126] a connection between political universality and social particularity. Social legislation, just like votes on the budget (which influence social structures by setting the basis for taxes) thus contributes to operating the necessary *political* mediation of civil society. At the same time, although social policy, like finance law, may pass through the

121. *RPh*, § 298, *GW* 14.1, p. 247 (*Elements*, 336; see *Outlines*, 284).
122. *RPh*, § 299 Anmerkung, *GW* 14.1, p. 247 (*Elements*, 337; see *Outlines*, 285).
123. Georges Gurvitch, *L'idée du droit social* (Paris: Sirey, 1931), esp. 153.
124. See *RPh*, §§ 246–48, *GW* 14.1, pp. 195–96 (*Elements*, 267–69; see *Outlines*, 222–23).
125. See *RPh*, §§ 308–11, *GW* 14.1, pp. 254–57 (*Elements*, 346–50; see *Outlines*, 294–97).
126. *RPh*, § 302, *GW* 14.1, p. 250 (*Elements*, 342; see *Outlines*, 289).

law, it is above all a *"government matter."*[127] It comes from the police rather than from legislation.

The Limits of the State of Law

We can see what distinguishes Hegel from liberalism by establishing what separates his understanding of civil society as "state of law" from *Rechtsstaat* theories.[128] We must first emphasize the strict limits that, in Hegel's eyes, the formalism of the rule of law and legal procedures entails. To a large extent, this formalism does no more than transcribe the formalism of abstract law itself. It echoes the conversion of law in itself, which is formal because it is abstract,[129] into socially actualized statute law. As a consequence, the latter has a limit that cannot be exceeded, the limit of a "state of law" reduced to its fundamental structure. At the same time, there is an insufficiency not in law itself (the abstraction of abstract law has positive content) but in its context of actualization. The formalism of the legal order stems from the properties of its field of actualization: civil society, the "abstract moment of the *reality* of the Idea, which is present here only as the *relative totality* and *inner necessity* of this external *appearance.*"[130]

Within civil society, no matter how rigorous the law is in its abstract universality, it must apply to "relationships . . . in their endlessly increasing diversity and complexity."[131] Therefore, tribunals must maintain a significant power of interpretation in order to properly apply the statute law; "it thereby enters the sphere of the *quantitative*, which is not determined by the concept."[132] This is one of the reasons why civil law cannot achieve definitive rationality; it "is primarily a product of its time and of the current condition of civil society."[133] However, the fundamental limit of the state of law is that it merely enacts *pri-*

127. See *Enzykl*, § 544 Anmerkung, *GW* 20, pp. 520–22 (*Encyclopedia* 244).

128. The diagnosis of Hegelian "antiliberalism" has been discussed in detail by Losurdo in *Hegel e la libertà dei Moderni*.

129. See *Enzykl*, § 487, *GW* 20, p. 481 (*Encyclopedia* 219): "*Law* as such is *formal, abstract* law."

130. *RPh*, § 184, *GW* 14.1, p. 160 (*Elements*, 221; see *Outlines*, 182).

131. *RPh*, § 213, *GW* 14.1, p. 178 (*Elements*, 244; see *Outlines*, 202).

132. See *RPh*, § 214, *GW* 14.1, p. 178 (*Elements*, 245; see *Outlines*, 202).

133. *RPh*, § 218 Anmerkung, *GW* 14.1, p. 182 (*Elements*, 251; see *Outlines*, 207). It is a "German affliction" to demand of legislation a perfection of which private law is incapable (*RPh*, § 216 Anmerkung, *GW* 14.1, p. 180 [*Elements*, 248; see *Outlines*, 205]).

vate law through *civil* society. As we know, civil society is the moment of ethicality's exteriority to itself, the moment of the merely external conjunction of the particular and the universal; it is based on the separation of needs, aspirations, and particular interests on the one hand and on the formal universality of economic regulations and legal procedures on the other.[134] Thus, it lends itself to a differentiated — and, in actual fact, differentiating — actualization of the universal legal and abstract norm.

The system of production and trade requires that civil society be structured by law. This system includes a dynamic whose socializing function (it makes social actors, who are rational egoists, dependent on one another) and desocializing effects (it creates inequality and social marginalization) must both be taken into account. The system of needs, thanks to its organization of production, which is all the more refined for not being planned, tends to ensure the satisfaction of the often-contradictory expectations of economic actors and of needs that, multiplied by the system of production, have but a distant relation to "nature." The satisfaction of these needs, amplified by the vertigo of *"representational thought [Vorstellung],"*[135] implies the dependence of each on each and on all. An invisible, virtual hand continuously adjusts how needs are satisfied and thus transforms them, but it also engenders undeserved inequalities that are perceived as unjust and that the law has neither the vocation nor the power to correct. The system of needs is structurally inegalitarian: *"inequalities in the resources and skills* of individuals" are the necessary consequence of its logic.[136] The dynamics of the system of production and resource allocation are thus full of conflicts that are even more disquieting because to solve them might require going beyond the resources of society, the legal order, and perhaps even the state — this issue will be addressed in the following chapter. However that may be, the competition between individuals (with all that it entails in terms of alienation and injustice for the poor but also in terms of what is positive regarding economic rationality and social productivity) takes place along the virtual axis of a class war or a "worldwide civil war"[137] that would certainly have very little to do with a state of law.

---

134. See *RPh*, §§ 182–184, *GW* 14.1, p. 160 (*Elements*, 220–21; see *Outlines*, 180–82).

135. *RPh*, § 194, *GW* 14.1, p. 167 (*Elements*, 230; see *Outlines*, 189).

136. *RPh*, § 200, *GW* 14.1, pp. 169–70 (*Elements*, 233; see *Outlines*, 192).

137. See Carl Schmitt, "Die Einheit der Welt" in Schmitt, *Frieden oder Pazifismus?* (Berlin: Duncker und Humblot, 2005), 841–52.

The state of law reduced to its essential feature is respect for fundamental subjective rights (especially freedom rights) under the guarantee of civil statute laws. As diverse as its characteristics are, they are made coherent by the structural link it has to bourgeois civil society insofar as it has (partially) detached itself from the state during a recent phase in modern history. This state of law is thus principally *apolitical*. From this we can understand Hegel's nuanced assessment of it and his reservations concerning the liberal dogma that grants it absolute value. This state of law, just like civil society itself, has the value of a *moment* in the process that is *Sittlichkeit*. It thereby has necessity and legitimacy, but it cannot be made absolute without its own principle of actualization being weakened at the same time. For, if the rights of the "bourgeois" are made absolute, not only is the political existence of cocitizenship weakened but so is society itself. If, as in the libertarian dream, the political dimension of the social bond could be eliminated, civil society would head toward self-destruction and social anarchy would end in political violence.

➔ 6 ⬅

"Ethicality Lost in Its Extremes"

In his preface to the volume of the *Jubiläumsausgabe* that included the first edition of the *Encyclopedia* (1817), Hermann Glockner notes that the parts of that work that underwent the most changes in the later two editions were the middle sections, sites of mediations par excellence: these are the sections on the philosophy of nature, the logic of essence, and the doctrine of objective spirit.[1] Glockner's statement has merely informative value and cannot be confirmed down to the last detail. In terms of objective spirit, it was the presentation of *Sittlichkeit* that most significantly changed. The most remarkable of these changes—one that we now know was made during the year the first *Encyclopedia* was published, in the 1817–1818 course on "Natural Law and Science of the State"—was Hegel's introduction of the distinction between family, civil society, and the state, which implies moving away from the dualism characteristic of both the Aristotelian perspective (the separation between the *oikos* and the *polis*) and the perspective of modern natural law (the separation between the state of nature and the state of society).[2] Certainly, the most remarkable aspect of this change was Hegel's redefini-

1. *SW*, 6:xxxv–xxxvi.
2. See above, preliminary to part 2.

tion of the classical concept of *bürgerliche Gesellschaft*, still present in the first edition of the *Encyclopedia*, which very classically contrasts the "fiction" of the state of nature with "the state constituted by society and the State" and maintains that "society, by contrast, is the condition in which only the law has reality";[3] here, society must be understood as the state of society, *political* society, and not what would later be called "civil society." This reworking confirms Glockner's assessment: indeed, within *Sittlichkeit*, civil society is "the sphere of mediation"[4] and consequently a critical space, a center of tensions. Surprisingly, this remark, which came from Hegel's course at the Nuremberg gymnasium,[5] was left unchanged in a short addition included in later editions, where the term *Gesellschaft* has a completely different meaning.[6] In the present chapter, the gradual formation of the concept of civil society and the distinction between civil society and the state will serve as my guiding thread for analyzing the changes made to the doctrine of *Sittlichkeit* and the structural difficulties that doctrine involves — difficulties of which Hegel seems to have become aware only gradually.

From Objective Spirit to *Sittlichkeit*

The very notion of *objective* spirit shows how different Hegel's concept of spirit is from common conceptions of it as well as from earlier philosophical understandings. The notion is already tacitly present in the *Phenomenology of Spirit*, in particular in chapter 6, where the figures of spirit are presented as "shapes of a world"[7] in contrast to consciousness, self-consciousness, and reason and where spirit itself is defined as an "ethical substance" in which consciousness "opposes to itself as an objective, actual world."[8] However, the expression itself first appeared in the Heidelberg *Encyclopedia*. In that text, the definition of objective spirit is succinct: subjective spirit, arriving at consciousness of what constitutes its determination (i.e., freedom willing itself), opens itself

---

3. *Enzykl* 1817, § 415 Anmerkung, *GW* 13, p. 228 (*Encyclopedia 1817*, 245).

4. Hegel, *Vorlesungen über Naturrecht und Staatswissenschaft*, 113; Hegel, *Lectures on Natural Right*, §89A, 162.

5. See *Propädeutik*, *W* 4, p. 247.

6. See *Enzykl*, § 502 Anmerkung, *GW* 20, p. 488 (*Encyclopedia* 223).

7. *PhG*, *GW* 9, p. 240 (*Phenomenology*, ¶ 441).

8. *PhG*, *GW* 9, p. 238 (*Phenomenology*, ¶ 439).

up to the necessity—implied by the concept of freedom as being at home with oneself in the other—of self-relinquishment, of alienation within an objectivity that at first appears to be a purely contingent given. This requirement that subjectivity be expressed in otherness, which is speculatively grounded in the *Logic*, is inseparable from the understanding of dialectics that from 1800 onward organized Hegelian philosophy. In the *Encyclopedia*, it is expressed above all in relation to *Sittlichkeit*.

Beginning with the *Philosophy of Right* (in fact, beginning with the 1817–1818 course), objectivization becomes the distinctive characteristic of spirit in general and practical spirit in particular: spirit's freedom is measured by its aptitude to "remain *with itself* in this objectivity."[9] Freedom, the generic determination of spirit, thus receives "the *form of necessity*."[10] If we recall that the transition from objective logic (being and essence) to subjective logic (concept) is presented as an *Aufhebung* of necessity into freedom, then we get a sense of the dramatic change implied by the concept of objective spirit. It seems to reverse the decisive logical argument that freedom is "the *truth of necessity*."[11] But this is only in appearance. Indeed, in the *Logic*, the *Aufhebung* of necessity—a category that encapsulates the entire process of the "objective" logic of being and essence—by freedom, which characterizes the "subjective" dynamism of the concept, only takes on its full meaning (suppressing while maintaining, surpassing while conserving) when the concept recreates in itself the dimension of objectivity and necessity without which it would be "merely subjective"—subjective in a trivial sense. The shift from subjective concept to objectivity and from logic to nature—and thus, the conversion of freedom into necessity—is therefore decisive proof of the freedom of the concept. The *Encyclopedia*'s "Philosophy of Spirit" repeats the chiasmic organization of the logic of the concept, ballasting it with the weight of actuality. Indeed, the doctrine of objective spirit reproduces and reverses the general organization of the philosophy of spirit. There, the sequence subjective spirit–objective spirit–absolute (subjective-objective) spirit is reversed, and the sequence runs objectivity (abstract law)–subjectivity (morality)–subject-

9. *RPh*, § 28, *GW* 14.1, p. 45 (*Elements*, 57; see *Outlines*, 46).

10. *Enzykl*, § 484, *GW* 20, p. 478 (*Encyclopedia* 217).

11. See *WdL* 3, *GW* 12, p. 12 (*Science of Logic*, 509): "*freedom* reveals itself to be the *truth of necessity* and the *relational mode of the concept*." Cf. *WdL* 3, *GW* 12, p. 14; *Enzykl*, §§ 158, 159 Anmerkung, *GW* 20, pp. 174–76.

objectivity (*Sittlichkeit*). From this we see, at least at the formal level, the need for the theory of objective spirit to include a theory of moral subjectivity quite different from the doctrine of subjective spirit.[12] In general, the Hegelian system both as a whole and in its parts is based on a truly unprecedented organization of subjectivity and objectivity, an organization that requires deep changes to be made to these notions.

Before 1830, the presentation of objective spirit underwent significant modifications. For example, in order to explain the claim, which is crucial for understanding *Sittlichkeit*, that "Freedom, shaped into the actuality of a world, acquires the form of necessity,"[13] the final edition of the *Encyclopedia* includes an extra paragraph that develops and alters the end of section 485 from the earlier edition. The earlier version read

> The rational will is not only in itself, nor internal, nor simply what is immediately natural, but rather its content is known and valid only as positive law and custom within the spiritual.[14]

The gist of the argument is clear. Objective spirit is freedom developed into a world, but this objective world is a *spiritual* world, which overcomes the abstract contradiction between subjectivity apprehended through the categories of reflection and objectivity conceived in terms of natural immediacy. However, by putting "positive laws" (which, posited by the will of an authority, connote exteriority) and customs (which add the sanction of lived—though not subjective or individual—adherence) on the same level, the 1827 text erases or at least attenuates the characteristic tension within objective spirit between the positive or implicit rules of the *system* of ethicality and the way in which these rules are *lived* by subjects and incorporated and validated in practices.

Paragraph 485, added to the 1830 edition, clarifies the difference between law and custom. The determinations of objective spirit are manifested "in the form of necessity," a "unity of the rational will with the particular will"; the latter is "the immediate and peculiar element of the operation of the rational will." But their content may appear to consciousness as either a "valid power" or as "impressed on the subjective will, not in the form of feeling and urge,

---

12. See chapter 10 below.

13. *Enzykl*, § 484, *GW* 20, p. 478 (*Encyclopedia* 217).

14. *Enzykl* 1827, § 485, *GW* 19, p. 353.

but in its universality, as the will's habit, disposition and character ... custom."
In the first case, objective spirit takes on the externally rational form of *law*;
in the second, the form of *ethical custom* (*Sitte*), the objective incorporation
of the rational into sensible (*sensées*) practices.[15] The tension between subjectivity and objectivity that characterizes objective spirit is expressed in the
possibility that individual and collective behaviors might not fit the universal pronounced by the law or that the law might not be internalized and lived
positively by individuals. The concept of *Sittlichkeit* explicitly addresses this
tension. Even when the "laws and powers" of *Sittlichkeit* are accepted by subjectivity, they compel it to give up its claim to complete autonomy, for "ethical
substance" has "absolute authority and power" over subjectivity.[16] The ethical subject (human, bourgeois, citizen) must give up his or her spontaneous
(and illusory) representation of freedom or free will, a representation that is
expressed in the language of morality.

The 1830 *Encyclopedia* explains the double subjective and objective dimension of objective spirit in terms that in the *Philosophy of Right* apply to *Sittlichkeit* alone. In 1820, Hegel defined *Sittlichkeit* as "*the concept of freedom which
has become the existing world and the nature of self-consciousness*"[17]; ethicality
unites and reconstructs the objective formalism of law and the subjective formalism of moral consciousness. But this unity, while overcoming the abstract
opposition between the two, does not abolish "consciousness of the difference of these moments"[18]—the difference between the universal concept of
free will and its particular concrete existence. Ethicality is first and foremost
a world of objectivity whose determinations form a "circle of necessity." But
individuals are not mere passive "accidents" of this substance; the system of
objective determinations that comprises *Sittlichkeit* is a *lived* world that has
actuality only if it is an "object of knowledge"[19] or at least of belief for individuals. Unlike the laws of physical nature, the laws of ethical nature have
validity only through "representation": their validity is based on individuals'
knowledge and recognition of them:

---

15. *Enzykl*, § 485, *GW* 20, p. 479 (*Encyclopedia* 217).
16. *RPh*, § 146, *GW* 14.1, p. 138 (*Elements*, 190; see *Outlines*, 155).
17. *RPh*, § 142, *GW* 14.1, p. 137 (*Elements*, 189; see *Outlines*, 154).
18. *RPh*, § 143, *GW* 14.1, p. 137 (*Elements*, 189; see *Outlines*, 154).
19. *RPh*, § 146, *GW* 14.1, p. 138 (*Elements*, 190; see *Outlines*, 155).

The fact that the ethical sphere is the *system* of these determinations of the Idea constitutes its *rationality*. In this way, the ethical sphere is freedom, or the will which has being in and for itself as objectivity, as a circle of necessity whose moments are the *ethical powers* which govern the lives of individuals. In these individuals—who are accidental to them—these powers have their representation [*Vorstellung*], phenomenal shape [*erscheinende Gestalt*], and actuality.[20]

Thus, the subject's relation to the objective structures of the ethical world reproduces the double aspect of this world. On the one hand, "the ethical substance, its laws and powers," are and appear to individuals to be completely out of reach; in this regard, their authority is "infinitely more firmly based than the being of nature."[21] On the other hand, the power of ethical objectivity also implies that the subject finds "self-awareness [*Selbstgefühl*]" in it and recognizes his or her own essence in it. Objectivity is only *ethical* to the extent that it is not something "*distinct* [from the subject]" and expresses "the actual living principle of self-consciousness."[22] Thus, individuals' relation to the conditions and norms of their action, which is still external when it takes the form of a legal or moral obligation, is fully internalized when it becomes *Sitte*. Ethical custom, as a "general mode of behavior,"[23] as a practice objectively based on the universal, manifests subjects' adherence to the universality that constitutes them. Consequently, it is *Sittlichkeit*, more than morality—or anyway more clearly than morality—that reveals the decisive role of *subjectivity* within objective spirit: objective spirit is not only the "ground in which the concept of freedom has its concrete existence [*Existenz*]," it is the mode of "existence of the concept which is adequate to it."[24] Objective spirit only conforms to its concept—which is to be "a *world* produced and to be produced by it; in this world freedom is present as necessity"[25]—if particular subjectivity actualizes and verifies such a conversion. But this can only happen if, unlike moral consciousness, which is still plagued by the vertigo of radical autonomy, ethical

20. *RPh*, § 145, *GW* 14.1, pp. 137–38 (*Elements*, 190; see *Outlines*, 154–55).
21. *RPh*, § 146, *GW* 14.1, p. 138 (*Elements*, 190; see *Outlines*, 155).
22. *RPh*, § 147 and Anmerkung, *GW* 14.1, p. 138 (*Elements*, 191; see *Outlines*, 155–56).
23. *RPh*, § 151, *GW* 14.1, p. 141 (*Elements*, 195; see *Outlines*, 159).
24. *RPh*, § 152 Anmerkung, *GW* 14.1, p. 142 (*Elements*, 196; see *Outlines*, 160).
25. *Enzykl*, § 385, *GW* 20, p. 383 (*Encyclopedia* 20).

subjectivity recognizes the primacy of the universal-objective norm and accepts that its own aspirations be relativized. In objective spirit, the normative content to which subjectivity gives actuality by adhering to it is not *first* posited by this adherence: that content is the substance of that subjectivity, but as substance it is always presupposed by its action. Ethicality, which is "*second nature*,"[26] is of course radically different from external nature, for it is freedom expressing itself in the forms of necessity, not the blind reign of necessity. Nevertheless, as it is spontaneously perceived, it is still *nature*: it speaks the language of necessity.[27]

We must not be too surprised by the fact that in the 1830 *Encyclopedia* the definition of objective spirit corresponds to the definition of ethicality in the *Philosophy of Right*. Ethicality is not a part of objective spirit, juxtaposed to law and morality. Only ethicality, "self-conscious *freedom* become nature,"[28] corresponds completely to the definition of objective spirit by carrying out, in the realm of objectivity, the reconciliation between the unilateral objectivity of law and the unilateral subjectivity of morality.

The Concept of *Sittlichkeit* and Its Modifications

Hegel's development of the concept of objective spirit completed his efforts, begun in 1803–1804, to "reconcile himself with the times" by conceptualizing the modern world in its specificity: the world of the Reform, the market economy, and the French Revolution. There were two aspects to this development, which was directly linked to his rejection of the model of the *polis*.

The notion of objective spirit gives speculative ground to the efforts Hegel had been making since Jena and even since Frankfurt to break with the framework of modern practical philosophy and natural law, whose "empirical" version (Hobbes, Grotius, Locke, Rousseau) as well as its "formalist" version (Kant-Fichte) the 1802 article mercilessly deconstructs. But, unlike the path Hegel took in the earliest Jena writings, the notion of objective spirit does not imply a rehabilitation of the classical, finalist, and naturalist conception

---

26. *RPh*, § 151, *GW* 14.1, p. 141 (*Elements*, 195; see *Outlines*, 159). This same expression, which clearly comes from Aristotle, is used to refer to the sphere of the law or objective spirit in general: see *RPh*, § 4, *GW* 14.1, p. 31 (*Elements*, 35; see *Outlines*, 26).

27. We are here at the heart of the debate over the degree of autonomy that Hegelian institutionalism recognizes in the individual; see chapter 12 below.

28. *Enzykl*, § 513, *GW* 20, p. 495 (*Encyclopedia* 228).

of ethical-political life, for that conception was definitively rendered null and void by Christianity's affirmation of the principle of autonomy and, more generally, by the "higher principle of modern times, that the ancients, like Plato, did not know."[29] The problematic of objective spirit is the means by which Hegel is able to overcome the antithesis confronting modern thought between nature and freedom (or—though this is just a variation of the same—between natural freedom and rational freedom).

From a point of view internal to the system, the distinction between subjective spirit and objective spirit clears space for the Hegelian conception of *absolute* spirit; we may even say that it necessarily calls for it. Of course, the Hegelian conception of absolute spirit had already been defined, but it posed many problems when one takes account of the systematic program presented in the preface to the *Phenomenology of Spirit*: to rise from the point of view of *"substance"* to that of *"subject."*[30] In truth, it is the unprecedented concept of subjectivity used by the logic of the concept that shows the path to resolution: this resolution is now no longer a property of the particular subject but first and foremost of the concept developing in a manner immanent to its determinations within an element of objectivity constituted by it. The world that is objective spirit can then be understood as "the system of determinations of freedom," although—or rather because—with objective spirit freedom "receives the *form of necessity.*"[31] And, so that this objectivity does not remain abstractly contraposed to subjectivity—as it does in the Kantian or Fichtean perspective that opposes law and morality (or law and ethics)—it receives the guarantee of *absolute* spirit, whose concept puts the true affirmation of freedom in scission and negativity:

> For this reason, formally the *essence* of spirit is *freedom*, absolute negativity of the concept as identity with itself. In accordance with this formal determination, spirit *can* abstract from everything external and from its own externality, from its very existence [*Dasein*]; it can endure the negation of its individual immediacy, infinite *pain*, i.e. it maintains itself affirmatively in this negativity and is identical for itself.[32]

29. *GW* 8, p. 263.
30. *PhG, GW* 9, p. 18 (*Phenomenology*, ¶ 17).
31. *Enzykl*, § 484, *GW* 20, p. 478 (*Encyclopedia* 217).
32. *Enzykl*, § 382, *GW* 20, p. 382 (*Encyclopedia* 215, modified).

It is therefore appropriate to examine the forms that, within objective spirit, the overcoming or sublating (*Aufhebung*) of the opposition between nature and freedom takes insofar as this opposition can be regarded as final.[33]

In the Jena texts, despite many indications that the concept had evolved, the reference point for *Sittlichkeit* remains the Greek *polis*, or at least Hegel's representation of it. The distinctive trait of the "kingdom of ethicality" is that "each one is *custom*, immediately one with the universal."[34] This *immediate* unity of the universal and the particular corresponds to a narrowly political understanding of ethicality: following a tradition established in the first book of Aristotle's *Politics*, Hegel bases his conception of ethicality on the traditional divide between economics and politics, between the *oikos* and the *polis* (or *societas civilis*). The expulsion of activities of production and exchange from the ethical-political sphere is explicit in the article on natural law, which denounces the "political nullity" of the bourgeois;[35] it is less explicit in the *System of Ethicality*,[36] where we still find what Hyppolite called a "heroic conception of freedom."[37] According to such a view, war is the eminent, and even exclusive, form of the *politeueien*.

This political and war-based vision of ethicality is still dominant in the *Phenomenology of Spirit*, chapter 5 of which paints an enthusiastic picture of such communion with the universal, the self-forgetting that comprises *Sittlichkeit*.[38] However, Hegel was already convinced that the model of the *polis* was outdated, but he continued to see it as the eminent form of ethicality. The 1805–1806 *Philosophy of Spirit* offers a striking example of this attitude, but it also points to the way out of these ambiguities. On the one hand, in an already nostalgic mode, it evokes the *Sittlichkeit* of antiquity, where "the beautiful public life was the custom of all"; on the other hand, one line further, it contrasts, for the first time, this model with the "*the higher principle of modern times*,"

---

33. See Manfred Riedel, "Freiheitsgesetz und Herrschaft der Natur," in Riedel, *Zwischen Tradition und Revolution*, 65–84.

34. *GW* 8, p. 262.

35. See *Naturrecht, W* 2, p. 495 (*Natural Law* 103). This entire passage emphasizes the connection between ethicality, nobility, and war.

36. In this text, in fact, the state of rectitude (the "bourgeois" state of artisans and merchants) is recognized as having "*relative ethicality*" while remaining strictly subordinate to the absolute state, the only truly political state. See *SS, GW* 5, p. 331.

37. Jean Hyppolite, *Introduction à la philosophie de l'histoire de Hegel* (Paris: Éditions du Seuil, 1983), 94.

38. See *PhG, GW* 9, pp. 194–96 (*Phenomenology*, ¶¶ 349–53).

which requires a differentiation, if not a dislocation, of the compact unity of each with all and with the whole.[39] Even more explicitly, chapter 6 of the *Phenomenology of Spirit* establishes the need to break with this still overly compact figure of "the true spirit" — *immediately* true — that the unsophisticated ethics of the *polis* embodies. This ethics must protect itself against any risk of division, and the quest for private happiness represents a major one; because it is based on the repression of individuality, this ethics cannot withstand the affirmation of individuality, including such politically innocent forms as Antigone's. In Sophocles' play, the analysis of the conflict between human law and divine law shows the contradiction that undermines a community that "can only maintain itself by suppressing this spirit of individualism."[40] From the moment this spirit of particularity occurs — and it does so, significantly, in a woman who, in the strongest and most tragic sense, embodies "the everlasting irony of the community" — the collision offers the comic or lamentable spectacle of an "absolute which is opposed to itself,"[41] divided by a scission it cannot survive. The ancient figure of the "beautiful totality" is thus not factually but rather essentially over and done with because of its denegation of the scissions and contradictions that are the wellspring of all life. No matter how painful, the "working one's way out of the immediacy of substantial life"[42] is unavoidable. In addition, it is fecund, for "it [spirit] only wins its truth . . . within its absolute disruption,"[43] that is, in fully experiencing the trial of its own negativity. The *speculative* reason for abandoning the model of the *polis* and the conception of ethicality it leads to is thus that model's inadequacy to the concept of spirit developed, notably, in the *Phenomenology of Spirit*. But this reason can only be given retrospectively, once Hegelianism reaches its full expression in the *Logic* and the *Encyclopedia*.

First of all, the principle of subjective autonomy, which Christianity proclaimed[44] but which was already present in Socrates,[45] shows the fragility of the substantial ethicality of the *polis*. Socrates destabilized the city, and a Christian destabilized the empire quite simply because, even without contest-

---

39. *GW* 8, p. 263.
40. *PhG, GW* 9, p. 259 (*Phenomenology,* ¶ 474).
41. *PhG, GW* 9, p. 252 (*Phenomenology,* ¶ 464).
42. *PhG, GW* 9, p. 11 (*Phenomenology,* ¶ 4).
43. *PhG, GW* 9, p. 27 (*Phenomenology,* ¶ 32).
44. See *RPh,* § 124 Anmerkung, *GW* 14.1, p. 110 (*Elements,* 151; see *Outlines,* 122).
45. See *RPh,* § 138 Anmerkung, *GW* 14.1, p. 121 (*Elements,* 166; see *Outlines,* 134).

ing the ends proclaimed by city or empire (Socrates was an exemplary soldier), they recognized *other* ends. No matter how contestable some forms of subjective freedom may be (e.g., the moral view of the world, or the figure of the beautiful soul, wallowing in its "solitary divine service"), it can no longer be ignored or repressed, so much so that for moderns, subjective freedom is the same as freedom "in the European sense [of the word]."[46]

The second reason for giving up the model of the *polis* lies in Hegel's critique of the French Revolution—not its principle, of course, which is the principle of political modernity itself, that is, "objective" freedom, but rather the deviation implied by unilaterally affirming this freedom. Indeed, the ideal of absolute freedom appears as an actualization of the ideal of an undivided ethical community and thus of the paradigm of the beautiful totality. But it does this within the conditions of modernity—whose recognition of an inalienable right to privacy is an essential characteristic—and this makes the revolutionary actualization of this paradigm far more formidable for individuals who can no longer *believe* in it wholeheartedly than it ever could have been within the universe of antiquity's more simple certainties.

The third reason is that the elucidation of the logic of the system of needs (the market economy or the "extended order" in Hayek's sense) by Anglo-Saxon authors convinced Hegel that the closed model of the *oikos*, the counterpart to that of the *polis*, was outmoded (in fact this outmodedness was already old: it dates back to the constitution of "world-economies"[47]). The Jena texts expose the dissonance between the logic of the system of needs (the logic of the division of labor, mechanized and parceled out, and of commercial trade) and the belief in an exclusively political constitution of the common good. From then on, the focus is on giving place to the abstract universality of economic regulation while maintaining the primacy of the concrete (political) universal. By positing in 1805 that "the same individual" is both "bourgeois" and "citizen,"[48] Hegel makes an observation that requires developing a differentiated concept of *Sittlichkeit*, making room for its nondirectly political dimensions. That concept, the crowning piece of the doctrine of objective spirit, emerges from the

46. *Enzykl,* § 503 Anmerkung, *GW* 20, p. 489 (*Encyclopedia* 224).

47. See Fernand Braudel, *Civilization and Capitalism 15th–18th Century,* vol. 1, *The Structures of Everyday Life* (New York: Harper Collins, 1985). See also Fernand Braudel, *La dynamique du capitalisme* (Paris: Arthaud, 1985), 84–89.

48. *GW* 8, p. 261. See chapter 4 above.

deeper understanding of the historical and dialectic nature of spirit developed in chapter 6 of the *Phenomenology of Spirit*. This is also what allows Hegel to systematically articulate the reasons—present but not coordinated in the Jena writings—that make it necessary to renounce the paradigm of the *polis*.

The new concept of *Sittlichkeit* developed in Hegel's mature writings implies that the sphere of objective spirit, which is marked by the separation between unilateral subjectivity and equally unilateral objectivity, finds *in itself* (and no longer, as in the *Phenomenology of Spirit*, in the higher spheres of religion and absolute knowing) the resources for an authentic reconciliation. It is not a matter of making objective spirit a world closed on itself, for the very concept of spirit excludes this possibility. Instead, it is a matter of teasing out the possible conditions for an *immanent* surpassing of the contradiction specific to finite spirit. In the *Phenomenology of Spirit*, spirit, certain of itself and having reached the end of its process—that is, having been historically actualized as world—does not possess the "strength to alienate" the knowledge it has of itself as "beautiful soul":[49] thus, the authentic reconciliation of its self-consciousness and consciousness is located beyond its own sphere. On the other hand, in the *Encyclopedia* and the *Philosophy of Right*, ethicality performs the objective *Aufhebung* of the scission between subjectivity and objectivity that affects objective spirit and even finite spirit in general. Indeed, ethicality is objectivity as lived by particular subjects whose identity is constituted by their living relationship to this objective totality; inversely, this totality only exists through their actions and internal dispositions.[50] From this it results that ethicality actually *coincides* with objective spirit in its totality even though conceptually the objective and subjective dimensions it includes still appear to be separate. In reality, law and morality are not so much separate parts or components of objective spirit as they are its *moments*: they are consistent only if they are articulated within the concrete unity of *Sittlichkeit*—this is why Hegel calls both of them abstract. From a systematic point of view, the third moment of a process is never the sum of the two previous ones (even if it is understood as a surpassing) but is rather the actual totality—in reality, primary—from which they result through a kind of operation of ideal decomposition. Of course, law and morality are not beings of reason! But they are *abstract* insofar as achieving their concept presupposes concepts foreign to their

49. *PhG, GW* 9, p. 360 (*Phenomenology,* ¶ 668).
50. See *Enzykl,* §§ 514–15, *GW* 20, p. 495 (*Encyclopedia* 228).

own principle: the actualization of the law is not only legal, and achieving the aim of morality requires that ethical objectivity be recognized in the norms that subjectivity claims to give itself by itself. Objective spirit, in the form of these two abstract moments, is thus unilateral. This unilateralism consists in "having its freedom immediately in reality, therefore in the external, the thing, partly in having it in the good as an abstract universal."[51] Because ethicality is both subjective and objective, it overcomes this unilateral separation, but that does not mean that the characteristic traits of legal normativity (the relationship of a legal person to the thing he or she owns) and of moral normativity (the relationship of a subject to a norm when acting) disappear there. To the contrary, it is there that they receive the guarantee of their actuality.[52]

Unlike abstract law and morality, *Sittlichkeit* overcomes the division between *Sein* and *Sollen*: the actuality of the Good resides in the world, which is instituted and transformed by the actions of subjects. The Good has no essence distinct from the process of its objective actualization, and this takes place in the concrete behavior of subjects who, recognizing this preestablished though not transcendental horizon, choose the ethical-political "living Good" as the norm of their practices rather than the abstract Good of morality. Thus in principle ethicality resolves the contradictions of morality by making objectivity the immanent presupposition of subjects' actions rather than an ideal perspective: the *"existing world,"* which itself is the work of freedom becoming objective is, at the same time, the "nature of self-consciousness."[53] This ethical solution of course requires giving up any particular subjectivity's illusory claim to radical autonomy, but it does not replace this claim with ethical objectivism or naturalism, as if norms were things present before it. If ethicality is "the completion of objective spirit, the truth of subjective and objective spirit itself,"[54] this is because within it, subjectivity, just like objectivity, receives an inalienable albeit circumscribed right.[55] This explains the importance of subjective disposition (*Gesinnung*) in this sphere—that is, the relationship, subjectively lived and simultaneously objectivized in regulated behaviors (cus-

51. *Enzykl*, § 513, *GW* 20, p. 494 (*Encyclopedia* 228).

52. Regarding law, see *RPh*, §§ 208, 217, *GW* 14.1, pp. 174, 181 (*Elements*, 239, 249; see Outlines, 197, 206); regarding morality, *RPh*, §§ 207, 242, *GW* 14.1, pp. 174, 193 (*Elements*, 238–39, 265; see *Outlines*, 197, 220).

53. *RPh*, §§ 207, 242, *GW* 14.1, pp. 174, 193 (*Elements*, 238–39, 265; see *Outlines*, 197, 220).

54. *Enzykl*, § 513, *GW* 20, p. 494 (*Encyclopedia* 228).

55. See part 4 below.

toms, mores), between individuals and the objective universality that they find already there but that they continually actualize by their actions:

> The *ethical* is a subjective disposition, but of that law which has being in itself. . . . Law and the moral self-consciousness can be seen in themselves to return to this Idea as their own *result*.[56]

Thus, there are specific subjective attitudes for each type of objective universality put into play by ethicality: Hegel gives these dispositions the general name of *Tugend* (virtue) or *Rechtschaffenheit* (rectitude).[57] Within the family, ethical virtue takes the form of love;[58] in civil society, it takes the form of honor attached to estate (*Standesehre*), which is embodied in the spirit of corporation;[59] and finally, in the state, it takes the form of political disposition (*politische Gesinnung*), which is the true meaning of what is called patriotism.[60] Liberated from the false absoluteness of moral consciousness, individuals' subjective dispositions are integral parts of the ethical sphere, although the objectivity of structures—familial, social, and political institutions—plays a determining role. In fact, these institutions draw their strength from individuals' subjective determinations, which guarantee *"the rooting of the particular in the universal."*[61]

Civil Society as an Objective Answer to the Problem of Mediating the Subjective and the Objective

The Hegelian conception of ethicality must satisfy two requirements that at first glance appear contradictory. First, it gives full weight to the objective components of spirit. *Sittlichkeit* is the *"existing world,"*[62] a "substance";[63] its objec-

---

56. *RPh*, § 141 Anmerkung, *GW* 14.1, pp. 135–36 (*Elements*, 186, modified; see *Outlines*, 152).

57. See *RPh*, § 150 A, § 252, *GW* 14.1, pp. 140–41, 197 (*Elements*, 193–94, 270–71; see *Outlines*, 157–59). See also *Enzykl*, § 527, *GW* 20, pp. 499–500 (*Encyclopedia* 231).

58. *RPh*, § 158, *GW* 14.1, p. 144 (*Elements*, 199; see *Outlines*, 162).

59. *RPh*, §§ 207, 253 A, 289 Anmerkung, *GW* 14.1, pp. 173, 198, 242 (*Elements*, 238, 272, 329–30; see *Outlines*, 196–97, 225–26, 278–79).

60. *RPh*, §§ 267–68, *GW* 14.1, pp. 211–12 (*Elements*, 288–89; see *Outlines*, 240–41). See chapter 11 below.

61. *RPh*, § 289 Anmerkung, *GW* 14.1, p. 242 (*Elements*, 330; see *Outlines*, 279).

62. *RPh*, § 142, *GW* 14.1, p. 137 (*Elements*, 189; see *Outlines*, 154).

63. *RPh*, §§ 144, 152, *GW* 14.1, pp. 137, 141–42 (*Elements*, 189, 195–96; see *Outlines*, 154, 160).

tivity differs from that of law, which merely spells out the abstract or formal conditions of free personality. *Sittlichkeit* (an idea now congruent with that of modernity) appears as a world that is in a sense inaccessible to the action of individuals and independent of their representations: a quasi nature. But second, this quasi naturalness of ethicality allows individuals to affirm their subjectivity without that attempt being hollow, as in the perversions of moral discourse that Hegel so forcefully denounces. Ethicality allows particular subjectivity to be fully itself and at the same time to understand that in its very self-affirmation it is subjected to the objectivized and universalized figure of its own freedom. Thus, ethical freedom is only *concretely* objective freedom because of the activity of subjective individuality, when this individuality "lives [in ethical objectivity] as in its element which is not distinct from itself" and in it finds "its *self-awareness* [*Selbstgefühl*]."[64]

Whereas up until the Jena period the paradigm of "beautiful ethicality" corresponded to individuals' *immediate* identification with the political totality, in the final problematic, this identification, while remaining necessary, supposes a set of mediations that are both subjective and objective. Indeed, the particular trait of modern *Sittlichkeit* is that in it political being ceases to be taken for granted. According to Hegel's point of view at Jena, it was necessary to separate the bourgeois' particular interest from the universal vocation of the citizen and to confine the "system of property and law" and the "universal private right"[65] it creates to limits that prevent them from being valid for themselves. On the other hand, in the *Philosophy of Right*, particular interests and the system that emerges from their random interactions constitute the mediation that articulates individuality with the statist universal. Civil society is thenceforth the "ground of mediation"[66] par excellence.

What is missing from the Jena and Nuremberg writings, and even from the first edition of the *Encyclopedia*, is the idea that the mediations that join a particular subjectivity to the "ethical substance" are neither solely nor essentially political mediations. We can find confirmation of this in a passage from the *Science of Logic*. Presenting the syllogistic structure of the absolute mechanism, Hegel takes an example borrowed from what would soon be named objective spirit:

---

64. *RPh*, § 147, *GW* 14.1, pp. 138 (*Elements*, 191; see *Outlines*, 155).

65. *Naturrecht*, *W* 2, p. 492 (*Natural Law*, 102).

66. Hegel, *Vorlesungen über Rechtsphilosophie*, 3:567.

Similarly, the *government*, the *individual citizens*, and the *needs* or the *external life* of these, are also three terms, of which each is the middle term of the other two. The *government* is the absolute center in which the extreme of the singulars is united with their external existence; the *singulars* are likewise the middle term that incites that universal individual into external concrete existence and transposes their ethical essence into the extreme of actuality. The third syllogism is the formal syllogism, the syllogism of reflective shine in which the singular citizens are tied by their *needs* and external existence to this universal absolute individuality; this is a syllogism that, as merely subjective, passes over into the others and has its truth in them.[67]

In this text, the government — which must be understood in the broad sense it had in the Jena texts (i.e., as the "universal government" and the "absolute government" from the *System of Ethicality*) and not in the narrow sense of "governmental power" — is charged with a task that, beginning in the 1817–1818 lectures, Hegel attributes instead to the mechanism of the system of needs and the division of labor: the mediation between individuals and their needs. Is this perhaps a throwback to the *System of Ethicality*, where the system of needs, of justice, and of discipline (which clearly prefigures the later division of civil society into the system of needs, the administration of law, and the police) were grouped under the heading "universal government"? In any case, this passage appears to maintain the political conception of ethicality found in the Jena writings, which in the 1805 *Philosophy of Spirit* was expressed in the doctrine of the *Gesinnungen* specific to each estate. The characterization of the mediation between individuals and the universal through needs as merely a "formal" syllogism that has its "truth" in the two other syllogisms shows that as late as 1816 Hegel did not see the system of needs and civil society more broadly as the "ground of mediation." The mediation was still *political*.

In the *Encyclopedia*, this same example concerning government, individuals, and needs undergoes a series of revealing changes. In the first edition, it is gone; this may have been a result of the text becoming more concise, but it also corresponds to the fact that the understanding of *Sittlichkeit* this example illustrates (and which dates back to Jena) is now in crisis. The second and third editions once again provide an ethical-political illustration of the absolute mechanism, but the presentation is different:

67. *WdL* 3, *GW* 12, pp. 144–45 (*Science of Logic*, 642).

Like the solar system, the state, for instance, is, in the practical sphere, a system of three syllogisms. (1) The *singular individual* (the person) joins itself through its *particularity* (physical and spiritual needs, what becomes the civil society, once they have been further developed for themselves) with the *universal* (the society, law, statutes, government). (2) The will, the activity of individuals, is the mediating factor which satisfies the needs in relation to society, the law, and so forth, just as it fulfills and realizes the society, the law, and so forth. (3) But the universal (state, government, law) is the substantial middle [term] in which the individuals and their satisfaction have and acquire their fulfilled reality, mediation, and subsistence.[68]

This passage is based on the new architecture of *Sittlichkeit*, which in the interim had been presented in detail in the *Philosophy of Right*. As far as the structure and significance of the doctrine of objective spirit, three points must be emphasized. First, the mediation between the individual and the universal (i.e., the state or political society) is now guaranteed by *civil society* and even by what at first glance is the least spiritual and most alienating within it: the system of needs. In fact, if civil society, the "system of all-round interdependence,"[69] is the site of a split between the particular and universal and consequently of a "loss of ethicality,"[70] it is also the condition for their true reconciliation. Second, the reconciliation of the particular and the universal is at first purely objective, since it takes place through the regulation of individual actions by the "invisible hand." Thus, this reconciliation is not seen by actors in the system as liberation but rather as "the *necessity* whereby the *particular* must rise to the *form of universality*."[71] As the third syllogism emphasizes, true ethical reconciliation requires a mediation that is not solely objective but is, rather, both subjective and objective: that of the state, the institutional (objective) figure of (subjective) freedom. Third, the second syllogism, where the will of individuals mediates the universal (the state) and the particularity of social needs and interests, confirms what is indicated (somewhat surprisingly at first) at the beginning of the "Morality" section in the *Philosophy of Right*: within the economy of objective spirit, *subjective* will is the

---

68. *Enzykl*, § 198 Anmerkung, *GW* 20, pp. 206–7 (*Encyclopedia* 273, modified).
69. *RPh*, § 183, *GW* 14.1, p. 160 (*Elements*, 221; see *Outlines*, 181).
70. *RPh*, § 181, *GW* 14.1, p. 159 (*Elements*, 219; see *Outlines*, 180).
71. *RPh*, § 186, *GW* 14.1, p. 162 (*Elements*, 224; see *Outlines*, 184).

"aspect of concrete *existence* [of freedom]," or "the real aspect of the concept of freedom."[72] But it is only when the necessity and consistency of the objective (social and political) bodies of mediation have been established that this observation takes on its full meaning and thereby justifies the inclusion of moral subjectivity in the theory of objective spirit.

The comparison between these two parallel texts, one from 1816 and the other from 1827–1830, shows the scope of the change that occurred in the doctrine of *Sittlichkeit* if not in the entire doctrine of objective spirit. In the *Science of Logic*, the third syllogism of absolute mechanism, in which individuals and the universal are connected by needs, or rather by the objective coordination of these needs in civil society, is described as "the syllogism of reflective shine."[73] In the second and third editions of the *Encyclopedia*, this same syllogism, now presented first, gives access to the economy of the whole insofar as it is placed under the sign of mediation:

> Since the mediation joins each of the determinations with the other extreme, each joins itself precisely in this way together with itself; it produces itself and this production is its self-preservation.[74]

Beyond its empirical justification, the systematic reason for introducing the concept of civil society into the doctrine of objective spirit seems to be to give consistency to the mediations capable of overcoming the tensions that structurally affect that sphere and consequently to give concrete content to the prospect of reconciliation that orients the thematic of *Sittlichkeit*. However, some questions remain unanswered, in particular, the following:

(1) Does the *objective* mediation of subjectivity and objectivity make it possible to satisfactorily handle the tension that might exist between these two dimensions, a tension that expresses the latent contradiction between the point of view of law and the point of view of morality?

(2) Can this mediation resolve the problems that the earlier version of *Sittlichkeit* left open, in particular, that of the place granted to subjective autonomy?

---

72. *RPh*, § 106 Anmerkung, *GW* 14.1, p. 99 (*Elements*, 135; see *Outlines*, 109).
73. *WdL* 3, *GW* 12, p. 145 (*Science of Logic*, 642).
74. *Enzykl*, § 198 Anmerkung, *GW* 20, p. 207 (*Encyclopedia* 273).

The Incompleteness of Objective Spirit: The Rabble as Symptom

Ethicality is "the *Idea of freedom* as the living good."[75] This phrase, which evokes and in a sense hijacks the vocabulary of morality, reminds us that ethical norms, made objective in institutions, have actuality only through the action of concrete subjects who follow these norms when formulating their plans to act. However, the statement also indicates that such action merely follows "given" norms, which are unavailable to actors. In this respect, the ethical solution to the contradictions of the moral point of view perhaps remains inconclusive. The gap between the weight of objectivity and the weight of subjectivity, including within the sphere of *Sittlichkeit*, entails the possibility of an imbalance. To use a vocabulary that is not Hegel's own, we might say that ethicality can only claim to resolve the tension or contradiction between the system and the lived world if we consider the latter to already be more or less in conformity with the requirements of the functioning of the system.[76] Of course, according to Hegel, the hypothesis of a complete discordance between the subjective and objective dimensions of objective spirit must be rejected. The intersubjectivity achieved in the ethical-political field relies on the process of recognition being carried out on the basis of objective, systemic conditions. This indicates how we should interpret the following remark from the *Encyclopedia* regarding the original, though not foundational, nature of violence:

> The struggle for recognition and the subjugation under a master is the *appearance* in which man's social life, the beginning of *states*, emerged. *Force*, which is the basis in this appearance, is not on that account the basis of *law*, though it is the *necessary* and *legitimate* moment in the passage of the *condition* of self-consciousness engrossed in desire and individuality into the condition of universal self-consciousness. This moment is the external beginning of states, their *beginning it appears*, not their *substantial principle.*[77]

---

75. *RPh*, § 142, *GW* 14.1, p. 137 (*Elements*, 189; see *Outlines*, 154).

76. I am borrowing these notions from Habermas: see Jürgen Habermas, *The Theory of Communicative Action*, vol. 2, *Lifeworld and System: A Critique of Functionalist Reason* (Boston: Beacon, 1987), chap. 6.

77. *Enzykl*, § 433 Anmerkung, *GW* 20, p. 431 (*Encyclopedia* 160, modified).

Of course, the harmony between the system and the lived world—or to use more traditional vocabulary, the harmony between law and custom—cannot always be achieved *in fact* but is nevertheless the horizon of *Sittlichkeit*. But what guarantees that this reconciliation will always be actual, which is a requirement for the coherence of the concepts of ethicality and objective spirit? I argue that such a guarantee cannot be offered by the sphere of objective spirit itself, where the agreement between institutions and subjective dispositions, between law and customs, between the objective and the subjective, always remains precarious.

This becomes clear in the very place where harmony should be objectively produced and maintained by the mechanical mediations of the market and the institutional mediations of the legal system, the police, and corporations: in civil society. Civil society should provide a corrective for the imbalance that affected the earlier (political) understanding of *Sittlichkeit* by introducing a series of objective mediations between individuals and the universal; however, civil society itself is the site of a possible pathological devolution. This is indicated in a famous passage from the *Philosophy of Right*:[78] a disintegration of the ethical nature of ethicality could result from the formation, within civil society, of a nonsocialized or desocialized fraction of the population whose material situation makes it impossible for them to possess the subjective dispositions required by a life in conformity with the social system and the exigencies of its reproduction. According to Hegel, first among the dispositions required is *Standesehre*, "the *honour of belonging to an estate*," that is, awareness of belonging to an institutionally recognized social group.[79] This is exactly what the "rabble" (*Pöbel*) lacks; suffering causes members of this group to lose the "feeling of law, integrity [*Rechtlichkeit*], and honour."[80] The poverty of the masses and the creation of an army of underprivileged endanger not only the other strata of civil society but above all the very idea of *Sittlichkeit* and the reconciliatory perspective it opens within objective spirit. Hegel takes this phenomenon very seriously and with great lucidity assesses the acute contradiction it creates at the very heart of civil society, specifically within the most developed and most modern civil society: Great Britain in the midst of the Industrial Revolution. The conclusion is clear:

78. See *RPh*, §§ 241–45, *GW* 14.1, pp. 192–94 (*Elements*, 265–67; see *Outlines*, 219–22).
79. See *RPh*, § 253 Anmerkung, *GW* 14.1, pp. 197–98 (*Elements*, 271–72; see *Outlines*, 225–26).
80. *RPh*, § 244, *GW* 14.1, p. 194 (*Elements*, 266, modified; see *Outlines*, 221).

This shows that, despite an *excess of wealth*, civil society is *not wealthy enough* — i.e. its own distinct resources are not sufficient — to prevent an excess of poverty and the formation of a rabble.[81]

The question then arises of the status of the anxious observations found in the *Philosophy of Right* and other texts from Berlin on the matter: are these remarks circumstantial, or do they mean that the phenomenon in question is a necessary consequence of civil society in its most recent development? Furthermore, is it possible to remedy this disturbance within the framework of civil society as Hegel understands its operation? The answer to these questions depends on whether one considers this social pathology to be circumstantial (and thus specific to the particular historical, political, and social circumstances of the English Industrial Revolution) or rather inherent to civil society as such (which brings Hegel's analysis strikingly close to Marx's later arguments). In any case, the solution to this dilemma requires a precise understanding of the role Hegel attributes to corporations as forms of institutionalization of social life. Can corporations contain the risk of explosion that accompanies the polarization of civil society into integrated and nonintegrated elements? Hegel's answer is complex, if not wavering.

On the one hand, Hegel seems to think that the existence of the rabble (which would soon be named the *Lumpenproletariat*) is a *necessary* effect of the development of civil society, an effect that in significant part escapes the concerted action of public authorities (in Hegel's terms, the police) as well as what Karl Polanyi names the strategies of self-protection of institutionalized social groups ("corporations").[82] Indeed, "as the connection [*Zusammenhang*] of human beings through their needs is *universalized*," this simultaneously — and contradictorily — creates "the *accumulation of wealth*" on one hand and "*dependence* and *want*" on the other.[83] Of course, the rabble Hegel speaks of must not be confused with the industrial proletariat: in his lectures, he uses the example not of the English working class, at the time in the midst of being formed, but rather the Neapolitan *lazzaroni*,[84] which certainly can-

81. *RPh*, § 245, *GW* 14.1, p. 194 (*Elements*, 267; see *Outlines*, 222).
82. See in particular chapter 11 of Karl Polanyi, *The Great Transformation: The Political and Economic Origin of Our Time* (Boston: Beacon, 1985).
83. *RPh*, § 243, *GW* 14.1, p. 193 (*Elements*, 266; see *Outlines*, 220–21).
84. See Hegel, *Vorlesungen über Rechtsphilosophie*, 4:609.

not be considered a product of industrial capitalism. However, it is only regarding this segment of "the excluded" and the "wealthy" who face them that Hegel speaks of "class" (*Klasse*) rather than estate (*Stand*), as if the novelty of the phenomenon required new vocabulary. It is the Industrial Revolution, an essential component of the formation of civil society in the Hegelian sense, that transforms what was a vaguely exotic curiosity into a structural consequence of social modernization.

However, on the other hand, Hegel never doubts the relevance or actuality of the reconciliatory horizon of his concept of ethicality. As he exposes the "dialectic" that pushes civil society "beyond itself," he analyzes the fundamental contradiction that affects civil society in terms that appear to presage Marx and Lenin: civil society can only deal with this contradiction by exporting it as part of an indefinite expansion, which itself generates new contradictions.[85] But immediately after, he presents the institution of the corporation as the means by which "*the ethical returns* to civil society as an immanent principle."[86] This leads him, against the apparent current of history, to advocate not only maintaining but also developing this type of institution. For him, the corporation (which is not the *Zunft* of old, fixated on its privileges, but rather the modern form of institutionalizing socioprofessional groups that make up "*the estate of commerce*"[87]) is the necessary counterweight to the deregulation of work and social life expressed by the phrase "freedom of enterprise." Thus, in the Berlin lectures he says,

> The municipality, the corporation, is the big point that currently must be negotiated in the world with regard to the constitution. It has against it the principle of abstract equality, and this conflict is the point around which, in the present state of the culture of understanding, our interest turns. The corporation is closely linked to the issue of the freedom of enterprise. The task on the agenda is to form corporations; but one does not want to do it; the need exists, but there is also a fear of acting on principles that are abstract.[88]

A note dating from the 1820s indicates the opposition:

---

85. See *RPh*, §§ 246–49, *GW* 14.1, pp. 195–96 (*Elements*, 267–70; see *Outlines*, 222–24).
86. *RPh*, § 249, *GW* 14.1, p. 196 (*Elements*, 270; see *Outlines*, 224).
87. *RPh*, § 204, *GW* 14.1, p. 172 (*Elements*, 236; see *Outlines*, 195).
88. Hegel, *Vorlesungen über Rechtsphilosophie*, 4:619.

Commercial freedom is nowadays the opposite of what [was] formerly the legal freedom of a city, village, guild [*Zunft*] — freedom of industry [was] the privilege a trade had. Now commercial freedom [means] that a trade has no rights, one can practice [it], more or less, without any conditions or rules.[89]

However, neither the institutionalization of social life (even if it is successful) nor the rootedness of social life in the political-state universal suffice to explain the presence of a perspective of reconciliation in the very place where objective spirit seems to have lost its rationality; that is, where its mechanisms of regulation no longer work, as is the case in the phenomenon of mass poverty, if it is not merely temporary. Ultimately, from the point of view of Hegelianism itself, the agreement between the system and the lived world, between the objective and subjective components of ethicality, cannot be guaranteed by the resources of *objective* spirit alone, because this, as *finite* spirit, remains marked by a "disproportion between the concept and the reality"[90] (just as subjective spirit is). The figures of finite spirit — even the highest ones, even the earthly divine, are but "stages of its liberation."[91] Their specific coherence is thus precarious and is subordinate to the guarantee of *absolute spirit*, the infinite and living form of this spiritual freedom. But if this is true, we are justified in wondering whether when Hegel presents the concept of ethicality that he adopted after renouncing "nostalgia for Greece" in the *Philosophy of Right* and in the *Encyclopedia*, he is not attributing to it a power of reconciliation between subjectivity and objectivity that is greater than what the economy of the system allows him to recognize de jure and de facto. In this respect, Hegel's demonstration of the structural imbalances of civil society is a remarkable indicator. It is precisely at that level of *Sittlichkeit* — which for *Sittlichkeit* is certainly a moment of alienation but which conversely must offer political universality an objective basis that it lacks in the premodern context — that the precariousness of objective ethical mediations is made manifest. It is true that reconciliation only takes on its full meaning with the state, which is the conscious institution of the universal. But the state — at least the *modern* state, which alone is capable of it — can only guarantee the reconciliation between subjectivity and objectivity (by creating appropriate subjective dispositions,

89. Hegel, *W* 11, p. 567.
90. *Enzykl*, § 386, *GW* 20, p. 383 (*Encyclopedia* 22).
91. *Enzykl*, § 386, *GW* 20, p. 383 (*Encyclopedia* 22).

which in return strengthen it) because it has its roots in civil society and its institutions, which are "the firm foundation of the state and . . . the pillars on which public freedom rests."[92] For the rational state to be able to carry out its vocation, that is, to ensure *objective* reconciliation, the possibility of an insurmountable fracture in the social body must be foreseen; furthermore, this possibility cannot be ruled out absolutely. Hegel tells us many times that the state cannot possibly claim to definitively resolve the constantly reoccurring tension between itself and modern society, or else it risks abdicating its vocation, which is to produce a specifically political, universalizing form of reconciliation, and becomes a "social" or "economic" state. Through the pathologies produced by its development, civil society introduces a crack into ethicality that the state does not have the means to fill. Consequently we must recognize that the actuality of an *ethical* reconciliation of objectivity and subjectivity—which indeed seems to be the end toward which all conceptualization of objective spirit is aimed—ultimately requires a metaethical and metaobjective guarantee. Hence, no doubt, the inclusion within this sphere of a philosophy of history whose final moment, the *Weltgeist*, is, in spite of its objectivity, nothing other than the mundane figure of absolute spirit.

92. *RPh*, § 265, *GW* 14.1, p. 211 (*Elements*, 287; see *Outlines*, 239).

PART III

The State and the Political

It is not without reason that Hegel's theory of the state is the part of his doctrine of objective spirit that has received the most attention: the topic of "Hegel and the state," ever since Rosenzweig's book by that name (*Hegel und der Staat*, 1920) and even since Haym's *Hegel und seine Zeit*, has been one of the most written-about subjects within Hegelian studies. One of the most critical topics as well, for the rather unattractive image of Hegel as the "philosopher of the Prussian state" has persisted, despite efforts to rectify it. It would not be an exaggeration to say that there is no interpretation in this vein, no matter how absurd, that has not been proposed by some commentator or another: Hegel as a precursor to Hitler, to Lenin or Stalin, but also to liberal democracy, and so on and so forth. The following chapters will neither seek to denounce this fable once again—though the following preliminary section will discuss it—nor offer a systematic interpretation of Hegel's political philosophy, which would require an entire work.[1] I will instead deal with three specific issues that provide a way to access what is most innovative and stimulating

---

1. The elements of such an interpretation are presented in the introduction to my translation of the *Philosophy of Right*, "L'institution de la liberté," in Hegel, *Principes de la philosophie du droit*, trans. Kervégan (Paris: Presses Universitaires de France, 2013), 1–109.

for contemporary thought in Hegel's philosophy[2]: his diagnosis of modernity through the silent dialogue between Tocqueville and Hegel (chap. 7); the problem of political representation, which has become central since the end of the eighteenth century and on which Hegel's unique views shed caustic light (chap. 8); and finally, his critique of democracy, in which we can find elements that anticipate what, much later, would be called the crisis of representative democracy (chap. 9).

2. An example of a fruitful reactualization of Hegel's political philosophy can be found in Axel Honneth's books *Suffering from Indeterminacy*, and *Freedom's Right: The Social Foundations of Democratic Life* (New York: Columbia University Press, 2014).

The Enduring Myth of the
Philosopher of the Prussian State

"Hegel's *system* is the philosophical home of the spirit of the Prussian restoration."[1] Rudolf Haym turned this proposition into a self-evident fact, and a lasting one. Through a kind of historical overwriting, the presentation of the rational state has been made to appear as an anticipatory apology for a conservative, warlike, Bismarkian Prussia. In reality, things are more complex. True, Hegel went to teach in a state that in his eyes had become the "center" of Germany,[2] but of a changing Germany, in contrast to reactionary Austria. What attracted him to Prussia—when he was anything but Prussian in mind or manner[3]—was that since 1805–1806 that country had not only gained power but, in a Germany dominated by Metternich, was at the forefront of progress. Hegel joined a state carrying out an ambitious policy of social and political reforms: serfdom was abolished, primary education was made mandatory, the privileges of the old corporations were curtailed in view of introducing free enterprise (which Hegel criticized), and a system of com-

---

1. Haym, *Hegel und seine Zeit*, 359.

2. "I came here to be in a center, and not in a province." See Hegel's letter to his friend, Niethammer in 1821, in Hoffmeister, *Briefe von und an Hegel*, 2:271.

3. See Otto Pöggeler, "Hegels Begegnung mit Preussen," in *Hegels Rechtsphilosophie im Zusammenhang der europäischen Verfassungsgeschichte*, ed. H. C. Lucas and O. Pöggeler (Stuttgart: Frommann-Holzboog, 1986), 311–51.

munity self-administration was established. Humboldt provided the sciences with prestigious institutions, thus allowing them to escape from the overly restrictive oversight of the authorities (i.e., the university and the Academy of Sciences in Berlin). Finally, Prussia was on the point of inaugurating a constitutional regime, which for Hegel was the eminent expression of the "eternal rights of reason."[4] Thus, the state to which Hegel offered the support of his philosophical speculations was, within a Germany in the midst of Restoration, a center of resistance, of "French ideas" (e.g., the principles of 1789).

However, at the very moment of his move to Berlin, Prussia, in the wake of the 1819 Carlsbad decisions made by the Germanic Confederation, adopted a clearly retrograde course that could not have suited the new professor of philosophy, well known for his liberal ideas. From the moment of his arrival in Berlin, where the hunt for "demagogues" (as liberals were called, in particular the leaders of student 'corporations, whose positions, tainted with anti-Semitism, were rather ambiguous) was going full throttle, Hegel found himself somewhat at odds. He did not openly oppose the authorities' repressive measures; thus, shortly after arriving, he refused to take part in raising funds for his colleague De Wette, who had been fired for making imprudent statements. But, in his teaching, he attempted to save what could be saved and to distance himself from certain aspects of the new politics. An example: when, in 1819, the king abandoned his repeatedly made promise to give the country a constitution (this would not happen until 1851, following the great movement that swept through Europe in 1848), Hegel described constitutional monarchy as "a constitution of *developed* reason."[5] From this example and the many others like it we see how distorted the image of Hegel as a reactionary philosopher of the Prussian state is.

In dedicating a copy of the *Philosophy of Right* to Chancellor Hardenberg (who was on the way out at the time), Hegel affirmed that his intent was to make philosophy "of immediate assistance to the beneficial intentions of the government."[6] But he was addressing the last great minister of the era of reforms, the head of a government that would disappear with him; Humboldt, the symbol of the temporary alliance between power and knowledge, had already been forced to resign. From then on, it was no longer Hardenberg,

---

4. Wurtemberg, *W* 4, p. 496; *Proceedings*, in *Hegel's Political Writings*, 274.

5. *Enzykl*, § 542, *GW* 20, p. 516 (*Encyclopedia* 241).

6. Hoffmeister, *Briefe von und an Hegel*, 2:242.

Humboldt, or Altenstein, Hegel's protector, who had the favor of the court, in particular of those in the entourage of the future Frederick William IV. They listened instead to the reactionary Haller, whom Hegel attacked virulently;[7] to Ancillon, an ideologue of the Restoration and soon to be minister of foreign affairs;[8] and to Savigny, Hegel's colleague and enemy and a fierce opponent of the codification about which Hegel said that to believe a nation incapable of it would be "among the greatest insults one could offer."[9] Even at the height of his glory, the "philosopher of the Prussian state" was never in the Prussian court, and he gave the "benediction of the concept," to use Haym's expression, to ideas that had either been discredited or remained distant dreams. From the height of his Berlin chair, Hegel maintained his old conviction: "the world spirit of the time has given the order to advance."[10]

7. *RPh*, § 258 Anmerkung, *GW* 14.1, p. 204 ff. (*Elements*, 278 ff.; see *Outlines*, 231ff).

8. In January of 1820 Hegel was advised not to attack him "since (1) he lives under the same roof as him, (2) he has more influence than him, and (3) because he is beneath all criticism." See Hoffmeister, *Briefe von und an Hegel*, 2:223.

9. *RPh*, § 211 Anmerkung, *GW* 14.1, p. 177 (*Elements*, 287; see *Outlines*, 200).

10. Hoffmeister, *Briefe von und an Hegel*, 2:231, 85–86.

7

Tocqueville-Hegel

A Silent Dialogue on Modernity

Is there any sense in establishing a parallel between the works of Tocqueville and Hegel, even if we reduce their work to what they have in common? Other than the vague, general fact that both were concerned with the fate of post-revolutionary societies — in Hegelian terms, the modern state in relation to civil society; in Tocqueville's, the democratic social condition — such rapprochement is not self-evident. It does not appear that the two ever encountered one another, either personally or intellectually. Hegel, it is clear, never heard of the young French aristocrat who only gained fame with the publication of the first part of his *Democracy in America* four years after Hegel's death in 1831. As for Tocqueville, he did mention Hegel's name once,[1] but his work gives us no reason to think that he had ever read him. There is, at the beginning of the first volume of *Democracy in America* (1840), an allusion to Germans who introduced pantheism into philosophy,[2] but it is extremely vague

---

1. In 1854 he wrote to F. de Corcelle: "You undoubtedly know the role of philosophy in Germany for fifty years and particularly the school of Hegel. You are probably aware that the latter was protected by governments, because his doctrine established in its political consequences that all the facts were respectable and legitimate simply because they occurred and [thereby] deserved obedience." Alexis de Tocqueville, *Correspondance* (Paris: Gallimard, 1983), xv-2, 107–8.

2. Tocqueville, *Democracy in America*, trans. Arthur Goldhammer (New York: Literary

and most likely refers to those involved in the *Pantheismusstreit* rather than to Hegel himself. Nothing in *Democracy in America* suggests that Tocqueville had any interest in German philosophy or political history. That changed with *The Old Regime and the Revolution*, but only as far as Germany's political and constitutional histories were concerned, not its philosophy. Moreover, Tocqueville must have thought the same thing about German philosophy as he did about French Enlightenment philosophy, which he contrasted to the political reality studied by economists: "philosophers rarely got beyond very general and very abstract ideas about government."[3] This assessment would surely have applied to Hegel. However, the very things that set the two apart also link them together in a silent conversation in which the very status of social and political modernity is at stake.

Tocqueville against Hegel?

On many issues Tocqueville and Hegel seem to take opposite sides — so much so that one could call Tocqueville the anti-Hegel; and indeed, those seeking to rehabilitate the liberal tradition against all forms of socialism often say as much. The following two examples illustrate this opposition.

The first concerns the historical role of America. Near the end of his introduction to the *Lectures on the Philosophy of History*, Hegel lists the distinctive characteristics of American civilization, and in many respects the list agrees with what we find in the first volume of *Democracy in America*, for example, the decisive role of commerce, that "very abstract principle."[4] Hegel concedes that the United States' "republican constitution" does indeed provide "universal protection of property" and guarantees the existence of a formal legal order.[5] But he adds that "this formal justice is devoid of integrity"[6]: the ethical vitality

---

Classics of the United States, 2004), 39; *De la démocratie en Amérique*, pt. 1 of *Oeuvres complètes* (Paris: Gallimard, 1961), 1:37.

3. Alexis Tocqueville, *Tocqueville: The Ancien Régime and the French Revolution*, trans. Arthur Goldhammer (Cambridge: Cambridge University Press, 2011), 143; *L'ancien régime et la révolution*, pt. 2 of *Oeuvres complètes* (Paris: Gallimard, 1952), 1:209.

4. Hegel, *Die Vernunft in der Geschichte*, 208; *Lectures on the Philosophy of World History*, 168 (modified).

5. Hegel, *Die Vernunft in der Geschichte*, 207; *Lectures on the Philosophy of World History*, 168.

6. Hegel, *Die Vernunft in der Geschichte*, 207; *Lectures on the Philosophy of World History*, 168.

that the state ensures or ought to ensure is lacking from this formal order. In short, the United States is not yet "a real state";[7] at most, it is a civil society in formation precisely because there is not (or not yet) a marked difference between social estates or conditions—in other words, because there is what Tocqueville calls a democratic social condition. Hegel adds,

> North America cannot yet be regarded as a fully developed and mature state, but merely as one which is still in the process of becoming; it has not yet progressed far enough to feel the need for a monarchy.[8]

It would be easy to focus only on the irony of this prognosis, but it is coherent with Hegel's often-repeated argument that constitutional monarchy (which is distinct from patriarchal monarchy and feudal monarchy) is the political formula best suited to the modern world.[9] At the same time, we may wonder whether the later development of presidential power in the United States (a power that Tocqueville considered to be both subordinate to and constantly threatened by the legislature) has not in part proved Hegel right. But ultimately this is not so important. For Hegel, "America is a country of the future";[10] similarly, for Tocqueville, it is, like Russia, "marked out by the will of heaven to sway the destinies of half the globe."[11] But the conclusions they draw from this diagnosis are quite different. For Tocqueville, America is of interest because it foreshadows the probable fate of societies: "in America, I saw more than America; I sought the image of democracy itself."[12] Hegel, to the contrary, concludes his presentation of America with this lapidary judgment: "it is of no interest to us here, for prophecy is not the business of the

---

7. Hegel, *Die Vernunft in der Geschichte*, 207; *Lectures on the Philosophy of World History*, 168.

8. Hegel, *Die Vernunft in der Geschichte*, 207; *Lectures on the Philosophy of World History*, 169.

9. See *Enzykl*, § 542, *GW* 20, p. 516 (*Encyclopedia* 241). Cf. Hegel, *Die Vernunft in Der Geschichte*, 147; *Lectures on the Philosophy of World History*, 119. The distinction between three types de monarchy (ancient or patriarchal, feudal, constitutional) is specified in the *Philosophy of Right*: *RPh*, § 273 Anmerkung, *GW* 14.1, p. 228 (*Elements*, 311; see *Outlines*, 262).

10. Hegel, *Die Vernunft in Der Geschichte*, 209; *Lectures on the Philosophy of World History*, 171.

11. Tocqueville, *Democracy in America*, 476; *De la démocratie en Amérique*, 1:431.

12. Tocqueville, *Democracy in America*, 15; *De la démocratie en Amérique*, 1:12.

philosopher."[13] True, the theoretical position of Tocqueville, a sociologist of politics and a historian of ideas and passions, is different from that of the philosopher seeking to "recognize reason as the rose in the cross of the present"[14] and looking for only "what is eternal"[15] in the present. But it is precisely this difference in orientation that is instructive and that perhaps renders any attempt at rapprochement vain.

A second example is even more general in scope: the two authors' assessments of the future of democracy.[16] Tocqueville thought that the "democratic revolution" was the "generative fact" of modernity,[17] and from the outset he proclaimed that his book was "written under constant preoccupation with a single thought: the future coming—irresistible—of universal democracy in the world."[18] Hegel, on the other hand, considered democracy to be fundamentally untimely in that the reign of (political) virtue toward which it tends on principle shows itself to be incompatible with the liberation of "the powers of *particularity*"[19] that is the defining trait of modernity. This is why any attempt at actualizing the democratic principle—for example, the French Revolution—necessarily unleashes tyrannical violence against those forces of particularity in a vain attempt to silence them. However, it is easy to explain the differences between the two authors here through their differing conceptions of democracy. Whereas Hegel sticks to the traditional (Greek) concept of democracy and tacitly assumes what goes along with it (an exclusively political definition of living together and a rejection of the division between private and public practiced by modernity), Tocqueville introduces a new definition of democracy as the *social condition* of equality; thus, he proposes a *nonpolitical* (in the classical sense of the word) concept of democracy that breaks with the conception used in Hegel's analysis. Despite these clear differences, it is possible that Hegel and Tocqueville intersect in their analyses, and each have much to suggest to present estimations of democracy.

13. Hegel, *Die Vernunft in Der Geschichte*, 210; *Lectures on the Philosophy of World History*, 171.

14. RPh, GW 14.1, pp. 15–16 (*Elements*, 22; see *Outlines*, 15).

15. RPh, GW 14.1, pp. 15–16 (*Elements*, 22; see *Outlines*, 15).

16. Regarding Hegel, see chapter 9 below.

17. Tocqueville, *Democracy in America*, 3 (modified); *De la démocratie en Amérique*, 1:1.

18. *De la démocratie en Amérique*, forward to the 12th ed. (Paris, Pagnerre, 1848), xliii.

19. RPh, § 273 Anmerkung, GW 14.1, p. 228 (*Elements*, 310; see *Outlines*, 261).

Two Perspectives on "Democratic Tyranny"

Let us begin by discussing a point that is revealing though not decisive. Tocqueville and Hegel both preserve the traditional classification of forms of government and distinguish between monarchy, aristocracy, and democracy without omitting their deviant forms—wholly in keeping with Aristotle or Polybius. We may think here of Hegel's mention of ochlocracy[20] or Tocqueville's constant play on the good and bad forms of aristocracy or democracy, as in his famous phrase, "on whether we next have democratic freedom or democratic tyranny, depends the destiny of the world."[21] But they immediately relativize the relevance of this kind of classification and emphasize its inadequacy to the conditions of political and social modernity.

First, a quote from Hegel:

The old classification of constitutions into *monarchy, aristocracy,* and *democracy* presupposes a *still undivided and substantial unity* which has not yet attained its *inner differentiation* (as an organization developed within itself) and which consequently still lacks *depth* and *concrete rationality*.[22]

According to this text, constitutional monarchy is neither a variant of classical monarchy nor a fourth type of constitution; rather, it sums up and relativizes the unilateral moments that classical constitutions represent, and it is their integrative unity, for its internal organization makes room for democratic aspects (parliamentary representation) and aristocratic ones (governmental administrations) as well as for the specifically monarchic aspect of state power. In this way, political philosophy's traditional question—what is the best regime?[23]—becomes obsolete. The question is even more obsolete because it is an illusion to think that a political regime can be chosen by a deliberate decision, as in the constitutional debate Herodotus imagines taking place

---

20. RPh, § 278 Anmerkung, GW 14.1, p. 231 (*Elements*, 316; see *Outlines*, 266). The word *ochlocracy* appears in Polybius (*The Histories*, trans. W. R. Paton [Cambridge, MA: Harvard University Press, 1922], 2:38, 6) to refer to the perverted form of democracy, which Aristotle called *democracy* in order to distinguish it from authentic *politeia*.

21. *De la démocratie en Amérique*, xliv.

22. *RPh*, § 273 Anmerkung, GW 14.1, p. 226 (*Elements*, 309; see *Outlines*, 259).

23. See Strauss, *What Is political philosophy?*, 34. Cf. *Vorlesungen über die Philosophie der Weltgeschichte* (Hamburg: Miner, 1955), 1:140.

in Persia.[24] For Hegel, "each nation . . . has the constitution appropriate and proper to it."[25] Instead, it is more fitting to see the succession of regimes as belonging to the process of historical development of objective freedom through successive, unilateral forms. This is why

> No lessons can therefore be drawn from history for the framing of constitutions in the present. For the latest constitutional principle, the principle of our own times, is not to be found in the constitutions of the world-historical nations of the past.[26]

As for Tocqueville, he spends little time on the typology of political regimes. In *Democracy in America* we find only scattered remarks on the subject. For example, unlike Hegel (at least the letter of Hegelian texts), Tocqueville maintains that the democracies of antiquity must be distinguished from modern democracy. Of the first, he indicates that "those so-called democracies consisted of elements very different from ours, with which they have nothing in common but the name,"[27] but he says no more. Cross-referencing this with other passages shows that Tocqueville considered ancient democracy, slave holding and bellicose, to be an aristocracy in disguise. Another passage, this time from the first volume of *Democracy in America*, repeats, over the course of a discussion on the institution of the jury, the original classification of regimes presented at the beginning of *The Spirit of the Laws* and classes aristocracy and democracy as two species of the genus republic, contrasting them both to monarchies.[28] But it is clear that this is not essential to Tocqueville's argument. What is essential is his increasingly clear-cut opposition between aristocratic and democratic societies. The systematic comparison of their properties,[29] the observation that government by a single ruler can go with both aristocratic society (as in the monarchy of the ancien régime) and with

24. Herodotus, *The Histories*, 3.80.

25. *RPh*, § 274 Anmerkung, *GW* 14.1, p. 229 (*Elements*, 312; see *Outlines*, 263).

26. Hegel, *Die Vernunft in der Geschichte*, 143; *Lectures on the Philosophy of World History*, 120.

27. Tocqueville, *Democracy in America*, 716; *De la démocratie en Amérique*, 2:230.

28. Tocqueville, *Democracy in America*, 233; *De la démocratie en Amérique*, 1:284. See Montesquieu, *The Spirit of the Laws*, trans. and ed. Anne M. Cohler, Basia Caroly Miller, and Harold Samuel Stone (Cambridge: Cambridge University Press, 1989), 1:2, 10–21 (*Spirit of the Laws* citations give book and chapter followed by modern translation page number).

29. See Tocqueville, *De la démocratie en Amérique*, 1:242–43 and 2:293 ff.

democratic society (the Napoleonic Empire and the July Monarchy)—these show that for Tocqueville, too, the classification of regimes is neither topical nor relevant. What is important for him, especially in the second volume, is to fully assess and draw out all the consequences of the gap between aristocratic and democratic societies; it is to establish what distinguishes aristocratic passions from democratic passions, what distinguishes the aristocrat from the democrat. Here, Kant had pointed the way for Tocqueville (and for Hegel) by maintaining that the question of *Regierungsform* is, in the conditions of modern society, which is dominated by the selfish quest to satisfy individual aspirations, less important than that of *Regierungsart*, that is the mode—liberal (in Kant's vocabulary, republican) or despotic—of government.[30]

Nevertheless, democracy is not only a "social condition," it is also a political regime. What are its characteristics in this regard? What is the specific nature of governing democracy, its properly political definition? The answer is almost trivial: it is the sovereignty of the people. However, there must be no mistaking the meaning of this notion; the stereotypes and ambiguities it generates must be eliminated. "Disentangled . . . from the many fictions with which it has elsewhere carefully been wreathed"[31]—particularly in France—the dogma of popular sovereignty fundamentally means that political power in no way transcends the social body or the governed; it refers to nothing other than "the slow and tranquil action of society upon itself."[32] In other words, no matter how subtle or complex the mechanisms of representation or the organized balance of powers (the American Constitution, following the canonical definition contained by the *Federalist Papers*, is a model in this regard), ultimately it is the opinion of the majority—whose "quiet reign[33] Tocqueville observes—that holds sway in democracy, where "the opinions, prejudices, interests, and even passions of the people" cannot be hindered "from making their influences felt on the daily direction of society."[34] In short, beyond constitutional fictions, the sovereignty of the people means that "the majority governs in the name of the people." This is the root of what Tocqueville sees as am-

30. Kant, *Frieden*, Ak. 8, pp. 352–53; *PP*, pp. 324–25.
31. Tocqueville, *Democracy in America*, 64; *De la démocratie en Amérique*, 1:56.
32. Tocqueville, *Democracy in America*, 456; *De la démocratie en Amérique*, 1:412.
33. Tocqueville, *Democracy in America*, 456; *De la démocratie en Amérique*, 1:413.
34. Tocqueville, *Democracy in America*, 197; *De la démocratie en Amérique*, 1:177.

bivalent and even troubling in popular sovereignty and thereby in democracy itself. The second volume of *Democracy in America* returns to this question over and over again: the power of the majority, which has influence over individual judgments and sentiments, constantly threatens to become tyrannical. "Democratic tyranny,"[35] exerted by a "power [that] is absolute, meticulous, regular, provident, and mild,"[36] is, as the *Federalist Papers* foresaw, the main danger threatening modern democracy.

Hegel is just as hesitant about the sovereignty of the people as Tocqueville — completely normal for a declared adversary of democracy. But what is more surprising is that his argument intersects with the French liberal's in significant ways. One can only critique the sovereignty of the people if one recognizes what is inevitable about this principle in the political configuration of modernity. The right to vote, that "sole act of the 'sovereignty of the people,'" is like the symbol — and often it is no more than just that — of the inalienable right of individuals insofar as they also constitute "the people," to "participate in public affairs and in the highest interests of the state and government."[37] This is why that right is prominently featured in the "elementary catechism" of modern politics, the Declaration of the Rights of Man and Citizen.[38]

From the foregoing we can see how Hegel and Tocqueville are both similar and different on the matter of the sovereignty of the people. They are similar — and this is the main aspect — in that they both recognize certain characteristics (to which we shall return) in the postrevolutionary world that make the sovereignty of the people, or at least certain forms of it, inevitable. Their promotion of this dogma is a response to the effacement of all transcendent principles of legitimacy (God, dynasty), and it expresses the immanence of political power to the social body. In this respect, for Hegel as well as for Tocqueville, democracy (in the weak sense) is the destiny of modern societies. However, they clearly diverge in how they understand this new principle.

Tocqueville, not without some anxiety, rallies to the new conception of democracy (new in comparison to the conception expressed by eighteenth-century authors such as Montesquieu and Rousseau) embodied by the insti-

---

35. *De la Démocratie en Amérique*, p. xliv.
36. Tocqueville, *Democracy in America*, 818; *De la démocratie en Amérique*, 2:324.
37. Hegel, *Reformbill*, W 11, p. 112; *Reform Bill*, in *Hegel's Political Writings*, 318.
38. Hegel, *Wurtemberg*, W 4, p. 49; *Proceedings*, in *Hegel's Political Writings*, 270.

tutions of the United States: checks and balances, administrative decentraliza-
tion, and the practices of local self-administration that had been the anchor of
political life there since the beginning of colonization. In the words of the *Federalist Papers*, we have here a republican government "on which the scheme of
representation takes place" and that is entirely different from classical democracy, where "the people meet and exercise the government in person."[39] An
attentive reader of the *Federalist Papers*, Tocqueville is keenly aware of the risk
contained in the principle of popular sovereignty even when a powerful representational corrective is implemented: this is the risk of the oppression of
minorities.[40] But since there is no alternative — and we shall see why — to the
democratization of society, there is no choice but to contain this risk, which
means "new remedies must henceforth be sought for new disorders." Tocqueville summarizes the remedies for democratic tyranny thus:

> To set broad but visible and immovable limits on social power; to grant cer-
> tain rights to private individuals and guarantee their uncontested enjoyment
> of those rights; to preserve what little independence, strength, and origi-
> nality is left to the individual; to raise him up alongside and support him
> vis-à-vis society.[41]

Though Hegel agrees with Tocqueville that since the French Revolution, unequal conditions are no longer appropriate in society, he refuses to see what
was not yet named representative democracy as an adequate response to the
problems of the modern world and first and foremost to the problem posed
by social polarization and the heightening of class conflicts. The democratic
vision of the political order is based on a fiction inherited from natural law
theories and actualized by political economy: the fiction of a society of individuals constituted by themselves and abstractly equal. Hegel and Tocqueville
are simultaneously similar and different in that they start off from similar diag-
noses of modernity but propose antithetical solutions to its challenges. But
what precisely was this diagnosis, and to what extent do they share it?

39. *The Federalist Papers*, no. 14, p. 68.
40. See *The Federalist Papers*, no. 10.
41. Tocqueville, *Democracy in America*, 829 (modified); *De la démocratie en Amérique*, 2:334.

Love of Liberty, Passion for Equality?

The question on which Tocqueville and Hegel at first seem to differ most directly is that of the role of the respective values of freedom and equality in the modern world as well as the institutions and norms that promote them. The debate is significant, for it concerns not only the way the two authors situate themselves with respect to the problematic of the rights of man and the text of the 1789 Declaration but also their fundamental analysis of modern society, their assessment of its negative tendencies, and their hypotheses about its future.

An *Anmerkung* from the *Encyclopedia* that I have already mentioned discusses at length the complex relationship between these "simple categories that have often been [used to sum up] what should constitute the fundamental determination and the final goal and result of the constitution,"[42] a clear allusion to the preamble to the 1789 Declaration. First, as regards *equality*, Hegel considers that this principle, clumsily expressed by the phrase "men are equal by nature" (for to the contrary, men are naturally unequal and it is precisely up to law, society, and the state to correct this immediate naturalness), has a social rather than political meaning. If it is applied in a consistent and coherent way, "the principle of equality rejects all distinctions, and thus allows no political condition to subsist."[43] Indeed, any political order introduces a functional hierarchy between rulers and the ruled, and thus an inequality, even if this inequality does not correspond to any statutory difference between those who "by nature" rule and those who "by nature" obey—which is also the case in many aristocratic societies in Tocqueville's sense. Contrary to a widespread illusion, the principle of equality does not have political significance but rather legal and social meaning: to say that men are equal (and it is only in modern societies that such a thing can be said) is to proclaim that they are equal as persons before the law, which is the same as affirming the existence of a "*lawful condition in general.*"[44] But—and this is where Hegel's argument becomes profound—the normative principle of the equality of persons before the law, which implies eliminating restrictions that premodern societies put on ac-

---

42. *Enzykl*, § 539 Anmerkung, *GW* 20, p. 509 (*Encyclopedia* 237).
43. *Enzykl*, § 539 Anmerkung, *GW* 20, p. 509 (*Encyclopedia* 237).
44. *Enzykl*, § 539 Anmerkung, *GW* 20, p. 510 (*Encyclopedia* 238).

quiring personhood,[45] has value only insofar as individuals are otherwise unequal: if not, this would not be a norm but rather a trivial factual statement. They are, in fact, unequal: they are so naturally on account of their psychological and physical makeups; they are so also socially because of the positions they occupy within the flexible space of civil society. In other words, and even though this appears to go against the general principles of the Declaration of Rights, "as regards the concrete, apart from their personality the citizens are equal before the law only in those respects in which they are in any case equal *outside the law*."[46] But for all that, it would be imprudent to count Hegel as a reactionary hostile to equality. It is simply that his realism forbids him from attenuating the distance that separates the level of *Sollen* from that of *Sein* and from confusing legal normativity with concrete reality.

As for freedom, Hegel disentangles this notion from the subjectivist and individualist interpretations that dominate modern thought. Such interpretations are connected to a conflation of freedom and free choice. The introduction to the *Philosophy of Right* indicates that free choice is merely a subordinate moment in the fully developed concept of freedom.[47] To that philosophically unsatisfying and politically suspect understanding of freedom Hegel contrasts "objective freedom," which "could grow to such a height only in modern times."[48] And this objective freedom, of which political freedom (the power recognized in individuals to take part in public affairs) is only one dimension, is precisely structured and guaranteed by the rule of law. Indeed, "every genuine law is a freedom, for it involves a rational determination of objective spirit, and so a content of freedom."[49] In this way, political obligation is not to be understood as a restriction on the freedom individuals originally have but rather as what allows their aspiration to freedom to have institutional grounding and thereby to overcome the unilateral nature of a merely subjective free-

---

45. Even if this is a retrospective generalization (Max Kaser, *Das römische Privatrecht*, 1:234), we may think of the triple conditions of status required by Roman law to achieve personhood: *status libertatis* (personal freedom), *status civitatis* (citizenship), *status familiae* (being head of a family).

46. *Enzykl*, § 539 Anmerkung, *GW* 20, p. 510 (*Encyclopedia* 238).

47. See *RPh*, §§ 14–17, *GW* 14.1, pp. 38–40 (*Elements*, 47–50; see *Outlines*, 37–40).

48. *Enzykl*, § 539 Anmerkung, *GW* 20, p. 512 (*Encyclopedia* 239). On this notion of objective freedom, see also *RPh*, § 258 Anmerkung, *GW* 14.1, p. 202 (*Elements*, 276; see *Outlines*, 229).

49. *Enzykl*, § 539 Anmerkung, *GW* 20, p. 511 (*Encyclopedia* 238).

dom — that is, freedom "taken partly in a negative sense against the willfulness of others and lawless treatment" and thus contrary to "rational freedom."[50]

Hegel deduces from this a judgment that at first glance seems to oppose the thesis of *Democracy in America* point for point:

> Thus it has also been said that modern peoples are capable only of equality, or more capable of *equality* than of *freedom*. . . . On the contrary, it has to be said that it is just the great development and cultivation of modern states that produces the supreme concrete *inequality* of individuals in actuality, whereas, through the deeper rationality of laws and reinforcement of the lawful condition, it brings about a freedom that is all the greater and more firmly entrenched, a freedom that it can allow and tolerate.[51]

Thus, the modern, postrevolutionary state guarantees the triumph of freedom over equality. But the argument seeks above all to clarify the confusion plaguing "current conceptions" of freedom and equality. For according to Hegel, freedom properly understood, the objective freedom produced and guaranteed by the legal order (the *Rechtszustand*), is equality itself or rather its condition: without political freedom, without a constitutional state guaranteeing the rule of law, there can be no true legal and social equality among citizens; there would be only a society stratified into castes or estates. In other words, civil equality, the characteristic trait of a society freed of the ancien régime's strict barriers between estates, lands, and professions, is the *consequence* of political freedom understood objectively and not only as an individual right to exercise active citizenship. *Freedom properly understood is equality properly understood,* for it is precisely to the extent that individuals are politically unequal (rulers and ruled/active citizens and passive citizens) and socially unequal (rich and poor) that they must imperatively be legally equal, which is only possible if the political order is a vehicle for freedom.

Tocqueville seems to take the opposite view, for he maintains — and this is even the central theme of *Democracy in America* — that *equality of conditions,* a "providential fact," [52] is the defining trait of democracy, or rather of the demo-

50. *Enzykl,* § 539 Anmerkung, *GW* 20, p. 512 (*Encyclopedia* 238).
51. *Enzykl,* § 539 Anmerkung, *GW* 20, p. 511 (*Encyclopedia* 238).
52. Tocqueville, *Democracy in America,* 6; *De la démocratie en Amérique,* 1:4.

cratic social condition in modern societies. The "passion for equality"[53] that equality arouses simultaneously engenders and opposes the aspiration to personal and political freedom, which is why "democratic peoples show a more ardent and enduring love of equality than of liberty."[54] The deepening of civil equality and the tendency to leveling it creates can undoubtedly lead to the "ideal," which would be the conjunction of perfect equality and complete freedom; but it can also lead—and this is clearly what Tocqueville considers most likely—to the disappearance of political freedom. Once it has been posited that equality is the "first passion"[55] of democratic societies—and we know that this expression designates the "state" of society rather than the political regime—we see that the "ills that liberty sometimes brings on,"[56] and whose effects are more immediate than those of extreme equality, can lead to the sacrifice of freedom. From equality to servitude the distance is not so great, and administrative centralization, one of the core tendencies of modern societies, brings them even closer.[57] Thus, we see the outline of the threat of "democratic tyranny," the dangerous alternative to "democratic freedom."[58] And it is clear that Tocqueville takes this threat very seriously:

> When I think of the state in which several European nations already find themselves and toward which all the others are tending, I am inclined to believe that soon there will no longer be room in Europe for anything but democratic liberty or the tyranny of the Caesars.[59]

However, equality and freedom cannot simply be understood as the terms of an alternative, as certain schools claiming (erroneously) to follow Tocque-

---

53. See Tocqueville, *Democracy in America*, 584; *De la démocratie en Amérique*, 1:334. See also "Democratic institutions awaken and flatter the passion for equality without ever being able to satisfy it to the full." *Democracy in America*, 226 *De la démocratie en Amérique*, 1:204.

54. *Democracy in America*, 581; *De la démocratie en Amérique*, 2:101. Chapter title. On the same page, Tocqueville reminds us that "the first and most intense of the passions to which equality gives rise is love of equality itself."

55. *Democracy in America*, 581; *De la démocratie en Amérique*, 2:101.

56. *Democracy in America*, 583; *De la démocratie en Amérique*, 2:103.

57. "I am convinced, moreover, that no nation is more likely to succumb to the yoke of administrative centralization than one whose social state is democratic." Tocqueville, *Democracy in America*, 109; *De la démocratie en Amérique*, 1:97.

58. *De la démocratie en Amérique*, xliv.

59. Tocqueville, *Democracy in America*, 363; *De la démocratie en Amérique*, 1:329.

ville would have it. A passage at the end of *The Ancien Régime and the French Revolution* analyzes in dialectical terms the two "principal passions" driving the history of modern France: equality and freedom. The love of equality, or rather the "violent, inextinguishable hatred of inequality" is certainly "older and more deeply rooted." But it also arouses and feeds the passion for freedom, which is more fragile because it is "more recent and less deeply rooted."[60] The Revolution, at least at the beginning, offered an astonishing example of the interaction between the two because the passion for equality powerfully encouraged the emergence of institutions of freedom, and in that case, the institutions of constitutional monarchy. Tocqueville comments that it was then that "the French were proud enough of their cause and of themselves to believe that they could enjoy freedom and equality together" and that "alongside democratic institutions they therefore created free institutions everywhere."[61]

But the passion that "has continued to dwell deep within the hearts it was first to capture" is indeed the passion for equality.[62] Therefore, even though equality can aid in the development of political freedom, it can also destroy it, and this is what most often occurs. This is what is demonstrated by the events of the Revolution, which Tocqueville analyzes in terms Hegel would not have repudiated. The reversal of freedom into despotism (the emperor's despotism followed naturally from the despotism of freedom) was made even easier by the fact that administrative centralization, which the Revolution inherited from the ancien régime and which Napoleon perfected, "offered remarkable assistance to despotism."[63] Thus, in the span of a few decades, the democratic passion for equality both encouraged spectacular progress in political freedom and paved the way for its greatest threat: centralization and administrative despotism. And yet, within the conditions of all modern states, there is no other remedy for this threat than freedom itself:

---

60. Tocqueville, *The Ancien Régime and the Revolution*, 182; *L'ancien régime et la révolution*, pt. 2, p. 247 (III/8).

61. Tocqueville, *The Ancien Régime and the Revolution*, 183; *L'ancien régime et la révolution*, pt. 2, p. 247 (III/8).

62. Tocqueville, *The Ancien Régime and the Revolution*, 184; *L'ancien régime et la révolution*, pt. 2, p. 248 (III/8).

63. Tocqueville, *The Ancien Régime and the Revolution*, 183; *L'ancien régime et la révolution*, pt. 2, p. 248 (III/8).

But I maintain that to combat the evils that equality may engender, there is only one effective remedy: political liberty.[64]

In the postrevolutionary world, it is decidedly not a question of choosing between equality and freedom (Tocqueville observes that the enemies of equality are not necessarily supporters of political freedom) but rather of arriving at an exact understanding of the tense connection that unites them.

We can see that beyond their differences, the two thinkers' arguments regarding freedom and equality in state and society are responses to a concern they share: what might the shape of the political be in the aftermath of the two revolutions (French and American) that marked the beginning of a new era? What institutional forms can ensure the maintenance and development of political freedom in a world stamped by equality: equal rights, equal conditions, equal aspirations? The convergence of problematics between Tocqueville, a democrat in principle[65] and an opponent of administrative centralization, and Hegel, a partisan of liberal monarchy and the bureaucratic state, is more decisive than the divergence of their particular judgments. At bottom, this convergence stems from their similar approach to the nature of modern society.

Civil Society and Political Democracy

The polysemous nature of Tocqueville's conception of democracy has often been noted.[66] However, the defining moment in his analysis is his definition of democracy not as a political regime or as a form of exercising power but rather as a *social condition*. This moment comes in the first volume of *Democracy in America*[67] and even more so in the second volume, where it is con-

---

64. Tocqueville, *Democracy in America*, 594; *De la démocratie en Amérique*, 2:112.

65. "In that case, the gradual growth of democratic manners and institutions should be regarded, not as the best, but as the only means of preserving freedom; and without liking the government of democracy, it might be adopted as the most applicable and the fairest remedy for the present ills of society." Tocqueville, *Democracy in America*, 1:328; *De la démocratie en Amérique*, 1:329.

66. See H. Laski, introduction to the first volume of *De la démocratie en Amérique*, xxix, and throughout. See also Pierre Manent, *Tocqueville et la nature de la démocratie* (Paris: Fayard, 1993), 18 ff.

67. "The social condition of the Anglo-Americans is essentially democratic." See Tocqueville, *Democracy in America*, 52 (modified); *De la démocratie en Amérique*, 1:45.

stantly assumed. The social condition of democracy is characterized by equal conditions, the "basic fact" of the "great democratic revolution [that] is taking place among us,"[68] in other words, the fact that "when citizens are divided into castes and classes, not only are they different from one another, but they have neither the taste nor the desire to look alike."[69] This definition of democracy in social rather than political terms is Tocqueville's major theoretical innovation. It explains his replacement of the classical typology of regimes with a distinction between aristocratic and democratic societies — a distinction remarkable above all because it does not admit the possibility of a third alternative. This distinction is the backbone of the second volume of *Democracy in America*, which develops an unrelenting comparison between the properties of aristocratic societies (inegalitarian) and democratic ones (egalitarian).

This social definition of democracy is made necessary by a thesis that is very interesting in comparison with what Hegel says:

> For in the long run, political society cannot fail to become the expression and image of civil society, and it is in this sense that one may say that there is nothing more political about a people than its civil legislation.[70]

This is remarkable from the point of view of the history of the political lexicon: in 1835–1840 Tocqueville uses the distinction between civil society and political society that Hegel was the first to have explicitly drawn around the year 1817, and he does so as if the distinction is self-evident. In the space of a few years, the concept of civil society, which had undergone such a profound transformation, became perfectly familiar and even indispensable all across Europe. Tocqueville's work aims to account for this fact by showing to what extent the democratic social condition transforms classical representations of politics.

But if Tocqueville seems to be similar to Hegel because he invokes the distinction between the state and civil society, he is not at all Hegelian in the way he uses the distinction; he is closer to Lorenz von Stein and even to Marx,

---

68. Tocqueville, *Democracy in America*, 3; *De la démocratie en Amérique*, 1:1.

69. Tocqueville, *Democracy in America*, 780n; *De la démocratie en Amérique*, 2:288n.

70. Tocqueville, *Democracy in America*, 686n; *De la démocratie en Amérique*, 2:201n. See also the important subtitle of chapter 3 of part 1 of volume 1: "Political Consequences of the Social Condition of the Anglo-Americans."

which may seem surprising. In Hegel, the distinction between civil society and the state goes along with the clear subordination of the former to the latter. It is extremely important for him — and in this he remains a classical author — to preserve the rights of the political and to avoid not only conflating the state with civil society but also, and above all, subordinating the state to the representations and modes of regulation that reign in civil society. This is what Tocqueville does when he writes that the social condition determines (in a way that is not entirely clear) the political configuration:

> There is no doubt in my mind that sooner or later we will come, as the Americans have come, to an almost complete equality of conditions. I do not conclude from this that we will one day be compelled to draw the same political consequences as the Americans from our similar social state. I am not at all convinced that they have hit upon the only form of government that a democracy may adopt. If, however, the same root cause has given rise to new laws and customs in both countries, then that is reason enough for us to take an immense interest in finding out what effects that cause has produced in each.[71]

While Hegel affirms the normative primacy of the political over the social, Tocqueville proclaims the primacy of the "social condition"; the "form of government" is not its mere reflection or "consequence," but it cannot contradict it for long, for it is the social condition that is the cause "influencing the manners of the country." If it is true that the move toward a democratic social condition is inevitable, we must ask what the inevitable consequences of this phenomenon are for the political sphere.

Regardless of the scope of their differences, Hegel and Tocqueville define civil society in similar terms. For Tocqueville, the equality of conditions, the fact that no one is attached by birth to a specific estate, is the sole generator of the democratic social condition, or in Hegelian terms of modern civil society. For Hegel, equality is not what characterizes civil society above all; civil society, resulting from the interaction of particular actors, an interaction orchestrated by various universalizing controls (the market, the law), represents, within *Sittlichkeit*, "the degree of *difference*,"[72] because there particular

---

71. Tocqueville, *Democracy in America*, 14; *De la démocratie en Amérique*, 1:11.
72. *RPh*, § 181, *GW* 14.1, p. 159 (*Elements*, 219; see *Outlines*, 180).

interest is subjected to the universal rather than freely converging with it. But in reality, the "requirement of *equality*"[73] is directly implied by civil society's distinctive trait: the needs and activities of each individual intertwine with the system of needs to help create the well-being of all; the *"legal constitution"*[74] of this society presupposes strict legal parity between social actors. Of course, this equality of position and rights does not exclude strong economic and social inequalities; it even goes along with their reinforcement. Hegel, in discussing the "objective *right of particularity*" emphasizes that it

> does not cancel out [*nicht aufhebt*] the inequality of human beings in
> civil society—an inequality posited by nature, which is the element of
> inequality—but in fact produces it out of the spirit itself and raises it to an
> inequality of skills, resources, and even of intellectual and moral education.[75]

Tocqueville says the same: equal conditions are not incompatible with the persistence of strong inequalities, in particular on the economic level; such equality, spread and magnified by "public opinion" is a "sort of imaginary equality."[76] Equality, including what may be phantasmagoric about it, is thus indeed the characteristic proper to civil society (in Hegel's sense) or the democratic social condition (in Tocqueville's sense).

However, there is a corollary to the equality of conditions: the *mobility* of individuals and social structures themselves. Hegel equates the man of civil society (the bourgeois) with man tout court.[77] What is the reason for this surprising identification of man per se with the bourgeois who is separated from his own existence as political citizen? It results from the fact that civil society, by stripping the individual of all the statutory attributes that would grant him a fixed, immobile position in the political universe, has literally invented *man in general*; it has thus given concrete basis to the abstract discourse of the rights of man. One of the consequences of this abstraction (of the democratic social condition) is that there, all else being equal, the individual is free to choose his estate. Far from being rigidly determined by factors out of individuals' control

---

73. *RPh*, § 193, *GW* 14.1, p. 167 (*Elements*, 230; see *Outlines*, 189).

74. *RPh*, § 157, *GW* 14.1, p. 143 (*Elements*, 198; see *Outlines*, 162).

75. *RPh*, § 200 Anmerkung, *GW* 14.1, p. 170 (*Elements*, 233–34; see *Outlines*, 192).

76. Tocqueville, *Democracy in America*, 674; *De la démocratie en Amérique*, 2:189.

77. See *RPh*, § 190 Anmerkung, *GW* 14.1, p. 166 (*Elements*, 228; see *Outlines*, 188).

(birth, etc.), "for the subjective consciousness . . . [the choice] has the shape of being the product of its own will,"[78] and this will is contingent and fluctuating. Consequently, mobility, in all the senses of the word, is implied by the very nature of civil society insofar as it disregards the political bond and political hierarchies.

At the very moment when he introduces his doctrine of the representation of social interests, quite undemocratic in itself, Hegel evokes the "*changing element in civil* society."[79] This can be compared to what Tocqueville writes in the second volume of *Democracy in America* regarding the "mobility" and "agitation" of democratic society:

> In enlightened and free democratic centuries, there is nothing to separate men or keep them in their place. They rise or fall with singular rapidity. All classes have one another constantly in view because they live in close proximity. They communicate and mingle every day and emulate and envy one another. To the people this suggests a host of ideas, notions, and desires they would not have if ranks were fixed and society immobile.[80]

In conclusion, despite the differences in emphasis that stem from the two authors' specific national and intellectual histories (a good example of which is the issue of corporations), Hegel's "civil society" and Tocqueville's "democratic social condition" refer to similar realities, though perhaps grasped in a different light (for Hegel, economical-legal; for Tocqueville, political-ideological). But above all, their analyses reveal surprisingly convergent concerns. Each one strives to measure *the consequences of the autonomization of the social for the political and for the state*, though it is clear that their orientations and proposed solutions are far from identical. This process is what they focus on, for it has given modernity its particular features, both fascinating and disquieting. The common point between these two approaches is thus the following question, which in many ways is my question as well: What happens to the political in a society where politics in the traditional sense (i.e., the institutionalized form of the relation between command and obedience) no longer determines, or no longer solely determines, how humans live together?

78. *RPh*, § 206, *GW* 14.1, p. 172 (*Elements*, 237; see *Outlines*, 195–96).
79. *RPh*, § 308, *GW* 14.1, p. 254 (*Elements*, 346; see *Outlines*, 294). See chapter 8 below.
80. Tocqueville, *Democracy in America*, 520; *De la démocratie en Amérique*, 2:45.

8

A Theory of Representation

Preliminaries: Sovereignty and Representation

In an openly anti-Hegelian declaration, Carl Schmitt wrote that "The elevation of the concept of the State to the rank of universal conceptual norm . . . probably will soon end with the era of the state-form itself."[1] In any case, the "era of the European state-form" opened with the proclamation of the supremacy of the political—the specifically modern form of which is an abstract entity, the state—over other spheres of human existence. The state also tends to overcome the religious universe, where the deep fracture that followed the Reformation required that religion somehow be neutralized. Furthermore, the state separates the world of work from technical-economic interaction (what comes to be termed *civil society*) and similarly profoundly transforms the closed space of the family. The political does not only free itself from these spheres, it imposes its law on them. The concepts of *sovereignty* and *representation*, though they have different origins and statuses, are the cardinal points of modern thinking about the state, which began to take form (at the same time as the state itself) in the sixteenth century. The state's first representatives, in very different genres, were Machiavelli and Bodin. With the concepts of sov-

---

1. Carl Schmitt, *Verfassungsrechtliche Aufsätze aus den Jahren 1924–1954: Materialien zu einer Verfassungslehre* (Berlin: Duncker und Humbolt, 1953), 376. See also *Der Begriff des Politischen*, 10–11 (this is from the 1963 preface, not translated in *The Concept of the Political*).

ereignty and representation, modern political philosophy began to attempt to think through the advent of the state.

The notion of sovereignty is typically modern: considered a property of the state rather than of the person or persons at its head, it is characteristic of the process of depersonalization and rationalization that according to Weber defines the modern form of the political.[2] Bodin famously defined sovereignty as "the absolute and perpetual power of a Republic."[3] This definition shows that even if for Bodin it was almost a given that this power would be held and exercised by a monarch, the person of the sovereign was henceforth understood on the basis of his or her office; the actual person became secondary with regard to the abstract essence of sovereignty. We should note that here the church paved the way for the state: the canonical distinction between person and office made the impersonal definition of power required by the modern state possible. In any case, during the period when the "state-form" ruled uncontested, sovereignty was its essential predicate, and it is not surprising that those who, beginning in the nineteenth century, wanted, like Cassirer, to denounce the "myth of the state" criticized the metaphysical nature of that notion.

Unlike sovereignty, representation is not *first* a political notion: it comes from theology, and more specifically from ecclesiology. In fact, it was over the course of the debate within the church between the supporters of conciliar representation and supporters of papal representation that its eminently political meaning was revealed.[4] But it was the modern theory of the sovereign state that gave this concept its most fecund applications. A state, regardless of its type of government or regime, implements forms of representation. Whether deliberation and decision are collective or whether a single person speaks for all, the state is the representative of the political community, of the

2. See Weber, *Economy and Society*. On legal-rational domination, see Catherine Colliot-Thélène, *Le désenchantement de l'Etat* (Paris: Minuit, 1992), 224 ff.

3. Bodin, *Les six livres*, I/8, 1:179. Olivier Beaud emphasizes the innovative nature of Bodin's doctrine of sovereignty insofar as it founds a "monopolization of positive law by the state." In Beaud, *La puissance de l'état*, 29–196, esp. 50–52.

4. On the prehistory of the modern concept of representation, see Hasso Hoffman, *Repräsentation: Studien zur Wort und Begriffsgeschichte* (Berlin: Duncker und Humboldt, 1990), especially chapter 5 ("Repraesentatio identitatis"), 191 ff., and the beginning of chapter 6 about Nicolaus Cusanus ("De Concordantia Catholica"), 286 ff. See also Giueseppe Duso, *La rappresentanza politica: Genesi e crisi del concetto* (Milan: F. Angeli, 2003), especially chapters 1 and 2.

people. Not, however, in the sense that the state is their mandated or commissioned agent: if that were the case, it would merely be a tool for carrying out a preexisting will, a government in the modern and restrictive sense of the word. The state, by its institutional existence and its action, represents or symbolizes the unity of the community, the common will.

The convergence between the theme of sovereignty, connected to the rise of absolutism, and that of representation, which opposed centralization (whether in conciliarism or in early adversaries of absolutism) and the monopoly of power, is surprising at first; it implies that each of these concepts underwent profound changes. This is perceptible in the *Leviathan*, where Hobbes develops a theory of sovereign political representation based on the concept of authorization in order to resolve certain problems in his earlier political philosophy. According to Hobbes, the sovereign represents the people, but not in the sense that the people delegates to the sovereign the people's own power, for that would imply that the people exists as such by nature, that it is already a subject capable of willing. But if that were the case, the problem that the doctrine of sovereignty seeks to solve — the problem of the constitution of political unity out of heterogeneous diversity — would be nonexistent, and the sovereign would be either fictive or useless. In reality, the sovereign represents in the particular sense that he creates, *constitutes*, the subject he renders present, just as in speech acts meaning does not preexist expression. Thus, the expression from *De Cive* must be understood literally: "in a monarchy . . . the king (although this seems paradoxical) *is the people*."[5] It means that the represented do not logically or chronologically preexist the sovereign but rather that their being, their identity, is constituted by the very act in which they acquire a representative. This is what the theory of authorization explains. By illustrating the mechanism of the constitution of sovereignty through the distinction between author and actor, Hobbes concludes that "it is impossible to conceive of unity other than by the form of representation."[6] Indeed, the difference between a disunited multitude and *a* people is created by the operation in which — as in the illusion of theater — the author, who is neither seen nor heard in person, speaks through the mouth of the actor and thereby is constituted as the author of the piece being played or represented. In other words, "it is the *unity* of the representer, not the *unity* of the represented, that

5. Hobbes, *De Cive: English Version*, 12:8, 190.
6. Hobbes, *Leviathan*, 2:248.

maketh the person *one*."[7] This is the paradoxical or miraculous essence of representative sovereignty.

This theory of representative sovereignty does not necessarily imply a predilection for monarchy. Thus, we find the theory in Rousseau, where it serves an entirely different purpose. The first chapter of book three of the *Social Contract* mobilizes the political concept of representative sovereignty to characterize the relationship between the prince (government, executive), the sovereign (the active political body), and the people (the same body understood as passive, as subject). Rousseau writes that there must be an "intermediate body established between the subjects and the sovereign for their mutual correspondence"[8]—a mediation between the active whole and the passive whole, between the sovereign and the people. Representation refers to the relationship a human group has with itself once it has political existence, once it gives itself a common will. The matter cannot be reduced to the presence of "representatives," elected or otherwise, of the people, of social groups, or of individuals within the institutions of the state, for that is just one aspect, wrongly isolated and foregrounded, of the general problem of political representation.

And in fact, the relationship between sovereignty and representation took on a different meaning with the French and American Revolutions, when a new idea of representation was born, or rather—since the idea was already present in Whig constitutionalism, and in particular in Burke[9]—when the idea surged to the forefront. This transformation first appeared with the American founding fathers, who developed a new conception of the republic guided by the ideal of an "empire of laws and not of men,"[10] thanks to which the notion of representation acquired the content we now recognize in it. The authors of the *Federalist Papers*, establishing the constitutional doctrine

7. Ibid.

8. See Rousseau, *Oeuvres complètes*, 3:396; *Social Contract*, 3:1, 194.

9. In his address to the electors of Bristol (1774), Burke presents the doctrine of "free mandate" and attacks the idea that representation can be a commission: "Parliament is not a congress of ambassadors from different and hostile interests ... but ... a deliberative assembly of one nation, with one interest, that of the whole." Edmund Burke, *The Works of Edmund Burke* (London: Rivington, 1803), 3:20.

10. John Adams, "Thoughts on Government," in *The Works of John Adams*, ed. Charles F. Adams (Boston: Little, Brown, 1951), 4:194.

of the United States in 1787, wrote that a republican government is "a government in which the scheme of representation takes place";[11] it is clear that for them a representative regime has nothing to do either with the absolutism of Hobbes's sovereign-representative or with a regime in which "the people meet and exercise the government in person."[12] The change in the concept of representation is just as clearly visible in Sieyès. Much has been made — too much, perhaps — of the innovation of distinguishing between constituting power and constituted power(s). For the most part, this distinction extends Rousseau's distinction in the *Social Contract* between sovereignty and government. Sovereignty, explains Rousseau, once again faithful to Hobbes, can be neither delegated nor constituted by delegation, for "sovereign power, which is in fact a collective being, can be represented only by itself."[13] The sovereign may of course have officials or commissioners — this is precisely the status of the government[14] — but not representatives who would hold *plenitudo potestasis*. It is that very cardinal principle of the doctrine of sovereignty that Sieyès upsets when he proclaims that if what he calls extraordinary representatives (i.e., those who exercise constitutive power) are legitimately constituted, then they are "put in the place of the nation itself," and "it is sufficient for them to will as they would will in the state of nature."[15] This literally reverses the doctrine of representative sovereignty: the nation's delegation of its sovereign power to a body of representatives does not at all imply a lessening or diversion of this sovereign power. To the contrary: it is *only* through the mediation of representation that the diffuse national will is expressed and becomes authentically sovereign. Henceforth, "the object or purpose of the representative assembly ... cannot be different from that which would propose the nation itself, if it could meet and confer in the same place."[16] Popular sovereignty is inalienable — this is Rousseau's argument — but the people itself cannot exercise it, it *must* be represented in the very act that constitutes it as a people; this is Sieyès's contribution.

This theory of sovereign representation is at the basis of what may be

---

11. *Federalist Papers*, no. 10, p. 52.
12. Ibid., no. 14, p. 68.
13. Rousseau, *Oeuvres complètes*, 3:368; *Social Contract*, 170.
14. See Rousseau, *Social Contract*, bk. 3, §§ 1, 15, 17.
15. Emmanuel-Joseph Sieyès, *Qu'est-ce que le tiers état?* (Geneva: Droz, 1970), 185.
16. Ibid., 204.

termed the *republican* problematic of power (in spite of Sieyès's own distaste
for the word). As the political history of the nineteenth century shows, this
theory can span widely different political options. Schematically, we can note
a *liberal* variant (after Burke and the founding fathers, Constant and Tocqueville were spokesmen for this version) and a *democratic* variant (which, quickly
stifled after the French Revolution, regained its strength around 1848 but
henceforth with a new current to work with: socialism). Despite the clear
opposition between these two variants, in particular with respect to the scope
and terms of suffrage, they were based on shared convictions regarding the
relations between the sovereignty of the people and political representation.
The divergence lay in whether emphasis was put on the first term (the democratic position) or on the second (the liberal position). The Hegelian theory of
representation is located upstream of this divergence. It seeks to overcome the
alternative confronting modern thinking about the state: between representative sovereignty (Hobbes, Rousseau) and sovereign representation (Sieyès,
the founding fathers).

A Politics of Representation

Hegel does not have a systematic theory of the relations between sovereignty
and representation. However, his political philosophy (in the strict sense of a
theory of the state in its internal aspect) is based on a particular articulation of
these two concepts that implies reshaping them: sovereignty is considered the
exclusive attribute of the state, which is distinct from the monarch, the people,
and "national" representation;[17] the task of representation is to guarantee mediation between the state and civil society. But in approaching this question,
we cannot limit ourselves to the writings that express the principles of Hegel's
political philosophy, that is, the *Philosophy of Right* and the doctrine of objective spirit in the *Encyclopedia*; we must also take into consideration the political writings that in a sense present a politics of representation.

Before Hegelian philosophy achieved its true originality (in 1802, as we
know), his text on the German constitution (1798–1800) developed a merciless critique of the premodern conception of representation on which the

---

17. This is what Hegel calls "the idealism" of sovereignty (*RPh*, § 278 Anmerkung, *GW* 14.1,
p. 231 [*Elements*, 315; see *Outlines*, 239]).

"imaginary state" (*Gedankenstaat*),[18] officially known as the Holy Roman Empire of the German Nation, rested. But Hegel makes an instructive comparison between this outdated vision and the one cultivated by political liberalism. In the wake of the French Revolution, German liberals contrasted the demand for a "representative constitution" (*Repräsentativ-Verfassung*) with the "constitution of estates" (*ständische Verfassung*) proper to the old regime and to the empire in particular. As for Hegel, he emphasizes that these two institutional options, which are opposed in practice, in fact share a common theoretical basis. The representative principle, regardless of the goal of its implementation, expresses in his eyes (at least it did at that moment) the rootedness of the constitution in the feudal system, which implies reducing public law to private law:

> Representation is so deeply interwoven with the essence of the feudal constitution in its development along with the rise of the *bourgeois* estate that we may call it the silliest of notions to suppose it an invention of the most recent times.[19]

The entire modern history of Germany shows that in the hands of the "provinces"—the most powerful of which had become true sovereign states—representation had become a weapon against imperial power, and it contributed to undermining the political unity of the empire. As Hegel reminds the reader in the course of the homage he renders to Machiavelli in this text, "freedom is possible only when a people is united into a state by legal bonds."[20] However, at the same time that he locates the cause of the imperial pseudo-state's political impotence in a certain system of representation, Hegel maintains—showing his unflagging adherence to the principles of 1789—that in the absence of representative institutions guaranteeing "cooperation of the general will in the most important affairs of state which affect everyone," "free-

18. "Verfassung," W 1, p. 507; "German Constitution," in *Hegel's Political Writings*, 180 (modified).

19. "Verfassung," W 1, p. 536; "German Constitution," in *Hegel's Political Writings*, 206 (modified). Regarding the reduction of public law to private law, see "Verfassung," W 1, pp. 454–56 (passage not included in the English translation).

20. "Verfassung," W 1, p. 555; "German Constitution," in *Hegel's Political Writings*, 220.

dom is no longer thinkable," so that representation "has become part of sound common sense."[21]

We see that *two* notions of representation, with opposite connotations, coexist in the young Hegel's manuscript. These correspond to two different German terms: *Repräsentation*, the constitutive relationship of the political community to itself, and *Vertretung* or *Stellvertretung*, the designation of authorized representatives of particular interests. Later, Hegel would explicitly draw on this distinction. In the remark to section 303 in the *Philosophy of Right*, he criticizes the "atomistic . . . view" that it is up to individuals to exercise legislative power, either on their own or through the intermediary of "representatives" (*Stellvertreter*).[22] To the contrary, the remark to section 311 uses the vocabulary of *Repräsentation* to justify a parliamentary system based on the representation of social interests. Hegel specifies that in this case "representation no longer means the *replacement* of one individual *by another*."[23] In his early writings, things are not so clear: there, Hegel contrasts *two* models of representation that are politically and theoretically opposed. The *first* one is the "feudal" (more precisely, *ständisch*) notion of representation, based on the schema of a mandate (*Stellvertretung*) borrowed from private law, which subordinates the representative (the emperor) to the represented (the electoral princes or dignitaries at the head of the territories of the empire); the so-called electoral capitulations, by which the represented impose the conditions of their support on candidates for imperial dignity, are an example of this kind of understanding of representation.[24] In short, because the empire is based on a conception of representation that reduces sovereignty, the distinctive trait of the state, to a mere empty word, it resembles "a heap of round stones which are piled together to form a pyramid."[25] But to combat the foregoing, "The German Constitution" also turns to the *second*, new model of representation as the vehicle for forming the general will. This truly revolutionary model—and it was as such that the young Hegel took it up—was illustrated by the 1791 Constitution[26] and justified in the writings of Sieyès. However, insofar as we can judge from the fact that the manuscript was never completed,

21. "Verfassung," *W* 1, p. 572; "German Constitution," in *Hegel's Political Writings*, 234–35.
22. *RPh*, § 303 Anmerkung, *GW* 14.1, p. 252 (*Elements*, 343–44; see *Outlines*, 291).
23. *RPh*, § 311 Anmerkung, *GW* 14.1, p. 256 (*Elements*, 350; see *Outlines*, 297).
24. See chapter 9.
25. "Verfassung," *W* 1, p. 504; "German Constitution," in *Hegel's Political Writings*, 180.
26. "The nation, from which alone emanates all the powers, can exercise them only by dele-

in 1800 Hegel did not yet have the conceptual means to overcome this contradiction between the two views of representation.

The article titled "Proceedings of the Estates Assembly in the Kingdom of Württemberg, 1815–1816" is dedicated entirely to the question of representation and in particular to the difficulties, in a country that had not experienced a revolution, of shifting from a traditional system to a postrevolutionary system of "national representation." The text develops a meticulous and engaged analysis of the debate in the Diet convoked by King Frederick II of Württemberg after the end of the French occupation in order to ratify a liberal constitution (in the mind of leading circles, it was to correspond to the model of the charter "granted" by Louis XVIII to the French); it includes significant notes regarding the articulation of representation and sovereignty. Let us go through the argument in this text, in which Hegel demonstrates his talent as a political chronicler. By opposing in every way the plans of the king—who, by multiplying the concessions to liberal ideas (which we must remember had penetrated Germany by means of France's military victories), was seeking to make the elites accept a crown he owed to Napoleon—the States of Wurtemberg adopted a typically reactionary attitude. In their attempt to fight the king's plans and to restore the "good old law" (*das alte gute Recht*), that is, the legal and political structures of a society of privileges, they thought of themselves as the General Estates of 1789, but, as Hegel scathingly put it, "only the roles are reversed."[27] Borrowing a phrase from Talleyrand, he adds, "one might say of the Wurtemberg estates what has been said of the returned French *émigrés*: they have forgotten nothing and learnt nothing."

This article does something the article on the constitution of the empire did not: it contrasts two distinct types of representation, "traditional representation" and "true national representation."[28] The true vocation of representation is—the *Philosophy of Right* returns to this theme—to be "the mediating body between the prince and the people."[29] However, the attitude of the estates—in particular, the attitude of delegates of what Hegel calls the bourgeois aristocracy—hindered the exercise of this function. This is why, since it is not

---

gation. The French constitution is representative, the representatives are the Legislative Body and the King" (Heading III, Article 2).

27. *Wurtemberg, W* 4, p. 507; *Proceedings,* in *Hegel's Political Writings,* 282.

28. *Wurtemberg, W* 4, p. 588 (passage not translated in *Hegel's Political Writings*).

29. *Wurtemberg, W* 4, p. 533 (passage not translated in *Hegel's Political Writings*). See *RPh,* § 302 Anmerkung, *GW* 14.1, p. 251 (*Elements,* 342–43; see *Outlines,* 290).

possible to give a priori a constitution to a people when its presumed representatives do not want one, one can only hope that the gathering of the estates was at least the occasion for "self-education,"[30] for an authentic *political* education in politics, offering representatives, who were clinging to the particularity of the interests they represented, the ability to accede the universal: "the ascent to the universal belongs to the formal aspect of the political education of a new assembly of the states."[31] But though he roundly criticized supporters of traditional representation, Hegel did not join the camp of those who supported the representative constitution—that is, in general, liberals or those presumed to be liberals.[32] To the contrary, the article includes in-detail criticism of *"French abstractions,"*[33] which Hegel would later expand on in the *Philosophy of Right*. The ultimate reasons for this criticism lie in the Hegelian conception of civil society and its relations to the state. The 1817 article sketches what would become the Hegelian analysis of representative mediation: the authentic vocation of representation is to institute the people, which, in its immediate being, is politically amorphous. In other words, as indicated in the lectures Hegel was giving at the same time in Heidelberg, which formed the first draft of the *Philosophy of Right*, without the "articulation" that representation introduces into the midst of the people, they lack the "rationality" that gives them a state and political meaning and are no more than a "mass."[34]

The connection between the system of representation and social and political equilibrium within the state is the theme of Hegel's last political article, "On the English Reform Bill," which appeared in April-May 1831 in the *Allgemeine preussische Staatszeitung*, though without its final third, which was

---

30. *Wurtemberg, W* 4, p. 582 (passage not translated in *Hegel's Political Writings*). See Christoph Jamme, "Die Erziehung der Stände durch sich selbst," in *Hegels Rechtsphilosophie im Zusammenhang der europäischen Verfassungsgeschichte*, ed. Otto Pöggeler and Hans-Christian Lucas (Stuttgart: Frommann-Holzboog, 1986), 149–73.

31. *Wurtemberg, W* 4, p. 591 (passage not translated in *Hegel's Political Writings*).

32. For reasons having to do with the economic and political conditions particular to nineteenth-century Germany, German liberalism combined progressive and regressive traits. Lothar Gall, "Liberalismus und 'bürgerliche Gesellschaft,'" *Historische Zeitschrift* 220, no. 2 (1975): 350 ff. The positions analyzed by Hegel are an example of this.

33. *Wurtemberg, W* 4, p. 483; *Proceedings*, in *Hegel's Political Writings*, 263.

34. Hegel, *Vorlesungen über Naturrecht und Staatswissenschaft*, 223; Hegel, *Lectures on Natural Right*, 273.

censored for being too critical of Great Britain.[35] Through an analysis of the situation in Great Britain the text examines the bill brought by the Whig prime minister Lord Grey before Parliament; the bill was passed in 1832 (thus, after Hegel's death) and would profoundly change English political life by eliminating the "rotten boroughs" and introducing more a balanced representation of the population (but not universal suffrage) that took into account social and demographic changes. Hegel's point of view here has sometimes been described as reactionary; since Rudolf Haym, that qualification has been a constant among liberal adversaries of Hegelianism. For didn't he, at the end of the day, oppose a reform that he himself showed to be indispensable and that common sense and parity seemed to demand? However, the matter is more complex if we examine it from the point of view of a theory of political representation. Hegel's reasons for opposing the system of representation Great Britain was preparing to implement stemmed from what we might call his political sociology. He refuses to see representation and its modalities from a strictly technical or political-moral point of view; instead, he analyzes it in relation to the legal, social, and political structures of a Great Britain undergoing the effects of the "great transformation," to borrow Karl Polyani's words. Hegel does not have words harsh enough to fustigate the "anomalies and absurdity of the English constitution."[36] England's situation, which he had long been familiar with thanks to his regular reading of the English press,[37] made reforms indispensable, especially in the system of representation. But Hegel thought that the reformation of electoral law would aggravate the situation by opening Parliament to new social strata—not the proletariat, but rather the radicalized petty bourgeoisie, followers of Bentham and demanders of democracy—but without transforming either a social structure that would remain deeply inegalitarian or an incoherent and outdated civil law. Hegel's

---

35. The historical and theoretical context of this analysis is discussed in Christoph Jamme and Elisabeth Weisser-Lohmann, *Politik und Geschichte: Zu den Intentionen von G.W.F. Hegels Reformbill-Schrift* (Bonn: Bouvier, 1995). See also Walter Jaeschke, "Hegel's Last Year in Berlin," in Hegel's *Philosophy of Action*, ed. Lawrence Stepelevich and David Lamb (Atlantic Highlands, NJ: Humanities Press, 1983), p. 31 ff.

36. *Reformbill*, W 11, p. 84; *Reform Bill*, in *Hegel's Political Writings*, 296.

37. See Michael J. Petry, "Hegel and the Morning Chronicle," *Hegel-Studien* 11 (1976): 11–80; Norbert Waszek, "Hegels Exzerpte aus der *Edinburgh Review* 1817–1819," *Hegel-Studien* 20 (1985): 79–112.

diagnosis: instead of (political) reform, the Reform Bill could spark (social and political) revolution, and this is the primary reason why it should not be adopted.[38]

Against the individualist understanding of representation that emerges from the principles of 1789 and that seems to have guided Lord Grey's plan, Hegel sets the *representation of social interests*. The representation of the "various great interests of the nation"[39] must be promoted, for only this can set "political life" on its "real basic constituents"[40] — the competition of organized interests within civil society. Whether one likes it or not, civil society, in its diversity and conflicts, is the *presupposition* of the process of unification that takes place on the terrain of the political, and it must be institutionally recognized as such; otherwise, one "leaves political life hanging, so to speak, in the air," and it is better to recognize this fact than to deny it in the name of abstract principles such as the right to individual suffrage.[41] It thus becomes clear that the argument in the 1831 article is not simply retrograde. Rather, Hegel shows himself for what he had long if not always been: an authoritarian liberal, a supporter of top-down reform as it was carried out in Prussia during the era of reforms (1806–1819) by enlightened ministers (Freiherr vom Stein, chancellor Hardenberg, Wilhelm von Humboldt).[42] What Hegel, like them, wants is for the initial program of the French Revolution to be realized (equal rights to certain fundamental goods guaranteed for all, a civil society freed from the rigidity of orders and privileges, a strong, liberal state) — but without revolution. This requires an adequate politics of representation, one entirely different from the risky politics of English liberals. We must now specify the theoretical basis for such a politics.

The Representation of Interests

Why must there be *representation* within the state in the sense that the term had taken on since the eighteenth century — that is, one or more assemblies of

---

38. See *Reformbill, W* 11, p. 128; *Reform Bill*, in *Hegel's Political Writings*, 330.

39. *Reformbill, W* 11, p. 105; *Hegel's Political Writings*, 312.

40. *Reformbill, W* 11, p. 107; *Hegel's Political Writings*, 314.

41. *RPh*, § 303 Anmerkung, *GW* 14.1, p. 252 (*Elements*, 344; see *Outlines*, 292).

42. On this period, see Reinhart Koselleck, *Preussen zwischen Reform und Revolution* (Stuttgart: E. Klett, 1967). Koselleck emphasizes the convergence between Hegel's point of view and that of Prussian reformers.

"representatives of the people"? In other words, what makes Hobbes's solution (the unity of the sovereign creates, on its own, the unity of the people represented) insufficient? Once again, the answer stems from the changes entailed by the separation of civil society and the state. Once the socioeconomic is distinguished from the political, a separation that is the defining trait of modern *Sittlichkeit*, in order to prevent this differentiation from becoming a dangerous competition, it is necessary to invent procedures of dynamic *integration* for a social universe increasingly divided into particular, antagonistic interests.[43] Among these procedures, representation — in the technical sense of the term — plays a decisive role: through it, as Hegel says, "the private estate attains a *political significance* and function."[44] In other words, representation guarantees the presence of the social world — divided, as it is, into divergent and even antagonistic interests — within state institutions and at the same time makes it possible to reaffirm the supremacy of the political universal — which is only concrete if it is not isolated from what contradicts it — over social particularity. But the political integration of social diversity can only be achieved if it takes into account — or better yet, bases itself on — actual divisions in civil society, which are institutionalized by corporations. Whence the surprising choice of representation of social interests instead of representation based on the free suffrage of individuals, which corresponds to an atomistic vision of civil society that does not conform to its reality.[45] This explains why representation is *necessary* to the world that emerged from the French Revolution and from the industrial and capitalist revolutions (and also shows how far Hegel's reasons are from the points of view of liberals as well as of democrats). In such a world, the separation of the political and the social and the tensions that run through the latter require a mechanism that guarantees the *institutional* integration (not left to the spontaneous regulations of the market) of social diversity, that is, essentially, parliamentary representation, which allows the people, faced with its impassable diversity, to be "face to face with a lively presence of spirit."[46]

From this we understand the reason for the political representation of social interests. It fits with a particular understanding of the organization of

43. See Rudolf Smend, "Verfassung und Verfassungsrecht," in *Staatsrechtliche Abhandlungen: Und andere Aufsätze* (Berlin: Duncker und Humblot, 1968), 154.

44. *RPh*, § 303, *GW* 14.1, p. 251 (*Elements*, 343; see *Outlines*, 291).

45. See *RPh*, § 308, *GW* 14.1, p. 254 (*Elements*, 346–47: see *Outlines*, 294).

46. *Wurtemberg*, *W* 4, p. 516 (passage not translated in *Hegel's Political Writings*).

244 · Chapter Eight

powers: for Hegel, the various powers among which the state's action is distributed are interactive moments of its organism and thus cannot exist or act
independently, as the common understanding of their separation would suggest. Princely power, the power of the hereditary monarch, has the authority
of ultimate decision; it closes the deliberative process with the *"I will"* that
initiates "all activity and actuality."[47] Within the state, governmental power is
the moment of particularity. It has a double role, both deliberative and executive. Composed of expert bureaucrats with precise knowledge of the concrete
conditions in which the state acts, the government is in charge in particular
of administrative tasks and economic and social regulation—of "policing." By
virtue of these characteristics, the government is a moment of mediation between the prince and the legislative power just as its administration of concrete situations contributes to creating the never-stabilized link between the
social world and the political universe. Finally, the legislature decrees universal norms, laws, for the ethical-political community. Thus, it defines—though
only at a general level—the relations between individuals and social groups on
the one hand and with the state on the other.[48] We see, thus, that state powers
differ in terms of their functions, not the people or bodies charged with carrying them out. This is why the prince and the government also participate in
legislative work alongside assemblies.[49] This participation is not limited to a
right of initiative: they make actual contributions to legislation on the basis of
their technical expertise and their sense of the state. Here, Hegel is faithful to
his refusal of the separation of powers, though he does make one exception,
which is not negligible: only with regard to the legislative power does he explicitly mention the interpenetration of the three powers, which should also
apply to the two others. Clearly one may be tempted here to suspect him of
wanting to restrict as much as possible the influence of the people's representatives within the state. But that interpretation supposes that Hegel shares the
common view of their mission, which is far from the case. Regardless, statutory representation is but one of the elements of legislative power.

Above all else, Hegel emphasizes the role representative institutions play
in mediation; I will return to this shortly. Thus, he presents in detail the bases
of an original bicameral system. The general principle is as follows: because

47. *RPh,* § 279 Anmerkung, *GW* 14.1, p. 233 (*Elements,* 317; see *Outlines,* 267).
48. *RPh,* § 299, *GW* 14.1, p. 247 (*Elements,* 337; see *Outlines,* 285).
49. See *RPh,* § 300, *GW* 14.1, p. 248 (*Elements,* 339; see *Outlines,* 287).

the representative assemblies—the "estates" in traditional terminology—mediate between the political state (*der Staat*) of which they are a part and a people that itself is socially divided into social estates, political representation must reflect the actual elements of civil society and base itself on the divisions within it:

> In the *Estates*, as an element of the legislative power, the *private estate* attains a *political significance* and function. In this capacity, the private estate cannot appear either as a simple undifferentiated mass or as a crowd split up into atomic units. It appears rather as *what it already is*, namely as an *estate* consisting of two distinct parts. . . . Only in this respect is there a genuine link between the *particular* which has actuality in the state and the universal.[50]

Thus, social differentiation, which in modern society results from the technical division of labor, can structure political representation. Thanks to representative institutions, the state gives concrete shape to one of its missions, which is to guarantee the political mediation of civil society with itself. This is the main reason why Hegel preserves the vocabulary of "estates," which by 1820 was completely outdated: because one and the same word (*die Stände*) refers to both socioprofessional groups and to the assemblies that exercise legislative power or at least participate in it.

Bicameralism reflects the opposition between the city and the country, between the capitalist industrial and commercial world and the rural world, between the modern and the premodern: these are the two "ethical roots" of the state.[51] The quasi-natural element that within civil society forms the estate of landowners is politically expressed in a high chamber, comparable to the British House of Lords or the Chamber of Peers of the French Restoration.[52] However, it must be noted that these landowners are members of this high chamber not because they belong to the nobility but rather because of their economic and social role. The second chamber is made up of mandated agents (*Vertreter*) of the "*changing* element in *civil* society,"[53] that is, social groups

---

50. *RPh*, § 303, *GW* 14.1, p. 251 (*Elements*, 343; see *Outlines*, 291).

51. See *RPh*, § 255 and 256 Anmerkung, *GW* 14.1, pp. 199–200 (*Elements*, 272–74; see *Outlines*, 226–27).

52. See *RPh*, §§ 304–307, *GW* 14.1, pp. 252–54 (*Elements*, 344–46; see *Outlines*, 292–93).

53. *RPh*, § 308, *GW* 14.1, p. 254 (*Elements*, 346; see *Outlines*, 294).

that make up the urban world. More specifically, this chamber emerges from cooperative associations (*Genossenschaften*), communities, and corporations that are the "*particular circles*" of civil society."[54] Hegel considers these various groups to have "the same right as the others to be represented."[55] The question of the person and mode of selecting deputies becomes secondary with respect to the question of the representation of the "special needs" and "particular interests" of the social body.[56] Through this type of representation, the universal (the state) includes within itself the particular social moment in its diversity. However, deputies are not mere mandated agents of a particular interest and must not act as such. This is why Hegel rejects the Jacobin doctrine of the imperative mandate, which according to its supporters allows electors to control the elected and is similar to the liberal theory of free mandate as Burke, for example, advanced it:

> Since deputies are elected to deliberate and decide on matters of *universal* concern, the aim of such elections is to appoint individuals who are credited by those who elect them with a better understanding of such matters than they themselves possess. It is also the intention that these individuals will not subordinate the universal interest to the particular interest of a community or corporation, but will give it their essential support. Their position is accordingly not that of commissioned or mandated agents, especially since the purpose [*Bestimmung*] of their assembly is to provide a forum for live exchanges and collective deliberations in which the participants instruct and convince one another.[57]

Although deputies come from particular groups and guarantee that these have political existence, they are first and foremost agents of the universal. The necessary political representation of the social world cannot be an institutional endorsement of lobbying.

The Hegelian state grants parliament, and in particular the lower chamber,

54. *RPh*, § 308 Anmerkung, *GW* 14.1, p. 254 (*Elements*, 347; see *Outlines*, 294). It is interesting to note the similarity in vocabulary between Hegel and Gierke's theory of *Genossenschaftsrecht*, which was presented as an anti-Hegelian reaction; this, in any case, is how it is commonly interpreted, for example by Gurvitch (see *L'idée du droit social*).

55. *RPh*, § 311 Anmerkung, *GW* 14.1, pp. 256–57 (*Elements*, 350; see *Outlines*, 297).

56. *RPh*, § 311, *GW* 14.1, p. 256 (*Elements*, 350; see *Outlines*, 296–97).

57. *RPh*, § 309, *GW* 14.1, p. 255 (*Elements*, 348, see *Outlines*, 295).

the role of mediating between the government and the people, between the state and civil society. But this mediation must be understood in its truth. It is both a way for a differentiated and even fractured social body to accede to political being and an organ for the continual politicization and repoliticization of civil society, which is constantly undermined by the conflicts of interest that run through it. In other words, if the state in general is a mediation of society with itself, if it is the authority that confers on it an ethical identity, it is above all up to the specific body of representation (parliament and its chambers) to solder the identity of the state, symbolized in the person of the monarch, and the divided social multitude. Contrary to what liberals claim, the mission of assemblies is not only to make the views of civil society heard within the state and ultimately to subordinate the state to civil society. They must also, and above all, allow the point of view of the state to penetrate society and practice a sort of political pedagogy toward their mandators through the publicity of debates:

> The determination of the Estates as an institution does not require them to achieve optimum results in their deliberations and decisions on the business of the state *in itself*. . . . They have the distinctive function [*Bestimmung*] of ensuring that, through their participation in [the government's] knowledge, deliberations, and decisions on matters of universal concern, the moment of *formal* freedom attains its right in relation to those members of civil society who have no share in the government. In this way, it is first and foremost the moment of *universal* knowledge [*Kenntnis*] which is extended by the *publicity* with which the proceedings of the Estates are conducted.[58]

As the article on the Estates of Wurtemberg indicated, parliamentary debate is above all the instrument of civil society's political "self-education" through those who represent its interests; representation is the work of the political.

A Philosophy of Representation

Neither individual suffrage nor a vote based on estate but rather socioprofessional representation of *Berufstände*, of "guilds": this, according to Hegel, is the third way, the reformist way, between the revolutionary views of demo-

---

58. *RPh*, § 314, *GW* 14.1, p. 258 (*Elements*, 351–52; see *Outlines*, 298).

crats that were unfortunately adopted by French and English liberals and the reactionary views of those who wanted to restore an old regime whose social bases had collapsed. Rejecting the usual arguments for political representation, Hegel secures an unprecedented *philosophical* basis for it: within the rational state (and of course not every state deserves to be called rational), representative institutions have a "mediating function."[59] This mediation actually has multiple forms: it occurs between the monarch and his subjects, between the state and civil society, and between the people and itself. For many, what justifies the creation of a mechanism of representation is the need to limit the monarch's power with the power of the people; thus, a great Prussian reformist minister wrote in 1806 that "the state has no constitution, as the supreme power is not shared by the head of state and delegates from the nation."[60] But this argument—leaving aside the fact that it proposes a very precarious compromise between two possible attributions of sovereignty (to the people or to the monarch)—rests on the presupposition that the people knows what it wants and must have the means to express it. Hegel contests this. He does not attach much importance to the classical argument of the people's fickleness, which is empirical. No, if the people does not know what it wants, it is because it is not *immediately* what it is, *a* people rather than a multitude. Representation, which gives body, thought, and voice to this "formless mass,"[61] allows the people to reach political *being*, to overcome its contradictory diversity, its particularity turned in on itself. At the same time, political representation appears as the decisive condition of sovereignty—and we know that Hegel prefers to speak of sovereignty of the state rather than sovereignty of the people[62]—if it is true, as Hermann Heller said, that sovereignty is the rule of the people united over the people as plurality.[63]

The people does not exist naturally, it is *politically constituted*. This constitution presupposes a mediation, and this mediation is representation. In order to become what it must be—that is, a political unity and not merely a "heap" (*Haufen*) of individuals or of groups considered to be natural (we

59. *RPh*, § 302 Anmerkung, *GW* 14.1, p. 251 (*Elements*, 342; see *Outlines*, 290).

60. Freiherr vom Stein, *Briefwechsel, Denkschriften und Aufzeichnungen* (Berlin: Heymann, 1937), 76.

61. *RPh*, § 279 Anmerkung, *GW* 14.1, p. 234 (*Elements*, 319; see *Outlines*, 269).

62. See *RPh*, § 278, *GW* 14.1, p. 230 (*Elements*, 315; see *Outlines*, 265).

63. Herman Heller, *Die Souveränität (1928)*, in *Gesammelte Schriften* (Leiden: Sijthoff, 1971), 2:97.

may think here of the traditional definition of the state as a group of families, which is still found in the Nuremberg lectures[64]) — the people needs representative mediation. The deep meaning of mediation as conceived by Hegel is not that a subject would be represented by an other and for an other (which is its common justification) but rather that this subject, the people, would arrive at itself, become a political community. *Representation is the mediation of identity*; it corresponds to the fact that a community (a *nation* in Hegel's vocabulary) or multiple communities juxtaposed within a society do not on their own form a political entity, a state. This is representation understood not as an individual's or group's delegation of power (whether real or supposed) but rather as a mediation that institutes political identity. And this political constitution of the people functions better through the institutional representation of social interests than through the abstract mechanisms of personal suffrage.[65]

Thus, the Hegelian theory of the state is structured by the idea of representative mediation. Representation ensures a dynamic relationship between the people as a group of individuals (the *masses*), the people as a diversity of social and cultural interests (the *nation*) and the political people (the *state*). A people stops being a collection of individuals or atoms, "an aggregate of private persons"[66] in an "arbitrary and inorganic situation"[67] when it constitutes itself as a state — that is, when it *puts itself into representation*. The meaning of the expression goes beyond the simple fact of the people giving itself representatives: it designates the constitutive act itself, a primary and permanent act, the continuous creation of political unity. The constitution is not only the definition of the organization of powers (the constitutional text): a people, just like an individual, always has a constitution, even "the constitution appropriate and proper to it."[68] It would be an exaggeration to say that the identity of a people is exclusively political or state based, for its economic, social, and cultural dimensions are also important. But the constitution of a collective identity necessarily implies the basis of state institutions. The definition of community is political before all else. This explains why Hegel, going against the trend of his time, refuses to give the state national or racial grounding. The

---

64. See *Propädeutik, W* 4, p. 62: "Extending the natural society that is the family leads to the universal society that is the state."

65. See *Reformbill, W* 11, pp. 110–14; *Reform Bill,* in *Hegel's Political Writings,* 317–20.

66. *Enzykl,* § 544 Anmerkung, *GW* 20, p. 518 (*Encyclopedia* 243).

67. *RPh,* § 279 Anmerkung, *GW* 14.1, p. 234 (*Elements,* 319; see *Outlines,* 269).

68. *RPh,* § 274 Anmerkung, *GW* 14.1, p. 229 (*Elements,* 312; See *Outlines,* 263).

nation is only the "natural principle of the people";[69] in order to achieve political meaning, it requires an operation of constitution, the author of which — and this is a point on which Hegel follows Sieyès and the writers of the French Constitution — can only be the people itself.

One of Hegel's earliest texts denounced, as Rousseau also did, the replacement of the point of view of the citizen, living for the universal, with the point of view of the bourgeois, glued to personal interest, the weakening of the state by the esprit de corps.[70] Inversely, his mature writings affirm that the culture of the universal, the spirit of citizenship, must be based on that esprit de corps, on organized and representative social interests.[71] This confirms the conclusion of my previous chapter, that the key to Hegelian *politics* is the discovery of the fact that for better or for worse, *civil* society is the central issue of modernity. It is the source of its upheavals (the Revolution) and of its internal pathologies (mass poverty), but it is also, in every sense of the term, the site of its wealth and possible flourishing. If in the postrevolutionary world the sovereignty of the state requires representative mediation, it is because this alone guarantees that social particularity, now become legitimate, will be included within the political universal that it decisively contributes to creating. However, and this is what will forever separate Hegel from political and economic liberalism, the *ethos* of citizenship can and must surpass institutionally structured social particularity. This is what democracy presupposes, which leads Hegel to tackle the concept of democracy.

---

69. Hegel, *Die Vernunft in der Geschichte*, 180; *Lectures on the Philosophy of World History*, 148.
70. Hegel, *W* 1, p. 57.
71. See Hegel, *Vorlesungen über Naturrecht und Staatswissenschaft*, 186ff; *Lectures on Natural Right*, 233 ff.

❧ 9 ❧

Beyond Democracy

It is clear that Hegel was not a democrat. This has contributed to the wide-spread negative assessments of his political philosophy. He also did a great deal to weaken his case—didn't his last published piece criticize an electoral form that was if not democratic at least equitable? The truth is more complex, and we cannot see Hegel as a simple "enemy" of an "open society" and the regime that naturally suits it, democracy.[1] His attitude is more nuanced than is often admitted, as his analysis of the French Revolution demonstrates. Hegel denounces the Terror and in particular the political principles of its actors; he openly declares himself in favor of reform and against revolution.[2] But he is even more resistant to the reactionary response that swept through Europe after 1815, and he mocks those who "seem to have slept through the last twenty-five years, possibly the richest that world history has had, and for us the most instructive, because it is to them that our world and our ideas belong."[3] As regrettable as the trajectory of the French Revolution was, it marked the beginning of a new era: henceforth, nothing could be as it was before, and

---

1. See Popper, *Open Society*, 2:27 ff. The argument is as follows: "I have tried to show the identity of Hegelian historicism with the philosophy of modern totalitarianism" (p. 78).

2. See *Reformbill*, *W* 11, p. 128; *Reform Bill*, in *Hegel's Political Writings*, 330.

3. *Wurtemberg*, *W* 4, p. 507; *Proceedings*, in *Hegel's Political Writings*, 282.

this "beautiful sunrise" was to be celebrated.[4] Strange words from a stalwart monarchist! But after all, Hegel's opinions on the Revolution and democracy bear no more philosophical importance than the prejudices on which they were based or which they opposed: the essential is elsewhere. His critique of democracy must be taken into consideration precisely because today, lacking any declared adversaries, the ideals of democracy seem exhausted and no longer up to the task of offering meek politicians a satisfactory principle of legitimacy. The considerations that constitute the basis of Hegel's rejection of democracy may shed light on the difficulties encountered by forms of democracy that he neither knew of nor wished for and whose development was accompanied by an obscuring of its concept.

The Concept of Democracy: From Aristotle to Hegel

Let us start from the Aristotelian definition, to which Hegel's argument tacitly refers: democracy creates an identity between the rulers and the ruled, or at least guarantees the equality of all with regard to the capacity to command and obey. It is thus the regime best suited to the definition of citizenship as the capacity for "knowing both how to rule and how to obey."[5] It is true that in principle this definition fits all good constitutions,[6] but there can be no doubt that it applies best to *politeia*, "constitutional government," and thus to the correct form of democracy. But this definition does not cover all of our usage of the term. For in our time, unlike in Hegel's, democracy has become a *normative concept* that can apply to any social situation: thus, we speak of democratic discussion, the democratization of culture or of the academy, and so forth. The intent behind such expressions may be laudable, but they contribute to clouding our understanding of the strictly political problem of commandment and obedience, the specificity of which Aristotle emphasized in the first book of his treatise. As for most of the usual definitions of democracy (government of the majority, the rule of freedom and equality, popular sovereignty, the reign of public opinion, etc.), they simply add to the imprecision of the notion. Thus, I will restrict myself to an abstract or nominal definition,

---

4. *Geschichte, W* 12, p. 529.
5. Aristotle, *Politics*, 3.1.1275b5–6. The definition of citizenship I cite is from 3.4.1277a27.
6. See Aristotle, *Politics*, 3.13.1283b40.

one Hegel shares: there is democracy when "all the people [are] the highest deliberative authority."[7]

Though Hegel was there to witness the rise of democratic demands in Europe during the Restoration, which were in part brought forth by liberals, he did not see the great awakening of the democratic principle in 1848. If we leave aside the case of revolutionary France, the only contemporary examples he mentions are the United States and Switzerland. The rarity of democracies in the modern world bolstered his conviction that democracy is a political form lacking *"rational form"*;[8] just like the aristocracy and traditional monarchy, it can only exist in an "undeveloped condition," and "there can be no further discussion of such a notion [*Vorstellung*] in face of the developed Idea."[9] But what do we mean by democracy? In spite of the homonymy between them, does the modern concept actually fit the same horizon of thought as it did for Aristotle? In fact, it is important to distinguish two visions of democracy that may be fundamentally opposed. *Classical democracy* is a political regime that for us (through a tenacious retrospective illusion) is conflated with the Greek city-state in general and that (second illusion) supposedly underwent an explosive renaissance during the French Revolution with Rousseau as its ultimate theoretician. This type of democracy implies that the political dimension of life has strong influence over its private aspects. *Modern democracy* is quite different in both spirit and form. The democratic aspirations of the nineteenth century were associated with mistrust of the liberal state, not only of the remnants of absolutism; those aspirations combined with an awakening of national consciousness that was not present in ancient democracy. Thus, there is a difference, if not an opposition, between the now-dominant representation of democracy and what was understood by the word at the end of the eighteenth century.

Hegel's explicit argument, the political language of which is rooted in eighteenth-century usages, concerns classical democracy. For him, as for Montesquieu, democracy has the traits of its Greek model: it rests on the *Gesinnung*, the political character, of its citizens, and this is what creates a problem "as the condition of society grows more advanced and the powers of *particu-*

---

7. Hegel, *Vorlesungen über Rechtsphilosophie*, 4:656.
8. *RPh*, § 308 Anmerkung, *GW* 14.1, p. 254 (*Elements*, 347; see *Outlines*, 294).
9. *RPh*, § 279 Anmerkung, *GW* 14.1, p. 234 (*Elements*, 319; see *Outlines*, 269).

larity are developed and liberated."[10] We could speak here of *pure* democracy, since the modern acceptation of the word today seems to monopolize the usage of the word taken on its own. Indeed, it would seem that one must now add a qualification to democracy when we use the word to designate anything other than a representative-parliamentary regime: for example, direct democracy or, inversely, authoritarian democracy, just as in the past — strange pleonasm! — one spoke of popular democracy. But these qualifications bowdlerize the radicalness of the democratic idea. Democratic government in the classical sense is not moderate government. To see this we need only look at certain consequences of the exercise by all of the power to command, that is, the hegemony of the *demos* as the "gathering of a multitude," as Cicero said,[11] with the understanding that this definition of the people may well exclude a large or small portion of the population. I will focus on four of these consequences that seem to me consonant with what Hegel understands by and critiques in democracy.

First, if everyone commands, then everyone obeys, and obeys in all things, and at least among citizens everyone obeys in all things. Democracy is thus at once egalitarian and discriminatory: "[Democracy] is thought by them to be, and is, equality — not, however, for all, but only for equals."[12] The modern reader's perplexity that this egalitarian definition of democracy can perfectly accommodate slavery shows how far our representations have moved away from such a strictly political conception of democracy.

Second, democracy is totalizing if not (as is often said) totalitarian;[13] it reduces the nonpolitical sphere to a minimum. In the Greek context, this was the sphere of the *oikos*, the enlarged family structure that included both the family and slaves and which was therefore the site of the elementary activities of production. The first book of the *Politics* is dedicated to distinguishing the properly political relationship of command and obedience, which is always based on similarity (the equality of equals) from interfamily relations

---

10. *RPh*, § 273 Anmerkung, *GW* 14.1, p. 228 (*Elements*, 310; see *Outlines*, 261).

11. The *populus* is "the gathering of a multitude associated with a legal act and the common good" (Cicero, *De republica*, 1.39). The distinction between people and multitude is also found in Hobbes, Spinoza, Rousseau, and Kant; it plays an important role in the modern political philosophy's idea of the people.

12. Aristotle, *Politics* 3.9.1280a12–13.

13. See for example Jacob L. Talmon, *The Rise of Totalitarian Democracy* (Boston: Beacon, 1952).

(man-woman, parent-child, master-slave), which are all based on natural inequality. Aristotle emphasizes what separates "political" power from the "despotic" power of the head of family: "the rule of a master is not constitutional
rule, and . . . all the different kinds of rule are not, as some affirm, the same as
each other."[14] From this we understand why ancient democracy was destabilized by the incursion of the economy—which "normally" belonged to the
autarchic operation of the *oikos*—into the public space, which was supposed
to be purely political: whence Aristotle's exclusion of chresmatics, in the narrow sense of lucrative forms of production and exchange, from the category
of legitimate modes of acquisition.[15]

Third, democracy reduces the role of representation in political life as
much as possible and even tends to annul it. The state does not represent the
city: it is the universalized expression of the common will, and it is the community, subject and object of the general will, that is sovereign. As Aristotle
says, the city is the citizens. Regardless of the difficulties in implementing it,
"direct" democracy is the authentic form of democracy, in which all individuals can declare what they think is the general interest and participate in acts of
sovereignty.[16] In a democracy, Hegel writes, "*all* individuals ought to participate in deliberations and decisions on the universal concerns of the state."[17]
Of course, one must then distinguish, as Rousseau did, between acts of sovereignty properly speaking, which occur "when the whole people decree concerning the whole people" and bring together in the form of law "the universality of the will with the universality of the object,"[18] from acts of government
in the narrow sense, the administrative acts that emanate from the "executive
power" as the "intermediate body established between the subjects and the
sovereign for their mutual correspondence."[19] In the *Philosophy of Right*, it is
in this classical sense of the subsumption of the particular under the political
universal (the law) that Hegel speaks of government. To the contrary, the *En-*

14. Aristotle, *Politics* 1.7.1255b16–18.

15. See Aristotle, *Politics* 1.9.1257b. Chresmatics refers both to the art of acquisition in general and to its speculative perversion.

16. Direct democracy corresponds to "the happiest nation in the world," where "troops of
peasants" decide "the affairs of the State under an oak and always . . . wisely." Rousseau, *Oeuvres
complètes*, 3:379; *Social Contract*, 4:1, 227.

17. *RPh*, § 308 Anmerkung, *GW* 14.1, p. 254 (*Elements*, 347; see *Outlines*, 294).

18. Rousseau, *Oeuvres complètes*, 3:379; *Social Contract*, 2:6, 179.

19. Rousseau, *Oeuvres complètes*, 3:379; *Social Contract*, 3:1, 194.

cyclopedia defines government in general as "the continual production of the state in general and of its constitution,"[20] and there the executive is no more than a "*particular* governmental power."[21]

Fourth, strictly speaking democracy precludes the separation of powers. The popular will is singular, for it actualizes the unity of the political community. Unless the sovereign is to be a "fantastic being, formed of disparate parts,"[22] the sovereign can speak with only one voice; hence, the unified will of the people has undivided power. The idea of a balance of powers contradicts the democratic principle. The *Federalist Papers* makes this an argument against "pure democracy": republican government, "in which a scheme of representation takes place," differs by nature from democracy, in which "the people exercise the government in person."[23] Consequently, in democracy, as Rousseau says,[24] not only is the government simply an officer or commissioned agent of the sovereign general will (which it is in any case), but the very power to judge, which is exercised "in the name of the people," is also in principle a political attribute of sovereignty.

Untimely Democracy

More than any other form of government, democracy implies an expansion of the political sphere and an intensification of the forms of life that develop in it. It demands a mobilization of the people and citizenry, which can be observed both in Athens and in the French Revolution. However, this tendency does not easily align with the modern world's representation of freedom, which is completely different from the Greek notion of Ἐλευθερία, or with the importance it attaches to it. Freedom, writes Aristotle, is "the end of democracy."[25] Unlike the slave, who is subject to economic necessity and "despotic" violence, a free man is sui juris and can thus live any way he likes.[26] But we must not pro-

---

20. *Enzykl*, § 541, *GW* 20, p. 514 (*Encyclopedia* 240).

21. *Enzykl*, § 543, *GW* 20, p. 517 (*Encyclopedia* 242).

22. Rousseau, *Oeuvres complètes*, 3:379; *Social Contract*, 2:2, 171.

23. *Federalist Papers*, no. 10, p. 52.

24. Rousseau, *Oeuvres complètes*, 3:379; *Social Contract*, 2:6.

25. Aristotle, *Rhetoric* 1.8.1366a.

26. See Aristotle, *Politics* 6.2.1317 to 40 ff. and 5.9.1310a25–33. See also Thucydides, *Peloponnesian War* 2.37, and Plato, *Republic* 8.557b and 562b–c.

ject the modern notion of free will onto this locution. To live freely means to be able to dispose, as one likes, of the part of existence that does not belong to the public space; that is, not to be a slave. But freedom also and above all includes the political sense of being by turn ruler and ruled and thus acceding to the magistracy and taking part in the exercise of the people's supreme power within a community of equals.[27] In contrast, the modern idea of freedom has a strong antistate connotation. Freedom is a quality of the individual and essentially is achieved in a nonpolitical context. To put it briefly, the modern view of freedom, which is fundamentally individualist, is in consonance with the existence of a social space detached from the political (state) sphere; thus, it provides an anthropological, legal, and moral basis for free enterprise and its logic of differentiation. In a democratic perspective, freedom is "based on equality."[28] Of course, democratic equality has a strictly political meaning, and does not imply social or economic equality: civic equality is not the same as equality of fortunes. But it does suppose that the eventual political effects of wealth (or poverty) are neutralized. This explains why partisans of democracy judge it to be incompatible with strong social differentiation, and in fact it is difficult for democratic institutions to withstand the expansion of economic activities and the private sphere (classical Athens is an example of this).

It is understood that Hegel, a thinker of the separation between the social and the political, considers democracy to be foreign to the modern world, even more so than the aristocracy or the old (patriarchal or feudal) forms of monarchy. Indeed, the entire classical typology of forms of government and the problematic underlying it seems obsolete to him in the postrevolutionary context. The appearance of a new and superior form of government, constitutional monarchy, different in every way from classical monarchy,[29] is a sign of this obsolescence. But it is Hegel's analysis of the deep structures of modernity that establishes that democracy is ill suited to it; democracy is an *untimely* idea and reality. Indeed, democracy demands not only the subordination but also the sacrifice of personal individuality and personal goals

27. See Aristotle, *Politics* 2.2.1261 to 30–1262b6 and 6.2.1317b2.

28. Aristotle, *Politics* 6.2.1317b16. According to Cicero, "there is no freedom that is not equal" (*De republica* 1.47).

29. See *RPh*, § 273 Anmerkung, *GW* 14.1, pp. 226–27 (*Elements*, 308–9; see *Outlines*, 259), as well as *Die Vernunft in der Geschichte*, 147. Constitutional monarchy is the "true monarchy" (*Enzykl*, § 544 Anmerkung, *GW* 20, p. 518).

to the substance that, so to speak, carries them: the city, its institutions, and its *ethos*. The heroism of citizens of democracy comes from the supremacy of the political practice over all other dimensions of existence. Montesquieu emphasized that virtue (Ἀρετή) is the principle of democracy.[30] Obviously this is not moral virtue but rather the eminently political virtue or excellence that consists in the individual fully acquiescing to the universal by fusing subjective mental dispositions with the traditions, mores, and customs that structure the community and its memory. Classical citizenship corresponds to this democratic requirement, though the cities that adopted and conserved a democratic regime were quite rare. For Athenian or Spartan citizens, to be free was not, as it is for modern people, to be master of one's person and opinions; it was not the ability to dispose freely of one's property; instead, it meant being a citizen of a just city with good laws.[31] Democratic virtue consisted in taking part in the destiny of the community. Hegel's youthful writings glorified this civic ethics, renewed by the French Revolution. But we know that during his stay in Jena, he became aware of the inadequacy of this ethics to the modern conditions of individual life, both social and political.[32] What explains Hegel's effacement of the model of a *Sittlichkeit* structured by the values of the *polis*, by the democratic paradigm? It is the fact that Greek citizens' mode of existence has become foreign to us. Three elements contributed to making this the case.

The first break with the intellectual universe of classical democracy was caused by Christianity, which made the autonomy of the subject a fundamental value:

> The right of *subjective freedom* is the pivotal and focal point in the difference between *antiquity* and the *modern* age. This right, in its infinity, is expressed in Christianity, and it has become the universal and actual principle of a new form of the world.[33]

---

30. Montesquieu, *Spirit of the Laws*, 3:3, 21–31. See *RPh*, § 273 Anmerkung, *GW* 14.1, pp. 437–38 (*Elements*, 310; see *Outlines*, 261).

31. *RPh*, § 153 Anmerkung, *GW* 14.1, p. 142 (*Elements*, 196. See *Outlines*, 160). The phrase comes from Xenophon (*Memorabilia* 1.1.3), who attributes it to Socrates, or from Diogenes Laertius (8.16), who refers to Xenophiles the Pythagorean. Cf. *PhG*, *GW* 9, p. 195 (*Phenomenology*, ¶ 352).

32. See chapter 4 above.

33. *RPh*, § 124 Anmerkung, *GW* 14.1, p. 110 (*Elements*, 151; see *Outlines*, 122).

The constitution of subjective consciousness as an autonomous normative moment, which was perfected by a "Protestant consciousness" that combined religious and ethical dimensions,[34] had significant political consequences. It made slavery unacceptable and thereby condemned the social and political organization of the ancient world. It also laid the groundwork for the bourgeois reign of property:

> It must be nearly one and half millennia since the *freedom of personality* began to flourish under Christianity and became a universal principle for part — if only a small part — of the human race. But it is only since yesterday, so to speak, that the *freedom of property* has been recognized here and there as a principle.[35]

In short, the (Christian) principle of subjective (personal) freedom gradually became part of the order of things, until it came to seem the very core of the law; this explains, by the way, why in Hegel's philosophy of *objective* spirit, moral *subjectivity* is placed between abstract law and ethicality.[36] Two effects of this reshaping of the deep structures of objective spirit may be mentioned here. First, although theories of social contract misunderstand the true nature of the political bond, they do show awareness of the modern requirement that the individual consent to belong to a collectivity. The second effect of Christianity's promotion of subjectivity is that it renders obsolete the ancient mode of the individual's fusional adhesion to community values and to the absolute will of the *demos*. The *"right of the subjective will,"*[37] whose premises, nevertheless, can be found in Greek philosophy, was thus the condemnation of the Greek political idea.

The second factor rendering democracy foreign to modern times is the redefinition of public space that began with the Enlightenment.[38] The site of

---

34. *Enzykl*, § 552 Anmerkung. We find here an early version of Weber's analysis of Protestant ethics in the Lutheran rather than Calvinist version.

35. *RPh*, § 62 Anmerkung, *GW* 14.1, p. 68 (*Elements*, 92; see *Outlines*, 74).

36. See chapter 10 below.

37. *RPh*, § 107, *GW* 14.1, p. 100 (*Elements*, 136; see *Outlines*, 110).

38. See Jürgen Habermas, *The Structural Transformation of the Public Sphere* (Cambridge, MA: MIT Press, 1989), in particular chapters 3 and 4. For a counterpoint, see Reinhart Koselleck, *Critique and Crisis* (Oxford: Berg), 1988.

public life was no longer the *ecclesia*, the gathering of citizens on the *agora*, but rather public opinion, a "relatively harmless nemesis" that can also be "base and spiteful."[39] The public sphere was no longer conflated with the political sphere and even less with the system of the state's functions and operations.

In modern societies, public opinion is clearly political. Along with representative institutions, which Hegel studies directly before turning to public opinion, it guarantees the mediation between "the universal in and for itself" and "its opposite," "the *particular opinions of the many*," insofar as the latter, no matter how majoritarian, are constitutively particular.[40] Public opinion is not so much the sentiment of the *populus* grasped in its identity as it is the judgment—often unfounded but still critical and thereby necessary—that civil society in its diversity makes of political institutions. Thus, public opinion is a "self-contradiction,"[41] and for that it "deserves to be *respected* as well as *despised*."[42] Whether they like it or not, rulers must take it into account, for it expresses, even if in a confused way, the representation a divided community has of its identity, its needs, its aspirations, and even the "eternal and substantial principles of justice."[43] One cannot rule against it for long even if its expression takes the form of prejudices or ideology, which is of course always the case. But rulers must also despise public opinion not only because of its changeability and frequent superficiality but above all because it is affected by particular interests and the centrifugal tendencies that run through a community that must, and yet cannot be, politically unified. Many political decisions must be made in spite of it or against its immediate sentiment, for often "the people is deceived *by itself*."[44] This argument cannot merely be chalked up to Hegel's supposed aversion to democracy, for Rousseau says more or less the same thing:

> the general will is always right and always tends to the public good; but it does not follow that the deliberations of the people always have the same rectitude.[45]

39. *RPh*, § 319 Anmerkung, *GW* 14.1, p. 263 (*Elements*, 358; see *Outlines*, 304).

40. *RPh*, § 316, *GW* 14.1, p. 258 (*Elements*, 353; see *Outlines*, 299).

41. *RPh*, § 316, *GW* 14.1, p. 258 (*Elements*, 353; see *Outlines*, 299).

42. *RPh*, § 318, *GW* 14.1, p. 260 (*Elements*, 355; see *Outlines*, 301).

43. *RPh*, § 317, *GW* 14.1, p. 259 (*Elements*, 353; see *Outlines*, 299).

44. *RPh*, § 317 Anmerkung, *GW* 14.1, p. 260 (*Elements*, 354; see *Outlines*, 300).

45. Rousseau, *Oeuvres complètes*, 3:371; *Social Contract*, 2:3, 172. See also 4:1 and 4:2.

Thus, public opinion may be compared to the will of all, which, when it separates from the general will, "has regard to private interests, and is merely a sum of particular wills."[46] In any case, its existence is a fact that rulers must reckon with. It is no longer enough for us to have good laws; we must, at the risk of erring, put them to the test of public opinion, the collective judgment.

The third, and probably decisive, reason why democracy is untimely is the creation of a depoliticized space that is susceptible to organization and regulation independent of state tutelage: *civil* society. In precapitalist societies, economic circuits, social relations, and family or interindividual relations were symbolically or statutorily coded in a way that was immediately political. It's not that they were subject to the regulatory power of an administrative apparatus such as the one the modern state has. But all the matters that we call social were completely political, just like warfare, justice, and taxes; conversely, what would later be called the state did not have a monopoly on these activities. In the feudal state or the *Ständestaat*, the postfeudal state to which the complicated structures of the empire gave surprising longevity, there was thus no clear boundary between what was political and what was not. The status of corporations or free cities was political, as were relations of vassalage, servitude, and the church's jurisdictional powers. The notion of privilege (*lex privata*) expresses a politicization of the social bond that has gradually become both incomprehensible and inadmissible: for does it not contradict the principle of individual freedom and the imperatives of competition and social mobility if every individual is assigned—as was formerly the case—an "estate" with statutory qualifications largely independent of the individual's actual activity and merits? Modernity is defined by an ever-increasing differentiation between statuses, functions, and social positions, and Hegel attempts to account for this transformation while formally maintaining the old vocabulary. Thus, for example, he writes that "the essential determinant" of an individual's belonging to such or such social "estate" "is *subjective opinion* and the *particular arbitrary will*," which "for the subjective consciousness . . . has the shape of being the product of its own will."[47] Of course it is not a matter of subordinating the state, in charge of the universal, to the egotistical and opposing goals of individuals and social groups, which as "partial associations"

---

46. Rousseau, *Oeuvres complètes*, 3:371; *Social Contract*, 2:3, 172. See also 4:1 and 4:2.

47. *RPh*, § 206, *GW* 14.1, p. 172 (*Elements*, 237; see *Outlines*, 195).

are necessarily "to the detriment of the whole":[48] "in relation to the spheres of civil law [*Privatrecht*] and private welfare, the spheres of the family and civil society, the state is . . . the higher power."[49] But the state must take into consideration this increasing differentiation in civil society that, as we know, justifies the political representation of social interests.[50] Furthermore, the modern understanding of politics as a particular function of society, assigned to an institution that claims a monopoly to it (the state), contradicts the principles of democracy.

Let us go one step further. If we consider that the *telos* of the modern world is the "catallactic"[51] functioning of a society without a state, the state must abstain from getting involved in the social process and must limit itself to the external conditions (legal, in particular) of its operation. Individual freedom, and above all the freedom to property and enterprise, requires that the state refrain from stepping into a social sphere next to which it is merely juxtaposed. The exercise of its traditional functions hinders economic progress and is a factor of social injustice, if that term can have meaning here. A self-organized society needs politics to be dethroned and the state — though it may have to subsist to carry out some minimal functions — to be stripped of its prestige and mysteries. It is clear that Hegel does not share this liberal, even libertarian view. He rejects it soundly, for it turns the state into a mediocre extension of civil society, "an arrangement dictated by necessity [*Not*],"[52] an institution of necessity and not of freedom. For Hegel, the liberals' night watchman state, the minimal or ultraminimal state in Robert Nozick's sense[53] is, like the civil society he is satisfied with serving, a "state of *necessity* and of the *understanding*";[54] in other words, it is merely a nonstate. However, like the liberals, Hegel saw that the increasing autonomy of civil society from the state made true democracy impossible, for democracy requires the identification of

48. Rousseau, *Oeuvres complètes*, 3:371; *Social Contract*, 2:3, 173.

49. *RPh*, § 261, *GW* 14.1, p. 208 (*Elements*, 283; see *Outlines*, 235–36).

50. See chapter 8 above.

51. See Hayek, *Law, Legislation and Liberty*, 2:207. He also speaks of an "extended or macro-order," which he distinguishes from "organizations" such as the state (*Fatal Conceit*, 37).

52. *RPh*, § 270 Anmerkung, *GW* 14.1, p. 219 (*Elements*, 298; see *Outlines*, 249).

53. See Robert Nozick, *Anarchy, State, and Utopia* (New York: Basic Books, 1974), 26. The positions of Hayek and Nozick seem moderate in comparison to those of a radical libertarian such as Murray Rothbard, for whom the state is no different than a band of gangsters: see Rothbard, *The Ethics of Liberty* (Atlantic Highlands, NJ: Humanities Press, 1982), 161–72.

54. *RPh*, § 183, *GW* 14.1, p. 160 (*Elements*, 221; see *Outlines*, 181).

individual aspirations with the goals of the political community; it is therefore incompatible with modern civil society—a powerful factor in the dispersion of interests and wills. The modern state can no longer be the *"undivided and substantial unity"*[55] presupposed by the democratic city-state. The state, *"the whole, articulated into its particular circles"*[56] recognizes the relative independence of society and bases itself on its institutions;[57] the state is a continuous political *process* of the recomposition of a society that never stops differentiating itself, decomposing itself; it is, in the dynamic sense of the term, *"union as such."*[58] Thus, Hegel agrees with liberals in considering that the modern individual is *"a son of civil society"* before he is a citizen of the state.[59] But unlike them he thinks that the particular social properties of this individual nourish a political "vocation," a *Beruf* that carries him beyond these properties. The political universal is the truth of a social space dedicated to the particularity of interests and the competition of passions, whether joyful or sad: this is what liberalism refuses to see. But this universal finds in social differentiation a supplementary reason for existing, and this is what condemns the ideal of pure democracy.

In the French Revolution, modern history experienced a grandiose attempt at actualizing the democratic principle. Hegel does not contest this, and no doubt that is where he originally drew the reason for his adherence to the Greek model, which, like many others, he saw as being reborn in revolutionary France. But in reality things are more complex. In the Hegelian texts there is a double reading of the major event of his time: the Revolution has a *liberal* as well as a *democratic* orientation, and in the end Hegel considers that the former is its most durable legacy. The democratic orientation of the Revolution manifested itself above all in its radical phase. The Jacobin Constitution of 1793, which was to go into effect at the end of the state of emergency caused by the war but which the Thermidorian reaction made obsolete, was authentically democratic: it organized the participation of all citizens in major political decisions. Hegel's article on the *Reform Bill* mentions the Constitution of the Year I, whose Articles 56–60 called for at least tacit ratification of all planned

---

55. *RPh*, § 273 Anmerkung, *GW* 14.1, p. 226 (*Elements*, 309; see *Outlines*, 259).

56. *RPh*, § 308 Anmerkung, *GW* 14.1, p. 254 (*Elements*, 347; see *Outlines*, 294).

57. See *RPh*, § 255, *GW* 14.1, p. 199 (*Elements*, 272; see *Outlines*, 226): "The *family* is the first ethical root of the state; the *corporation* is the second, and it is based in civil society."

58. *RPh*, § 258 Anmerkung, *GW* 14.1, p. 201 (*Elements*, 276; see *Outlines*, 229).

59. *RPh*, § 238, *GW* 14.1, p. 192 (*Elements*, 263; see *Outlines*, 218).

laws by citizen assemblies.[60] Up until the excesses of the Terror, the revolutionary government was a *democratic* dictatorship of virtue:

> Robespierre established the principle of virtue as the highest principle, and that man was serious about virtue. Now, *virtue* and *terror* prevail.[61]

But the Revolution was also, and perhaps above all, an insurrection of civil society and its forces against the absolutist political order and estate society, and that is what survived the upheaval. In this sense, unknown to those who were directly involved in it, its effect was more social than political, and its orientation was liberal rather than democratic. After all, its most lasting achievement was the proclamation of the rights of man, which set forth the principles of liberal individualism and abolished privileges and all the ancien régime's obstacles to free enterprise. On this point Hegel's argument anticipates Marx's, who describes the "supposed rights of man" as those of "an individual separated from the community, withdrawn into himself,"[62] basically, of the bourgeois and not of the citizen.

The Jacobin attempt to restore the vocabulary and democratic mores of the *polis* was destined to fail for at least two reasons. The first reason was the distance between the abstract principles it claimed and actual political action. Liberty, equality, and fraternity do not institute a politics. In other words, "men of principles," doctrinaires, are not ipso facto "statesmen" whose "knowledge, experience, and business routine" is required to introduce principles of "life as it is lived."[63] For Hegel as for Marx, there cannot be a *politics* of the rights of man, for they concern *social* existence above all else. The second reason, on which the first probably depends, is that the democratic tendency of the Revolution, embodied by Robespierre, Marat, and Saint-Just, betrays a misunderstanding of the social and cultural conditions of modernity, in particular those conditions that contribute to the emancipation of the political sphere and the

---

60. *Reformbill, W* 11, p. 11 (not translated in *Hegel's Political Writings*). See Jacques Godechot, *Les constitutions de la France depuis 1789* (Paris: Garnier-Flammarion, 1970), 87. On this matter the Montagnard text adopted in 1793 is less democratic than Condorcet's Girondin plan, which called for the Primary Citizens' Assemblies to sit at all times rather than intermittently.

61. *Geschichte, W* 12, p. 533.

62. Marx, "On the Jewish Question," 43. This critique of the rights of man constantly draws on the Hegelian distinction between the state and (bourgeois) civil society.

63. *Reformbill, W* 11, p. 122; *Reform Bill*, in *Hegel's Political Writings*, 326.

retreat of the state. This is why the dream of direct democracy rapidly turned into the political dictatorship of the Jacobins and created the conditions for its own destruction. The directorate and the empire are in certain respects civil society's revenge against a democratic politics that threatened its autonomous development even though it also freed it from the hindrances of the ancien régime. The Restoration, that "farce that lasted fifteen years,"[64] did not change the fundamentals of the situation.

However, although Hegel considered democracy outdated, his critique of one of the capital institutions of the representative democracy to come—universal suffrage—and its conceptual basis—the idea of the sovereignty of the people—shows that for him the question of democracy is not merely a historically bygone question. Beyond his choice of constitutional monarchy, which reminds us that philosophy cannot project itself ahead of its time, there are in Hegel elements of a critique of modern democracy that may have something to teach us.

Universal Suffrage

Too often, Hegel's assessment of universal suffrage and elective procedures is isolated from its context. In fact, his rejections of them can be explained by the problematic of political representation and the theory of the exercise of sovereignty that results from it. It should also be specified that his critique of the "*democratic* mode of election"[65] in reality applies not to classical democracy, which used lots rather than elections to choose representatives,[66] but rather to what would later be called representative democracy, where what he questions is the idea of citizens' delegation of their will to an assembly. The various forms taken by the elective process include two irreconcilable presuppositions: all individuals must take part in political life by exercising their right to vote but at the same time the people (understood as a group of citizens) must be represented within the state as if on foreign territory. On this point we should note that what Hegel rejects is not so much the *universal* vote (which anyway was rejected by the liberal bourgeoisie during the first half of the nineteenth

---

64. *Geschichte, W* 12, p. 534.

65. *Enzykl,* § 544 Anmerkung, *GW* 20, p. 520 (*Encyclopedia* 244).

66. See Aristotle, *Politics* 4.9.1294b8–9: "the appointment of magistrates by lot is thought to be democratic, and the election of them oligarchical."

century) but the *individual* vote. His critique was of "democratic formlessness [*Unförmlichkeit*],"[67] where a "whole dissolve[s] into a heap"[68] or a multitude targets both selective or capacity-based suffrage (dear to Sieyès), which subordinates the right to vote to an "external condition,"[69] and universal suffrage. Thus, Hegel condemns both democratic egalitarianism and selective oligarchy, for they share the erroneous belief that the general will is exclusively formed by the agglomeration of individual preferences. In a striking expression, Hegel writes that such an understanding, which deprives political life of a "[social] foundation that is stable," "leaves political life hanging, so to speak, in the air."[70]

There are three specific reasons behind Hegel's harsh judgment of the elective process. The first is that the individual vote convinces the voter of his or her political near nullity, "weakening his idea of its importance and consequentially his interest in exercising this right."[71] This has two effects. First, the voter is tempted to refrain from taking part in "universal life" and to retreat to private existence, where he or she is aware of being active and effective. Second, the individual vote favors active minorities and can in fact lead to an organized party taking control of the state:

> In the earlier years of the French Revolution the zeal and the behavior of the Jacobins at elections disgusted peaceful and decent citizens and even made it dangerous for them to cast their votes. So faction alone held the field.[72]

In such cases, the very vocation of a universal politics is compromised, as Rousseau notes when he condemns ruses.[73]

Second, Hegel's critique of the elective system was sparked by the implosion of the political and verbal monstrosity that was the Roman Empire of the

---

67. *Wurtemberg, W* 4, p. 485; *Proceedings,* in *Hegel's Political Writings,* 265.

68. *Wurtemberg, W* 4, p. 482; *Proceedings,* in *Hegel's Political Writings,* 262.

69. *RPh,* § 310 Anmerkung, *GW* 14.1, p. 256 (*Elements,* 349; see *Outlines,* 296).

70. *RPh,* § 303 Anmerkung, *GW* 14.1, p. 252 (*Elements,* 344; see *Outlines,* 292).

71. *Reformbill, W* 11, p. 115; *Hegel's Political Writings,* 320. See also *RPh,* § 311 Anmerkung, *GW* 14.1, pp. 256–257 (*Elements,* 350; see *Outlines,* 297).

72. *Reformbill, W* 11, p. 114–115; *Hegel's Political Writings,* 320. See also Hegel, *Vorlesungen über Rechtsphilosophie,* 4:717.

73. Rousseau, *Du contrat social,* in *Oeuvres complètes,* 3:371; *Social Contract,* 2:3, 173.

German Nation (Römisches Reich deutscher Nation), the Holy Roman Empire's last and final name. It was good and dead even before Napoleon signed its official death notice in 1806. One of the reasons for Hegel's bitter observation in 1800 that "Germany is a state no longer"[74] was its status as an elective empire (*Wahlreich*). Hegel's experience of its disintegration explains his conviction that the *Wahlreich* is "the worst of institutions."[75] In fact, it subordinated the state to the particular, self-interested, and competing wills of voters and was surely brought to ruin by the transformation of the political constitution into a cartel of interests protected by electoral capitulations. These capitulations, which had existed since Charles V was elected, were conventions by which the Empire's electors used their votes to gain an ever-expanding sphere of privileges. Hegel emphasizes that this institution is harmful to the state's political unity and to the autonomy of the political sphere from the procedures of private law: "German constitutional law is not a science derived from principles but a register of the most varied constitutional rights acquired in the manner of private rights."[76] This historical background—the outdatedness of which was emphasized by the French Revolution and Empire—sheds unique light on Hegel's support for a hereditary constitutional monarchy.

Finally, Hegel thinks that one's status as a "member of a state" (citizenship) is an "*abstract* determination,"[77] while one's status as member of civil society (being bourgeois) is not. At first glance this is surprising, since it seems to make the political more abstract than the social, whereas the entire analysis of *Sittlichkeit* makes the state the universally concrete truth, the "*true* ground" of the competitive world of abstract social particularity.[78] But the *Logic* provides a way of overcoming this apparent difficulty. In the logical process, the result is both mediated and absolutely immediate so that beyond its apparent beginning and end, the process is itself both origin and end.[79] The same is true in the ethical-political sphere. The state results from civil society in the sense that civil society is the negative and particular mediation that its

---

74. "Verfassung," *W* 1, p. 46; *Hegel's Political Writings*, 143.

75. *RPh*, § 281 Anmerkung, *GW* 14.1, p. 238 (*Elements*, 324; see *Outlines*, 274).

76. "Verfassung," *W* 1, p. 468; *Hegel's Political Writings*, 149. See also "Verfassung," *W* 1, pp. 454–55 (not included in *Hegel's Political Writings*): "by its original legal basis, German constitutional law is actually private law."

77. *RPh*, § 308 Anmerkung, *GW* 14.1, p. 254 (*Elements*, 347; see *Outlines*, 294).

78. *RPh*, § 256 Anmerkung, *GW* 14.1, p. 199 (*Elements*, 274; see *Outlines*, 227).

79. See *WdL* 3, *GW* 12, p. 243 ff. (*Science of Logic*, 743ff).

universal identity presupposes; for this reason, political citizenship is built on particular social affiliations and remains an abstract quality if it is separated from these affiliations. Conversely, the state is the *"true* ground" of civil society, which can only be *thought* as the product of a historical process of the differentiation of the ethical-political totality. Thus, there is a sort of chiasmus: the state, the moment of the concrete universal, is the logical foundation of civil society, which is the "abstract moment of the *reality* of the Idea,"[80] but social being constitutes the real basis of the citizen's political being.

However, we must not think that Hegel makes citizenship a mere consequence of social status. To the contrary, it is essential for him that each individual be recognized as having identical political being from which obligations *and rights* derive even if the equality thus ushered in remains abstract. This is the whole difference between the modern state and ancient democracy. The latter had slaves, and "slaves have no duties because they have no rights, and vice versa."[81] But Hegel also takes his distance from a principle that was becoming dominant at the time: "one man, one vote." For him, citizenship cannot consist in bracketing or denying social inequality; it must recognize it in order to accomplish its *Aufhebung*. On this view, I do not have political being insofar as I am an abstract individual, a legal atom, or a private person; it is, rather, because of my social position, my concrete and particular rootedness that comes from having an estate (*Stand*). In the modern world, the individual is a citizen neither *in spite of* his or her social determination nor *because of* it; he or she is a citizen *with* it:

> The concrete state is *the whole, articulated into its particular circles*. Each member of the state is a *member* of an *estate* of this kind, and only in this objective determination can he be considered in relation to the state. His universal determination in general includes two moments, for he is a *private person* and at the same time a *thinking* being with consciousness and volition of the *universal*. But this consciousness and volition remain empty and lack *fulfillment* and actual *life* until they are filled with particularity, and this is [to be found in] a particular estate and determination.[82]

80. *RPh*, § 184, *GW* 14.1, p. 160 (*Elements*, 221; see *Outlines*, 182).
81. *RPh*, § 261 Anmerkung, *GW* 14.1, p. 209 (*Elements*, 284; see *Outlines*, 237).
82. *RPh*, § 308 Anmerkung, *GW* 14.1, pp. 254–55 (*Elements*, 347; see *Outlines*, 294–95).

Thus the political and the social are neither conflated nor separate; they are moments that mutually presuppose and engender one another. On the one hand, my political being is shaped by my social being: it is only as a member of one of the "particular circles" of civil society that I can access actual political existence. On the other hand, the political universal is the condition of social particularity, the foundation that allows the "external state" to survive. Political identity, guaranteed by the institutions of the state, anticipates the ever-possible devolution of social competition into civil war. (Co)citizenship keeps civil society from returning to a state of nature. In this way, Hegel's critique of universal suffrage, even if it targets classical democracy, shakes one of the foundations of liberal political philosophy.

The People and the Multitude: Where Is the Sovereign?

The state is the rational condition of freedom. In the absence of a strong state, the simply agonistic logic of civil society risks devolving into a war of all against all.[83] For this reason it acts as a constraint on the abstract will, when it compels individuals to abandon the summary representation they may have of their freedom and, as Rousseau puts it, forces them to be free.[84] Thus, the individual is both citizen (*Staatsbürger*) and subject (*Untertan*). Two understandings of the notion of a people, and above all two theories of sovereignty, correspond to this double relation between the state and the individual. Indeed, whose sovereignty is proclaimed when it is said to belong to the people or to the nation? Basing himself on the distinction between *populus* and *multitude* found in Cicero and Hobbes,[85] Hegel contrasts the political people, the "organized people" understood in its unity (*das Volk*) with the "aggregate" "of private persons," the collection of individuals and groups thought to exist on their own that he calls the *vulgus* and which, if it could exist as such, would unleash "a shapeless, wild, blind force, like that of the stormy, elemental sea."[86]

83. See chapter 6 above.

84. See Rousseau, *Oeuvres complètes*, 3:364; *Social Contract*, 1:7, 165–66.

85. See Cicero, *De republica*, 1.39: a people is not a "group of men gathered in any way." According to Hobbes, in contrast to the multitude, an aggregate to which "any action or any right" can be attributed, a people is "something which has a will, and to which action can be attributed" (*De Cive: English Version*, 12:8, 190).

86. *Enzykl*, § 544 Anmerkung, *GW* 20, p. 518 (*Encyclopedia* 244).

The unity of the *populus*, however, is not natural; it is continuously produced and reproduced by political mediation, in particular through mechanisms of representation. Thus, a notion like the sovereignty of the people ultimately has no meaning—and Hegel is very hesitant to use an expression with such strong connotations in the political debates of his time—unless one gets rid of the "garbled notion" of the people as a "formless mass"[87] that in a sense stands across from the political institution. Hegel writes that such a mass *"does not know* [*its*] *own will,"*[88] because no rational will can emerge from a particular group, no matter how majoritarian. Hegel points out that this "inorganic" representation of what a people is is held in particular by those belonging to the "rabble." It is telling that hostility toward the state is attributed to those who have reason to think that the state is hostile toward them.

There is even reason to distinguish two variants of the apolitical understanding of the people as multitude. In the first version, it is a mass that stands across from rulers. This is the trivial *democratic* interpretation of the principle of popular sovereignty. But such an unorganized mass cannot have a unified political will. Rousseau, who based his theory of sovereignty on the distinction between the atomized multitude, incapable of willing, and the "common self" that is born with the political body, understood this well.[89] But he thought that in order to explain the passage from one to the other, it was necessary to preserve the fiction of the social contract. This amounts to presupposing the state as a given, which Hegel, too, would grant, albeit on other premises. The second version is of the people as a conglomerate of individuals, each with his or her own plan or will. This is a *liberal* view of what a people is, in which the will of the people is the will of the majority of individuals. Hegel rejects this understanding even more clearly than he does that of the democrats: first, because it rests on the incorrect postulate of the independence of the particular will, and second, because it makes the political bond itself, *"unity* as such," unthinkable.[90] Liberal individualism includes a deeply antipolitical orientation, one that is not only antistate; in this respect it espouses the point of view of civil society kept separate from its political foun-

---

87. *RPh*, § 279 Anmerkung, *GW* 14.1, p. 234 (*Elements*, 319; see *Outlines*, 269).
88. *RPh*, § 301 Anmerkung, *GW* 14.1, p. 249 (*Elements*, 340; see *Outlines*, 288).
89. Rousseau, *Oeuvres complètes*, 3:361; *Social Contract*, 1:6, 163–64.
90. *RPh*, § 258 Anmerkung, *GW* 14.1, p. 201 (*Elements*, 276; see *Outlines*, 229).

dation. Liberal individualism, thinking it is fighting absolutism, ruins the very idea of sovereignty and of the state. As important a liberal thinker as Constant recognized this clearly:

> Sovereignty exists only limitedly and relatively. At the point where independence and individual existence begin, the jurisdiction of sovereignty ends.[91]

Thus, it would be a simplification to say only that Hegel rejects popular sovereignty; it is more accurate to say that he rejects the disfiguring, parallel interpretations that democrats and liberals have of it. For doesn't he write, regarding the right to vote, that

> it is in this right that there lies the right of the people to participate in public affairs and in the highest interests of the state and the government. . . . This right and its exercise is, as the French say, the act, the sole act, of the "sovereignty of the people."[92]

It is remarkable — and here one will see either the mark of Hegel's ambiguousness or the proof of his lucidity — that the article on the Reform Bill, which criticizes "French abstractions"[93] more than ever before and denies that legislation or a constitution can be based on the rights of man and citizen,[94] so solemnly proclaims the principle of the sovereignty of the people. But it is insofar as individual elements of the people, the *populus*, is united through representative mediation — thus, insofar as the people is the *state* — that it is sovereign:

> We may also say that *internal sovereignty* lies with the *people*, but only if we are speaking of the *whole* [state] in general, in keeping with the above demonstration . . . that sovereignty belongs to the *state*.[95]

91. Constant, *Political Writings*, 177.

92. *Reformbill*, W 11, p. 112; *Hegel's Political Writings*, 318.

93. See in particular *Reformbill*, W 11, pp. 117–18, 122; *Hegel's Political Writings*, 322, 325. The first passage criticizes some of Sieyès's views regarding constitutions.

94. *Reformbill*, W 11, p. 127; *Hegel's Political Writings*, 329.

95. *RPh*, § 279 Anmerkung, *GW* 14.1, p. 234 (*Elements*, 318; see *Outlines*, 268).

This identification of the sovereign people with the state is combined with an initially enigmatic definition of sovereignty as the *"universal* thought of this ideality" of the state.[96] But context provides the key. Ideality corresponds to the fact that the various powers of the state have their principle, their "ultimate roots," in "the unity of the state as their simple self."[97] This implies the impossibility of any division of sovereignty, as Rousseau and Hobbes already asserted. The sovereignty of the state is ideal because the state itself is an ideality: it is the life of all, the moving identity of a multiplicity, "unity as such." Here we arrive at the reason for the refutation of both variants of the doctrine of the sovereignty of the people: each one reduces the *populus* to the *vulgus* or the *multitudo*. But these should instead be thought of as the poles (identity and atomization) between which the process of constituting the political takes place. From this perspective, sovereignty has no foundation other than itself: the state is sovereign because it is the only foundation of its own power. The immediate objection that this legitimates all tyranny ignores the fact that tyranny has nothing in common with the very real "idea" of the state, for it does not *unify*. Sovereignty, however, the identity of identity and difference, implies the differentiation of the state's power. And if by constitution (*Verfassung*) is meant the necessary self-differentiation of the state into distinct but not independent powers, the idea of sovereignty coincides with that of constitutionality:

> Sovereignty is to be found specifically under lawful and constitutional conditions as the moment of ideality of the particular spheres and functions [within the state]. In other words, these spheres are not independent or self-sufficient in their ends and modes of operation, nor are they solely immersed in themselves; on the contrary, in these same ends and modes of operation, they are determined by and dependent on *the end of the whole* (to which the indeterminate expression "the *welfare of the state*" has in general been applied).[98]

State, people, sovereignty, and constitution are so many different expressions, each with their own specific connotation, of the idea that the political is the

---

96. *RPh*, § 279, *GW* 14.1, p. 232 (*Elements*, 316; see *Outlines*, 267).

97. *RPh*, § 278, *GW* 14.1, p. 230 (*Elements*, 315; see *Outlines*, 265).

98. *RPh*, § 278 Anmerkung, *GW* 14.1, p. 231 (*Elements*, 316; see *Outlines*, 266).

infinite process of a community's creation of identity. But we must add that sovereignty needs to be embodied in a concrete existence that is physically and subjectively individual: "The personality of the state has actuality only as a *person*, as *the monarch*."[99] Even in democracy, an individual must detach from and take upon himself the actualization of the general will; otherwise, it would have to be up to blind fate or various forms of divination to choose the opportune moment (*kairos*).

Liberalism and Democracy

If, as Hegel said (and he was not the only one), democracy is so foreign to the postrevolutionary world, why did this notion acquire such a normative charge in later political vocabulary, including our own? For what regime, what political school, does not claim democracy? To understand this paradox, we must take into account two interdependent circumstances. First, the concept of democracy underwent a profound transformation and ultimately became almost synonymous with "representative government." Whereas in Rousseau, Kant, and Hegel, democracy is construed on the (idealized) model of the Athenian city-state of the fifth and fourth centuries and is therefore incompatible with the new problematic of representation, toward the end of the eighteenth century there occurred what Thomas Paine called an "ingrafting" of representation onto "simple democracy" that deeply affected the latter. [100] Second, it so happens that starting in the middle of the nineteenth century, political liberalism gradually reconciled with democracy, whereas up until 1848, it was highly distrustful of it — and the fact that the content of the concept of democracy had been radically altered played, of course, a role in this shift. In both cases, it is clear that the matter of the individual vote (whether universal or restricted) was a powerful means of convergence.[101]

99. *RPh*, § 279 Anmerkung, *GW* 14.1, p. 233 (*Elements*, 317; see *Outlines*, 267).

100. Paine, *Rights of Man*, 232. As early as 1777, one of the future authors of the *Federalist Papers* spoke of "representative democracy" (A. Hamilton, *Papers*, vol. 1 [New York: Columbia University Press, 1961], 255).

101. Kant illustrates the safeguards of original liberalism against democracy, for he considers democracy to always be despotic and thinks it is incompatible with the "republican constitution" (see *Ak.* 8, pp. 352–53; *PP*, pp. 324–25). In 1848, Guizot heard in the cry for a democratic republic "the echo of an old social war cry" (*De la démocratie en France* [Paris: Masson, 1849], 39–40).

For Hegel, "philosophy is . . . *its own time comprehended in thoughts*";[102] thus, it is normal that his political philosophy takes part in the lively debate that developed during the postrevolutionary period between liberalism and democracy. His argument reveals a number of fundamental differences between liberal and democratic views of the political order, though during the 1820s these were not always clearly perceived. True, the immediate object of Hegel's critique of democracy was ancient democracy, in which, as Rousseau said, the people is both sovereign and magistrate. But it can also apply to the new idea of *representative democracy* that emerged from the American and French Revolutions. Then, the argument turns against liberal political philosophy, with which Hegel, however, shares some premises. Thus, it is as if in contributing to the argument liberals made against both those who supported a return to the old order and those who wanted a democratic radicalization of the principles of 1789, Hegel undermines the very foundations of liberal political discourse by displaying its tacit assumptions (the article on the Reform Bill is exemplary on this point).

Hegel does not conflate the liberal state of law with democracy; he is well aware that political liberalism was created in reaction to both democracy, assimilated with the Terror, and to restored monarchy. But his critique of the point of view that, in confusing the state with civil society, makes the sole purpose of the former the "security and protection of property and personal freedom," that is, "*the interest of individuals [der Einzelnen] as such*,"[103] indirectly contributes to thinking about what is called the crisis of representative democracy. I have already described what distinguishes the state in the *Philosophy of Right* from the liberal state. The latter is an external organ of civil society: its only necessity stems from marginal conditions of self-regulation of economic and social processes as well as civil society's possible dysfunctions. For liberals, the state is a necessary evil and it certainly is not the objectivization of freedom. It is a constant threat to individuals and commerce, not their condition of being. This is why liberal democracy strives to erect safeguards against the power of the state. Two elements contribute to this: the problematic (which became powerfully ideological) of the fundamental and inalienable rights of the human person, and the constitutional doctrine

102. *RPh, GW* 14.1, p. 15 (*Elements*, 21; see *Outlines*, 15).
103. *RPh*, § 258 Anmerkung, *GW* 14.1, p. 201 (*Elements*, 276; see *Outlines*, 228).

of the separation of powers.[104] The rights of man circumscribe the sphere of inalienable independence of the legal person and the social subject, the bourgeois; they are thus guaranteed by the process of constituting or reconstituting the nonpolitical dimension of human existence. As for the separation of powers, which is completely different from the necessary differentiation of power within the constitution of the rational state, its clearly restrictive intention with regard to a state perceived as a threat to fundamental freedoms can lead to "the destruction of the state."[105] Fortunately, this view of things is an illusion: when there is a clash between the powers of the state, one of them will quickly reconstitute its unity to its benefit.

Weber noted with lucidity that "as soon as mass administration is involved, the meaning of democracy changes so radically that it no longer makes sense for the sociologist to ascribe to the term the same meaning."[106] Today's democratic states are certainly quite far from classical democracy, which on principle could not accept the delimitation or weakening of the governance of men. However, they do bear resemblance to Hegel's version of the liberal state (or nonstate) as a counterpoint to the speculative theme of the rational state. Democracies make the liberal principle of delimitation of the political sphere their own. Henceforth, the true subject of power is perhaps not the *demos*, though the principle of popular sovereignty is proclaimed. It is here that Hegel's double critique of democracy and liberalism (which for him are clearly two very distinct things) turns out to be very fertile.

Among the aspects of Hegelian politics that have been most harshly judged are his condemnation of democracy, his rejection of universal suffrage, and his corporative interpretation of parliamentary representation. As his adversaries indeed saw, these aspects form a system, but in general it has not been understood why. Hegel's reason for thinking that the total democracy certain actors in the French Revolution planned to implement was illusory is first and foremost *theoretical*. Fundamentally, the democratic project in the strict sense is incompatible with the way in which the modern world

104. "Basic rights and separation of powers denote, therefore, the essential content of the *Rechtsstaat* component of the modern constitution." Schmitt, *Verfassungslehre*, 127; *Constitutional Theory*, 170.

105. See *RPh*, § 272 Anmerkung, *GW* 14.1, p. 225 (*Elements*, 307; see *Outlines*, 258).

106. Weber, *Economy and Society*, 951.

differentiates between the social and the political, especially in light of the development of an economy of free enterprise, with its mandate to exceed the territorially closed limits of the state. But this argument becomes unintelligible (including its controversial aspects) if one posits the state and society as two adversaries whose perspectives can at best be reconciled. The center of gravity of Hegel's *political* theory is the creation of a *not immediately political* organization of the social world. Thus, his theory leads us to contemplate one of the paradoxes of modernity: even though the institutionally political space is based on the fluidity of the social world, in order for the latter not to succumb to the contradictions that animate it, it requires the mediation of that which it mediates. Therein lies the impossibility of overcoming the political.

PART IV

Figures of Subjectivity in Objective Spirit
Normativity and Institutions

The doctrine of objective spirit deals with subjectivity as well. This seems paradoxical only if one does not understand Hegel's reshaping of the notion in the wake of Kant and the post-Kantians. As the doctrine of the concept in the *Logic* shows, for Hegel, subjectivity and objectivity are inseparable and must be thought of as moments of a primary "subject-objectivity" that is proper to what he calls the *Idea*.[1] This definition obviously affects the theory of finite subjectivity as it is presented in the doctrine of subjective spirit. But it also affects objective spirit, which is inseparable from subjective spirit, the two combining together to form the sphere of *"finite* spirit";[2] this is why "we must not regard the distinction between subjective and objective spirit as a rigid distinction."[3] Thus, it is not surprising that subjectivity is not absent from objective spirit. It is even constantly present in it, in forms that extend and enrich the forms of subjective spirit: using the example of the objective figure of the

---

1. See *Enzykl,* § 214, *GW* 20, p. 216 (*Encyclopedia* 284–85): "The idea can be grasped as . . . subject-object . . . because in it [the idea] all relationships of the understanding are contained, but in their infinite return and identity in themselves." The term, as we know, is borrowed from Schelling (see Hegel, *Lectures on the History of Philosophy, W* 20, p. 430).

2. *Enzykl,* § 386, *GW* 20, p. 383.

3. *Enzykl,* § 387 Zusatz, *W* 10, p. 39 (*Encyclopedia* 26, modified).

subject that is the legal person in his or her constitutive relationship to an object owned, Hegel notes that

> Here we see a subjective entity that is aware of itself as free, and, at the same time, an external reality of this freedom; here, therefore, spirit attains to being-for-itself, the objectivity of spirit receives its due.[4]

Thus, we can say that every level of objective spirit corresponds to a specific form of subjectivity engaged in a relationship to objectivity that itself is spiritual (e.g., not "natural"): legal personhood, moral consciousness, familial love, the "bourgeois" consciousness of members of civil society, the political subjectivity of citizens.

But precisely because it (re)surges within *objective* spirit, this subjectivity is fed by the objectivity of the world of spirit. It is my theory that within objective spirit, what carries and nourishes subjective consciousness is its *institutional* structuration. In other words, it is as an institution or a system of institutions — the sense of which must still be specified — that objective spirit brings forth the specific figures of subjectivity I have just listed. How? By giving birth to *normative* configurations, the institutions of objective spirit "manufacture" subjectivity. This obliges us to revise the conventional idea of Hegel as a fierce opponent of Kantian normativism. A distinctive feature of the Hegelian doctrine of objective spirit is that it includes an original theory of normativity and a conception of the forms of subjectivity it calls forth. I will establish this by looking first at Hegel's critique of Kant's moral philosophy and then at the positive aspect of his critique, the doctrine of *Moralität* (chap. 10). I will then turn to the Hegelian understanding of political subjectivity, an indispensable complement to the theory of political institutions (chap. 11). Finally, I will show how the complex relationship between subjects, norms, and institutions allows us to conceive an ethical life in the strong sense of the term (chap. 12).

---

4. *Enzykl*, § 385 Zusatz, *W* 10, p. 34 (*Encyclopedia* 21, modified).

Strong and Weak Institutionalism

What are we to understand by "institutionalism"? With some reservations, let us begin with Carl Schmitt's characterization of it—though Schmitt himself prefers the name "concrete-order thinking" in order to distinguish it from the "decisionism" he first adopted and from "normativism," which he consistently rejects:

> Every jurisprudential thought works with rules, as well as with decisions, and with orders and formations ... the three kinds of thinking—*rules* and *statutes, decision,* and concrete *order* and formation—are distinguished according to the various ranks each confers ... on the three types of jurisprudential thought.[1]

I do not intend to assess the relevance of this classification, which can easily be labeled simplistic; I am merely borrowing a definition of institutionalism from Schmitt. Whereas normativism (illustrated by Kelsen's pure theory of law) postulates that every order is based on a norm, and decisionism con-

---

1. Carl Schmitt, *Über die drei Arten des rechtswissenschaftlichen Denkens* (Berlin: Duncker und Humbolt, 2006), 7; *On the Three Types of Juristic Thought*, 43 (modified).

siders that "every order is based on a decision"[2] that cannot be reduced to a rational basis: "institutional legal thinking unfolds in institutions and organizations that transcend the personal sphere."[3] Institutional legal thinking subordinates norms and decisions to an order (an institution or a complex of institutions) that establishes their coherences and gives them vitality and duration: from this perspective, institutions are identified with the legal order itself, of which they are the objective manifestation and the "concrete and real unity."[4] As Maurice Hauriou, the major French representative of the institutionalist school, writes, the institution understood as the realization of an "arch-idea" "possesses an objective existence," a "proper and autonomous life."[5] It thereby demonstrates the "objective nature of the idea,"[6] forming a kind of "objective soul"[7] that is refracted in every individual, as if "incorporated into the things around us." It is in a sense an idea-made thing, a quasi nature that offers individuals a clear framework for their actions: to use Rudolf Smend's vocabulary,[8] this "block of incontestable ideas" guarantees their "integration" into a suprapersonal totality that is a "totality of life," that is, both living and lived.

We see that the idea-made thing, the institution in the sense of Hauriou, Romano, or Smend, or the concrete order in Schmitt's sense, have traits that undeniably bring them close to what Hegel calls objective spirit: that is, to use one of his definitions, spirit "in the form of reality, as a world produced and to

2. Schmitt, *Politische Theologie*, 16; *Political Theology*, 10. The English translation erroneously has "every legal order."

3. *Politische Theologie*, 8; *Political Theology*, 3. This is the preface added by Schmitt in November 1933, thus, after he had rallied to National Socialism.

4. Santi Romano, *L'ordre juridique* (Paris: Dalloz, 2002), 7, 29–31.

5. Maurice Hauriou, "L'ordre social, la justice et le droit," in *Aux sources du droit: Le pouvoir, l'ordre et la liberté*, ed. Maurice Hauriou (Caen: Centre de philosophie politique et juridique, 1986), 76.

6. Maurice Hauriou, "La théorie de l'institution et de la foundation," in Hauriou, *Aux Sources Du Droit*, 101.

7. Ibid., 108.

8. Schmitt's contemporary, Smend, is the author of the "theory of integration," which attempts to define the process by which the incorporation of individuals into a unified whole is ensured in such a way that "the unity that is achieved is more than the sum of the parts together." See Smend, "Integration," in Smend, *Staatsrechtliche Abhandlungen*, 482. Along with Hauriou and Romano, Smend is one of the major representatives of the legal institutionalism that developed in the interwar period in response to positivism and its normativist variant (Kelsen, *Pure Theory of Law*).

be produced by it; in this world freedom is present as necessity."[9] Thus. it is not surprising that these jurists willingly refer to Hegelian objective spirit or to certain of its supposed properties when they present their doctrines as well as when they describe the "cunning of reason" at work in processes of institutional integration.[10] The question then becomes whether the Hegelian doctrine of objective spirit can be called institutionalist, and if so, in what sense.

In Dieter Heinrich's introduction to a *Nachschrift* from the 1819 to 1820 lectures, he maintains that the doctrine of objective spirit is *strong* institutionalism. I quote:

> The doctrine animating Hegel's *Philosophy of Right* ought to be understood
> as an "institutionalism." The minimum conditions for calling something
> an institutionalism are met when it is accepted that a theory of law that is
> based on the principle of the autonomous will also has to recognize its con-
> ditions of possibility and its origin in an order of things that allows for the
> realization of any such principle. But Hegel's theory is a strong institution-
> alism: it teaches that the freedom of the individual cannot be realized in an
> order where the objective itself does not possess the form of the rational will,
> where the will is not encapsulated entirely within its conditions, albeit with-
> out alienation. The individual will, which Hegel calls "subjective," is wholly
> integrated into the order of institutions and is justified only insofar as they
> are themselves.[11]

In what follows, Heinrich asks whether — given that strong institutionalism has consequences unacceptable to contemporary consciousness, in particular at the ethical and political levels (since it implies the unilateral subordination of individuals, their choices, and their behavior to the institutional conditions

---

9. *Enzykl*, § 385, *GW* 20, p. 383 (*Encyclopedia* 20).

10. See Smend, "Integrationslehre," in Smend, *Staatsrechtliche Abhandlungen*, 476: "the integration process takes place through unpremeditated legality, through a 'cunning of reason.'" Schmitt explains that the classic parliamentary system implements a "cunning of the idea or the institution" that elevates the representative of a particular interest for the purposes of general interest. See Carl Schmitt, *Die Hüter der Verfassung* (Berlin: Duncker und Humboldt, 1985), 88. Schmitt also stresses that Smend's (institutionalist) theory of integration has its roots in Hegel's thought, with Lorenz von Stein's distinction between "constitution" and "order" of the state serving to connect the two. Schmitt, *Verfassungslehre*, 6; *Constitutional Theory*, 62.

11. See Dieter Henrich, "Vernunft in Verwirklichung," in Hegel, *Philosophie des Rechts*, 31.

of their existence)—it is possible to add a corrective while still maintaining the general framework of the Hegelian system and giving relevance to the theme of objective spirit.[12] His answer is a cautious yes: it should be possible to replace strong institutionalism with a moderate institutionalism that gives more room to individual rights on the condition that the connection between objective spirit, subjective spirit, and absolute spirit be emphasized better and more strongly than it was by Hegel himself.[13]

As for myself, I contest the observation at the basis of this analysis and therefore would like to modify the conclusion. Does the acknowledgment of a "right of the world" restrict the *"right of the subjective will,"*[14] or is it rather the condition of its actuality (weak institutionalism)? In my opinion, Hegel's philosophy of law and right does not fall under *strong* institutionalism as defined by Heinrich, meaning that it does not *necessarily* imply a unilateral subordination of the subjective will to the objective will embodied in institutions, and equally, it undoubtedly excludes any inversion of the priority of objective ethical institutions. To convince oneself of this, one must study how the doctrine of objective spirit transforms, or at least modifies, the conception of subjectivity developed in the doctrine of subjective spirit, notably by developing a theory of *moral* subjectivity that is distinct from Kantianism yet shares its fundamental intention, and a theory of subjectivity that involves complex interactions between subjects, norms, and institutions.

12. Henrich's approach is therefore similar to that of Vincent Descombes, who, starting from an analytical standpoint, legitimizes some of the premises of Hegelian institutionalism—those summed up in the concept of objective spirit. See Vincent Descombes, "Y at-il un esprit objectif?," *Les Etudes Philosophiques* (1999): 347–67; *Institutions of Meaning*, passim.

13. Henrich, "Vernunft in Verwirklichung," in Hegel, *Philosophie Des Rechts*, 33.

14. *RPh*, § 33, *GW* 14.1, p. 48 (*Elements*, 62; see *Outlines*, 50).

10

The Truth of Morality

The guiding idea of German idealism is the autonomy of reason in the strong sense given to it by Kant in the *Critique of Practical Reason*: reason, and reason alone, is (under certain conditions) capable of producing its objects itself and thereby of foregoing all passivity ("receptivity") and becoming pure activity ("spontaneity"). Hegel thinks that this idea "must from now on be regarded as a universal principle of philosophy" but that it has also become "one of the prejudices of our time."[1] If there is a divergence between the two philosophers, it has to do with how widely the principle of rational autonomy can apply. In Kant's eyes, the meaning and scope of this principle is exclusively moral. Although pure reason is one and the same in its theoretical and practical usages,[2] the principle of autonomy is only foundational when it comes to its practical-normative usage, not its theoretical-cognitive usage; moreover, the fundamental interests of reason are ultimately practical.[3] Fichte considerably expanded the principle of rational autonomy by extending it to

1. *Enzykl*, § 60 Anmerkung, *GW* 20, p. 97 (*Encyclopedia* 108).
2. "It is still only one and the same reason that, whether from a theoretical or a practical perspective, judges according to a priori principles." (*KpV, Ak.* 5, p. 121; *PP*, p. 237).
3. See *KpV, Ak.* 5, p. 121; *PP*, p. 238: "all interest is ultimately practical."

the entirety of the subject's field of activity, which he understands as practical in a renewed sense of the term. Reason is practical because it is pure self-activity and because "determining its activity and being practical, are one and the same."[4] He is fully aware of the revision of the Kantian concept of practice this implies:

> It is a familiar proposition: reason is practical; and I promised to show the equivalence of this Kantian assertion with my own. [For Kant] this means first: that reason is, among other things, practical and yet sometimes, in certain circumstances, not. I affirm the opposite: reason is only practical, and there is only one purely practical reason.[5]

As for Hegel, he gives maximal scope to the self-determination of reason by striving to reconcile theoretical interest and practical interest in the unity of speculative reason. The very meaning of what he calls the *absolute idea* is that reason is inseparably knowing and willing, oriented toward both the true and the good: the "speculative or absolute" idea is in fact "the unity of the theoretical and practical idea"[6] not in the sense that it is their retrospective synthesis but rather in the sense that the subjective-objective unity of the "objective world" and the "subjectivity of the concept"[7] is secretly presupposed by acts of knowing and willing *finis* (bound up with the duality of the subject and object).

Kant and Hegel on the Principle of Practical Philosophy: Proximity and Distance

Ultimately, it is in the practical field, understood in the narrow (say, Kantian) sense that the consistency of the idealist principle of rational autonomy is determined. We must be careful to specify the vocabulary we use here, for between Kant and Hegel (to limit ourselves to these two philosophers) there are

---

4. Fichte, *Sittenlehre, Werke*, 4:57.
5. Fichte, *System der Sittenlehre* (1812), *Werke*, 11:37.
6. *Enzykl*, § 235, GW 20, p. 228 (*Encyclopedia* 299).
7. *WdL* 3, GW 12, p. 235 (*Science of Logic*, 734).

differences that can lead to serious confusion. Hegel underscores the innovation contained in his distinction between *Moralität* and *Sittlichkeit*:

> *Morality* and *ethicality*, which are usually regarded as roughly synonymous, are taken here in essentially distinct senses. Yet even representational thought [*Vorstellung*] seems to distinguish them; Kantian usage prefers the expression *morality*, as indeed the practical principles of Kant's philosophy are confined throughout to this concept, even rendering the point of view of *ethicality* impossible and in fact expressly infringing and destroying it. But even if morality and ethicality were etymologically synonymous, this would not prevent them, since they are now different words, from being used for different concepts.[8]

I will return to Hegel's claim that Kant's moral philosophy makes "the point of view of *ethicality* impossible"; I believe that at bottom it is less one sided and misguided than is often claimed. But first we must note that Kant himself does not confuse *Moral* and *Ethik*, at least in his late practical philosophy. The treatise on *Perpetual Peace* formally distinguishes "moral as doctrine of law" from "moral as ethics."[9] In *The Metaphysics of Morals*, Kant reinterprets the distinction made in the *Critique of Practical Reason* between legality and morality in the sense that legality is the distinctive trait of "rightful lawgiving," while morality is the specific mark of ethical lawgiving.[10] Thus, we may schematically state the following: whereas in Hegel, ethicality (*Sittlichkeit*) is the concrete totality within which the two abstract moments of law and morality (*Moralität*) can be distinguished, in Kant, ethics (*Sittenlehre*) and law (*Rechtslehre*) are both species of the genus morality (*Moral*). Clearly, in comparing their positions we must keep this terminological difference in mind (while also admitting that it may turn out to be more than just a difference in vocabulary).

In terms of their conceptualizations of the moral or ethical domain (i.e., the practical field), I will start from the following paradoxical observation: it is in this domain that Hegel turns out, sometime unwittingly, to be closest to

---

8. *RPh*, § 33, *GW* 14.1, p. 49 (*Elements*, 63; see *Outlines*, 51).
9. Kant, *Frieden*, *Ak.* 8, pp. 383–86; *PP*, p. 349–51 (modified).
10. Kant, *MdS*, Einleitung, *Ak.* 6, p. 219; *PP*, p. 383 ff.

Kant, but it is here that he fights against him most strenuously. I will quickly review the two sides of the issue.

Proximity

German idealism refuses to construct a "material ethics" that would try to determine the ends that the moral subject should set for him- or herself. Thus, it completes the modern break with the traditional conception of a teleological order that just needs to be discovered so that the subject can conform to it by adding the idea of rational self-determination that foregoes any material element. Kant's discovery lies here: pure reason and *it alone* is practical on its own,[11] which means that the moral problem has less to do with the objects or ends that reason pursues and more with the form it adopts in order to do so — in this case, the form of self-determination. Any instrumental or prudential determination is proscribed or at least relegated to second place with regard to the principle of autonomy, which is illustrated by the "fundamental law of pure practical reason: so act that the maxim of your will could always hold at the same time as a principle in a giving of universal law"[12] and other (derivative) formulations of the categorical imperative. In any event, the advice of prudence and instrumental rationality are practical determinations only in a weak sense: they are actually theoretical propositions applied to the domain to free actions (thus, they belong to the "knowledge of nature [theory]"[13]) and not the rational promulgation of norms intended to frame these actions themselves. Thus, the determination of the ends of action, that is to say the objects of practical reason, is if not secondary then at least second with respect to the foundational act of practical normativity as it is experienced in awareness of obligation in respect for the very idea of normativity. This explains the reversal of the structure of the Analytic in the second *Critique*: principles first, then concepts.[14] The real practical question, the only one relevant from the normative point of view, is thus the question of what ultimately determines the will to will (pure reason or various pathological interests) and not the ends or goals of action. This results in a rejection of all forms of eudemonism, that is, of

11. Kant, *KpV*, Ak. 5, p. 31; *PP*, p. 164.
12. Kant, *KpV*, Ak. 5, p. 30; *PP*, p. 164.
13. Kant, *Erste Einleitung in die Kritik der Urteilskraft*, Ak. 20, pp. 199–200 / 3C, p. 6.
14. See Kant, *KpV*, Ak. 5, p. 89 ff. ("Critical Elucidation of the Analytic"); *PP*, p. 211 ff.

any material definition of morality. It also explains Kant's tendency, palpable in his later texts, to simply identify the will with practical reason and to accentuate the difference between the rational will and mere free choice:

> The will is therefore the faculty of desire considered not so much in relation to action (as choice is) but rather in relation to the ground determining choice to action. The will itself, strictly speaking, has no determining ground; insofar as it can determine choice, it is instead practical reason itself.[15]

Hegel's insistent critique of the formalism of practical reason has sometimes led readers to believe that he strays from the Kantian path; according to some, the distinction between *Moralität* and *Sittlichkeit* implies a return to the principle of happiness and a conception of ethics based on teleological ends or substance. This is not at all the case, at least at the level of morality properly speaking, insofar is it concerns the relationship between an acting subjectivity, a norm (the good), and the actual world, which also has rights to be asserted. Hegel's critique of the classical (external) conception of finality and his concomitant valorization of the Kantian theme of internal finality[16] indicates that he is most certainly not reintroducing into practical philosophy what the *Logic* rejects even more radically than Kant does: finalism understood according to the traditional technical paradigm and the naively ontologizing perspective, denounced in the appendix to the first part of the *Ethics*. Thus, in the moral domain, Hegel takes up for his own the Kantian refutation of the principle of happiness or well-being (*das Wohl*), adding that there can be no question of sacrificing law to the quest for personal happiness (which is not illegitimate in itself).[17] There is indeed a place for this quest, but at a subordinate level where neither morality nor ethicality are fully developed. If civil society is dedicated to the (partly illusory and partly contradictory) quest for particular well-being, it is precisely because particularity and abstraction are its principle; and while particular happiness must be recognized as a moment

---

15. Kant, *MdS*, Einleitung, *Ak.* 6, p. 213; *PP*, p. 375. See also Religion, *Ak.* 6, pp. 3–4.

16. "Through the concept of inner purposiveness, Kant re-awakened the idea in general and that of life in particular" (*Enzykl*, § 204 Anmerkung, *GW* 20, p. 210 [*Encyclopedia* 277]). See also *WdL* 3, *GW* 12, p. 154 ff. (*Science of Logic*, 654ff).

17. *RPh*, § 126 and Anmerkung, *GW* 14.1, pp. 111–12 (*Elements*, 153–54; see *Outlines*, 124–25).

in the development of ethicality,[18] it cannot provide it with a principle. As in Kant, rational autonomy, *"the free will which wills the free will,"*[19] is the only foundation for legal, moral, or ethical norms.

Distance

Hegel opposes Kant most strongly and consistently in the domain of practical philosophy. This is expressed in the terminological change I have already mentioned: the elevation of ethicality (*Sittlichkeit*) to the level of the concrete truth of the abstract norms of law and morality. But this shift goes along with a transformation of the very meaning of these concepts. In Kant, the distinction between law and ethics has meaning only on the basis of the sole formal principle of morality: we must distinguish an action's external conformity to a norm (legality) from the fact that the obligation attached to a norm is the motive for the action (morality). Consequently, *ethics*, the doctrine of obligatory ends, the legislation of which can only be internal to the subject, must be distinguished from *law*, the doctrine of external obligations. But both are founded on the self-determination of practical reason, which means that ethical norms and legal norms are both, as norms, "laws of freedom," categorical imperatives.[20] Hegel profoundly alters a terminology that in his eyes reveals a conceptual defect. For him, ethicality (*Sittlichkeit*) is the *"unity* and *truth* of these two abstract moments,"[21] that is, law and morality; it reconciles the objective abstraction of law and the subjective abstraction of morality within a concrete totality, itself divided into strata that correspond to various institutional shapes. Thus, ethicality becomes foundational in the sense that it gives rational actuality to the two spheres, the moral and the legal, where the formalism of abstract normativity reigns. But this clearly corresponds to a radical transformation of the meaning of the term, one that fits the general problematic of objective spirit. Ethicality in Hegel no longer refers to a domain or type of normativity but rather to the institutional field within which (legal

18. On "particular welfare" as the aim of the "external state," see *RPh*, §§ 183, 230, *GW* 14.1, pp. 160, 189 (*Elements*, 221, 259–60; see *Outlines*, 181, 215).

19. *RPh*, § 27, *GW* 14.1, p. 45 (*Elements*, 57; see *Outlines*, 46).

20. Kant, *MdS*, Einleitung, *Ak.* 6, pp. 214, 218–21; *PP*, pp. 375, 383–85. The distinction between legality and morality is, however, not the same as that between law and ethics. See Reflection 6764, *Ak.* 19, p. 154: "legality is either juridical or ethical."

21. *RPh*, § 33, *GW* 14.1, p. 48 (*Elements*, 62; see *Outlines*, 50).

and moral) normativity becomes actual for subjects who only access concrete subjectivity insofar as they inscribe their actions (or their plans to act) within this requisite institutional framework that is like second nature to them.[22] The terminological shifts are thus both an indication and an effect of reshaping the field of practical philosophy. They also imply a judgment of the Kantian project to base ethics on the principle of the self-determination of pure practical reason.

The Three Vices of Kantian Morality

Hegel makes three reproaches to the Kantian theory of moral normativity: the definition of practical philosophy is tainted by *formalism*; it is condemned to *inactuality* because of the opposition it establishes between ought and is; and it reveals the *dualism* characteristic of philosophies of the understanding. This triple failure dooms Kant's moral philosophy to be no more than a finite thought of finitude.

1. The imputation of formalism in Kant's moral philosophy is based on the letter of his texts. The Analytic of pure practical reason establishes that

> since material principles are quite unfit to be the supreme moral law . . . the *formal practical principle* of pure reason (in accordance with which the mere form of a possible giving of universal law through our maxims must constitute the supreme and immediate determining ground of the will) is the *sole* principle that can *possibly* be fit for categorical imperatives, that is, practical laws (which make actions duties), and in general for the principle of morality.[23]

Within the deontological perspective, which Kant considers the only perspective that can allow for the constitution of a rational morality, this open formalism is based on the demonstration that it is impossible to found apodictic ethical norms on any material principle whatsoever.[24] Because any definition of

---

22. See *RPh*, § 4 and 151, *GW* 14.1, pp. 31, 151 (*Elements*, 35, 195; see *Outlines*, 26, 159).

23. *KpV*, Ak. 5, p. 41; *PP*, p. 173. See also *MdS*, Tugendlehre, Vorrede, Ak. 6, pp. 376–77, as well as *Gemeinspruch*, Ak. 8, p. 282: "the law with respect to what is formal in choice is indeed all that remains when I have left out of consideration the matter of choice."

24. See *KpV*, Ak. 5, pp. 21–22; *PP*, pp. 154–55.

obligation based on its content—that is, on the ends it prescribes—implies a heteronomy of choice, the rational foundation of normativity, in keeping with the principle of autonomy, requires that the form of universality (the "form of the law) be the ultimate (if not sole) foundation of the determination of the will. From Kant's point of view, the formalism of practical reason is simultaneously the result of the critique of the eudemonism that any material ethics ultimately amounts to and the consequence of defining reason as the power to actualize the universal in the particular, as the "faculty of principles."[25]

Hegel shares Kant's conviction that moral normativity must have a purely rational basis too much to invoke the common version of the antiformalist argument, which Péguy's wisecrack sums up neatly: the Kantian subject's hands are clean, but he/she has no hands. This is why Hegel takes seriously the requirements to which the deontological formalism of practical reason corresponds:

> What Kant had denied theoretical reason, namely free self-determination, he explicitly vindicated for practical reason. It is principally this side of the Kantian philosophy that has won it great favour, and rightly so. In order to recognize the value of our debt to Kant in this respect, we need first to call to mind that shape of the practical philosophy and specifically the moral philosophy that he encountered as the dominant one. This was generally speaking the system of eudaemonism . . . in opposition to this eudaemonism that dispenses with any firm hold within itself and opens the door to every whim and passing mood, and he enunciated in this way the requirement of a universal determination of the will that was equally binding on everybody.[26]

Hegel recognizes the advance implied by the formalism of the Kantian understanding of moral normativity when it is properly understood: it simply expresses the founding principle of idealism, rational autonomy—the fact that "for the will . . . there is no other aim than that derived from itself, the aim of its freedom."[27] Hegel expresses this by saying that "the absolute determination

---

25. Kant, *KrV, Ak.* 3, B 356 / 1C, p. 387: "we defined the understanding as the faculty of rules; here we will distinguish reason from the understanding by calling reason the faculty of *principles.*"

26. *Enzykl,* § 54 Zusatz, *W* 8, pp. 138–39 (*Encyclopedia* 102–3).

27. *GdP, W* 20, p. 367 (*Lectures on the Philosophy of World History,* 459).

or, if one prefers, the absolute drive, of the free spirit is to make its freedom into its object [*Gegenstand*]."[28]

Hegel contests Kantian formalism for a reason other than the formalism of (moral) normativity, a reason directly connected to his own concept of speculative reason. "Bad" formalism is in reality a legacy of theoretical philosophy. The rejection, within Kant's idealism, of the constitutive use of rational ideas in favor of merely regulative usage makes the function of theoretical reason simply to order the knowledge that the understanding produces; reason "does not create any concepts (of objects) but only orders them."[29] This restriction condemns speculative reason to engender abstract universals (transcendental ideas) that are separate from the particular material and tools of true knowledge (the concepts — possibly pure — of objects, produced by the understanding); Kant himself describes the rational idea as *focus imaginarius*.[30] For Hegel, on the other hand, true, concrete, speculative universality is the universality constituted in the process of its own self-differentiation. True reason works within the finite acts of the understanding, and it is to emphasize the imbrication between the two that Hegel evokes "what reason and its understanding have labored to produce over several thousand years"[31] and attributes to the latter an "absolute power" that lies in the analytic work that its "activity of dissolution" practices on "familiar" representations.[32] Because Kant's practical reason ignores this and does not call into question the separation between understanding and reason established in the first *Critique*, it "does not advance beyond the formalism that is supposed to be the ultimate standpoint of theoretical reason." At the same time, it keeps the understanding in isolation and therefore does not manage to actually go beyond "*abstract identity* of the understanding."[33]

Making use of Hegel's distinction between two aspects of moral subjectivity's formalism, which stems from the two senses (passive and active) that

---

28. *RPh*, § 27, *GW* 14.1, p. 44 (*Elements*, 57; see *Outlines*, 46).

29. Kant, *KrV*, Ak. 3, B 671 / 1C, p. 590.

30. Kant, *KrV*, Ak. 3, B 672 / 1C, p. 591.

31. *RPh*, Vorrede, *GW* 14.1, p. 10 (*Elements*, 16; see *Outlines*, 9).

32. *PhG*, *GW* 9, p. 27 (*Phenomenology*, ¶ 31). The preface also praises *Verständlichkeit*, the intelligibility of understanding; see *PhG*, *GW* 9, pp. 15–16 (*Phenomenology*, ¶ 13).

33. *Enzykl*, § 54, *GW* 20, p. 93 (*Encyclopedia* 102). The *Phenomenology*, at the end of its analysis of the famous example of the "thing entrusted": "It is not, therefore, because I find something is not self-contradictory that it is right" (*PhG*, *GW* 9, p. 237 [*Phenomenology*, ¶ 437]).

the notion of form can have,[34] we may say for simplicity's sake that the formalism of Kantian reason has both positive and negative meaning. The problem is that there is a break between the positive meaning of this formalism — it illustrates the power of reason's self-determination, the fact that it is pure spontaneity — and the negative meaning, the reduction of the universal to abstract noncontradiction, to the principle of identity that the *Logic* shows implies precisely what it intends to proscribe — contradiction. However, we may also say that the first meaning leads to the second. For it is the very requirement of reason's unconditioned autonomy that, due to the lack of tools that would be speculatively suited to its fulfillment, leads to the formalist distortion of rationality. This ambiguity of Kantian formalism is emphasized in a Remark in the "Morality" section of the *Philosophy of Right*:

> However essential it may be to emphasize the pure and unconditional self-determination of the will as the root of duty — for knowledge [*Erkenntnis*] of the will first gained a firm foundation and point of departure in the philosophy of Kant, through the thought of its infinite autonomy — to cling on to a merely moral point of view without making the transition to the concept of ethicality reduces this gain to an *empty formalism*, and moral science to an empty rhetoric of *duty for duty's sake*. From this point of view, no immanent theory of duties is possible. One may indeed bring in material *from outside* and thereby arrive at *particular* duties, but it is impossible to make the transition to the determination of particular duties from the above determination of duty as *absence of contradiction*, as *formal correspondence with itself*, which is no different from the specification of *abstract indeterminacy*; and even if such a particular content for action is taken into consideration, there is no criterion within that principle for deciding whether or not this content is a duty. On the contrary, it is possible to justify any wrong or immoral mode of action by this means.[35]

The analysis may seem curt. Nonetheless it is true that the formal law, as a principle for discriminating between subjective maxims, aims to proscribe what cannot be willed, and beyond that, what cannot be thought without contradiction.

---

34. See *RPh*, § 108, *GW* 14.1, p. 100 (*Elements*, 137; see *Outlines*, 110–11).
35. *RPh*, § 135 Anmerkung, *GW* 14.1, p. 118 (*Elements*, 162; see *Outlines*, 130–131, modified).

However, the critique of formalism only takes on its full meaning in light of Hegel's reading of the *Critique of Judgment*, a text that in his eyes includes Kantianism's most fertile speculative potential. According to Hegel, the doctrine of internal finality that Kant develops in that work would have made it possible to reconstruct practical philosophy on other bases. Through it, Kant could have renounced the formal concept of the good upheld in his moral philosophy and thus would have avoided the trap of the ought and (bad) formalism:

> Through the concept of inner purposiveness Kant has resuscitated the idea in general and in particular the idea of life. He liberated practical reason from external purposiveness only insofar as he recognized the formal element of the will, self-determination in the form of generality, as absolute. The content, however, is indeterminate. Purposive action is conditioned by material and accomplishes only formal goodness, or, what amounts to the same thing, realizes only the means.[36]

The hypothesis of an intuitive understanding—which Kant merely affirms is not contradictory[37]—makes it possible to reconstruct what Kantian ethics could have been if not for the limitations it set on itself. Such an intuitive understanding (the equivalent of what Hegel calls speculative reason) would be able to actually and "synthetically" produce the particular from the universal and thus to deduce concrete ethical obligations from the formal principle of autonomy. This is not the case in Kantian morality, where normative content is given by "common reason" or "the most ordinary understanding" and is tested by practical reason only for its universalizability. Thus, had Kant taken this hypothesis seriously, he would have had the means to go beyond "bad" formalism in his practical philosophy without thereby returning to ethical principles that entail heteronomy.

2. Hegel's second criticism concerns the inactuality of the moral principle: the only perspective for the realization of the highest good, the object and end of pure practical reason, offered by the postulates is that of an indefinite ought. His analysis in the *Phenomenology of Spirit* of the displacements or distortions (*Verstellungen*) of the moral vision of the world and the (un-

---

36. *Enzykl* 1817, § 155 Anmerkung, *GW* 13, p. 95 (*Encyclopedia* 1817, 124–25, modified).
37. See Kant, *KU*, § 77, *Ak.* 5, pp. 405–8.

suspected) contradictions practical reason runs into in determining the ultimate end (*Endzweck*) of moral action is well known.[38] According to Kant, the
doctrine of the postulates of practical reason responds to the requirement of
accomplishment that drives practical action, and they are intended to overcome, asymptotically, the discordance between the end that the will is obliged
to prescribe for itself (the realization of the highest good in the world) and the
"external relations within which alone an object as end in itself (as moral final
end)" would be "produced in conformity with these incentives."[39] Though the
doctrine of the highest good and of the postulates must be dissociated from
the determination of the *principle* of morality (the "fundamental law of pure
practical reason"), it illustrates the contrast between the practically constitutive value of rational ideas and their merely regulatory theoretical usage;
thus, it expresses the necessity that results from the critique of the powers of
reason to "deny knowledge in order to make room for faith."[40] In this sense,
the theme of the ought, the *Sollen*, is not the mark of an insurmountable gap
between what is and what should be according to the requirement of abstract
reason (Hegel's interpretation); to the contrary, it is the principle of a tendency to actuality that, resulting from the rational necessity of action, guarantees it an indefinitely open perspective. Kant is clearly quite aware of the
objections that this problematic of the *Sollen* as an indefinitely open perspective on action can raise. But in his eyes, it alone can reconcile the autonomy of
rational willing with the achievements of the critique of speculative reason. A
passage from the third *Critique* illustrates this conviction:

> Moral laws must be represented as commands (and the actions that are in
> accord with them as duties), and that reason expresses this necessity not
> through a be (happening) but through a should-be, which would not be the
> case if reason without sensibility (as the subjective condition of its application
> to objects of nature) were considered, as far as its causality is concerned, as a
> cause in an intelligible world corresponding completely with the moral law,
> where there would be no distinction between what should be done and what

38. See *PhG*, *GW* 9, p. 332 ff. (*Phenomenology*, ¶ 616 ff.).
39. Kant, *Gemeinspruch*, Ak. 8, p. 280n; *PP*, p. 282.
40. Kant, *KrV*, Ak. 3, B xxx / 1C, p. 117.

is done, between a practical law concerning that which is possible through us and the theoretical law concerning that which is actual through us.[41]

In Hegel's eyes there are two flaws in this determination of the practical field and of the horizon — considered necessary — of moral action. First, from a *logical* point of view, it ignores the speculative determination of infinity as a process that works immanently within the finite itself. As the *Logic* establishes, the theme of the ought implies a finitization of true infinity, an operation analogous to that of a mathematician who, ignoring the truth in effect in his own practice, represents infinity as the beyond of the finite:

> In the ought the concept of finitude and then the transcendence of the finitude, infinity, begins. The ought is that which, in the subsequent development, in accordance with the said impossibility, will display itself as a progress to infinity.[42]

Second, from a *practical* point of view, the doctrine of the postulates, which refers the concordance between happiness and morality to an indefinite horizon, inaugurates an insurmountable gap between universal-rational volition, the apodictic power of self-determination of which is expressed by the moral law, and the particular-empirical volition of the pathologically determined subject; for the latter, the conditions of effectiveness of action necessarily lie beyond his or her action. Practical reason requires the realization of the highest good, the immortality of the soul, and the existence of a divine administrator of the world, but at the same time it also requires the nonrealization of these conditions, for their realization would deprive the moral purpose of the *meaning* it holds for empirical human subjects.[43] There is thus a contradiction between the objective content of morally determined behavior and the meaning it has for the subject of this behavior, between universality and particularity, and between freedom and nature. Kant's point of view plunges the

41. Kant, *KU*, § 76, *Ak.* 5, pp. 403–4 / 3C, p. 273.

42. *WdL* 1², *GW* 21, p. 121 (*Science of Logic*, 105, modified).

43. We may note apropos of this analysis that finality constitutes a link between the problematic of practical reason, centered around rational action, and that of reflective judgment, which has to do with "a lawfulness of the contingent as such" (*Erste Einleitung in die Kritik der Urteilskraft, Ak.* 20, p. 217 / 3C, p. 20).

moral subject into an *inextricable* contradiction, for the subject's action both presupposes the aporia and, unknown to the subject, is its practical resolution:

> Actin therefore in fact immediately brings to fruition what had been put forward as not taking place at all, that is, what was only supposed to be a postulate, merely an other-worldly beyond. Consciousness therefore expresses through its deed that it is not serious about its own act of postulating, since what the action means is that it brings into the present what was not supposed to be in the present.[44]

In the *Philosophy of Right*, the doctrine of morality presents the positive lesson to be drawn from the equivocations of the moral view. If moral consciousness is not to succumb to its contradictions, it must be understood in such a way that it ceases to always be within or beyond itself: it must include an immanent principle of actuality. But to define this rule of actualization it is necessary to go beyond the space of moral subjectivity properly speaking. The true actuality of practical reason is located in the sphere of the concrete objectivization of action for which Hegel reserves the name *Sittlichkeit*, thus breaking with the Kantian usage of the term. At bottom, the problems with Kantian practical philosophy illustrate the fact that moral subjectivity cannot be thought of as self-sufficient, for it is not able to actualize by itself what it must necessarily strive for. If practical reason is doomed to contradiction, it is ultimately because of a structural deficiency, "not only the one-sidedness of this subjectivity but subjectivity in general."[45] The solution to the aporia of the ought is not to abandon the expectations of moral subjectivity, let alone of rationality itself; rather, it lies in the objectivization of subjective reason, the true "reason of understanding," and in the promotion of morality to ethicality (in the Hegelian sense!).

3. The third criticism of practical philosophy actually goes beyond the moral-practical problem and leads to a general judgment on the Kantian system; this critique has to do with the *dualism* of Kant's philosophy. This dualism brings with it the contradictions contained in the moral view of the world:

---

44. PhG, GW 9, p. 333 (*Phenomenology*, ¶ 618). See also *Enzykl*, § 60.
45. *Enzykl*, § 234, GW 20, p. 228 (*Encyclopedia* 298).

> In every dualistic system, and especially in the Kantian system, its basic
> flaw reveals itself through the inconsistency of combining [*vereinen*] what
> a moment ago has been declared to be independent and thus incompatible
> [*unvereinbar*].[46]

Dualism—between the thing-in-itself and the phenomenon, the infinite
and the finite, the understanding and reason, freedom and necessity, subjective practical reason and its objective horizon—condemns Kant's project to constantly betray its own fundamental requirement of the radical self-
determination of reason freed of any *given* condition. The duality of *Sein* and
Sollen (which Kant attributes to the anthropological constitution of the subject, to the combination of spontaneity and receptivity within the subject) is
the effect of a structure of thought that of itself calls for its own surpassing.
Kantian dualism, precisely because it results in "nothing but the contradiction itself posited as perennially recurring,"[47] works unknown to itself toward
speculative rationality, toward true autonomy. If it is true that the understanding, by the judgment it makes of abstract difference, is the site of this always-
re-created contradiction, then Kant's philosophy is indeed the "completed
philosophy of the understanding."[48] But as we know, Hegel's judgment of the
understanding is far from unilaterally negative: doesn't it have "the most astonishing and mightiest of powers, or rather the absolute power"?[49] In a sense,
the understanding is extremely close to speculative reason, of which it is the
abstract, though decisive, moment. This sheds light on the nature of Hegel's
overall assessment of Kantian morality: to satisfy the requirement it rightfully
expresses (the self-determination of reason), Kant's subjective reason must
be replaced with a simultaneously subjective and objective rationality, which
develops the truth contained in the former by revealing the objective conditions of its actuality.

46. *Enzykl*, § 60 Anmerkung, *GW* 20, p. 97 (*Encyclopedia* 106).
47. *Enzykl*, § 60, *GW* 20, p. 96 (*Encyclopedia* 106).
48. *GdP*, *W* 20, p. 385 (*Lectures*, 476, translation modified).
49. *PhG*, *GW* 9, p. 27 (*Phenomenology*, ¶ 32).

The Fertility and Limitations of the Moral Point of View

The analysis of *Moralität* describes the complex relations between moral *subjects* and their *actions* (and thus, with the world to which subjects belong) and with the *norms* to which these actions must conform. For Hegel, it is not a matter of denying all value to "subjective morality" and replacing it with *Sittlichkeit* alone. It is true that his analysis is full of criticism: the Remark to section 140 — the longest one in the *Philosophy of Right* — contains a scathing denunciation of the ambiguous or perverse figures of a subjectivity that *"declares itself absolute"*[50] under the cover of subtle moral casuistry. It is also true that a famous passage in the *Phenomenology of Spirit* develops a vigorous critique of the "moral view of the world."[51] But we must not forget that after the wanderings of the "beautiful soul" and its "solitary divine service"[52] have been denounced, the critique culminates in the eminently positive figure of the pardon of Evil,[53] in which the entire odyssey of spirit is recapitulated, for this is what allows spirit in its history or world (the phenomenological equivalent to objective spirit) to transition to religion and absolute knowing, which in the completed Hegelian system are part of absolute spirit. This is why Hegel's denunciation of moral subjectivism, consistent since the earliest Jena writings, must not lead us to misunderstand the positivity that morality has for him when it is understood within its limits and brought back to the requirements of objectivity (the "right of the world"). Everything suggests that within the economy of objective spirit, the task of morality is to guarantee the connection between the abstract outline of objective spirit (law) and its concrete figures (political-ethical institutions). Why does this task of mediating between objective spirit and itself fall to moral subjectivity?

For Hegel as for Kant, the principle of morality is the rational self-determination of the subjective will:

> The will's *self-determination* is at the same time a moment of its concept, and subjectivity is not just the aspect of its existence [*Dasein*], but its own determination (see § 104). The will which is determined as subjective and free for

50. *RPh*, § 140, *GW* 14.1, p. 123 (*Elements*, 170; see *Outlines*, 138).
51. See *PhG*, *GW* 9, p. 324 ff. (*Phenomenology*, ¶ 599 ff.).
52. See *PhG*, *GW* 9, p. 353–4 (*Phenomenology*, ¶ 632–33).
53. See *PhG*, *GW* 9, p. 360 ff. (*Phenomenology*, ¶ 670).

itself, though initially only concept, itself has *existence* in order to become *Idea*. The moral point of view therefore takes the shape of the *right of the subjective will*. In accordance with this right, the will can *recognize* something or *be* something only in so far as that thing is *its own*, and in so far as the will is present to itself in it as subjectivity.[54]

This definition raises a preliminary question: why is the study of the "right of the *subjective* will" framed by the theory of *objective* spirit? The question is all the more pressing because within subjective sprit, practical spirit has characteristics that clearly make it akin to moral subjectivity: like moral subjectivity, it is initially bound by the characteristic structure of the ought of the norm it gives itself, but at the same time it is thereby involved in an indefinite process of objectivization by which its intrinsic limitation is surpassed. So then why separate the examination of practical spirit (the will) from that of its "right," morality? Precisely because morality, which connects the subjectivity of willing to norms that must be realized through actions, expresses the *right*—that is, the objective manifestation—of the internal principle that is free subjectivity. The necessary distinction between the principle of willing and the manifestation of this principle as right explains the inclusion of morality in the sphere of objective spirit or of law in the broad sense of the concrete existence, the objectivization of freedom.

However, we must not think that Hegel cuts morality off from principle, that is, in Kantian terms, the obligations of virtue (*Tugendpflichten*) from the rational autonomy of the practical subject. For practical spirit, which experiences itself as spirit through acts of volition, impulses, desires, and choices, is in reality merely the *abstract* support (in Kelsenian terms, the point of imputation) for the objectivized system of moral norms; thus, the doctrine of objective spirit constitutes the "rational system" of that which, for the subjective spirit as such, remains an "indeterminate demand."[55] In short, the principle of subjective autonomy is an objective principle, a "right" in the Hegelian sense:

> So the question of which are the *good*, rational inclinations and how they are to be subordinated to each other, turns into a presentation of the relationships that the spirit produces when it develops an *objective* spirit—a devel-

54. *RPh*, § 107, *GW* 14.1, p. 100 (*Elements*, 136; see *Outlines*, 110).
55. *RPh*, § 19, *GW* 14.1, p. 40 (*Elements*, 51; see *Outlines*, 40).

opment in which the *content* of self-determination loses its contingency or willfulness. The treatment of urges, inclinations, and passions in their genuine content is thus essentially the *theory* of legal, moral, and ethical *duties*.[56]

Conversely, the inclusion of morality in the doctrine of objective spirit gives the weight of actuality to abstractly objective determinations, in particular those of law in the narrow sense, for the formal universality of these determinations means that they need a concrete principle of actualization, which subjective consciousness guided by moral norms offers them. Whence the surprising affirmation (if we keep in mind Hegel's reproach that the moral view of the world is abstract and formal) that morality is the "real aspect of the concept of freedom" and that the subjectivity of willing is the only "aspect of *existence*" by which "freedom, or the will which has being *in itself*, [can] be actual."[57] What does this mean?

Within the structure of objective spirit, moral *subjectivity* has a function that corresponds to that of *objectivity* within the logic of the concept: it supplies a mediation through which the initially formal and abstract concept finds itself in the actual world of common representation, which appears foreign to it. There is nothing arbitrary about this seemingly paradoxical similarity. Just as in the doctrine of objective spirit the concept of law must be actualized as idea, so in the *Logic* the *"formal* concept" is transposed into objectivity, leaves its *"inwardness,"* and moves to "determinate existence"[58] so that the identity in process in each one, that is, its *idea,* can become manifest in its speculative truth. From this parallel structure (which in fact is a chiasmus since in it subjectivity plays the role that had fallen to objectivity, and vice versa) we must retain the fact that the presence of morality within objective spirit and its function there stem from the fact that *subjectivity,* whose natural language is morality, is an operator of actuality for objective spirit. Without the mediation that moral normativity, which is abstract *in itself,* provides for objective spirit, the gap between law and ethicality and between law and morality itself would be conceptually and practically insurmountable.

But in reality, subjectivity as such is not what drives the analysis of morality; *action* is, understood through the lens of its imputability to a subject and in

---

56. *Enzykl,* § 474 Anmerkung, *GW* 20, p. 472 (*Encyclopedia* 212, modified).
57. *RPh,* § 106 and Anmerkung, *GW* 14.1, p. 99 (*Elements,* 135; see *Outlines,* 109).
58. *WdL* 3, *GW* 12, p. 30 (*Science of Logic,* 527).

relation to the norms that structure action and the human world to which it belongs. In this way, Hegel's analysis of morality acquires positive content and turns out to be closer to Kant's than is often thought. The point of view of the moral subject, finite and abstract, perpetually renews the distance between what is and what should be. But it turns the subject into a *being of action*, for he or she must act in order to try to fill the gap between the norm prescribed by reason and the state of the world. Thus, action (*Handlung*), defined as "the expression of the will as *subjective* or *moral*,"[59] is the center of gravity of the Hegelian theory of morality. This, however, does not apply to just any act or "deed" (*Tat*) an individual may perform; it refers to a plan made by a subjectivity guided by a norm or normative configuration. Action lies at the intersection of a concrete individual's subjectivity, the (abstract) objectivity of a universal norm recognized by the subject as the supreme end of his or her action, and the (concrete) objectivity of a world present in the mode of factuality and immediacy and which involves other subjective individualities in the structure of action. Action, the vehicle of the subject's moral aim, is the contact point between the various components that the moral view of the world incorporates.

This is how we are to understand the astonishing expression from the *Philosophy of Right* that "what the subject *is*, is the series of its actions."[60] When the moral subject is engaged in the process of objective spirit, it is not through his or her subjectivity or interiority—which give free reign to the very moralizing absolutization Hegel denounces—but rather insofar as he or she is fully invested and present in the action. We can then understand why moral subjectivity is described as "the aspect of concrete *existence* [*Existenz*]" or the "real moment" of objective freedom;[61] only this dimension of subjectivity gives actual, lived density to freedom. In other words, objective freedom (realized as *Sittlichkeit*) requires real self-determination of moral subjectivity in action. The form of the ought, which affects subjectivity's relation to its actions and the norms that guide it, is thus not to be understood as a mere mark of incompleteness, for it also expresses the subject's need to act and thus to face other subjects and a world that resists.[62] This real and concrete aspect of subjective

59. *RPh*, § 113, *GW* 14.1, p. 102 (*Elements*, 140; see *Outlines*, 114).
60. *RPh*, § 124, *GW* 14.1, p. 110 (*Elements*, 151; see *Outlines*, 122).
61. *RPh*, § 106, *GW* 14.1, p. 99 (*Elements*, 135; see *Outlines*, 109).
62. On this subject, see Odo Marquard, "Hegel und das Sollen," in *Schwierigkeiten mit der Geschichtsphilosophie* (Frankfurt am Main: Suhrkamp, 1964), 37–51.

plans for action is fully expressed in the dialectic of conscience (*Gewissen*) and the good, the third moment in the analysis of morality. Indeed, unlike aim (*Vorsatz*) or intention (*Absicht*), conscience is directly and explicitly measured against the universal and constitutes for subjectivity the decisive test of its capacity to go beyond its constitutive limits — its finitude, its interiority, its inactuality — practically, in action. This is why

> *Conscience* expresses the absolute entitlement of subjective self-
> consciousness to know *in itself* and *from itself* what right and duty are,
> and to recognize only what it thus knows as the good; it also consists in
> the assertions that what it thus knows and wills is *truly* right and duty.[63]

If action is the core of Hegel's analysis of morality it is because he is concerned with showing the conditions of actuality of the moral aim and in thus showing its role in the process of objectivizing and concretizing freedom. The completed expression of this objectivization — ethicality — requires subjectivity to take on the requirements of the universal, that is, legal norms and the conditions of social and political life. The individual lives and thinks his or her practical relationship to the objective institutional conditions of his or her freedom in the subjective language of morality. This language undoubtedly contributes some confusion as to the true rationality of ethicality, but through it the abstract commands of law and the social and political requirements of rational freedom are actualized. For regardless of its value, "*the law* [itself] *does not act*; only an actual human being acts."[64] When the subject acts in conformity with the ends he or she must prescribe him- or herself, objective spirit takes on practical actuality, and its structures acquire lived value. Thus, subjectivity is the "*infinite form*"[65] through which alone the ethical substance appears concrete. In this way, the objective organization of ethicality does not make the principle expressed in moral action outmoded — to the contrary, it conceptually presupposes it. But conversely, the objectivity of ethical-political institutions orients moral subjectivity's formal aim toward the actual conditions of its fulfillment.[66]

---

63. *RPh*, § 137 Anmerkung, *GW* 14.1, p. 119 (*Elements*, 164; see *Outlines*, 133).
64. *RPh*, § 140 Anmerkung, *GW* 14.1, p. 130 (*Elements*, 178; see *Outlines*, 146).
65. *RPh*, § 144, *GW* 14.1, p. 137 (*Elements*, 189; see *Outlines*, 154).
66. See Joachim Ritter's classic demonstration in Ritter, "Moralität und Sittlichkeit."

The moral point of view constitutes objectively effective subjectivity through actions that subjectivity recognizes as its own and the ends it prescribes to itself; this is what justifies its inclusion in objective spirit. It even belongs to it inevitably, at least in the modern world, which, thanks to Christianity, recognizes the value of the "right of *subjective freedom*."[67] Of course, taking the "right of objectivity" into account at the various strata of *Sittlichkeit* leads to relativizing this point of view or rather to preventing its illegitimate absolutization. But it still has its right, and in this sense, morality, like abstract law, is unsurpassable: all rational action presupposes the noncoerced adhesion of subjectivity to the norms of reason and the real human world. But if subjectivity restricts itself to the moral requirement alone, it does not reach fulfillment and remains exposed to the fantasies of subjectivism, which are illustrated by the romantic exaltation of the self. This is why moral subjectivity, "formal conscience," is only completed by going beyond itself and becoming ethical subjectivity, or "true conscience":

> True conscience is the disposition to will what is good *in and for itself*; it therefore has fixed principles. . . . But the objective system of these principles and duties and the union of subjective knowledge with this system are present only when the point of view of ethics has been reached.[68]

No doubt it is here that Hegel truly takes leave of Kant: the moral point of view, analyzed through the lens of action, includes a limitation and even an "all-around contradiction."[69] Action presupposes a discordance between what is (the world as it is) and what ought to be (the world as it should be, which is none other than the concept of what it actually is); it strives to reduce this discordance through a normatively oriented act. The paradox of this "syllogism of action"[70] (which has three terms: the *agent*, the *norm*, and the *world*) is that the agent aspires (this is his or her "will") to realize an end (making the world conform to the norm or concept) and at the same time supposes that this end (the good) has not been reached, otherwise this will, which constitutes the subject's entire being as a practical agent, would itself disappear: if the world

67. RPh, § 124 Anmerkung, GW 14.1, p. 110 (*Elements*, 151; see *Outlines*, 122).

68. RPh, § 137, GW 14.1, p. 119 (*Elements*, 165; see *Outlines*, 134).

69. Enzykl, § 511, GW 20, p. 493 (*Encyclopedia* 227).

70. WdL 3, GW 12, p. 233 (*Science of Logic*, 732).

were as it should be, there would be no more will to transform it. But the solution to this paradox, and along with it the *normative* structure of action, lies in the very actualization of willing. *Action* is the practical solution to this contradiction from which moral *conscience* cannot extricate itself. It thereby implies the *Aufhebung* of morality and the passage to ethicality. Let us examine how.

The moral point of view emerges from the relation between three elements that at first are incongruent, each demanding their "right": the subject, the norm of action (the good), and the world as it is, in which the action takes place:

> Reflected from its external existence *into itself*, determined as *subjective individuality* [*Einzelheit*] in opposition to the *universal*—the universal partly as something internal, the *good*, and partly as something external, an *existent world*, with these two aspects of the Idea *mediated* only *through each other*; the Idea in its division or *particular* concrete existence, *the right of the subjective will* in relation to the right of the world and the *right* of the Idea—which, however, *has being* only *in itself*.[71]

The contradictions of morality stem from the fact that action must simultaneously honor these three rights. The subject must suppose his or her end realized, that is, a world in conformity with the good, in order to work to achieve this end in a world that must not be all that it should be but that is all that it must be. Thus, a mediation must be established between the autonomous subject and the two universals facing it, the norm of the good and the real. Action, as Kant says, must tend toward achieving the harmony of nature and morality; but it can only want to realize it if it supposes that it has not been realized—otherwise the action would be useless—and even that it cannot be realized. For the same reason, the subject cannot will the union between his or her particular end and the ultimate end that is the good; in that case as well, action and, consequently, morality itself would become obsolete. In order to act, the subject (who *must* act to actualize his or her freedom so that this freedom is not a pure ought) must postulate both the validity of the universal norm that guides him or her (i.e., the actuality of the good as an ultimate end to accomplish) and the incomplete nature of this achievement, which would deprive the action of meaning. In other words, the subject must affirm that he or she

---

71. *RPh*, § 33, *GW* 14.1, p. 48 (*Elements*, 62; see *Outlines*, 50).

is free while at the same time subjecting itself both to the real and to the moral norm, both of which are independent of his or her volition and possibly incompatible with it.

In reality, the aporias of the syllogism of action are the same as those the *Logic* describes in its analysis of external finality. Unlike internal finality, external finality presupposes the reciprocal externality of ends and means. This externality implies the finite nature of the content of the end in such a way that its accomplishment only produces a means in view of another end, and so on: it "only goes so far as to be a means, not to be an objective purpose."[72] Because this finality is external, it is caught in bad infinity. The same is true of the practical syllogism. The moral subject's inadequate representation of the ultimate end of action (the good) condemns this end, despite its "internal universality," to the "fate of" finitude:[73] it must be realized so that action has a moral nature, but it must also not be realized, so that this ultimate end will preserve its absolute nature. Thus, the imbalance between the ultimate end of action and the always-particular content of the subjective will makes the former spectral and the latter contradictory, and action itself becomes useless and uncertain. It is thus not without reason that the long remark concluding the *Philosophy of Right*'s study of morality is dedicated to the various perversions of moral conscience: hypocrisy, probabilism, bad conscience, and so forth. Indeed, because of moral conscience's presupposition of a finite aim for the finite, it is tempted to give up on all action in order to escape the contradictions it would be exposed to.

But the analysis goes further. Just as in the case of external finality, Hegel shows that the contradictions of the moral point of view stem not from its principle but rather from the subject's representations of his or her actions and ends. In the analysis of external finality, the way out of contradiction consists of recognizing that though one only ever achieves the means and not an ultimate end, the activity is nonetheless meaningful. The error would be to believe that means are less worthy of attention than the ends they are meant to serve; but "the means is higher than the finite purposes of external purposiveness."[74] In the same way, unknown to the subject, "*actual concrete* action"[75] contains

---

72. *WdL* 3, *GW* 12, p. 169 (*Science of Logic*, 666).
73. *WdL* 3, *GW* 12, p. 232 (*Science of Logic*, 731).
74. *WdL* 3, *GW* 12, p. 166 (*Science of Logic*, 663).
75. *RPh*, § 140, *GW* 14.1, p. 122 (*Elements*, 170; see *Outlines*, 138).

the speculative resolution to the contradictions to which his or her point of view leads. What makes the moral aim inactualizable is the fallacious representation of the absolute nature of its realization, a representation that makes this realization impossible: the good is always beyond individuals' plans, which thus have no value or importance. As he shows with regard to teleology, Hegel demonstrates that this representation is the true obstacle: for in order to try to realize the ultimate end — which is always the final goal of moral action — one must presuppose that this end is constantly realized through the actions of subjects. In short, one must renounce the prejudice of a radical dissonance between the existing world and the norm, between what is and what ought to be. By recognizing the actual world as the site of the realization of the good, never achieved but always already undertaken, the subject gives full value to his or her action but thereby gives up thinking of this action as an absolute origin, a pure self-determination, free of any presupposition. The truth of morality thus lies not in its "surpassing" — for, as the subject's point of view on his or her action, it is unsurpassable — but in the recognition it presupposes of a web of objective relations on which action must be based: "the objective world is thus in and for itself the idea precisely as it [the idea] at the same time eternally posits itself as purpose and through activity produces its actuality."[76] It would be wrong to see in this reminder of the "right of the world" a conservative or resigned reaction to the moral requirement of action expressed in the philosophies of Kant and Fichte. Hegel takes over this requirement, registered in the principle of rational autonomy, but he thinks that it can only be made right on the condition of renouncing the *formalist* representations that doom the moral project to fail. Morality always already supposes the world of ethicality, the objectivized figure of human action, and it must be based on the obviously partial accomplishments that this action has already given to its project.

From Morality to Ethicality

For Hegel, Kantianism is the completed form of a practical philosophy that limits itself to the "merely moral point of view without making the transition to the concept of ethicality."[77] Thus, the doctrine of *Sittlichkeit* appears as a response to the internal limitations of such a point of view. This shift has con-

76. *Enzykl*, § 235, *GW* 20, p. 228.
77. *RPh*, § 135 Anmerkung, *GW* 14.1, p. 118 (*Elements*, 162; see *Outlines*, 130–31).

sequences for the structure of morality itself. A long-dominant interpretation of the Hegelian doctrine of ethicality saw it as a pure and simple rejection of the moral point of view, making Hegel a precursor of *Machtstaat* theoreticians, a *Realpolitiker* who rejected all moral requirements in the name of state power—that is, in the name of factual violence. This is basically Heller's reading as well as Meinecke's in his book on the doctrine of the *Raison d'état*.[78] Otto Pöggeler has done justice to these imputations by highlighting the fact that they reflect the dominant concerns of a recently defeated Germany in 1918.[79] But some texts do seem to support such a view; for example, the Remark to section 337 in the *Philosophy of Right*. Hegel responds to Kant's claim that "true politics can therefore not take a step without having already paid homage to morals"[80] by saying that

> the immediate existence [*Dasein*] of the state as the ethical substance, i.e. its right, is directly embodied not in abstract but in concrete existence [*Existenz*], and only this concrete existence, rather than any of those many universal thoughts which are held to be moral commandments, can be the principle of its action and behavior.[81]

In similar fashion, Hegel refuses to subordinate politics to an abstract representation of justice as implied in the adage *fiat justitia, pereat mundus*, which Kant praises while also conceding that it is "rather boastful."[82] But Hegel doesn't reject moral norms; he just contests that they can offer a satisfactory principle for politics. Government is not a matter of "universal providence" but rather of "*particular wisdom*,"[83] for it always strives for the good of a certain community. Thus politics cannot claim the universal-abstract norms of morality without

78. See Hermann Heller, *Hegel und der nationale Machtstaatsgedanke in Deutschland* (Leipzig: Teubner, 1921); Friedrich Meinecke, *Machiavellism: The Doctrine of the Raison d'État and Its Place in Modern History* (New Haven, CT: Yale University Press 1957).

79. Otto Pöggeler, "Hegel et Machiavel: Renaissance italienne et idéalism allemand," *Archives de Philosophie* 41, no. 3 (1978): 435–67.

80. Kant, *Frieden*, Ak. 8, p. 380; *PP*, p. 347.

81. *RPh*, § 337 Anmerkung, *GW* 14.1, p. 272 (*Elements*, 370; see *Outlines*, 314). For Kant, this subordination of politics to morality is in reality a subordination to the law, to "morals . . . as doctrine of law" (*Frieden*, Ak. 8, p. 386; *PP*, p. 351).

82. Kant, *Frieden*, Ak. 8, p. 378; *PP*, p. 345. Cf. Hegel, *RPh*, § 130, *GW* 14.1, p. 114 (*Elements*, 157–58; see *Outlines*, 126–27).

83. *RPh*, § 337, *GW* 14.1, p. 271 (*Elements*, 370; see *Outlines*, 314).

hypocrisy. Politics thus has an *ethical* status, which does not mean that it cynically ignores all morality. Furthermore, the moral point of view—that is, the requirement of a normative autonomy of subjective reason—would suffer as much as politics (which is a sort of empirical ethical technique) from the confusion expressed in the moralizing politician's point of view (which is Machiavellian in the banal sense of the word). It is thus *moralism*, the perversion of political ethics, that Hegel rejects, and not morality as a form of objectivizing the normative expectations of subjectivity; it is moralism, not morality, that is based on "superficial notions [*Vorstellungen*] of morality, the nature of the state, and the state's relation to the moral point of view."[84]

The distinction between morality and ethicality thus implies a relativization or circumscription of the moral point of view, but certainly not its rejection. Otherwise, there would be no explanation for why the doctrine of objective spirit includes a theory of moral subjectivity or why the latter is the mediation between the abstract objectivity of law and the concrete objectivity of ethicality. The "moral view of the world" specifically contributes to the objectivization of spirit. In becoming objective, spirit loses its limited and futile subjectivity and adopts "the shape of a world."[85] But morality is the moment of the reflection of rational will in itself that makes possible the ethical, and essentially political, *actualization* of the formal and abstract objectivity of the system of legal norms.

Two points of view must, however, be distinguished. *Historically*, ethicality—that is, freedom made objective in institutional configurations—is the condition of morality. The exercise of the "right of *subjective freedom*" that is the "pivotal and focal point in the difference between *antiquity* and the *modern* age"[86] presupposes an appropriate political and social organization, since morality cannot be achieved in an ethical state of nature, to use Kant's words in a different sense than the one he gives them. If Christianity put forth the principle of moral autonomy, only the appearance of a "new form of the world" allowed it to become a "universal and actual principle."[87] It is thus thanks to the modern state that morality ceases to be an abstract demand for subjectivity, for the state has enough strength to "allow the principle of sub-

84. *RPh*, § 337 Anmerkung, *GW* 14.1, p. 272 (*Elements*, 370; see *Outlines*, 314).
85. *PhG*, *GW* 9, p. 240 (*Phenomenology*, ¶ 441).
86. *RPh*, § 124 Anmerkung, *GW* 14.1, p. 110 (*Elements*, 151; see *Outlines*, 122).
87. Ibid.

jectivity to attain fulfillment in the *self-sufficient extreme* of personal particularity, while at the same time *bringing it back to substantial unity*."[88] Logically, on the other hand, morality is the presupposition of ethicality, for the reflection into subjectivity of objective spirit is the mediation through which what might be alienating within this objectivity is overcome. Subjectivity gives life to the formal structures of objective spirit and thus makes possible its own ethical realization. Certainly ethicality is the *Aufhebung* of morality, but this dialectical succession means conservation and verification as much as surpassing and negation. *Sittlichkeit* accomplishes the subjective moral claim by liberating it from its own abstraction, but in this way it conserves it as its conceptual presupposition. In other words, the Hegelian doctrine of ethicality is not a rejection of the problematic of the practical autonomy of reason but rather its completion and extension. For Hegel, as for Kant, the objectivity and rationality of ethical-political configurations are connected to the possibility that individual subjectivity has of producing the norms of its actions or of consenting to them; they presuppose this possibility to the very extent that they condition its actualization.

There is a remarkable terminological indication of this complex relation between ethicality and morality: the distinction between two modes of moral conscience that Hegel draws at the end of the analysis of morality. *Formal moral conscience*, closed in on itself, suffers from a mismatch between the subjective principle of its autonomy and the objective nature of the norm it recognizes, the good—whence the characteristic form of its relation to this norm, the *Sollen*. Unable to overcome the gap between certainty and truth that affects all the figures of conscience and finite spirit, it is tempted to go beyond the rational formalism defined by Kant and take refuge in a subjectivism of intention or moral sentiment. Thus, in the *Phenomenology of Spirit*, the dialectic of the good and subjective moral conscience culminates in the "beautiful soul" deciding to give the full weight of truth to its certainty because it lacks "the force to empty itself, that is, lacks the force to make itself into a thing and to suffer the burden of being."[89] This is the high point of the subjectivism that in Hegel's eyes is one of the *possible* endpoints of Kantian moral philosophy. To the contrary, what Hegel calls *true* moral conscience is "the disposition to will

---

88. *RPh*, § 260, *GW* 14.1, p. 208 (*Elements*, 282; see *Outlines*, 235).
89. *PhG*, *GW* 9, p. 354 (*Phenomenology*, ¶ 658).

what is good *in and for itself.*"⁹⁰ In other words, moral subjectivity can only sat‑
isfy its own requirement by becoming part of a network of objective political
and social institutions. If subjectivity does not take into account this ethical-
political objectivity, it becomes virtually empty and risks leaving the ground of
true morality and succumbing to the dangerous charms of moralism.

But *Sittlichkeit* cannot be reduced to objective institutions and regulations,
to the structures that organize it. It integrates the subjectivity it relativizes at
the same time that it guarantees the actualization of its aim, its right: "the *ethi‑
cal* is a subjective disposition, but of that law which has being in itself."⁹¹ *Sitt‑
lichkeit* is ethical *life* because it is both subjective and objective.⁹² The active
presence of subjectivity within ethicality is manifested in what Hegel calls the
sittliche Gesinnung (the "ethical disposition"⁹³), or more classically virtue,
which here has ethical-political meaning and not merely the moral sense it
has in Aristotle: "virtues as the ethical in its particular application."⁹⁴ This
actualization of the subjective principle within an objective framework is the
true accomplishment of moral conscience, "true conscience." This means that
it is only in the institutional context of ethicality that subjectivity can fully
enjoy its normative role:

> Subjectivity, which is the ground in which the concept of freedom has its
> concrete existence [*Existenz*], and which, at the level or morality, is still dis‑
> tinct from this its own concept, is, in the ethical realm, that [mode of] exis‑
> tence of the concept which is adequate to it.⁹⁵

This disposition of ethical spirit (or true moral conscience) is illustrated
in two striking ways. The first is framed by civil society. The second, the politi‑
cal disposition, is the topic of the next chapter. Discussing civil society, Hegel
states that

> *Morality* has its proper place in this sphere, where reflection on one's own
> actions and the ends of welfare and of particular needs are dominant, and

90. *RPh*, § 137, *GW* 14.1, p. 119 (*Elements*, 164; see *Outlines*, 132).
91. *RPh*, § 141 Anmerkung, *GW* 14.1, p. 135 (*Elements*, 186; see *Outlines*, 152).
92. See chapter 12 below.
93. See *RPh*, § 207, *GW* 14.1, p. 173 (*Elements*, 238; see *Outlines*, 196).
94. *RPh*, § 150 Anmerkung, *GW* 14.1, p. 140 (*Elements*, 194; see *Outlines*, 158).
95. *RPh*, § 152 Anmerkung, *GW* 14.1, p. 142 (*Elements*, 196 see *Outlines*, 160).

where contingency in the satisfaction of the latter makes even contingent and individual help into a duty.[96]

At first glance the statement is surprising: isn't civil society the "field of conflict in which the private interests of each individual come up against those of everyone else"?[97] But we know that this society is not exactly the same as the spontaneous order of the market; it also includes an *ethical* dimension. Consequently, its organization must prevent, or at least limit, the effects of pure market socialization. This is not merely a vague duty to help the poor in order to compensate for the harshness of the system of needs. In reality, the truly social form of the ethical disposition (and consequently of morality) lies in what Hegel calls "the *honour of one's estate*," "rectitude" or "the spirit of the corporation."[98] This is one of the aspects of his institutionalism: Hegel gives institutions with more or less archaic names (like "corporation") a structuring role in the operation of modern civil society precisely because he thinks it is vital to counteract the disastrous effects that the competition between actors, entirely focused on and driven by the quest for their own personal well-being, can have on the social body. The corporation, the institutionalized form of a social estate (*Stand*), thus has a role as an ethical regulator. Thanks to it, virtue, initially indeterminate as to its content, receives concrete content: to enjoy the rights and fulfill the obligations that go along with the socioprofessional status guaranteed to each individual. Thus, after the family, the corporation is the "second *ethical* root of the state":[99] ethical and not only social and economic, for the practices it puts into place and the dispositions it cultivates among its members are the verified echo of the claim of freedom pronounced by subjective conscience in a partially inadequate moral language. Thus, subjectivity in its various forms remains the "moment of the *actuality* of the ethical."[100]

96. *RPh*, § 207, *GW* 14.1, p. 174 (*Elements*, 238–39; see *Outlines*, 197).

97. *RPh*, § 289 Anmerkung, *GW* 14.1, p. 241 (*Elements*, 330; see *Outlines*, 278).

98. *RPh*, § 150 and Anmerkung, 207, 252, 253 A. and 289 Anmerkung, *GW* 14.1, pp. 140, 173, 197, 198 (*Elements*, 193–94, 238, 271, 272; see *Outlines*, 157–58, 196, 224, 226, 278–79).

99. *RPh*, § 255, *GW* 14.1, p. 199 (*Elements*, 272; see *Outlines*, 226).

100. *RPh*, § 141 Anmerkung, *GW* 14.1, p. 135 (*Elements*, 185; see *Outlines*, 152).

11

The Conditions of Political Subjectivity

The concept of political disposition (*politische Gesinnung*) is described in sections 267 and 268 of the *Philosophy of Right*. But the question of the subjective forms of political being, which Hegel first discusses at the beginning of the section on the "state" through the themes of "piety" ("feeling [*Empfindung*] and ethicality governed by feeling") and "political virtue" ("the willing of that thought end which has being in and for itself")[1] is in reality the center of gravity of the text introducing the theory of the rational state, which deals with the relations between the state and the individual and with what may be called the subjective dimension of the political. The concept of political disposition refers to the fact that subjective consciousness recognizes in the institution of the state the objectivized form, and thus the condition, of its own freedom; the expression designates the spontaneously trusting attitude of a self-consciousness that knows that in the political universal it has "its essence, its end, and the product of its activity"[2] and is therefore favorably disposed toward it. Of course, civil society already offers the individual the opportunity to go beyond his or her egotistical interest — ultimately, to go beyond finitude. Undoubtedly socialization has a universalizing effect, which

---

1. *RPh*, § 257 Anmerkung, *GW* 14.1, p. 201 (*Elements*, 275; see *Outlines*, 228).
2. *RPh*, § 257, *GW* 14.1, p. 201 (*Elements*, 275; see *Outlines*, 228).

is due to the modern mode of production and exchange: the presence of kernels of universality within civil society (economic and monetary regulations enabling the creation of a market, the actions of corrective justice, the work of social institutions) allow it to be self-administrated in large part and makes it possible for individuals to consider themselves links in a chain they depend on for their material and cultural existence and that they must therefore will in order to will themselves. But only the state, turning the necessity that social life implements externally and mechanically into "the *shape* of freedom"[3] can create and maintain the individual's adherence to the ethical conditions of his or her being. Thus, on the very ground of subjective dispositions, the citizen is the truth of the bourgeois.

Political Subjectivity

The objective institutions of the state represent just one of its aspects. If the state is the developed, differentiated, and concrete expression of freedom, and thus the substance of free subjectivity that wills and affirms itself as such, it must be considered both "*subjective* substantiality," that is, "political disposition," and "*objective* substantiality," that is, the constitutional organization of powers within the "*organism* of the state."[4] These two dimensions, which mediate each other, are speculatively connected and have equal weight. "The state is the actuality of the ethical Idea,"[5] and we know that an idea, in the Hegelian sense, is the unity of the subjective concept and objectivity, or rather the process of harmonization that produces them, sets them against one another, connects them, and unifies them. A set of merely objective and material determinations, such as institutions in the common sense of the word, cannot therefore be an idea. The state is only an idea, an "ideality" of "necessity" embodied by social institutions,[6] if its structures are animated and confirmed by the will of individuals. This is the condition on which the state can ensure "*union* as such" and allow individuals to "lead a universal life." [7] This volition

---

3. *RPh*, § 266, *GW* 14.1, p. 211 (*Elements*, 288; see *Outlines*, 240).

4. *RPh*, § 267, *GW* 14.1, p. 211 (*Elements*, 288; see *Outlines*, 240).

5. *RPh*, § 257, *GW* 14.1, p. 201 (*Elements*, 275; see *Outlines*, 228).

6. *RPh*, § 267, *GW* 14.1, p. 211 (*Elements*, 288; see *Outlines*, 240). On social institutions as "the *constitution* . . . in the realm of *particularity*," see *RPh*, § 265, *GW* 14.1, 211 (*Elements*, 287; see *Outlines*, 239).

7. *RPh*, § 258 Anmerkung, *GW* 14.1, p. 201 (*Elements*, 276; see *Outlines*, 229).

for the universal as such is precisely what distinguishes the citizen's attitude from that of the social actor, the bourgeois, for whom the entirely abstract and external universality of economic regulations and civil laws is only ever a tool for private happiness. A state that depends solely on the coherence and strength of its material institutions necessarily becomes despotic: this was the fate of the monarchies of the ancien régime. Conversely, a state that bases itself on subjective virtue alone will be neither stable nor free. This, in Hegel's eyes, is the fatal flaw of democratic constitutions, which "[do] indeed depend on the *disposition* [of the citizens]": the virtue of the "people" and its leaders cannot replace "the *legally determined* activity of an *articulated* organization."[8] The Terror, a consequence of a politics of virtue, emphatically proves the logical and historical necessity of the constitutional (that is, institutional) objectivization of the state, as well as of the autonomous development of subjective particularity within a civil society that is itself "constituted." In the postrevolutionary world, the particular social being of the bourgeois guarantees the mediation between the objective constitution of the state and the subjective dispositions of the citizenry. But we must explain the content of the latter and specify the conditions for their emergence and enduring actuality.

The political disposition is defined as "certainty based on *truth*."[9] The general relationship of individuals to ethical objectivity in their "*subjective determination to freedom*"[10] is presented using the same vocabulary, borrowed from the *Phenomenology of Spirit*. Hegel's use of the concepts of certainty and truth shows that the political disposition is not a mere subjective opinion based on such or such a representation of what the state should be but is rather membership in and adherence to the universal: it expresses the fact that the state "ceases to be an other for me" and "in my consciousness of this, I am free."[11] Thus, the political disposition is not of the order of knowledge or even of the discernment of the understanding (*Einsicht*). In truth, it is only insofar as it is a lasting and stable aptitude (*hexis*) to act in conformity with the objective conditions of freedom that the political *ethos*, unknown to the individuals who act as its vehicles, includes a rationality that confirms and validates its properly ethical content, its "virtue."

---

8. *RPh*, § 273 Anmerkung, *GW* 14.1, p. 228 (*Elements*, 310; see *Outlines*, 261).
9. *RPh*, § 268, *GW* 14.1, p. 211 (*Elements*, 288; see *Outlines*, 240).
10. *RPh*, § 153, *GW* 14.1, p. 142 (*Elements*, 196; see *Outlines*, 160).
11. *RPh*, § 268, *GW* 14.1, pp. 211–12 (*Elements*, 288; see *Outlines*, 240).

Second, Hegel presents the political disposition as "volition which has be-come habitual."[12] This points to its kinship with mores or ethical customs (*Sitten*), which are the true cultural bases of political institutions. Ethical customs are described in strong terms:

> But if it is simply *identical* with the actuality of individuals, the ethical [*das Sittliche*], as their general mode of behavior, appears as *custom* [*Sitte*]; and the *habit* of the ethical appears as a *second nature* which takes the place of the original and purely natural will and is the all-pervading soul, significance, and actuality of individual existence [*Dasein*]. It is *spirit* living and present as a world, and only thus does the substance of spirit begin to exist as spirit.[13]

It is from this fertile ground that the will to live and to live together, *cocitizen-ship*, begins to grow: *mores*, the manifestation of an unreasoned but in no way irrational faith that the state presupposes and constantly recreates, are both the basis of institutions and the manifestation of their ethical rationality. Thus, they constantly recreate the living bond between the community and the indi-vidual, a bond that Hegel designates by the term *Sittlichkeit*. The political dis-position is thus a type of ethical virtue (*Tugend*) — defined as the reflection of ethicality into individual personality[14] — or of rectitude (*Rechtschaffenheit*). This ethical virtue means that although human beings are "naturally" attached to their own egotistical interests, they see observance of the rules of the social groups to which they belong and the fulfillment of the duties prescribed by the objective system of institutions not as obstacles or limitations but rather as the conditions of their own "substantial freedom" in which they "liberate [them-selves]" by conforming.[15] Ethical virtue, which produces social and politi-cal action in conformity with its reasons, is the lasting consciousness of reci-procity between subjective rights (which are made actual by being inscribed within a context of objectivity) and duties (which "are not something *alien* to the subject"[16] when they spell out what is "substantial" in subjective free-dom.) Thus, ethical virtue implies that the particular will, which is itself edu-

---

12. *RPh*, § 268, *GW* 14.1, pp. 211–12 (*Elements*, 288; see *Outlines*, 240).
13. *RPh*, § 151, *GW* 14.1, p. 141 (*Elements*, 195; see *Outlines*, 159).
14. See *RPh*, § 150, *GW* 14.1, p. 140 (*Elements*, 193; see *Outlines*, 157).
15. *RPh*, § 149, *GW* 14.1, pp. 139–40 (*Elements*, 192; see *Outlines*, 157).
16. *RPh*, § 147, *GW* 14.1, p. 138 (*Elements*, 191; see *Outlines*, 155).

cated and shaped by mores and customs, consciously sacrifices its primitive naturalness to its potential rationality, its abstractness to the objective conditions of its concrete actualization. The ethical is *"spirit* living and present as a world."[17] Its reality is thus inseparably *subjective* and *objective*: "the *ethical* is a subjective disposition, but of that law which has being in itself."[18]

The attunement of the subjective and objective components of the ethical (but not their immediate fusion, which would necessarily suppress subjective freedom, as in the example of the democratic *polis*) is a process that gives rational consistency to both the ethical and the state. When Hegel says that the ethical is the *living* good, this is not an observation but rather the indication of a task incumbent on modernity: to achieve freedom, including the freedom of subjective individuality in its potential egocentrism, on the terrain of historical-political objectivity. From this point of view, creating a new political *ethos*, a spirit of citizenship that, in spite of everything, was exemplified by the French revolutionaries' patriotism without nationalism, is as important as establishing the institutions of freedom, for the two correspond to one another.

Nonetheless it may seem surprising—especially if we do not bear in mind the Greek *and* French context of the argument—that Hegel simply identifies the political disposition with *"patriotism."*[19] It is obvious that Hegel means to reject the common representation of patriotism as a disposition to heroic sacrifice while at the same time claiming a notion inherited from the political legacy of the French Revolution, one that we know the Restoration loathed.[20] For Hegel, authentic patriotism is not revealed on the battlefield but rather "in the normal conditions and circumstances of life,"[21] and he understands it as a modest disposition toward cocitizenship, a peaceful civic-mindedness that strengthens the system of political institutions and supplies it with appropriate representations. Three observations should be made with regard to this argument.

First, this civic conception of patriotism relativizes Hegel's well-known and never-renounced opinions in the article on natural law concerning the

---

17. *RPh*, § 151, *GW* 14.1, p. 141 (*Elements*, 195; see *Outlines*, 159).

18. *RPh*, § 141 Anmerkung, *GW* 14.1, p. 135 (*Elements*, 186, modified; see *Outlines*, 152).

19. *RPh*, § 268, *GW* 14.1, p. 211 (*Elements*, 288; see *Outlines*, 240).

20. In response to the demand for German national unity, supported at the time by the left and some liberals, Metternich quipped, "Germany? It is merely a geographic notion!"

21. *RPh*, § 268 Anmerkung, *GW* 14.1, p. 212 (*Elements*, 289; see *Outlines*, 241).

ethical value of war, which "preserves the ethical health of peoples. . . . Just as the blowing of the winds preserves the sea from the foulness which would result from a continual calm, so also corruption would result for peoples under continual or indeed 'perpetual' peace."[22] The everyday patriotism valorized by the *Philosophy of Right* gives this initially bellicose proposition a clearly circumscribed scope. The "willingness to perform *extraordinary* sacrifices and actions" is only the superficial layer of "the genuine [political] disposition";[23] without the latter, the former would not exist for long. Furthermore, valor (*Tapferkeit*), the disposition required by war, is quite particular: though it is a virtue, it is a "*formal* virtue," the exercise of which (the sacrifice of life in combat) is not "in itself of a spiritual nature";[24] it cannot by itself provide a motive to act. Military valor has no meaning in itself; it only has value in the service of the supreme political end, the preservation of the state and its sovereignty. Thus, this virtue falls to a particular social group of professional soldiers and cannot be confused with the political virtue that the state expects of its members and works to instill in them. War exists, like power, and it demands valor. But this is neither what is essential nor most difficult: "human beings often prefer to be guided by magnanimity instead of by the law."[25] Hegel's conviction is that a state cannot be sustainably built on enthusiasm and the spirit of sacrifice, at least in the context of modernity. Moreover, even if he rejects the pacifism and cosmopolitanism of the Enlightenment, he rejects all nationalism, as is clear from his strictly political definition of a people. In contradiction to the usage that has since become dominant, Hegel thinks of the nation as a prepolitical and thus prehistoric reality. On the other hand, he completely identifies people and state:

> In the concrete existence of a people, the substantial aim is to be a state and to stay as such; a people without the form of a state (a nation as such) has no

22. *Naturrecht, W* 2, p. 482 (*Natural Law*, 93). Hegel cites this passage in the *Philosophy of Right* to support his argument that war is "the moment in which the ideality of *the particular attains its right and becomes actuality*"; see *RPh*, § 324 Anmerkung, *GW* 14.1, p. 266 (*Elements*, 361; see *Outlines*, 306–7).

23. *RPh*, § 268 Anmerkung, *GW* 14.1, p. 212 (*Elements*, 289; see *Outlines*, 241).

24. *RPh*, § 327, *GW* 14.1, p. 267 (*Elements*, 364; see *Outlines*, 309). The *System of Ethicality* defined courage as "indifference to the virtues" and concluded that "it is only a formal in-itself virtue" (*SS, GW* 5, p. 329).

25. *RPh*, § 268 Anmerkung, *GW* 14.1, p. 212 (*Elements*, 289, modified; see *Outlines*, 24).

proper history; people have existence before adopting the state form, and still others exist now as savage nations.[26]

We should note in passing that this represents a refusal to define the political on the basis of a limit situation such as war, confirming that although Hegel gives an eminent place to the moment of political decision—the necessity of which ultimately justifies the power of the prince, that "absolutely decisive moment of the whole"[27]—his rational politics fundamentally lacks any decisionist orientation.

Second, in the lectures on the philosophy of history, the "terrorist" inflection of the French Revolution is chalked up primarily to the Robespierrist exaltation of political virtue regardless of the external and internal threats to the young Republic:

> Virtue has now to rule against the many who are unfaithful to it because of their depravity, their old interests, or [merely] the excesses of freedom and passions. Virtue is here a simple principle and distinguishes only between those who have a good disposition (*Gesinnung*) and those who don't. The disposition can only be known and judged by a disposition. Suspicion therefore reigns, and virtue, when it becomes suspect is already condemned. . . . From Robespierre the principle of virtue was established as the highest, and one can say, that this man was serious about virtue. Now, virtue and terror prevail, because the subjective virtue that governs merely by disposition brings with it the most terrible tyranny. It exercises its power without legal forms, and its punishments are just as simple: death.[28]

This analysis does not call into question political disposition or political virtue ("the spirit of the whole") as such. But it reminds us that political subjectivity is but *one* component of the simultaneously subjective and objective totality of the ethical. If political virtue is separated from its indispensable comple-

26. *Enzykl*, § 549 Anmerkung, *GW* 20, p. 526. See also *RPh*, §§ 331, 349, *GW* 14.1, pp. 269, 276 (*Elements*, 366–67, 375; see *Outlines*, 311, 318); Hegel, *Die Vernunft in der Geschichte*, 180. The second *Philosophy of Spirit* says of the Germans that "they disappeared as a *people*, they were only a *nation*" (*GW* 8, p. 259).

27. *RPh*, § 279, *GW* 14.1, p. 232 (*Elements*, 317; see *Outlines*, 267).

28. *Geschichte*, *W* 12, pp. 532–33.

ment, free political and social institutions (let us say the institutions of a republic in the Kantian sense), it can become criminal, as the *Phenomenology of Spirit* shows through the figure of "Absolute Freedom and Terror"[29] and its continuations, "The Moral View of the World" and "The Beautiful Soul." The lesson to be taken from these texts and from the analysis of the French Revolution in the lectures on the philosophy of history is that virtuous political subjectivity does not contain its measure within itself but rather must be organized under a stable constitutional order that in return it enriches. "There is nothing more sacred or higher than the disposition [vis-à-vis] the state," on the condition, however, that it is properly understood as "the disposition according to which the laws and the constitution in general is what is stable, and that it is the supreme obligation of individuals to thereby subordinate their particular will."[30] Thus, what Hegel rejects is the patriotic voluntarism of the sansculottes and the Robespierrist cult of intransigent virtue along with the violence it implies against subjects by subjectivity and not the principle of political subjectivity itself, which is the very modern right to be not only a subject (in the sense of the German *Untertan*, the subject who obeys the sovereign) but also and above all a citizen.

Third, the theory of *politische Gesinnung* in a sense constitutes the Aristotelian moment of a thought that elsewhere calls into question the Greek political ideal (the "beautiful totality") in the name of the values of modernity. Just like Aristotle, Hegel refuses to dissociate even momentarily ethics from politics: ethical virtues (and even properly moral virtues) are to be exercised within the life of the city-state; they are "the ethical in its particular application."[31] It thus becomes clear that Hegel appreciates the Aristotelian definition of virtue: "Aristotle . . . judiciously defined each particular virtue as a mean between an *excess* and a *deficiency*."[32] Both thinkers connect virtue to a continuous process. According to the Stagirite, virtue, a habitual state (*hexis*),[33] is the fruit of habit (*ethos*); in the same way, for Hegel, virtue con-

---

29. *PhG, GW* 9, p. 316ff (*Phenomenology*, ¶¶ 582, 599).

30. *Geschichte, W* 12, p. 531.

31. *RPh*, § 150 Anmerkung, *GW* 14.1, p. 140 (*Elements*, 194; see *Outlines*, 158).

32. *RPh*, § 150 Anmerkung, *GW* 14.1, p. 141 (*Elements*, 194; see *Outlines*, 158). See Aristotle, *Nichomachean Ethics*, 1106.b.36 ff.

33. Aristotle, *Nichomachean Ethics*, 1106.a.11. On virtue, *hexis*, and *ethos*, see *Eudemian Ethics*, 1220.b.9–20 and 1222.b.5–14.

sists in observing the mores and laws of one's people because in them the universal substance "speaks its *universal language*."[34] Does this language that political subjects speak and bring to life in actualizing their ethical dispositions perhaps realize, on concrete political ground, the project for a "mythology of reason" that the young Hegel, the young Schelling, and the young Hölderlin thought would reconcile a people and its thinkers?[35]

However, we must be aware of a major difference between Aristotle's and Hegel's arguments regarding political virtue; this difference makes clear the separation between modern ethics and the ethics of the *polis*. For Aristotle, virtue (ethical or political) does not at all presuppose anything like subjectivity understood as an interiority that voluntarily rules behaviors; virtue is acquired not by working on oneself or practicing a technique of the self but rather by observing virtuous action and imitating the "prudent" or wise man.[36] To the contrary, modern *Sittlichkeit*, as Hegel conceives it, essentially brings subjectivity into play even if ethical subjectivity, by virtue of its being subordinated to the objective universality of laws and mores, is absolutely distinct from the "empty principle of moral subjectivity."[37] It is not "that indeterminate subjectivity which does not attain . . . the objective determinacy of action,"[38] but it is indeed a subjectivity, one that constitutes itself in action:

> Subjectivity is the absolute form and existent actuality of substance, and the difference between the subject on the one hand and substance as its object [*Gegenstand*], end, and power on the other is the same as their difference in form, both of which differences have disappeared with equal immediacy.[39]

Objective spirit *passes through* subjectivity: we are far from the Greek *polis*, which the young Hegel praised for being based on the elision of individuality

34. *PhG, GW* 9, p. 195 (*Phenomenology*, ¶ 351). See *RPh,* § 153 Anmerkung, *GW* 14.1, p. 142 (*Elements*, 196; see *Outlines*, 160).

35. "We need a new mythology, but this mythology must be in the service of the idea, it must become a mythology of *reason*" (*Systemfragment, W* 1, p. 236).

36. Aristotle, *Nichomachean Ethics*, 1106.b.36–1107.a.1. On the notion of "techniques of the self," see Michel Foucault, *The History of Sexuality*, vol. 2, *The Use of Pleasure*, trans. Robert Hurley (New York: Vintage Books, 2012).

37. *RPh,* § 148 Anmerkung, *GW* 14.1, p. 139 (*Elements*, 191; see *Outlines*, 156).

38. *RPh,* § 149, *GW* 14.1, p. 140 (*Elements*, 192; see *Outlines*, 157).

39. *RPh,* § 152, *GW* 14.1, p. 142 (*Elements*, 196; see *Outlines*, 160).

and the ignorance of interiority. Decidedly, the "superior principle of modern times" is not forgotten even and especially when subjective interiority is literally put back in its place.

"Patriotism" and Social Culture

How is the political *hexis* acquired? Where does the political disposition come from, and how is it instilled in individuals when everything, in particular their bourgeois social being, encourages them to turn away from the universal? True, their attitudes are shaped by mores and the *Volksgeist*, but this fact is too general to account for individuals' trust in and support of the state institution and its mode of operation. First of all, the "[*political*] disposition takes its particularly determined *content* from the various aspects of the organism of the state."[40] Since this organization of powers is inseparable from the mode of governance—in Kantian terms, its "despotic" or "republican" nature[41]—we may conclude that democracy, aristocracy, and monarchy require specific dispositions and virtues on the parts of rulers and ruled alike—an idea that Hegel acknowledges comes from Montesquieu. He writes, for example,

> Nevertheless, in this as in so many other instances, we must acknowledge Montesquieu's depth of insight in his famous account of the principles of these forms of government. . . . It is common knowledge that he specified *virtue* as the principle of *democracy*; and such a constitution does indeed depend on the *disposition* [of the citizens] as the purely substantial form in which the rationality of the will which has being in and for itself still exists under this constitution. . . . [But] we must avoid the misunderstanding of imagining that, since the disposition of virtue is the substantial form in a democratic republic, this disposition thereby becomes superfluous, or may even be totally absent, in a monarchy; and still less should we imagine that virtue and the *legally determined* activity of an *articulated* organization are mutually opposed and incompatible.[42]

40. *RPh*, § 269, *GW* 14.1, p. 212 (*Elements*, 290; see *Outlines*, 241).

41. Kant, *Frieden*, *Ak*. 8, p. 352; *PP*, p. 324. On Kant's definition of the republican constitution and Hegel's modification of it, see chapter 5 above.

42. *RPh*, § 273 Anmerkung, *GW* 14.1, pp. 227–28 (*Elements*, 310–11; see *Outlines*, 261). See Montesquieu, *Spirit of the Laws*, 3:3, 23.

Thus, there are subjective dispositions and virtues appropriate to the various types of regimes even if democracy (understood in the classical sense) most obviously supposes and mobilizes the political virtue of its citizens, who are immediately *actors* in the life of the state. But any regime, and in particular the "constitution of developed reason," constitutional monarchy, requires a certain mode of *politische Gesinnung*. This clarifies the claim that since a constitution is not created artificially, each people has the constitution appropriate to it.[43] That expression does not seek to legitimize every established order but rather indicates that a political regime is only *established*, and thus durable, if it bases itself on individuals' subjective dispositions and is able to kindle them by conforming to "the general spirit of the nation."

But this still does not explain where the political disposition comes from, for the state, no matter its regime, presupposes it more than creates it. We must therefore look elsewhere, in a direction very significant for the general economy of *Sittlichkeit*: the political disposition is "a consequence of the institutions within the state, a consequence in which rationality is *actually* present, just as rationality receives its practical application through action in conformity with the state's institutions."[44] We could take this to mean that political institutions, by performing a kind of practical pedagogy, create and maintain within individuals the attitudes suited to their own operation. But in addition to the fact that this functionalist interpretation is unsatisfying, it is not compatible with the letter of the text, for here, at the beginning of the section on the state, it is not yet a matter of the political institutions that form the "internal constitution for itself"[45] of the state. On the contrary, in the immediately preceding paragraphs,[46] the term *Institution* refers to prepolitical forms of ethical organization, the family and civil society, which are the "ethical root[s]"[47] of the state, although the state is at the same time their "true ground."[48] Thus, it is self-organized familial and social communities that can inspire the political disposition in individuals, and we have seen that without this virtue, the state is condemned to die or to misunderstand the rational free-

---

43. *RPh*, § 274 Anmerkung, *GW* 14.1, p. 229 (*Elements*, 312; see *Outlines*, 263): "Each nation . . . has the constitution appropriate and proper to it."

44. *RPh*, § 268, *GW* 14.1, p. 211 (*Elements*, 288; see *Outlines*, 240).

45. Title of subsection I: *RPh*, *GW* 14.1, p. 208 (*Elements*, 305; see *Outlines*, 256).

46. See *RPh*, §§ 263–65, *GW* 14.1, pp. 210–11 (*Elements*, 286–88. See *Outlines*, 238–39).

47. *RPh*, § 255, *GW* 14.1, p. 199 (*Elements*, 272; see *Outlines*, 226).

48. *RPh*, § 256 Anmerkung, *GW* 14.1, p. 199 (*Elements*, 273; see *Outlines*, 227).

dom it embodies and makes objective. The social estates (*Stände*) in particular contribute to engendering the political disposition: the individual is able to accesses them by free choice[49] and from them receives a specific disposition, a type of social virtue, "rectitude" or "the honour of one's estate"[50] that is adapted to the activity he or she practices and the social context to which he or she belongs.

We must recall that in the 1805 *Philosophy of Spirit*, the differences between estates was not based directly on the structures of production and exchange (i.e., on the objective configuration of the system of needs or the market economy) but rather on differences in the mental dispositions proper to each type of social activity.[51] The peasant's disposition was trust, the bourgeois's was honesty, the merchant's severity and intelligence, and the disposition of the universal estate was duty (or obligation). In the *Philosophy of Right*, this doctrine of *Gesinnungen* disappears, or at least ceases to be foundational. But if the distinction between estates is there based above all on the objective characteristics of processes of production and exchange,[52] it also implies a specification of the "theoretical and practical education" particular to each one of them.[53] Thus, Hegel continues to reject a definition of the estates that would be based solely on their function within the mode of production: a *Stand* is an ethical reality, not a grouping of economic interests. This is why it, along with civil society, is the true site of individuals' formation and flourishing: it is what gives determinate and specific content to the notion of ethical disposition. Thus, rectitude (*Rechtschaffenheit*), which is first defined abstractly as "the simple adequacy of the individual to the duties of the circumstances [*Verhältnisse*] to which he belongs,"[54] is explicitly instituted as a specific virtue of civil society in the form of honor attached to estate (*Standesehre*), which we could also call a form of "estate consciousness" by analogy to the concept of class consciousness:

49. See *RPh*, § 185 Anmerkung 206, 262, *GW* 14.1, pp. 161, 172, 210 (*Elements*, 223, 237, 286; see *Outlines*, 182–83,195–96, 238).

50. See *RPh*, §§ 150, 207, 252, *GW* 14.1, pp. 140, 173–74, 197 (*Elements*, 193, 238–39, 270–71; see *Outlines*, 157, 196–97, 224–25).

51. See *GW* 8, p. 266 ff.

52. See *RPh*, §§ 203–5, *GW* 14.1, pp. 171–72 (*Elements*, 235–37; see *Outlines*, 193–95).

53. *RPh*, § 201, *GW* 14.1, p. 170 (*Elements*, 234; see *Outlines*, 193).

54. *RPh*, § 150, *GW* 14.1, p. 140 (*Elements*, 193; see *Outlines*, 157).

The ethical disposition within this system is therefore that of *rectitude* and the *honour of one's estate*, so that each individual, by a process of self-determination, makes himself a member of one of the moments of civil society through his activity, diligence, and skill, and supports himself in this capacity; and only through this mediation with the universal does he simultaneously provide for himself and gain *recognition* in his own eyes [*Vorstellung*] and in the eyes of others.[55]

Thus, citizens' political virtue, accurately understood as everyday patriotism, is based on their belonging to a given social estate, to civil society and its institutions: "each member of the state is a *member* of an *estate*."[56] We should not be surprised by this rootedness of political subjectivity in the ethical mode of being of social institutions. Civil society, the external state, is the external *of* the state, *its* other, *its phenomenon*. As the *Logic* establishes, there is no essence that both goes together with its phenomenal manifestation and remains withdrawn from it. This explains the relationship between the rational political essence of *Sittlichkeit* and the moving and muddled diversity of the social world. It also, by the way, sheds light on Hegel's words regarding the rabble, who have sunk below a certain standard of living and therefore "that feeling of right, integrity [*Rechtlichkeit*], and honour which comes from supporting oneself by one's own activity and work is lost,"[57] and his obvious worry in seeing civil society engender a mass of disadvantaged, "asocial" elements who are condemned to poverty. This is not only a social problem but a political one, since the lack of defined social status and its correlative qualities and guarantees destroys the very possibility of political consciousness and a sense of community. From this perspective we also understand why for Hegel the basis of parliamentary representation is not the individual will but rather the social estate institutionalized by corporations.[58] Parliamentary assemblies ("estates" in the old terminology), which represent the "higher offices of the state," are, as we know, "a *mediating* organ"[59] between the state and the social body, between the universal and its moment of particularity. As the re-

55. *RPh*, § 207, *GW* 14.1, pp. 173–74 (*Elements*, 238; see *Outlines*, 196–97).
56. *RPh*, § 308 Anmerkung, *GW* 14.1, p. 254 (*Elements*, 347; see *Outlines*, 294).
57. *RPh*, § 244, *GW* 14.1, p. 194 (*Elements*, 266; see *Outlines*, 221).
58. See chapter 8 above.
59. *RPh*, § 302 and Anmerkung, *GW* 14.1, pp. 250–51 (*Elements*, 342; see *Outlines*, 289).

positories of this function, parliamentary assemblies provide a favorable opportunity for their members to develop within themselves "the *sense* and *disposition* of the *state* and *government*."[60] Their task consists first and foremost in representing the point of view of civil society and the particular interests that emerge within it to the government and the administration. But the sense of the state that they acquire through their function also allows deputies to perform a kind of political pedagogy for social actors by changing their naive point of view that the state is hostile toward them by nature. Thus, they play an important role in the formation and education of public opinion:

> *Public opinion* . . . arrive[s] for the first time at *true thoughts* and *insight* with regard to the condition and concept of the state and its affairs, thereby *enabling it to form more rational judgments on the latter*. In this way, the public also becomes familiar with, and learns to respect, the functions, abilities, virtues, and skills of the official bodies and civil servants. And just as such publicity provides a signal opportunity for these abilities to develop, and offers them a platform on which they may attain high honours, so also does it constitute a remedy for the self-conceit of individuals and of the mass, and a means — indeed one of the most important means — of educating them.[61]

Political disposition and civic virtue are thus exercised in this double circulation of meaning from the bottom up and from the top down, which culminates in the development within individuals — especially those who hold public office — of "the *sense of authority* and *political sense*."[62]

But when Hegel discusses "institutions within the state" in paragraph 268 of the *Philosophy of Right* — that is, the institutions of civil society — he refers more directly to *corporations* than to social estates, which are semi-institutional realities, so to speak. Corporations are institutions in the strict sense[63] both because they are statutory groupings constituted within civil society and because they in a way extend the state into the social world by carrying out, locally and partially, its function as a promoter and representa-

---

60. *RPh*, § 302 and Anmerkung, *GW* 14.1, pp. 250–51 (*Elements*, 342; see *Outlines*, 289).
61. *RPh*, § 315, *GW* 14.1, p. 258 (*Elements*, 352; see *Outlines*, 298).
62. *RPh*, § 310, *GW* 14.1, p. 255 (*Elements*, 349 see *Outlines*, 296).
63. See *RPh*, § 253 Anmerkung, *GW* 14.1, p. 198 (*Elements*, 271; see *Outlines*, 225;): "the institution of the corporation."

tive of the people's identity. This, in Hegel's mind, justifies the government overseeing their operation.[64] But corporations are not only the tools of the state's dominance over civil society, a means of social control, although they may *also* play that role. The corporation, precisely as an institution, exudes a dimension of universality within a civil society that seems doomed to the juxtaposition and confrontation of particular interests: it has, in particular, thanks to its power of regulation, a "wholly *concrete*" "universal end."[65] Thus the corporation is the social prefiguration of the political state. While it is true that the modern individual has "become a *son of civil society*,"[66] it is in his belonging to a "*second* family,"[67] the corporative institution, that this filiation can be expressed. Corporations, themselves a first overcoming of social particularity and also themselves social, are essential mechanisms for "*constitution* . . . in the realm of *particularity*,"[68] just as civil society is in the external state. Prefiguring the rational universality of the political constitution, they are the "firm foundation of the state and of the trust and disposition of individuals towards it."[69]

This explains the social provenance of the political disposition. The vocation to the universal appears and develops through participation in corporate life and the social virtues the latter generates: institutionalized professional honor inculcates the aptitude for a "way of life of a more general kind."[70] The corporate spirit, incorporated into regulated practices, institutes a sort of culture of the universal that will find its true vocation in civic participation in the life of the state. It also guarantees the prevalence of a political point of view in handling social situations and confrontations. In conjunction with the mechanisms of political representation, this social culture guarantees, or at least contributes to guaranteeing, the community's ethical-political identity.

64. See *RPh*, §§ 252, 288, *GW* 14.1, p. 197 ("under the supervision of the public authority") and p. 241 ("these circles must be subordinated to the higher interests of the state") (*Elements*, 270, 329; see *Outlines*, 224, 278). Hegel also justified government intervention in choosing their leaders, leaving them a limited autonomy to say the least.

65. *RPh*, § 251, *GW* 14.1, p. 197 (*Elements*, 270; see *Outlines*, 224).

66. *RPh*, § 238, *GW* 14.1, p. 192 (*Elements*, 263; see *Outlines*, 218).

67. *RPh*, § 252, *GW* 14.1, p. 197 (*Elements*, 271; see *Outlines*, 225).

68. *RPh*, § 265, *GW* 14.1, p. 211 (*Elements*, 287; see *Outlines*, 239).

69. *RPh*, § 265, *GW* 14.1, p. 211 (*Elements*, 287; see *Outlines*, 239).

70. *RPh*, § 253 Anmerkung, *GW* 14.1, p. 198 (*Elements*, 272; see *Outlines*, 225).

The spirit of the corporation, which arises when the particular spheres gain legal justification [*Berechtigung*], is now at the same time inwardly transformed into the spirit of the state.... This is the secret of the patriotism of the citizens.... In so far as the *rooting of the particular in the universal* is contained *immediately* in the spirit of the corporation, it is in this spirit that such depth and strength of *disposition* as the state possesses are to be found.[71]

Considered as social institutions, churches — which in this respect are corporations just like professional associations[72] — participate in the development of this culture of the universal which is the specific contribution of instituted social life to politics. Belonging to a church, independent of its doctrine, could even be an ethical-political obligation: the state can "require all its citizens to belong to such a community."[73] This holds true at least as long as the church does not come to consider the state as a mechanism external to true ethicality (which would then be essentially religious), as a mere means to ends that only the church would be able to reveal. This example shows that the rootedness of political subjectivity in the institutional structures of social life — and a church is such a structure, though it is not *only* that — must not be understood as the subordination of the state to civil society. To the contrary, social institutions depend on the political institution, a rational totality that guarantees their ethical nature; this is why they are subject to its control. Thus, the chain of causality within *Sittlichkeit* runs in opposite directions depending on whether we are looking at its subjective dimension or its objective configuration.

Political Subjectivity and Moral Consciousness

However, one question arises: why isn't it the state itself that engenders civic virtue among citizens and makes itself loved for itself to the point of convincing individuals to subordinate their particular ends to the universal? Why must there be, from the point of view of both subjects and the objective order, a social mediation of the political, just as there is a political mediation of the social? To understand the answer, we must briefly go back to Hegel's analysis

---

71. *RPh*, § 289 Anmerkung, *GW* 14.1, p. 242 (*Elements*, 329–30; see *Outlines*, 278–79).
72. *RPh*, § 289 Anmerkung, *GW* 14.1, p. 242 (*Elements*, 329–30; see *Outlines*, 278–79).
73. *RPh*, § 270 Anmerkung, *GW* 14.1, p. 216 (*Elements*, 295; see *Outlines*, 246).

of morality. It is clear that Hegel's attitude toward the moral point of view is far from unilaterally negative.[74] But there is reason to ask why the theory of moral subjectivity is included in a philosophy of objective spirit. Indeed, this theory has a tight relationship to the idea of the social rootedness of the political disposition.

The subjective taking-on of freedom gives this freedom actual content. In other words, *objective* freedom requires that the subject exercise his or her capacity for self-determination within normatively ordered action. The normative point of view of morality constitutes the effective reality of subjectivity: this is what justifies its inclusion in the doctrine of objective spirit. In civil society and the state, which are more concrete configurations than morality, this right of subjective will cannot be eliminated even if it can be relativized. The dialectic of moral consciousness certainly leads subjectivity to recognize that in order to will the good, it must suppose that the good is in a way realized in the human world; in this way, ethicality, in the entirety of its development, is the condition of actuality of the moral point of view. But it does not thereby strip it of its value. The subject's noncoerced adherence is presupposed by all action claiming actuality and rationality; at the same time, if one were to limit oneself to the point of view of an abstract ought, subjectivity would not achieve its concrete completion, which is political.

It is now possible to specify the relationship between moral consciousness, the ethical disposition, and the political disposition. The moral point of view raises the finite subject to a concrete reality that produces normatively oriented actions. Through it, the individual is truly *constituted*, for him- or herself and for other acting subjects. But, if the individual remains stuck in this point of view, his or her goal is doomed to remain inactual. If subjectivity does not nourish itself with the objectivity of the social world, it risks becoming idle. Only then will it succumb to moralism, the practical consequences of which can be terrifying. But moral consciousness remains the mode in which the individual becomes actual and strives to master the causes and effects of his or her action. In the modern world, the individual, precisely because he or she has the will to be an individual and not a mere result of objective forces, is led to live his or her relation to the real, and first and foremost to the ethical-political real, in the moral mode. The ethical disposition (social virtues) and the political disposition express the permanence of the point of view of sub-

74. See chapter 10 above.

jectivity within *Sittlichkeit*. Social and political individuality, each one of which is characterized by a type of virtue (corporate honor, the spirit of everyday civic-mindedness), are thus the completion of moral individuality, which they protect from itself by awakening it to its objective extensions. This elevation of morality to the rank of a mediation internal to objective spirit, this active presence of subjectivity within ethical configurations (society and state), where it must recognize its own rational actuality, can be considered the *Kantian moment* of the doctrine of objective spirit. If it is true that the theory of political disposition is its *Aristotelian* moment, we may then represent this thought as an effort not at arbitration but rather at reconciliation set against the background of the dialectical tension between two orientations considered incompatible: deontological morality and the ethics of virtue.[75]

75. See Alasdair MacIntyre, *After Virtue* (Notre Dame, IN: University of Notre Dame Press, 1981), esp. chaps. 2, 9 12; *Whose Justice? Which Rationality* (Notre Dame, IN: University of Notre Dame Press, 1988), esp. chaps. 7, 8.

12

Subjects, Norms, and Institutions

What Is an Ethical Life?

It is clear that the doctrine of objective spirit gives a major role to both social and political institutions, but what does this mean for the problem of normativity (which Hegel in no way dismisses, despite what is sometimes claimed) and for our understanding of the normatively structured actions of empirical ("finite") subjects within institutional networks that more or less restrict them? My hypothesis is that the Hegelian doctrine of *Sittlichkeit* inaugurates a very particular relationship between subjectivity and institutions, one that makes it possible to determine, by using an original conception of normativity, what it means for individuals to lead an *ethical life*. We must first define the vocabulary used here. Obviously "ethical life" must mean something other than biological life, which belongs to the philosophy of nature, or the life of the concept, the "logical life," discussed in the *Science of Logic*; however, ethical life presupposes and in a sense extends them. Insofar as it is understood in its most general sense as the "resolving of . . . contradictions," isn't life "speculative?"[1] Isn't it, as Hegel proclaimed in Frankfurt, "the binding of binding and nonbinding?[2] But ethical life (*das sittliche Leben*) must also not be confused with ethicality (*die Sittlichkeit*), though it presupposes it. If *Sitt-*

1. *Enzykl,* § 337 Zusatz, *W* 10, p. 33 (*Encyclopedia* 274).
2. *Systemfragment, W* 1, p. 422.

lichkeit consists in "lead[ing] a universal life,"[3] we still must understand how conforming to the rules of the *"universal language"* formulated in "customs and laws"[4] allows the individual to live a life that is ethical while also being his or her *own* life. In other words, how does observing the beliefs and practices normatively defined by a cultural and political community authorize and even encourage individuals to attain a self-representation and a practical autonomy without which, in the context of modernity, they would be no more than mere biological particulars—that is, precisely not *individuals*? To speak, as Hegel sometimes (though rarely[5]) does, of an ethical *life* is thus to suppose that the matter of the *institution* of individuality or subjectivity within the powerfully institutional context Hegel calls objective spirit has been resolved. This is the issue I will discuss here.

What Is *Sittlichkeit*?

It is generally accepted that Hegel's understanding of *Sittlichkeit* substantially changed between his Jena writings and his mature works. The earlier writings, which developed what Jean Hyppolite called a "heroic conception of freedom," were marked by strong criticism of the withdrawal into the "private individual"[6] and of the "political nullity"[7] characteristic of the modern bourgeois world. In these writings, the "repression" of individuality, or at least its subordination to the superior norm of the *politeuein*, of civic life, is the condition for true, "absolute"—not "relative"—ethicality. By contrast, the later writings, marked by Hegel's goal of "reconciling with the times," dismiss the ideal of the "beautiful and happy freedom of the Greeks"[8] and make the disentanglement of civil society and the state, of bourgeois life and political life, the defining feature of the modern world and the sign of its *ethical* superiority. Not only do these writings not make the "disappearance of the individual"[9]

3. *RPh*, § 258 Anmerkung, *GW* 14.1, pp. 201–2 (*Elements*, 276; see *Outlines*, 229). See *Naturrecht*, *W* 2, p. 489.

4. *PhG*, *GW* 9, p. 195 (*Phenomenology*, ¶ 351).

5. See in particular *PhG*, *GW* 9, pp. 197, 240 (*Phenomenology*, ¶¶ 440, 753); *Geschichte*, *W* 12, p. 56.

6. *Naturrecht*, *W* 2, p. 492 (*Natural Law*, 103).

7. *Naturrecht*, *W* 2, p. 494 (*Natural Law*, 103).

8. *GW* 8, p. 262.

9. Ibid., 263.

the condition of *Sittlichkeit*, they present the affirmation of the individual, with a few caveats, as a positive trait of modernity, including *political* modernity. Here we need only think of Hegel's eminently positive judgment of the "elementary catechism" that is the Declaration of the Rights of Man in his 1817 article on the Wurtemberg Assembly: he calls that declaration a declaration of the individual's "natural and inalienable" powers, and it is precisely for this reason that it expresses the "simple bases of political institutions."[10] However, it seems to me that what changed in the interim was not the concept of *Sittlichkeit* itself but rather Hegel's determination of the conditions of its actualization and his assessment of its effects on the structure of action and the constitution of subjectivity.

The clearest definition of *Sittlichkeit* as distinct from morality (which is the relationship of subjectivity to norms of actions that it prescribes itself autonomously) and from the law (the relationship of a person to things and, through them, to other persons) is in section 142 of the *Philosophy of Right*:

> Ethicality is the *Idea of freedom* as the living good which has its knowledge and volition in self-consciousness, and its actuality through self-conscious action. Similarly, it is in ethical being that self-consciousness has its motivating end and a foundation which has being in and for itself. Ethicality is accordingly the *concept of freedom which has become the existing* [*vorhandenen*] *world and the nature of self-consciousness.*[11]

What should we take from this definition of ethicality? First of all, it actualizes moral-practical normativity: in it, the idea of freedom takes on an *actuality* that it does not have on its own, and the abstract good to which moral subjectivity refers becomes a good that is *living* because it is embodied in shared community practices and representations. Second, ethicality is based on the interaction between objective universality (the universality of what Hegel calls "ethical being" or, later in the text, "ethical substance") and particular subjectivity (individuals' "self-consciousness"): the first is the "base" of the second, and the latter is the principle of actualization of the former. Third, objective spirit overcomes the seemingly fundamental scission between the subject and

---

10. *Wurtemberg, W* 4, p. 492; *Proceedings*, in *Hegel's Political Writings*, 270.
11. *RPh*, § 142, *GW* 14.1, p. 137 (*Elements*, 189; see *Outlines*, 154).

the world. Ethicality is a world that is imposed through a kind of immediate givenness (it is *vorhanden*, present in the mode of "that's how it is"), but it is a world of intersubjectivity, a world within which subjects are practically constituted in their double relationship to other subjects (with whom they are engaged in a complex game of recognition) and to a "given" that is always already there but that only *is* thanks to the individual subject and other subjects. It is thus immediately clear that *Sittlichkeit* involves an original relationship between objectivity and subjectivity. But before going into this matter, we should recall a few essential aspects of the Hegelian concept of ethicality.

As I have said, *Sittlichkeit* is not a "part" of objective spirit, juxtaposed to law and to morality; in reality, it alone truly corresponds to the Hegelian definition of objective spirit.[12] It is an objectivity lived by particular subjects; the identity of these subjects is constituted in the lived relationship they have with this objective totality, which, conversely, only exists through their actions and thanks to their inner dispositions. Ethicality thus coincides with objective spirit in its totality. Law and morality are not distinct layers but rather its abstract moments: they have substance only if they are articulated within the concrete unity of *Sittlichkeit*. Of course, they are not beings of reason, *Gedankendinge*. But they are *abstract*, since fulfilling their concept presupposes elements that are foreign to their own principle: the realization of law is not only legal, and that of the moral end assumes that ethical objectivity is conferred on the norms that subjectivity claims to give itself. Thus objective spirit, grasped from the standpoint of these two moments, maintains an incompleteness that it is up to ethicality to overcome. This does not mean that within ethicality the relations that characterize abstract/private law and morality disappear. To the contrary, it is there that they receive the guarantee of their actuality. Ethicality gathers together and reshapes the objective formalism of law and the subjective formalism of moral consciousness. But though this coming together overcomes the abstract opposition between the two, it does not abolish their difference. *Sittlichkeit* has first and foremost the traits of a world of objectivity whose determinations, forming a "circle of necessity," are the "*ethical powers* which govern the lives of individuals."[13] However, these individuals are not only "accidents" of this substance, for the system of objective de-

---

12. See chapter 6 above.

13. *RPh*, § 145, *GW* 14.1, pp. 137–38 (*Elements*, 190; see *Outlines*, 155).

334 · Chapter Twelve

terminations to which their actions belong is for them a *lived* world that only has reality when it is an "object [*Objekt*] of knowledge" or at least of belief on their part.[14] Unlike laws of nature, ethical laws have validity only because of the representations individuals have of them: their validity rests on subjects' knowledge and recognition of them.

This is why there are two sides to the relationship the subject maintains with the objective structures of the ethical world. On the one hand, for the subject, "the ethical substance and its laws and powers" have "absolute authority and power, infinitely more firmly based than the being of nature";[15] thus, like the laws of nature, they exist entirely outside of the subject's reach. On the other hand, this power of objectivity does not rule out the possibility of the subject finding his or her own place within it as long as the subject does not merely contrast his or her "virtue" to the "way of the world" and recognizes within objective spirit that which constitutes his or her own essence, that by which he or she can be a subject. In this way, the individual's relation to the conditions and norms of his or her actions, which is still external when it takes the form of the moral ought, becomes fully internal when it becomes *Sitte*: as a "general mode of behavior,"[16] ethical custom is a practice that expresses subjects' adherence to the universal that constitutes them. Thus, *Sittlichkeit* reveals the decisive role of *subjectivity* within objective spirit. Objective spirit only corresponds to its concept, which is to be a "*world* [*where*] freedom is present as a necessity,"[17] insofar as within it a particular subjectivity is the moment that validates the objective rules presiding over its constitution. But particular subjectivity only succeeds in this if, unlike "formal" moral consciousness, it recognizes the priority of objectivity, the "right of the world," and accepts that relativization of its own aspirations.

Within objective spirit, the normative content to which subjectivities give actuality by adhering to it is not *first* posited by this subjective adherence: it is *their* substance, but, as substance, it is always presupposed by their action. *Sittlichkeit*, a second nature,[18] is certainly radically different from external na-

---

14. *RPh*, § 146, *GW* 14.1, p. 138 (*Elements*, 190; see *Outlines*, 155).

15. *RPh*, § 146, *GW* 14.1, p. 138 (*Elements*, 190; see *Outlines*, 155).

16. *RPh*, § 151, *GW* 14.1, p. 141 (*Elements*, 195; see *Outlines*, 159).

17. *Enzykl*, § 385, *GW* 20, p. 383 (*Encyclopedia* 20).

18. See *RPh*, § 4, *GW* 14.1, p. 31, and § 151, *GW* 14.1, p. 141 (*Elements*, 35, 195; see *Outlines*, 26, 159).

ture, for it is freedom expressing itself in the form of necessity rather than the blind rule of necessity. However, insofar as it is spontaneously perceived, it remains a *nature*: it speaks the language of necessity. Although *Sittlichkeit* allows subjective individuality to recognize itself and complete itself, it is not spontaneously apprehended as such, especially once subjectivity has freed itself from the restrictions that previously applied to it. For the individual, reaching true freedom requires an education (*Bildung*), an apprenticeship in the universal through the "*hard work*"[19] it does on its immediate naturalness and its representation of freedom. Thus, the individual often resists a liberation that at first appears as an external violence. Consequently, in the sphere of objective spirit, the reconciliation between subjective spirit and objective spirit often remains (merely) objective. This is why, especially in the political-state domain, obligations appear to win out over rights — understood as subjective rights — even though the two are speculatively of equal weight and in truth are even reciprocal.[20] The "ethical disposition" and the "political disposition"[21] consist not in the subject's power of self-determination in conformity with rational norms established by his or her reason but rather in his or her trusting and naive acknowledgment of the authority of the state and its laws. Thus, *Sittlichkeit* does not depend essentially on the virtue of the individual's goals and behavior but rather on the fact that the individual is a "*citizen of a state with good laws.*"[22] However, the validity of these laws of ethical nature requires something other than passive submission from individuals. It is precisely because humans do not have "the innocence of a plant"[23] that second nature, unlike first nature, must be recognized and willed by subjective consciousness, which has been educated to do so. In the rational state, subjective freedom does not abdicate its rights. Thus, there must be some mediation between rights and obligations, between the state and subjective consciousness. This mediation is guaranteed by the substructures of the ethical sphere, which all share the feature of being *institutions*.

19. *RPh*, § 187 Anmerkung, *GW* 14.1, p. 163 (*Elements*, 225, see *Outlines*, 185).

20. See *RPh*, § 261, *GW* 14.1, p. 208 (*Elements*, 283, see *Outlines*, 236): "[Individuals] have *duties* toward the state to the same extent as they also have rights."

21. See chapter 11 above.

22. *RPh*, § 153 Anmerkung, *GW* 14.1, p. 142 (*Elements*, 196; see *Outlines*, 160).

23. See *Enzykl*, § 248, Anmerkung, *GW* 20, p. 238.

Institutions as the Syntax of Objective Spirit

So-called institutionalist theories aim to go beyond the choice between sub-jectivism and objectivism.[24] The Hegelian doctrine of *Sittlichkeit* shares this perspective even if it seems to lean toward the side of objectivity. This is pre-cisely where its profound coherence lies: beyond the apparent heterogeneity of the materials it brings together, its goal is to show the *institutional rooted-ness* of individual and collective practices, which law and morality reduce to abstract operations (the acquisition, transferal, and restitution of rights; the moral imputation of action and the normative networks it involves) and only envision in their individual dimension (law judges a person's acts; morality evaluates a subject's actions). This institutional anchoring can also be seen in the family (marriage, filiation, inheritance) and in the economic and social relations that connect classes of individuals in the depoliticized space of civil society; it is also at the heart of the theory of the state, whose laws and insti-tutions Hegel says are "will as *thought*."[25] Thanks to institutions (marriage, corporations, representative assemblies), the subject can submit to a univer-sal regulation without feeling dispossessed. This is the paradox that Hegelian institutionalism assumes and accounts for. The question must nevertheless be asked: does recognition of a "right of the world" impose a restriction on the "right of subjective will,"[26] or is it the condition of its actuality? The Hegelian philosophy of *Sittlichkeit* does not *necessarily* imply subordinating the subjec-tive will to the objective will lodged in institutions, but it is clear that it ex-cludes the opposite, for all institutionalism gives priority to objective struc-tures; this priority may be described as that of syntax over the semantics and pragmatics of the system of ethicality.

The complex relationship individuals have with their peers and with the objective ethical milieu in which they exist involves a paradox that must be accounted for. On the one hand, the "objective ethical element"—in other words, the social and political world—is like a "circle of necessity" that has "absolute authority and power"[27] over individuals and their representations

---

24. See the preliminary to part 4 above and Maurice Hauriou, "La théorie de l'institution et de la fondation (Essai de vitalisme social)," in *Aux sources du droit*, 89–128.

25. *RPh*, § 256 Anmerkung, *GW* 14.1, p. 200 (*Elements*, 274; see *Outlines*, 228).

26. For these two expressions, see *RPh*, § 33, *GW* 14.1, p. 48 (*Elements*, 62–63; see *Outlines*, 50–51).

27. *RPh*, § 145 and 146, *GW* 14.1, pp. 137–38 (*Elements*, 190; see *Outlines*, 154–55).

of themselves, others, and their milieu; on the other hand, however, these objective powers "are not something *alien* to the subject," for they guarantee "the right of individuals to their *particularity*"[28]—in other words, they institute their very individuality. Hegel describes this mutual constitution of subjects and the ethical world by using the Aristotelian idea of *second nature*. Ethical-political nature is nothing other than the *movement of the institution of the identity* that individuals claim as their own nature or freedom. In other words, for freedom to be more than a hollow claim, it must always already be mediated, structured by what appears to be its other but which in reality is nothing but the system of conditions of its reality and objectivity. Thus, objective spirit is a fully spiritual (let us say human) world but one that initially seems rife with impersonal objectivity. This corresponds to the spontaneous reaction of consciousness when it perceives the network of norms and institutions that frame its action as obstacles to its autonomy rather than as conditions of its freedom. Whence the paradox characteristic of objective spirit: in it, the subject finds its identity and constitutes itself in and through it, but it also exposes itself to the far-from-illusory risk of dispossession and alienation. Nothing, other than blind faith in the virtue of institutions (both static and dynamic), can entirely prevent the risk of individuals submitting to nonuniversalizable interests or the risk of social and political institutions—and therefore individual choices—becoming tainted by ideology, which is never more than a false consciousness of universality adopted by a particular form of being-self. Thus, even in adopting Hegel's premises, it is perhaps appropriate to pair the elucidation of the *structuring* conditions of subjectivity, which are located in institutions, with a critique of ideologies intended to prevent or combat particular corruptions of those institutions. It is here that critical theory, basing itself on Marx and Freud, took leave of Hegelian orthodoxy, which right-wing neo-Hegelianism proved could sanction some very unsettling derivations when "the dialectic of Enlightenment is transformed objectively in delusion."[29]

How are we to explain the paradoxical relationship by which subjectivity and objectivity, freedom and necessity, individuality and sociality mutually

---

28. *RPh*, § 147, *GW* 14.1, p. 138, and § 154, *GW* 14.1, p. 141 (*Elements*, 191, 197; see *Outlines*, 155, 161).

29. Max Horkheimer and Theodor W. Adorno, *Dialectic of Enlightenment* (New York: Herder and Herder, 1972), 204. On the critique of "fascist neo-Hegelianism," see Herbert Marcuse, *Reason and Revolution: Hegel and the Rise of Social Theory* (New York: Humanities Press, 1954), 402 ff.

construct and strengthen one another? We must introduce a third term, one that appears occasionally yet decisively in Hegel's text: the *institution*. Expressions of the "power of the rational in necessity,"[30] ethical institutions (political, social, familial), because they are, so to speak, always already there, guarantee not only the cohesiveness of the individual and the objective totality but also their common genesis. In a single movement—the one that creates "shared meanings," as Charles Taylor puts it, or, in Castoriadis's terms, the "imaginary institution of society"—institutions structure subjectivity *and* objectivity, the individual (along with the individual's very modern claim to freedom and autonomy) *and* the community (understood as a space of conversation that may be a site of conflict). For Hegel as for Hauriou, institutions are not artifacts; they are "geological layers," a kind of archaic basis for truth, on which mores, beliefs, and practices, intertwining to form the field of action, are based as if on a kind of nature. For instituted subjects, institutions are quasi things that furnish the world in which they move: they are there, seemingly eternal,[31] apparent because presupposed by the everyday behaviors for which they provide a horizon of meaning; they establish an "objective reason."[32] Thus, the church, the army, school, professional or associative organizations, as well as more abstract configurations such as marriage, the market, and language are institutions that produce meaning, truths, norms, and individuals. And yet they are not things, because there is nothing material about them: institutions are purely symbolic relations that structure the perceptions, utterances, and actions of subjects who only attain the status of subject by carrying out the rites that indicate their belonging to an institution and at the same time giving that institution the only reality it can have: symbolic— in other words, subjective-objective—reality. We can verify this by studying the role of familial and social institutions in constituting not only social but also political individuality.

Hegel says that social institutions (but we may generalize to all institutions) form "the *constitution* . . . in the realm of *particularity*."[33] In what sense

---

30. *RPh*, § 263, *GW* 14.1, p. 210 (*Elements*, 286; see *Outlines*, 23).

31. Legal institutions (*Rechtsinstitute*), says Savigny, are "always already prior to any given legal relationship" (*System des heutigen römischen Rechts* [Berlin, 1840], vol. 1, pt. 1, chap. 2, §7). It is tempting to apply this extraordinary definition to every institutional configuration!

32. Descombes, "Y at-il un esprit objectif?," 364 The expression can already be found in Hegel: see, for example, *Enzykl*, § 467 Zusatz, *W* 10, p. 287 (*Encyclopedia* 204–5).

33. *RPh*, § 265, *GW* 14.1, p. 211 (*Elements*, 287; see *Outlines*, 239).

are marriage and corporations (the first two institutions his analysis focuses on) institutions? In what sense do they constitute, and what do they constitute? To answer these questions, we must take the word *constitution* in its dynamic sense: something that institutes. Social institutions *constitute* "the trust and disposition of individuals"[34] in the realm of particularity specific to the institution. Marriage—love within an institution, if not institutional love (Hegel calls it "rightfully ethical love")[35]—is an *ethical* relationship insofar as it overcomes individual arbitrariness without thereby eliminating the vagaries of love's choices; the strength of the institution lies in its ability to channel the contingency of subjective choices without sacrificing that contingency to pure legal formalism, as Kant does. Hence, marriage institutes an interpersonal relationship—the union of the sexes—not by sacrificing the sex drive but by making it a "natural moment" of a relationship that is not essentially natural but rather ethical or spiritual; thus, it institutes personality (feminine as well as masculine) in its nonlegal or superlegal aspects.

As for corporations, once we understand that Hegel is referring to something entirely different from the *Zünfte*—the guilds and confraternities of the ancien régime whose sole function was to maintain their members' privileges and which contradicted the universalizing logic of the market in favor of particular interests—we see that they, too, play a constitutive role in individuality itself. The clearest text on this subject is the 1817 article on the Wurtemberg estates, which contrasts *Zunftgeist*, the "guild mentality" characteristic of the old corporations, with the modern institutionalization of social particularity that truly constitutes individuality (social *and* political) by allowing it to be "something," although taken on its own, it is "nothing."[36] In other words, social individuality (the representations, choices, and behaviors of a person or bourgeois) and, mediately, political individuality (those of the citizen), this "volition which has become *habitual*,"[37] are not given with the physical individual but are socially constructed, which means they are generated by institutionalized social life. But how?

---

34. *RPh*, § 265, *GW* 14.1, p. 211 (*Elements*, 287; see *Outlines*, 239).

35. *RPh*, § 161 Zusatz, *W* 7, p. 310 (*Elements*, 201; see *Outlines*, 164).

36. Hegel, *Wurtemberg*, *W* 4, p. 482; *Proceedings*, in *Hegel's Political Writings*, 263; the allusion to Sieyès's *What Is the Third Estate?* seems obvious. See also Hegel, *Vorlesungen über Naturrecht und Staatswissenschaft*, 168–70, 75; Hegel, *Lectures on Natural Right*, §§121, 25, 217ff, 24 ff.

37. *RPh*, § 268, *GW* 14.1, p. 211 (*Elements*, 288; see *Outlines*, 240).

The Institution of the Individual

While the dispositions of subjective spirit are *aroused* by the institutions of objective spirit, they are not *determined* by them in the sense that these institutions could be considered the superstructural reflection of these dispositions, and this is why something like an ethical life is possible: the Hegelian theory of the ethical constitution of subjectivity is not a theory of ideology in Marx's sense, even if it can (or must, according to Horkheimer and Adorno) be completed by such a theory. Hegel's weak institutionalism seeks to account for the institution of individuality without reducing it to a mere trace of what creates it, that is, objective familial, social, and political institutions. An individual's identity presupposes partial memberships — that is, institutions (the family, the corporation, but also the legal system and the market) that nourish individual identity by creating feelings of cobelonging: I am not only "a bourgeois" — that is, as Rousseau fiercely notes, "nothing"[38] — I am identified, including in my own eyes, by my belonging to a certain profession, a certain religious or cultural community, a certain territorial collectivity, and so on.

The conscious and active individuality required by the conditions of modern social and political life presupposes institutions and networks of belonging, but it never develops mechanically: my social identity (my *ethos*) and my political identity (my opinions and engagements) cannot be deduced from my objective properties in the institutional field, and this is why I am "free" (according to a summary understanding of freedom) when I take on the institutional rootedness of my particular individuality. I am free, first, in the common sense of the term: I am not (entirely) determined by the properties that individualize me. But I am also free in the specifically Hegelian sense of the word: if freedom consists in being at home with oneself (or arriving at oneself) in the other, in an "absolute affirmation" born out of "negativity that deepens itself within itself to the point of the utmost intensity,"[39] then it is clear why the actual freedom of the social and political (as well as moral) subject arises

---

38. See Rousseau, *Emile*, bk. 1: "He will be one of those men of our days; a Frenchman, an Englishman, a Bourgeois. He will be nothing." Rousseau, *Oeuvres complètes*, 4:250; *Emile*, 164. On the degradation of the spirit of citizenship in modern states, see also *Oeuvres complètes*, 3:361–62; *Social Contract*, 1:6.

39. *Enzykl*, § 87 Anmerkung, *GW* 20, p. 124 (*Encyclopedia* 140).

out of the formative infusion, which is cultural in the strong sense,[40] of objective spirit diffused by institutions and lodged in mores and customs. But this infusion "inclines without necessitating," as Leibniz might say. Thus, ethical and political freedom does not simply consist in recognizing necessity (embodied by institutions and the influence they have over individual representations and wills) but in sometimes confronting it, as, for example, in a context where an individual's honor is at stake in a confrontation with injustice, as in the French Revolution.

Let us now look at how, within the context of objective spirit, the various shapes of individuality are articulated: the legal person, the moral subject, the social human (the "*Bürger als* bourgeois" of the *Philosophy of Right*),[41] and finally, the political citizen. A linear reading (which goes along with a teleological understanding of *Aufhebung*) would lead us to think that each of these shapes surpasses the one before it, which is thus canceled out rather than preserved. But I believe that here (and in general)[42] *Aufhebung* signifies a regression toward what a position is based on (i.e., what legitimizes it *relatively*) rather than a progression toward what refutes it: as the *Logic* indicates, progression toward the result is also a regression toward the foundation,[43] since true immediacy is mediated by the mediations that proceed from it. The *Philosophy of Right* ratifies this "progressive-regressive" structure of the "method of truth": here, too, the "*result*" (the state) is the "*true* ground" of the moments that precede it in the "development of the scientific concept": the family and civil society.[44] Thus, the specifically political form of individuality (citizenship

---

40. "It is through [the] work of education that the subjective will attains *objectivity* even within itself, that objectivity in which alone it is for its part worthy and capable of being the *actuality* of the idea." (*RPh*, § 187 Anmerkung, *GW* 14.1, p. 163 [*Elements*, 225; see *Outlines*, 185).

41. *RPh*, § 190 Anmerkung, *GW* 14.1, p. 166 (*Elements*, 228; see *Outlines*, 188).

42. See *WdL* 1², *GW* 21, p. 94 (*Science of Logic*, 81–82): "The German 'aufheben' ('to sublate' in English) has a twofold meaning in the language: it equally means 'to keep,' 'to preserve,' and 'to cause to cease,' 'to put an end to.' . . . That which is sublated is thus something at the same time preserved, something that has lost its immediacy but has not come to nothing for that."

43. See *WdL* 3, *GW* 12, p. 251 (*Science of Logic*, 750): "It is in this manner that each step of the advance in the process of further determination, while getting away from the indeterminate beginning, is also a getting back closer to it; consequently, that what may at first appear to be different, the retrogressive grounding of the beginning and the progressive further determination of it, run into one another and are the same."

44. *RPh*, § 256 Anmerkung, *GW* 14.1, p. 199 (*Elements*, 274; see *Outlines*, 227).

and that which expresses it, "political disposition") is the logical result and the real foundation of the earlier shapes—the person, the subject, and the bourgeois. And in the same way that "the *state* in general is in fact the *primary* factor [and] only within the state does the family first develop into civil society,"[45] the citizen is the "true foundation" of the bourgeois and, mediately, of the person and the moral subject. What does this mean? It means that within the modern conditions of a functional differentiation between the social and political, political subjectivity or *ethos* is the condition of actuality (though not of possibility) of that in which it itself is rooted, that is, it is the condition of the prepolitical shapes (familial and social) of individuality. It is what delivers them from the abstraction they maintain within themselves, which means that outside of the political configuration of modernity (the postrevolutionary state), the legal person, the moral subject, and the social human have no actual existence. And, as we have seen, this political subjectivity is generated by "the institutions within the state."[46] Thus, we are dealing with a recursive scheme. Social (and political) institutions generate the spirit of citizenship, which in return carries out and nourishes the subjective dispositions (e.g., the "mentality of the corporation")[47] required by the proper functioning of the partial systems that are the family and civil society, which themselves actualize the "abstract" determinations of law and morality. In this way, subjective dispositions ("the spirit of the whole" as well as "esprit de corps"[48]) are indeed produced by the operation of institutions, but they themselves retroactively feed these institutions and allow them to operate, which in certain cases means that they contribute to their transformation.

One might object that if the dispositional components of *Sittlichkeit*—in other words, the various shapes of ethical subjectivity—are destined to consolidate the institutional structures that cause them to emerge, individuals' autonomy with regard to these institutions remains very limited. Two responses can be made to this objection. First, it is necessary to take into consideration the fact that Hegel (like Kant before him) rejects any solely negative defini-

---

45. *RPh*, § 256 Anmerkung, *GW* 14.1, p. 199 (*Elements*, 274; see *Outlines*, 227).
46. *RPh*, § 268, *GW* 14.1, p. 211 (*Elements*, 288; see *Outlines*, 240). See chapter 11 above.
47. See *RPh*, § 289 Anmerkung, *GW* 14.1, p. 242 (*Elements*, 329, modified; see *Outlines*, 278).
48. See Hegel, *Vorlesungen über Naturrecht und Staatswissenschaft*, 186; *Lectures on Natural Right*, §132 A, 237. See chapter 4 above.

tion of subjective freedom; from Hegel's perspective, it does not at all follow that an individual who diverges from the representations and practices that conform to institutions or who rejects them is eo ipso more free than one who, without being constrained, conforms to the obligations tied to his or her position.[49] To the contrary, Hegel maintains that

> The *right of individuals* to their *subjective determination to freedom* is fulfilled in so far as they belong to ethical actuality; for their *certainty* of their own freedom has its *truth* in such objectivity, and it is in the ethical realm that they *actually* possess *their own* essence and their *inner* universality.[50]

Hegel is convinced that the adherence of particular subjectivity to universal and objective norms (*"the laws and institutions which have being in and for themselves"*)[51] does not, within the differentiation of normative systems that defines modern ethicality, lead to any irremediable sacrifice of the "right of individuals to their *particularity*."[52] It is true that for him, this right is honored above all in the nonpolitical elements of *Sittlichkeit*, the family and civil society, where the principle of free choice (of one's spouse, of one's profession) plays an essential role, for it is there that the difference between modern society and the *altständische Gesellschaft* lies: the former is based to a certain extent on the principle of free enterprise, whereas the latter assigned each individual an immutable position within a rigid and hierarchical political-social space (the "three orders" making up the "feudal imagination").[53] To summarize:

> If it is supported by the objective order, conforming to the latter and at the same time retaining its rights, subjective particularity becomes the sole animating principle of civil society. . . . The recognition and right according to

49. This largely explains Hegel's aversion for the cult of the "dear Self" practiced, before Stirner, by German romanticism (Tieck, the Schlegel brothers, Novalis, Kleist . . .); see *RPh*, § 140 Anmerkung, *GW* 14.1, pp. 132 ff. (*Elements*, 180 ff.; see *Outlines*, p147 ff., as well as the review of Solger's *Posthumous Works: W* 11, pp. 205–74.

50. *RPh*, § 153, *GW* 14.1, p. 142 (*Elements*, 196; see *Outlines*, 160).

51. *RPh*, § 144, *GW* 14.1, p. 137 (*Elements*, 189; see *Outlines*, 154).

52. *RPh*, § 154, *GW* 14.1, p. 142 (*Elements*, 197; see *Outlines*, 161).

53. See Georges Duby, *The Three Orders: Feudal Society Imagined* (Chicago: University of Chicago Press, 1982).

which all that is rationally necessary in civil society and in the state should at the same time come into effect *through the mediation of the arbitrary will* is the more precise definition of what is primarily meant by the universal representation [*Vorstellung*] of *freedom*.[54]

Second, while it is patent that within objective spirit, subjectivity is constantly measured against the "right of the world" as it is expressed in ethical-political institutions and the sets of norms that go along with them, and if it is true that subjectivity is in a sense repressed by the "right of the world," it is also true that it is thanks to the historical work of "reason *which is*,"[55] the objective reason embodied in institutions, that subjectivity can constitute itself as an actual reality, including its most extreme and self-indulgent claims. Free subjectivity, which the theory of subjective spirit presents as if it were the culmination of the knowledge that spirit, atemporally, gains of itself, is in fact inscribed in history; it is a sort of trace of objective spirit within the very order of subjectivity. The subject who thinks and acts as if free—including with respect to the world and the limits it imposes—is, as both the *Encyclopedia* and the *Philosophy of Right* reiterate, a product of history (and a rather belated one at that).

What Does It Mean to Lead an Ethical Life?

As I said at the beginning of this chapter, it is important not to confuse ethicality (*Sittlichkeit*) with ethical life (*das sittliches Leben*). We can now see the philosophical reason for this philological distinction. *Sittlichkeit*, in which the objective components of objective spirit (institutions) play a driving role, creates the *conditions* for an ethical life by producing distinct and historically situated schemas for the actualization of subjectivity, but only the *individuals* whose constitution it enables can have such a life, that is, can *live* it coherently and reasonably *as if* this life were the result of their own autonomous choice. But, as Hegel learned from Kant, autonomy means recognizing and observing a normativity that is not imposed on subjects but is in a sense validated by them. The question is thus as follows: when can one say that an individual is

---

54. *RPh*, § 206 Anmerkung, *GW* 14.1, p. 173 (*Elements*, 238, modified; see *Outlines*, 196).

55. *Enzykl*, § 6, *GW* 20, p. 44. The preface to the *Philosophy of Right* speaks of "reason as present actuality" (*RPh*, *GW* 14.1, p. 15 [*Elements*, 22] See *Outlines*, 15).

a *subject* without falling into the subjectivism reviled[56] by Hegel and that his institutional understanding of objective spirit sought to eradicate? I am not sure that this question is clearly or explicitly answered in the texts, but we can find a series of elements that when brought together point in the direction of what the answer might be.

The first such element is *recognition*. One of Hegel's great strengths was to have linked the constitution of subjectivity to intersubjective recognition (or to its negation) and to have conceived of these on the basis of the theme of conflict. I am of course thinking here of his (too?) famous analysis of the "struggle for recognition" in the *Phenomenology of Spirit*, where what is at stake, we must remember, is the "self-sufficiency and non-self-sufficiency,"[57] as the title of the passage says—that is, reaching being-self, subjectivity. The struggle with death, the "absolute master," and the experience of brutal, *pre-political* domination at the hands of a master are the conditions of the "truth" that consists in "being recognized as a self-sufficient self-consciousness."[58] And it must be remembered that coerced recognition, like the recognition the master thinks he has gained, can only be inauthentic and precarious. This is why the struggle for recognition "can only occur in the *state of nature*";[59] it pre-cedes the symbolic institution of society and individuality, for which recognition of the other's humanity is the minimal condition. But this origin myth, in the strong sense of the term, is also there to remind us that recognition, and thus living together, and thus achieving subjectivity, is not something given or established, but rather is at stake in an open process: "part of this freedom is the possibility of nonrecognition and nonfreedom."[60] The possibility of non-recognition does not only concern the ideal-type called "the state of nature"[61]: it also concerns all the forms of social pathology that Hegel sketches out in the *Philosophy of Right* and which one current of contemporary political phi-

---

56. See Hegel's detailed analysis of the various "shapes" of "*subjectivity [that] declares itself absolute*," *RPh*, § 140 Anmerkung, *GW* 14.1, p. 123 ff. (*Elements*, 170ff; see *Outlines*, 138 ff.).

57. *PhG, GW* 9, p. 109 (*Phenomenology*, ¶ 178).

58. *PhG, GW* 9, p. 111 (*Phenomenology*, ¶ 187).

59. *Enzykl*, § 432 Zusatz, *W* 10, p. 221 (*Encyclopedia* 159).

60. *SS, GW* 5, p. 305.

61. See *Enzykl*, § 433 Anmerkung, *GW* 20, p. 431 (*Encyclopedia* 160), and *RPh*, § 349 Anmer-kung, *GW* 14.1, p. 277 (*Elements*, 375; see *Outlines*, 318).

losophy seeks to bring up to date on the basis of an expanded conception of recognition.[62]

The second element is *work*. We know how important this subject is in the Jena writings (and already in some of the Frankfurt writings), where it testifies to the influence that classical economists (Smith, Ricardo) and belated mercantilists (Steuart) had on Hegel. We also know how much "the reception of political economy" (M. Riedel) contributed to shaping Hegel's concept of civil society. I would like to quickly discuss something a bit less well known: the role of work in creating subjectivities capable of leading an *ethical life*. Of course, and especially because of Marx's influence, Hegel's critique of the alienation necessarily implied by modern forms of the organization of work has often been a subject of focus, in particular his analysis in the *Philosophy of Right* of the structural contradictions of "ethicality lost in its extremes."[63] But this must not obscure the fact that for Hegel, as for Marx, work not only generates alienation but is a decisive factor in constructing subjectivity and intersubjectivity; there is in Hegel, as Habermas would say, a substantial connection between work and interaction.[64] In the 1803–1804 *Philosophy of Spirit* and the *System der Sittlichkeit*, work is presented at the scale of a people as a "subjective activity" raised to a "universal rule."[65] It is thus a potent means of abstracting subjectivity from the particular context it is naturally in the grip of — all the more so because it requires no conscious planning to this end: thus work is a method of universalization. In other words, in the context of modern civil society, work is *simultaneously* a factor in relinquishment and a factor in the construction of subjectivity: to use the vocabulary of the 1802 article on natural law, it is both the tragedy and the comedy of ethicality.

The third element is *normativity*. The weak institutionalism of the doctrine

---

62. The importance of the theme of recognition and its fecundity were highlighted, after Kojève, by Ludwig Siep, *Anerkennung als Prinzip der praktischen Philosophie*, Munich: Alber 1979; Franck Fischbach, *Fichte et Hegel: La reconnaissance* (Paris: Presses Universitaires de France, 1999); Axel Honneth, *The Struggle for Recognition: The Moral Grammar of Social Conflicts* (Cambridge, MA: MIT Press, 1996); *Suffering from Indeterminacy*; Emmanuel Renault, *Mépris social: Éthique et politique de la reconnaissance* (Bordeaux: Le Passant ordinaire, 2000).

63. *RPh*, § 184, *GW* 14.1, p. 160 (*Elements*, 221; see *Outlines*, 182).

64. See Jürgen Habermas, "Arbeit und Interaktion," in *Technik und Wissenschaft als "Ideologie"?* (Frankfurt am Main: Suhrkamp, 1969), 9–47.

65. *GW* 6, p. 320.

of *Sittlichkeit* does not prevent it from including a *normative* structure. This bears repeating, for it goes against a reading that is still dominant: Hegel's critique of the "ought" and of the "moral view of the world," developed in particular in the *Phenomenology of Spirit*[66] and repeated in many forms in his later work, does not imply any rejection of normativity as such. I will not comment here on his famous analysis of the "moral vision of the world," but we have already seen that it is *"incomplete* morality" that Hegel criticizes from the point of view of what he calls in the *Philosophy of Right* "true moral consciousness," which coincides with ethical-political subjectivity.[67] In conformity with the structure of the ought and of the boundary (*die Schranke*) described in the logic of being, this incomplete morality calls for its own infinitization: the true infinity of the *Logic* thus corresponds to the ethical culmination of morality, or, in the register of the *Phenomenology of Spirit*, to the transition from the moral point of view to the "reconciling yes,"[68] thanks to which two consciousnesses recognize each other in confessing to and forgiving evil and thus overcome the aporia of formal moral consciousness and the guiles of the beautiful soul. At most, the normative configuration of action must be brought back to its limits, as an expression from the *Encyclopedia* emphasizes a contrario: "the idea . . . is not so impotent as to demand that it merely ought to be actual without being so."[69] But the base structure of normativity—the opposition between *Sein* and *Sollen*—if understood dynamically and procedurally, is perfectly compatible with the requirement of Hegelian philosophy. The *Logic* emphasizes the contradictory dynamic that lies within the idea of the ought: unlike a limit, which inexorably determines the being of the finite (*"something coincides with its limit"*[70]), the boundary (*die Schranke*) that affects a being signifies both a restriction and the exigency of overcoming this restriction such that "in the ought the transcendence of finitude, infinity, begins."[71] Of course, this going beyond the finite itself remains finite; this is why it takes the shape of the ought or the undefined. Nevertheless, the problematic of *Sollen* is fruit-

---

66. "Spirit that is certain of itself, morality," in *PhG, GW* 9, pp. 323 ff. (*Phenomenology*, ¶¶ 596 ff.).

67. *RPh*, § 137 Anmerkung, *GW* 14.1, p. 120 (*Elements*, 164–165; see *Outlines*, 133–34).

68. *PhG, GW* 9, p. 362 (*Phenomenology*, ¶ 671).

69. *Enzykl*, § 6 Anmerkung, *GW* 20, p. 46 (*Encyclopedia* 34).

70. *WdL* 1¹, *GW* 11, p. 69.

71. *WdL* 1², *GW* 21, p. 121 (*Science of Logic*, 105).

ful, as long as it is not taken as an ultimate horizon, for it contributes to adequately describing the relationship that finite subjects have with the given world they face:

> The *ought*, for its part, is the transcending of restriction, but a *transcending* which is itself only *finite*. It therefore has its place and legitimacy in the field of finitude, where it holds in-itself fixed over against what is restricted, declaring it to be the norm and the essential relative to what is null. Duty is an *ought* directed against the particular will, against self-seeking desire and arbitrary interest; it is the ought held up before a will capable of isolating itself from the truth because of its instability. . . . But in the actual order of things, reason and law are not in such a sad state of affairs that they only *ought* to be (only the abstraction of the in-itself stays at this).[72]

The fertility of the point of view of the ought or normativity finds its expression all the way to the sphere of the idea, which, however, is "not so impotent as to demand that it merely ought to be actual without being so." Indeed, the logical idea, when it has not yet been identified, as absolute idea, with the pure process of thought, includes a teleological structure manifested in particular by the "syllogism of action."[73] The surpassing of this teleological-normative structure is also the surpassing of the finitude of the subject itself and its will. It is not, of course, that the subject disappears and along with it the representations that gave meaning to its practical being. But it overcomes its own finitude by granting the actual, existent world the dignity that abstract normativism (Kelsen more so than Kant) reserves only for representations of what ought to be. By recognizing the rationality (the actuality!) of the world, the subject gives meaning to his or her rational action on it and posits him- or herself as a rational subject. But this is possible only because the subject has adopted the normative posture without which it could not posit itself as the *subject* of an action. This is precisely what happens in the analysis of objective spirit, at the turning point between *Moralität* and *Sittlichkeit*, and this is why the transition from the former to the latter includes an explicit reference to the analysis of the good in the *Logic*.[74] Just as in the *Logic*, the resolution of the

---

72. *WdL* 1², *GW* 21, p. 123 (*Science of Logic*, 107).

73. *WdL* 3, *GW* 12, p. 234 (*Science of Logic*, 732).

74. See *RPh*, § 141 Anmerkung, *GW* 14.1, p. 135 (*Elements*, 185; see *Outlines*, 152).

contradiction affecting action passes through a reminder of the actuality of the world,[75] so in the *Philosophy of Right* the aporias of moral subjectivity, illustrated by the perversions of subjectivism denounced in the Remark to section 140, are overcome by the recognition of the "right of the *world*," without which the "*right of the subjective will*," along with the "right of the idea," would remain inactual.[76] This right of the world is honored first and foremost in the institutions of ethicality, if it is true that ethicality is freedom become world and that its institutional constitution distinguishes it from the abstract spheres of legal and moral normativism.

Recognition that is not coerced and that must always be won again—the constitution of social intersubjectivity, in particular through work; the active internalization of the normative structures without which there can be no sensible action—these are the primary conditions, necessary but not sufficient, that (eventually) allow an individual to lead an ethical life, that is, simply to have "a life" of which he or she can be the subject. Hegel was neither the first nor the last to realize that these conditions cannot be achieved once and for all.

75. "This actuality is by presupposition determined to have only the reality of an appearance, to be in and for itself a nullity, entirely open to determination by the objective concept. As the external actuality is altered by the activity of the objective concept and its determination is consequently sublated, the merely apparent reality, the external determinability and worthlessness, are by that very fact removed from it and it is thereby *posited* as having existence in and for itself. In this the presupposition itself is sublated, namely the determination of the good as a merely subjective purpose restricted in content, the necessity of first realizing it by subjective activity, and this activity itself. In the result the mediation itself sublates itself; the result is an *immediacy* which is not the restoration of the presupposition, but is rather the presupposition as sublated. The idea of the concept that is determined in and for itself is thereby posited, no longer just in the active subject but equally as an immediate actuality; and conversely, this actuality is posited as it is in cognition, as an objectivity that truly exists. The singularity of the subject with which the subject was burdened by its presupposition has vanished together with the presupposition. Thus the subject now exists as *free, universal self-identity* for which the objectivity of the concept is a *given*, just as immediately *present* to the subject as the subject immediately knows itself to be the concept determined in and for itself." (*WdL* 3, *GW* 12, p. 235 [*Science of Logic*, 734–34]).

76. *RPh*, § 33, *GW* 14.1, p. 48 (*Elements*, 62; see *Outlines*, 50).

→ **Epilogue** ←

The Passion of the Concept

One of Hegel's best-known phrases is *"nothing great has been and nothing great can be accomplished without passion."*[1] At first glance, one might think (and it has been suggested) that this affirmation is part of a romantic reaction against the Enlightenment and against a form of rationalism that sees passion as merely the opposite of reason; on this reading, the phrase is an attack on the program of philosophy and the modern sciences. And indeed, there is a tradition of interpreting Hegel — at least some respects or parts of his work — as a romantic, or at least as a precursor of *Lebensphilosophie* and thus of a certain form of irrationalism. We may think here of Dilthey's reading of Hegel or Glockner's distinction between "pantragism" and "panlogism."[2] Of course, Hegel does not simply pit passion against reason; to the contrary, he tries to identify "genuine rationality"[3] within the complex of passions. But this rationality, which must be assessed in the light of Hegel's critique of *Verständigkeit*,

---

1. Hegel, *Die Vernunft in der Geschichte*, 85. See *Enzykl*, § 474 Anmerkung, *GW* 20, pp. 471–72 (*Encyclopedia* 211).

2. See *Die Jugendgeschichte Hegels*, in volume 4 of Wilhelm Dilthey, *Gesammelte Schriften* (Leipzig: Teubner, 1963). See also Hermann Glockner, *Hegel*, in Hegel, *SW*, vols. 21, 22.

3. *Enzykl*, § 474 Anmerkung, *GW* 20, p. 472 (*Encyclopedia* 212).

the formal rationality of the understanding, has little to do with the rationalism proclaimed by the dominant school of modern philosophy.

The Hegelian project of promoting a type of rationality superior to what is found in philosophies of the understanding can also be interpreted differently, especially when viewed in light of the theme of the "cunning of reason" — another *topos* of Hegelian commentary. We know that Hegel developed this theme in his lectures on the philosophy of history, but it is often forgotten that it first appeared in the *Logic*, where it is presented rather differently.[4] This well-known (in fact, too-well-known) motif offers a first view of what has sometimes been called Hegel's hyperrationalism. I do not intend to present or to refute the "Hegelian theory of the cunning of reason," which to my mind does not exist or at least does not have the all-encompassing significance sometimes attributed to it. I would just like to point out in passing that the critique of Hegelian hyperrationalism, part of an old interpretative tradition,[5] has been met with strong opposition from those who offer an immanent, or, if one prefers, orthodox, reading. It has recently been shown, for example, that the common interpretation of the cunning of reason is a result of confusing internal and external finality.[6] It cannot be denied, however, that the cunning of reason (or whatever other name is given to this structure of thought) constitutes a systematic problem within Hegelian philosophy. With it, the system includes the means (whether considered legitimate or not) of dissolving or at least mastering the irrational dross of the world — manifestations of contingencies and the works of passion. But the system then encounters a series of difficulties, and we may say that Hegel hesitates between a downright liberation of contingency and the powers of particularity and a tendency, which some consider irrepressible, to eliminate contingency or, as Adorno puts it, to subject difference to "the compulsion to achieve identity."[7] In an attempt to find a solution to these difficulties, I will now turn to examining the location

4. See *WdL* 3, *GW* 12, pp. 165–66 (*Science of Logic*, 663). Cf. Hegel, *Die Vernunft in der Geschichte*, 105.

5. As far as I know, this goes back to Ranke, who in his lectures to the Archduke Maximilian (1854) characterizes Hegelian philosophy of history as a "theory of puppets." See Leopold von Ranke, *Über die Epochen der Weltgeschichte*, vol. 2, *Aus Werk und Nachlass* (Munich: Historische Kommission bei der Bayerischen Akademie der Wissenschaften,1971), 64.

6. Mabille, *Hegel: L'épreuve de la contingence*, 163–70.

7. Theodor W. Adorno, *Negative Dialectics*, trans. E. B. Ashton (New York: Continuum, 1973), 157.

and significance of passions in the system of speculative reason, in particular, within the sphere of objective spirit. This question intersects with the question raised in the preface of this work regarding the metaphysical status of Hegel's philosophy.

The Passion of Subjectivity

The fate of the passage in the introduction to the lectures on the philosophy of history that deals with the role of passions in the dynamic of history has sometimes obscured the fact that the proper site of the Hegelian theory of passions is not the philosophy of history, that is, the ultimate sequence of the doctrine of objective spirit, but rather (and this is perfectly normal) the doctrine of subjective spirit, and more precisely, the section dealing with practical spirit; it is at the end of this section that Hegel expressly discusses urges (or inclinations) and passions.[8] This analysis of practical spirit is revisited and refined in the introduction to the *Philosophy of Right*, where it acts as the philosophical deduction of the concept of law,[9] or, more precisely, as the philosophical presupposition of the concept of objective spirit. Subjective will (spirit determining itself in volition) is in fact the sole presupposition of "objective will,"[10] which can be considered the guiding concept of the entirety of the doctrine of objective spirit or of law in the broad sense of "the *existence* of the *free will*."[11]

In terms of Hegel's treatment of passions in the context of subjective spirit, it must first be emphasized that the "*dialectic* of drives and inclinations"[12] has an essential relationship to free choice (*Willkür*). *Willkür*, insofar as it is the will still outside of itself, no doubt expresses the rational and active nature of spirit itself but in a deformed and contradictory manner. It is not "the will in its truth" but rather "the will as *contradiction*."[13] This is why in spite of its etymology and the context in which it usually signifies, passion is not

---

8. *Enzykl*, §§ 473–75, *GW* 20, pp. 470–73 (*Encyclopedia* 210–13).

9. See *RPh*, § 2, *GW* 14.1, p. 23 (*Elements*, 26, modified; see *Outlines*, 18): "the concept of law, so far as its *coming* into being is concerned, falls outside the science of law; its deduction is presupposed here and is to be taken as *given*." See chapter 1 above.

10. *RPh*, § 13 Anmerkung, *GW* 14.1, p. 37 (*Elements*, 47; see *Outlines*, 36). See above, preliminary to part 1.

11. See *RPh*, § 29, *GW* 14.1, p. 45 (*Elements*, 58; see *Outlines*, 46).

12. *RPh*, § 17, *GW* 14.1, p. 39 (*Elements*, 50; see *Outlines*, 39).

13. *RPh*, § 15 Anmerkung, *GW* 14.1, p. 38 (*Elements*, 48; see *Outlines*, 38).

merely an expression of the passivity of spirit; it must not be understood as the other that would come from the outside to restrict what is spiritual within spirit—that is, freedom as (self-)activity. This congruence between passion and the self-affirmation of the freedom of spirit—which at this stage is still one sided and confused—explains why Hegel refuses to accuse or condemn the passionate will. In truth, "passion is neither good nor evil,"[14] so it does not make sense to judge it morally. In the same way as *Willkür*, and with the same contradictions, passion means that "the subject is the activity of satisfying urges, of formal rationality, namely of translating the content, which in this respect is purpose, from subjectivity into objectivity, in which the subject joins together with itself."[15] It thus contributes to the process of determination whereby the practical subject (volition) overcomes the abstraction of its immediate natural concrete existence and, taking on the contingency and finite nature of its particular (if not arbitrary)[16] decisions, reaches true freedom and the infinity that consists in being at home with oneself in the other. This is why if we bracket the extreme form of passion that is madness, in which the subject loses itself in "the absolute unhappiness of contradiction,"[17] passion is not a pure and simple disorder of subjectivity. To the contrary, it is only through passion that subjectivity experiences the imbalance between its share of contingency and its share of rationality, between its self-destructive particularity and its affirmative universality; thus, passions and impulses "are nothing but the lifeblood of the subject."[18] As an expression of this "lifeblood" that can be formidable, passion has the right to claim a *truth*. But this internal truth of the passionate constitution only becomes actual when the subject is integrated into the order of objective spirit, in which it encounters other subjects also ruled by normative and institutional universality, the validity of which must be recognized by all.

Taken on the ground of subjective spirit alone, the resolution of passionate contradictions appears random. Because passion "has no yardstick within

---

14. *Enzykl*, § 474 Anmerkung, *GW* 20, p. 471 (*Encyclopedia* 211).

15. *Enzykl*, § 474 Anmerkung, *GW* 20, p. 471 (*Encyclopedia* 211).

16. See *RPh*, § 12, *GW* 14.1, p. 37 (*Elements*, 46; see *Outlines*, 36): "Inasmuch as the will, in this double indeterminacy, gives itself the form of *individuality*, it is a resolving will, and only insofar as it makes any resolutions at all is it an *actual* will."

17. *Enzykl* 1817, § 321 Anmerkung, *GW* 13, p. 296 (*Encyclopedia* 1817, 210).

18. *Enzykl*, § 475 Anmerkung, *GW* 20, p. 473 (*Encyclopedia* 212).

itself," it is up to "the contingent decision of arbitrariness (*Willkür*)"[19] to choose between opposing drives and to thus procure for the subject a precarious equilibrium between passions. Similarly, there is no convincing—that is, rational—assessment of a passion taken in isolation or of the general passionate constitution of subjects. At the same time, the classic question of whether human nature is good or evil is relativized, or rather decentered, giving rise to an original analysis, particularly in Hegel's courses on the philosophy of religion. In the classic debate between anthropological optimism and pessimism, which assumes that it is necessary to choose between these two options, Hegel's position at first seems very cautious: "one is as true as the other, but the key is contradiction."[20] Thus, the proposition that humans are made of "crooked wood,"[21] and must therefore be straightened, is as true as it is false, that is, as unilateral as what seems to result from an (obviously simplistic) reading of Rousseau's famous phrase that "man . . . is naturally good; I think I have demonstrated [it]."[22] In truth, it is the choice between the two that must be contested along with the conviction that there is necessarily a choice between good and bad inclinations. For in fact, the "nature" of the subject lies instead in the *contradiction* at the heart of the complex of passions. Thus, the resolution of this infinitely fruitful contradiction can only lie in the *Aufhebung* of the point of view of naturalness itself. No doubt humans are "by nature" good as well as bad. But humanity's rise to subjectivity, which in the *Encyclopedia* covers the whole process of subjective spirit and in the *Phenomenology* corresponds to the development leading from immediate sensory consciousness to the self-actualization of rational consciousness, consists precisely in the fact that the naturalness and consequently the contradictoriness of spirit are dissolved. In other words, the positive meaning of the *Aufhebung* of the contradictory nature of subjectivity is the dialectical construction of freedom, the full scope of which is revealed in the dialectic of moral conscience (*Gewissen*)

---

19. *RPh*, § 17, *GW* 14.1, p. 39 (*Elements*, 50; see *Outlines*, 39). See also *RPh*, § 18, *GW* 14.1, p. 40 (*Elements*, 50–51; see *Outlines*, 40).

20. *W* 17, pp. 251–56.

21. Kant, *Idee zu einer allgemeinen Geschichte in weltbürgerlicher Absicht*, Ak. 8, p. 23.

22. See the second discourse in Rousseau, *Oeuvres complètes*, 3:202; *Social Contract*, 139; Rousseau, *Discours*, note 9, *Oeuvres complètes*, 3:202. Rousseau's position is complex, as demonstrated by another claim, that men in the state of nature could "be either good or bad, and had neither vices nor virtues." (3:152, 105).

and normativity (the opposition between good and evil). This dialectic sheds light on "the mystery of freedom" or "[its] speculative aspect":[23] its capacity for opposites, or rather contradictions.

But the rational exit out of the dialectic of passions does not exist within the framework of subjective spirit alone. The passionate subject—in other words, the practical subject—has no internal authority allowing it to evaluate and master its misguided ways. The conflict between impulses and passions reflects the opposition within the subject between what it is *in itself* (a rational will, free in and for itself) and what it actually is (a will trapped in a contradictory naturalness). Subjective spirit is not capable of overcoming this opposition by its own means. Thus, the true resolution of the contradiction internal to subjective spirit consists in the insertion of this subjectivity into the normative and institutional framework of objective spirit. There is a shift from the idea that humans *have* of themselves as subjects (an idea that was born with Christianity)[24] to the idea that they *are*[25]—not as individual subjects but as members of an instituted ethical-political community. The truth of passionate subjectivity and the resolution of the contradiction inherent in the subject, which both endangers it and leads it to act—thus, to exist—lies in the noncoerced integration of subjectivity into an objective order whose structures and norms influence the individual will but also provide the systematic conditions for subjectively lived freedom. Therefore, we have the definition given in the *Encyclopedia* of objective spirit as freedom expressed in the register of necessity:

> Freedom, shaped into the actuality of a world, acquires the form of necessity, whose substantial interconnexion is the system of determinations of freedom, and its apparent interconnexion is power, recognition, i.e., its validity in consciousness.[26]

But such an ethical-political solution to the contradictions within subjective spirit is not at all definitive. The paradox in the definition of objective spirit

---

23. *RPh*, § 139 Anmerkung, *GW* 14.1, p. 121 (*Elements*, 167; see *Outlines*, 135).

24. See *RPh*, § 124 Anmerkung, *GW* 14.1, p. 110 (*Elements*, 151; see *Outlines*, 122); *Enzykl*, § 482 Anmerkung, *GW* 20, pp. 476–77 (*Encyclopedia* 215).

25. *Enzykl*, § 482 Anmerkung, *GW* 20, p. 477 (*Encyclopedia* 215).

26. *Enzykl*, § 484, *GW* 20, pp. 478–79 (*Encyclopedia* 217).

cited above—within it, freedom takes the shape of necessity—demonstrates that the objective ethical solution to the contradictions of subjectivity is incomplete. And yet this definition outlines what the doctrine of objective spirit must achieve: it must resolve the contradiction between objective and subjective freedom, between a system and a lived world. This solution must not be understood as the mere capitulation of subjectivity to the injunction of society; if this were the case, so-called objective freedom would be comparable to Oriental despotism, and subjective freedom would come close to the "freedom of a turnspit" described by Kant.[27] From the point of view of subjectivity, which only becomes *rational* by following this path, the solution to its contradictions consists in the recognition of the institutional conditions that give substance and actuality to its claim to freedom, which would remain hollow without them. But subjective spirit has not come to the end of its contradiction when it accustoms itself to objective spirit. To the contrary, the contradictions of the passionate subject reemerge within objective spirit. This persistence of the contradictory logic of finite subjectivity can be seen clearly in the mistaken ways of moral conscience, which are discussed in the Remark to section 140 in the *Philosophy of Right*, where moral conscience loses itself when it does not recognize that it is ruled by ethics, that is, when the subject does not rise from the position of "formal moral conscience" to that of "true conscience" (which is ethical-political).[28] But the contradictory logic extends well beyond the sphere of morality. The residual effect of the dialectic of passions is especially clear in Hegel's philosophy of history, where the passions play a driving role, but it is already present in the analysis of social processes.

Social Passions and the Historical Process

As I mentioned, Hegel's analysis of the cunning of reason in the lectures on the philosophy of history has often, if not always, been interpreted as a sign of his supposed hyperrationalism, for it appears to imply that the passions of historical figures, "great men," are in the service of an impersonal rationality they unwittingly serve—all the better because they do so unwittingly. Readers have sometimes looked to this theory of historical passions for proof of the

---

27. Kant, *KpV*, *Ak.* 5, p. 97; *PP*, p. 218.

28. See *RPh*, § 137 and Anmerkung, *GW* 14.1, pp. 119–20 (*Elements*, 164–65; see *Outlines*, 132–34).

potentially totalitarian nature of the Hegelian concept, thought to be guaranteed, from the outset, to triumph over contingent particularity and to make difference, as Adorno says, vanish or perish.[29] These common objections to the theory of the cunning of reason express a misunderstanding of the original type of rationality mobilized by the Hegelian system;[30] more precisely, they ignore the fact that this rationality constitutes an attempt to overcome conventional dichotomies (activity/passivity, subjectivity/objectivity, positivity/negativity, etc.) and the "either/or" logic that underlies them.[31] I will try to explain this unique type of rationality (which may be called dialectical-speculative) by commenting on the well-known arguments Hegel makes in the preface to the *Phenomenology of Spirit* regarding the dynamic of the concept. But first I would like to make a few observations about the nature and status of social passions within the doctrine of objective spirit.

Surprisingly, criticism of the totalitarian nature of the theory of the cunning of reason remains silent about one incontestable fact: this theory (which is perhaps not truly a theory, at least not in the sense intended by those who see it as the core of Hegelianism) is very close to the argument used by late eighteenth-century British philosophers that held that the "passions" and "interests" of humans serve ends of which humans are ignorant and together create "establishments, which are indeed the result of human action, but not the execution of any human design."[32] There is a clear kinship between the metaphor of the invisible hand and Hegelian cunning of reason, as a famous passage from *The Wealth of Nations* makes clear:

> He [the individual] generally, indeed, neither intends to promote the public interest, nor knows how much he is promoting it. . . . He intends only his

29. See "Synthesis"" in the second part of Adorno, *Negative Dialectics*, 157.

30. See H. F. Fulda, "Zum Theorietypus der Hegelschen Rechtsphilosophie," in *Hegels Philosophie des Rechts die Theorie der Rechtsformen und ihre Logik*, ed. Dieter Henrich and Rolf-Peter Horstmann (Stuttgart: Klett-Cotta, 1982), 393–427.

31. See *Enzykl*, Vorrede zur zweiten Ausgabe, *GW* 20, p. 9 (Hegel's note); *Enzykl*, § 32 Zusatz, *W* 8, pp. 98–99.

32. See Ferguson, *Ferguson: An Essay*, 119. On this subject, see Albert O. Hirschman, *The Passions and the Interests: Political Arguments for Capitalism before Its Triumph* (Princeton, NJ: Princeton University Press, 1997); John Greville Agard Pocock, *Virtue, Commerce, and History*, vol. 2.

own gain, and he is in this, as in many other cases, led by an invisible hand to promote an end which was no part of his intention.[33]

Many other texts by Scottish Enlightenment thinkers develop analogous arguments;[34] this is not the place to discuss them. However, I would like to emphasize the following: there is not only a symmetry of form or structure between the doctrine of "self love" that unintentionally contributes to the common good and the theory of the constitution of objective reason through the dialectic of egotistical interests and passions. We know that Hegel's theory of civil society was shaped by his original and precocious appropriation of Scottish social philosophy. Already in his Jena writings, Hegel, a reader of *The Wealth of Nations* and other writings (certainly those of Steuart and likely those of Ferguson), developed the concept of what would later be called a spontaneous order. This appropriation had significant effects on the concept of society within the dominant school of modern political philosophy. We know that it led Hegel to develop a concept of civil society explicitly distinct from the classical concept of κοινωνία πολιτική or *societas civilis*,[35] civic-political society, which takes on the central themes of Smith's (or the Scottish) view of the creation of a market society, in particular in analyzing the system of needs. This new concept of society is clearly presented in the 1817/1818 Heidelberg lectures:

> So civil society is in the first place the external state or the state as the understanding envisages it [*Verstandesstaat*], since universality does not as such take the form of purpose in and for itself, but of means for the existence [*Existenz*] and preservation of single individuals — the state based on need [*Notstaat*] — because the main purpose is to secure the needs [*Bedürfnisse*] [of individuals].[36]

33. Smith, *Inquiry*, bk. 4, chap. 2, p. 456. Smith also writes that "the private interests and passions of individuals naturally dispose them to turn their stock toward the employments which in ordinary cases are most advantageous to the society" (Smith, *Inquiry*, bk. 4, chap. 7, p. 630).

34. See in particular Smith, *Theory of Moral Sentiments*, and Ferguson, *Ferguson: An Essay*. See also Hirschmann, *The Passions and the Interests*.

35. See above, the preliminary to part 2.

36. Hegel, *Vorlesungen über Naturrecht und Staatswissenschaft*, 112; *Lectures on Natural Right*, §89, 161.

This passage also shows us where Hegel's argument diverges from that of his Scottish predecessors. In his work, social passions have both a negative and a positive role and thus generate complexity; they, along with civil society as a whole, call for *dialectical* analysis. On the one hand, "bourgeois" passions have a positive role, for together they help create "a system of all-round dependence,"[37] although they themselves are selfish and strive only for private well-being. In this sense, passionate ambivalence, the tension between "self love" and sympathy (to use Smith's vocabulary) plays as important a role in the dynamic of civil society as in the constitution of subjectivity itself. But, on the other hand, the increasing interaction between social actors leads to the multiplication and delimitation of selfish and contradictory desires, which can cause serious dysfunctions in social regulation. When that happens, "civil society affords a spectacle of extravagance and misery as well as of the physical and ethical corruption common to both."[38]

Thus, there are two sides to social passion: it has both a structuring and destructuring effect on society. On the one hand, "*subjective selfishness* turns into a *contribution towards the satisfaction of the needs of everyone else*."[39] Competition between egotistical appetites is a powerful factor in universalizing social particularity. On the other hand, the actualization of the universal remains confined within narrow limits: in civil society, the universal is externally coordinated with the particularity of needs and passions. Universality is present but in the form of necessity rather than ethical-political freedom. Lacking any immanent measure, the competition between passions traps society in an endless logic of envy and profit, which generates tensions and contradictions that cannot be *socially* overcome. The social distress and moral degeneration of the *lumpenproletariat* are the overwhelming but quasi-necessary results of the logic of market society.[40] Which of these two aspects of passionate competition — as a purveyor of cohesion and as a destructive force — is ultimately decisive? Hegel seems to waver in his answer to this question, and his uncertainty may in fact be the crux of the entire doctrine of objective spirit. I have already discussed this systematic difficulty,[41] but I would like to dwell on three points.

---

37. RPh, § 183, GW 14.1, p. 160 (*Elements*, 221; see *Outlines*, 181).
38. RPh, § 185, GW 14.1, p. 161 (*Elements*, 222; see *Outlines*, 182).
39. RPh, § 199, GW 14.1, p. 169 (*Elements*, 233; see *Outlines*, 191–92).
40. See *RPh*, §§ 243–44, *GW* 14.1, pp. 193–94 (*Elements*, 266; see *Outlines*, 220–21).
41. See chapter 6 above.

1. One thing is certain: from Hegel's point of view, the competition of interests, which is also a struggle for recognition, cannot reach a satisfactory outcome (i.e., one that does not threaten the social system's capacity for self-regulation) by means of market mechanisms alone. It is here that Hegel diverges from Scottish moral and social philosophy even as he appropriates its basic axioms. Evidence of this can be found in the paragraph in the *Philosophy of Right* that establishes that in spite of civil society's increasing wealth, it is not able to remedy the development of poverty, and that the various solutions imaginable (redistribution policies, proactive development of supply) are counterproductive.[42] Of course, this applies first and foremost to the merely material performance of civil society. But since the theory of the system of needs—that is, of the economic subsystem—is rooted in analysis of what I have called the competition of passions, its results necessarily have a moral, or more specifically ethical, effect. The "extravagance," "misery," and "want"[43] of the working class or a part of it (the "rabble") signify not only poverty but above all moral destitution and loss of the ethical surplus that social life should normally include.

2. From a socioeconomic point of view, the solution to the contradiction that weakens and undermines society lies first in the institutionalization of social processes by means of corporations (whose task is to manage social pathologies as best as possible) and second in the interventions made by government authorities (which, as vehicles of the political sense of the universal, have a real, though limited, capacity to regulate economic processes and handle social crises). Thus, for example, the state must ensure that all citizens are educated insofar as education conditions their "capacity to become members of society."[44] All this goes to show that in a modern market society (which is precisely not a pure market society), "the individual [*Individuum*] becomes a *son of civil society*":[45] the individual can no longer be raised and educated within the confines of the *oikos* or the tribe. Civil society (what we would today call

---

42. *RPh*, § 245, *GW* 14.1, p. 194 (*Elements*, 267; see *Outlines*, 221–22).
43. See *RPh*, § 185, *GW* 14.1, p. 161, and § 242, *GW* 14.1, p. 193 (*Elements*, 222, 265; see *Outlines*, 182, 220).
44. *RPh*, § 239, *GW* 14.1, p. 192 (*Elements*, 264; see *Outlines*, 219).
45. *RPh*, § 238, *GW* 14.1, p. 191 (*Elements*, 263; see *Outlines*, 218).

"the social") must therefore be seen as a *"universal family"* in the full sense.[46] However, we are right to wonder whether this interventionist liberalism is able to resolve the problems posed by the competition between social passions and interests — problems that are not merely economic or social but fundamentally *ethical* in the Hegelian sense.

3. The conviction Hegel constantly expresses that the historical (political) *Aufhebung* of social tensions and of the sterile dialectic of self-love/self-loss is the order of the day in the postrevolutionary world ultimately requires a metaethical and metaobjective guarantee. This means that Hegel's confidence in objective reason's power of reconciliation, which is exercised in the conflict of passion and which imposes its logic on this conflict, cannot be based on the intrinsic resources of *objective* spirit alone. In reality, *finite* spirit, whether subjective or objective, is unable to achieve full reconciliation with itself; this only occurs in the sphere of absolute spirit with manifest religion and then with philosophy, "the free and comprehended cognition of [the] truth,"[47] which the rational state allows to develop freely within itself. Does this mean that spirit's actual (absolute) reconciliation with itself brings with it the definitive appeasement of passion in the eternal repose of the idea? Such an optimistic and quietist solution must be rejected, for it does not fit the infinite dynamic of the concept.

The Passion of the Concept

Two points have been established so far. First, passion in the sense of a movement of irrationality plays a positive role in both the sphere of subjective and objective spirit: paradoxically, it creates order. This is schematically summarized in the ambiguous expression "cunning of reason." Second, the doctrine of finite (subjective and objective) spirit does not have the means to overcome, once and for all, the tensions that subjective and objective (social) passions arouse in their own sphere. Madness (the extreme point of subjective suffering) and poverty (the extreme suffering of society) are contradictions that remain unreconciled at their own level and probably cannot be truly *Auf-*

---

46. *RPh*, § 239, *GW* 14.1, p. 192 (*Elements*, 264; see *Outlines*, 219).
47. *RPh*, § 360, *GW* 14.1, p. 282 (*Elements*, 380; see *Outlines*, 323).

gehoben. To imagine the actual possibility of such a reconciliation, we must look to the doctrine of absolute spirit, and more specifically to what Hegel defines as the speculative — that is, affirmative — dynamic of the concept that raises rather than dissolves finite oppositions, that "grasps the unity of the determinations in their opposition."[48]

The speculative experience that true positivity only arises through the "sublating of the negative"[49] leads us to suspect the existence of something like a passion of the concept, a suffering of the idea. During his stay in Jena, through his debate with "philosophies of reflection" (in particular, Fichte's and Schelling's), Hegel conceived of the notion of a passionate disposition of the speculative concept, if we may thus describe the "higher dialectic of the concept," which constitutes the "work . . . accomplished by the reason of the thing [*Sache*] itself."[50] The *Phenomenology of Spirit* can be read as a presentation of this passionate aspect of thought, an aspect without which thought would remain riveted to the operations of the finite understanding, which are no doubt immensely fecund at their own level. Indeed, rational positivity, which results from the creative power of the concept, is only born because of the negative, thanks to the resistance that the world and (finite) thought itself set against it.

At bottom, the entire 1807 preface, except for its polemical arguments, deals with one issue: "the seriousness, the suffering, the patience, and the labour of the negative"[51] are the elements, the milieu in which one must "sojourn" so that the affirmative and creative, speculative life of spirit will arise — and this vitality of spirit cannot be measured by the dualities of consciousness or finite subjectivity. The structure of absolute knowledge, or, to use later terminology, of the logical idea, as well as its self-explication as absolute spirit, attribute a decisive role to passion, or rather to *suffering* — the role of a mediating negativity that is the only way spirit arrives at itself and can remain "at home in itself" (*bei sich selbst*). Spirit — that is, thought as the becoming-subject of substance — is not; rather, it *happens,* and it only happens insofar as it opposes itself, denies itself. Thus, spirit is also Goethe's "spirit that always negates" in a sense that is far from solely negative:

48. *Enzykl,* § 82, *GW* 20, p. 120 (*Encyclopedia* 132).
49. *WdL* 3, *GW* 12, p. 248 (*Science of Logic,* 747).
50. *RPh,* § 31 Anmerkung, *GW* 14.1, p. 47 (*Elements,* 60; see *Outlines,* 48).
51. *PhG, GW* 9, p. 18 (*Phenomenology,* ¶ 19).

The living Substance is being that is in truth Subject, or what amounts to the same thing, it is in truth actual only insofar as it is the movement of self-positing, that is, that it is the mediation of itself and its becoming-other-to-itself.[52]

The chapter on absolute knowing specifies this theme of the constitution of subjective interiority in and through externalization: spirit abandons itself to externality so as to find itself there. But, to think this dialectic tension that constitutes spirit, one must give up the dualist schema that contrasts the interiority of spirit with the externality of substance or worldly objectivity:

> Spirit, however, has shown itself to us to be neither merely the withdrawal of self-consciousness into its pure inwardness, nor the mere submergence of self-consciousness into substance, and the non-being of its [moment of] difference; but Spirit is this movement of the Self which empties itself of itself and sinks itself into its substance, and also, as Subject, has gone out of that substance into itself, making the substance into an object and a content at the same time as it cancels this difference between objectivity and content.[53]

The language of religion, and more specifically of Christianity, provides the most powerful representation of this process of the constitution of being at home with oneself in otherness. Hegel uses this language both in the preface and the final page of the *Phenomenology* when he describes the movement of thought as the infinite *Aufhebung* of negativity. "Comprehended organization," understood as the reconciliation of spirit, the timeless agent of knowledge, and its necessary externalization in time, is presented at the very end of the work as the "Golgotha of absolute spirit."[54] We find the same allusion to the Passion of Christ in a passage in the preface celebrating "the energy of thought," which consists in conforming to the "tremendous power of the negative." Hegel, fully aware of the theological background of the argument, indicates that

52. *PhG, GW* 9, p. 18 (*Phenomenology*, ¶ 18).
53. *PhG, GW* 9, p. 431 (*Phenomenology*, ¶ 804).
54. *PhG, GW* 9, p. 434 (*Phenomenology*, ¶ 808).

it is this power, not as something positive, which closes its eyes to the negative, as when we say of something that it is nothing false, and then, having done with it, turn away and pass onto something else; on the contrary, Spirit is this power only by looking the negative in the face, and tarrying with it. This tarrying with the negative is the magical power that converts it into being.[55]

It is this religious backdrop to the Hegelian conception of thought that the expression "passion of the concept" seeks to illustrate. Nowhere is this religious background more obvious than at the end of *Faith and Knowledge*, where Hegel defines the capacity of the "pure concept" to withstand the "infinite suffering" of a world without God by using the image of "speculative Good Friday,"[56] an image which, taken literally, implies that philosophy is the serene resurrection of freedom (which is actually its true birth) in the element of the concept.

The question then becomes whether a certain form of Christology is the matrix for Hegel's conception of absolute spirit and philosophy itself. Does Hegel, with his understanding of speculative thought, turn philosophy once again into an *ancilla theologiae*? The answer is no: despite the opinions of many great interpreters of Hegel and despite Hegel's own temptation to present Christianity as the *true* representation of the speculative,[57] it is rather the Hegelian understanding of the processuality of thought and in particular the role of negativity—the "passionate" component of the work of the concept— that determines his interpretation of all of religion, and in particular his Christology. This is not a Byzantine debate, for it is a matter of locating the center of gravity of the Hegelian doctrine of spirit and consequently of the entire system. It seems to me that the thematic of the "impediment (*Hemmung*)"[58] of thought by the "rigorous exertion of the concept"[59] as it is expressed in the speculative proposition (as distinct from the proposition of the understanding) contains the key to the doctrine of absolute knowing and consequently also that of absolute spirit. The sojourn through the negative of a thought that

---

55. *PhG, GW* 9, p. 27 (*Phenomenology*, ¶ 32).
56. *Glauben und Wissen, W* 2, pp. 432, 443.
57. See *Enzykl*, § 571, *GW* 20, p. 553 (*Encyclopedia* 265–66).
58. *PhG, GW* 9, p. 44 (*Phenomenology*, ¶ 64).
59. *PhG, GW* 9, p. 41 (*Phenomenology*, ¶ 58).

rises above identitarian representations, its immersion in contradiction or in the despair of a loss of meaning, are in truth the painful experiences by which *the concept*, the true subject — a subject in the making or in the process of becoming — becomes convinced of its actuality and reconciles with itself in its never-abolished separation from itself. The entire process of the *Phenomenology of Spirit*, and in particular the passage from rational self-consciousness to the historical world of spirit, demonstrates that *reconciliation* presupposes a taking-on, a constant internalization (but one that does not result from a preexisting interiority) of the negative, of being-other or the "becoming other to oneself" (*Sichanderswerden*) of being as well as of thought. *Speculative* thought culminates in the self-manifestation of reason as idea; this is why it is also *dialectical* thought, a thought that goes through the fruitful experience of the negative. But this experience of negativity and of its strength can only be decoded by *thought*, for it institutes what is most characteristic of thought: the concept as "infinite, fecund form that encompasses the fullness of all content within itself and at the same time releases it from itself."[60] No doubt it was possible to interpret the "passion of the concept" as a theological regression (or promotion) of philosophy. But we may also see it as proof of the fact that philosophy, as a speculative (i.e., positively rational) *utterance* of negativity and its powers has definitively freed itself from the ineffability of back-worlds.

60. *Enzykl*, § 160 Zusatz, *W* 8, p. 307 (*Encyclopedia* 233).

TRANSLATOR'S NOTE

Our aim in translating Kervégan's monumental work has been to give English readers access to Kervégan's argument while also providing them with references for his primary sources. In cases where Kervégan has cited a source available only in German, we have based our translations on the original German as opposed to the French (although we have consistently consulted Kervégan's French translation of the German in crafting our own English one). Where no English reference is cited, the translation is our own (whether French or German).

Below is a list of translations and abbreviations that we have employed throughout. Generally, we have tried to cite both German and English sources. We have generally avoided emending the English translations except in cases where we disagreed with the translation or where it was necessary to do so in order to make Jean-François Kervégan's point clear. In such cases, we have noted it. In addition to these few instances, the English translations have also been frequently emended at Jean François Kervégan's request and in consultation with him so as to make his reading of Hegel more clear (e.g., *law* often occurs instead of *right*, *spirit* instead of *mind*, and so forth). Because they are so frequent, these have not been noted. One example that should be cited immediately is that at his behest, we have consistently modified every English translation of *Sittlichkeit* to read as "ethicality" (instead of the often used "ethical life"); we have done this in order to make plausible and clear Kervégan's important discussion, pursued extensively in chapter 12, of the distinction between "ethicality" (*Sittlichkeit*) and "ethical life" (*sittliche Leben*). The same is true of the translation of *Recht* in the English translation of the *Philosophy of Right*: while English translators have generally rendered it as "right," Kervégan frequently gives it as "law," and we have generally followed his impulse in emending the English translations without noting it. One other notable and common issue is the translation of *droit privé*. We have generally rendered this as "private right" (*Privatrecht*) instead of the perhaps more proper translation as "civil right" or "civil law" (both of which we use occasionally). We've done this in order to maintain a parallelism with "private right" and "objective right" or "abstract right" since that is a parallelism that Kervégan frequently invokes. The reader can also find other words and phrases in the glossary located at the end of the book. Generally, our rule has been to translate for readability while maintaining consistency of translation, which we have aimed to do with key terms (so, e.g., *l'arbitre* and *Willkür* have been rendered always as "free choice").

However, with the very sticky and crucial Hegelian term *Aufhebung* we use several different terms (*sublate, overcome*) in keeping with the various English translations of Hegel cited. But we have always included *Aufhebung* in brackets and trust that the reader will understand our reasons for doing so.

Hegel's Texts

1. Hegel's Complete Editions

GW: *Gesammelte Werke*. Edited by the Rheinisch-Westfälischen Akademie der Wissenschaften. Hamburg: Meiner, 1968–.

SW: *Sämtliche Werke: Jubiläumsausgabe*. Edited by H. Glockner. 12 vols. Stuttgart: Frommann-Holzboog, 1927–1930.

W: *Werke in zwanzig Bänden*. Edited by E. Moldenhauer and K. M. Michel. Frankfurt: Suhrkamp, 1969–1971. CD-Rom, Berlin: Talpa.

2. Hegel's German Texts

Enzykl: *Enzyklopädie der philosophischen Wissenschaften*. 2nd ed. Heidelberg, 1827; 3rd ed., 1830. [*W* 8, 9, or 10]

Enzykl 1817: *Enzyklopädie der philosophischen Wissenschaften*. Edited by W. Bonsiepen and K. Grotsch. Heidelberg, 1817. [*GW* 13, 2000]

GdP: *Vorlesungen über die Geschichte der Philosophie*. [*W* 18–20]

Naturrecht: *Über die wissenschaftlichen Behandlungsarten des Naturrechts*. [*W* 2]

PhG: *Phänomenologie des Geistes*. [*W* 3]

PPD: *Philosophische Propädeutik*. [*W* 4]

RPh: *Grundlinien der Philosophie des Rechts*. [*W* 7]

SS: *System der Sittlichkeit* (1802/1803). [*GW* 5]

WdL 1^1: *Wissenschaft der Logik*. Vol. 1, bk. 1, *Das Sein*. 1812. [*GW* 11]

WdL 1^2: *Wissenschaft der Logik*. Pt. 1, vol. 1, *Die Lehre vom Sein*. 1832. [*W* 5]

WdL 2: *Wissenschaft der Logik*. Vol. 1, bk. 2, *Die Lehre vom Wesen*. [*W* 6]

WdL 3: *Wissenschaft der Logik*. Vol. 2, *Die subjektive Logik oder Lehre vom Begriff*. [*W* 6]

3. English Translations of Hegel

The most cited volume is Hegel's *Philosophy of Right*, of which we have used the Wood translation (although page numbers are also given for the Knox translation). For the *Phenomenology*, we have, for ease of reference, cited the Miller translation by paragraph numbers, although the Pinkard online translation has been used (which also uses the Miller paragraph numbers, albeit with a few differences; we have followed Pinkard). For the *Science of Logic*, we have cited the most recent translation by Di Giovanni. The *Encyclopedia* translation we have cited is the Harris and the Wallace, while for the 1817 *Encyclopedia*, we have cited the translation by Steven Taubeneck in the Continuum edition. Finally, although the English translation of the natural law essay (put out by University of Pennsylvania press in 1975) works off of a different German edition than cited here, we have included references to it for easy access to an English source.

Elements of the Philosophy of Right. Translated by H. B. Nisbet. Edited by Allen W. Wood. Cambridge: Cambridge University Press, 1991. [*Elements*]

The Encyclopedia Logic. Translated by T. F. Geraets, W. A. Suchting, and H. S. Harris. Indianoplis: Hackett, 1991. [*Encyclopedia* §§ 1–244]

Encyclopedia of the Philosophical Sciences in Outline, and Critical Writings. Translated by Steven A. Taubeneck. London: Continuum, 1990. [*Encyclopedia 1817*]

Hegel's Philosophy of Mind. Translated by William Wallace. Oxford: Oxford University Press, 2007. [*Encyclopedia* §§ 377–577]

Hegel's Philosophy of Nature. Edited and translated by M. J. Petry. London: Allen and Unwin, 1970. [*Encyclopedia* §§ 245–376]

Hegel's Political Writings. Translated by T. M. Knox. Oxford: Clarendon, 1964.

Natural Law: The Scientific Ways of Treating Natural Law, Its Place in Moral Philosophy, and Its Relation to the Positive Sciences of Law. Philadelphia: University of Pennsylvania Press, 1975. [*Natural Law*]

Outlines of the Philosophy of Right. Translated by T. M. Knox. Revised, edited, and introduced by Stephen Houlgate. Oxford: Oxford University Press. [*Outlines*]

Phenomenology of Spirit. Translated by A. V. Miller. Oxford: Oxford University Press, 1977. [*Phenomenology*]

Science of Logic. Translated by George Di Giovanni. Cambridge: Cambridge University Press, 2015.

4. Others

German

Fichte, *Werke*: Fichte, Johann Gottlieb. *Fichtes Werke*. Edited by I. H. Fichte. Berlin, De Gruyter, 1971. Reedited on CD-Rom, Berlin, 2002.

Kant, *Ak.*: Kant, Immanuel. *Gesammelte Schriften (Akademie-Ausgabe)*. Charlottesville, VA: Intelex, 1999. [Book and CD-Rom]

Kant, *Frieden: Zum ewigen Frieden*. [*Ak.* 8]

Kant, *Gemeinspruch: Über den Gemeinspruch: das mag in der Theorie richtig sein, taugt aber nicht für die Praxis*. [*Ak.* 8]

Kant, *KpV: Kritik der praktischen Vernunft*. [*Ak.* 5]

Kant, *KrV: Kritik der reinen Vernunft* [*Ak.* 3]

Kant, *KU: Kritik der Urteilskraft*. [*Ak.* 20]

Kant, *MdS: Metaphysik der Sitten*. [*Ak.* 6]

Kant, *Rechtslehre: MdS*, pt. 1, *Metaphysische Anfangsgründe der Rechtslehre*. [*Ak.* 6]

Kant, *Sittenlehre: MdS*, pt. 2, *Metaphysische Anfangsgründe der Sittenlehre*. [*Ak.* 6]

English

For Kant, we have employed the Cambridge translations exclusively.

Kant, Immanuel. *Critique of Pure Reason*. Translated by Paul Guyer and Allen W. Wood. Cambridge: Cambridge University Press, 1998. [1C]

———. *Critique of the Power of Judgment*. Translated by Paul Guyer and Eric Matthews. Cambridge: Cambridge University Press, 2000. [3C]

———. *Practical Philosophy*. Translated by Mary J. Gregor. Edited by Mary J. Gregor Cambridge: Cambridge University Press, 1996. [2C]

BIBLIOGRAPHY

Adams, Charles F., ed. *The Works of John Adams*. 10 vols. Boston: Little, Brown, 1951.

Adorno, Theodor W. *Negative Dialectics*. Translated by E. B. Ashton. New York: Continuum, 1973.

Andler, Charles. *Les origines du socialisme d'état en Allemagne*. Paris: Alcan, 1897.

Aristotle. *Aristotle's Nicomachean Ethics*. Translated by Robert C. Bartlett and Susan D. Collins. Chicago: University of Chicago Press, 2011.

Balibar, Étienne. *Equaliberty: Political Essays*. Durham, NC: Duke University Press, 2014.

———. "Les Universels." In *La crainte des masses*. Paris: Galilée, 1997.

Beaud, Olivier. *La puissance de l'état*. Paris: Presses Universitaires de France, 1994.

Beiser, Frederick *The Cambridge Companion to Hegel*. Cambridge: Cambridge University Press, 1993.

Bergbohm, Carl. *Jurisprudenz und Rechtsphilosophie*. Leipzig: Duncker und Humboldt, 1892.

Biard, J., D. Buvat, J. F. Kervégan, J. F. Kling, A. Lacroix, A. Lécrivain, and M. Slubicki. *Introduction á la lecture de la science de la logique de Hegel*. Vol. 1, *L'être*. Paris: Aubier-Montaigne, 1987.

Binder, Julius. "Der obligatorische Vertrag im System der Hegelschen Rechtsphilosophie." In *Verhandlungen des dritten Hegel-Kongresses*, edited by B. Wigersma, 37–59. Tübingen: Mohr, 1934.

Bloch, Ernst. *Natural Law and Human Dignity*. Cambridge, MA: MIT Press, 1986.

Bobbio, Norberto. *Studi Hegeliani*. Turin: Einaudi, 1981.

———. "Sulla nozione di società civile." In *Studi Hegeliani*. Turin: Einaudi, 1981.

Böckenförde, Ernst. "Entstehung und Wandel des Rechtsstaatsbegriffs." In *Recht, Staat, Freiheit*. Frankfurt am Main: Suhrkamp, 1991.

———. *Recht, Staat, Freiheit*. Frankfurt am Main: Suhrkamp, 1991.

———. *Staat und Gesellschaft*. Darmstadt: Wissenschaftliche Buchgesellschaft, 1976.

Bodin, Jean. *Les six livres de la république*. Paris: Fayard, 1986.

Bourgeois, Bernard. *Études Hégéliennes: Raison et décision*. Paris: Presses Universitaires de France, 1992.

———. *La pensée politique de Hegel*. Paris: Presses Universitaires de France, 1969.

———. *Le droit naturel de Hegel*. Paris: Vrin, 1986.

———. "Sur le droit naturel de Hegel (1802–1803)." In *Études Hégéliennes*, 178–79. Paris: Presses Universitaires de France, 1992.

Brandom, Robert. *Making It Explicit: Reasoning, Representing, and Discursive Commitment*. Cambridge, MA: Harvard University Press, 1994.

Brandom, Robert B. "Some Pragmatist Themes in Hegel's Idealism: Negotiation and Administration in Hegel's Account of the Structure and Content of Conceptual Norms." *European Journal of Philosophy* 7, no. 2 (1999): 164–89.

Braudel, Fernand. *Civilization and Capitalism 15th–18th Century*. Vol. 1, *The Structures of Everyday Life*. New York: Harper Collins, 1985.

Brunner, Otto, Werner Conze, and Reinhart Koselleck, eds. *Geschichtliche Grundbegriffe*. 8 vols. Stuttgart: Klett-Cotta, 1974–1997.

Burke, Edmund. *The Works of Edmund Burke*. 16 vols. London: Rivington, 1803–1827.

Cassirer, Ernst. *The Myth of the State*. Oxford: Oxford University Press, 1946.

Colliot-Thélène, Catherine. "Les origines de la théorie du *Machtstaat*." *Philosophie* 20 (1988): 24–47.

Constant, Benjamin. *Constant: Political Writings*. Cambridge: Cambridge University Press, 1988.

Croce, Benedetto. *What Is Living and What Is Dead of the Philosophy of Hegel*. Translated by Douglas Ainslie. New York: Macmillan, 1915.

d'Hondt, Jacques. "La personne et le droit abstrait selon Hegel." In *Droit et liberté selon Hegel*, edited by Guy Planty-Bonjour. Paris: Presses Universitaires de France, 1986.

Diderot, Denis. *Encyclopédie; ou, Dictionnaire raisonné des sciences, des arts et des métiers*. Paris, 1751–1765.

Dilthey, Wilhelm. *Gesammelte Schriften*. Vol. 4, *Die Jugendgeschichte Hegels und andere Abhandlungen zur Geschichte des deutschen Idealismus*. Leipzig: Teubner, 1963.

Dubarle, Dominique. *Logos et formalisation du langage*. Paris: Klincksieck, 1977.

Duby, Georges. *The Three Orders: Feudal Society Imagined*. Chicago: University of Chicago Press, 1982.

Duso, Giuseppe. *La rappresentanza politica: Genesi e crisi del concetto*. Milan: F. Angeli, 2003.

Elias, Norbert. *The Civilizing Process*. Oxford: Blackwell, 1982.

Engels, Friedrich. *Socialism: Utopian and Scientific*. New York: Pathfinder, 1972.

Engels, Friedrich, and Karl Marx. *Ludwig Feuerbach and the Outcome of Classical German Philosophy*. New York: International, 1941.

The Federalist Papers. London: Oxford University Press, 2008.

Ferguson, Adam. *Ferguson: An Essay on the History of Civil Society*. Cambridge: Cambridge University Press, 1995.

Fischbach, Franck. *Fichte et Hegel: La reconnaissance*. Paris: Presses Universitaires de France, 1999.

Forsthoff, Ernst, ed. *Rechtsstaatlichkeit und Sozialstaatlichkeit*. Darmstadt: Wissenschaftliche Buchgesellschaft, 1968.

Foucault, Michel. *The History of Sexuality*. Vol. 2, *The Use of Pleasure*. Translated by Robert Hurley. New York: Vintage Books, 2012.

Franklin, J. H. *Jean Bodin and the Rise of Absolutist Theory*. Cambridge: Cambridge University Press, 1973.

Fulda, Hans Friedrich. "'Spekulative Logik als die eigentliche Metaphysik': Zu Hegels verwandlung des neuzeitlichen Metaphysikverständnisses." In *Hegels Transformation der Metaphysik*, edited by Detlev Pätzold, 9–27. Cologne: Dinter, 1991.

Gall, Lothar. "Liberalismus und 'bürgerliche Gesellschaft.'" *Historische Zeitschrift* 220, no. 2 (1975): 324–56.

Gans, Eduard. *Das erbrecht in weltgeschichtlicher Entwickelung*. 4 vols. Berlin, 1824–1835.

Gernet, Louis. "Droit et société dans la Grèce ancienne." In *Droit et institutions en Grèce antique*, 7–119. Paris: Champs Flammarion, 1982.

Girard, Paul Frédéric. *Manuel élémentaire de droit romain*. Paris: A. Rousseau, 1929.

Godechot, Jacques. *Les constitutions de la France depuis 1789*. Paris: Garnier-Flammarion, 1970.

Goldschmidt, Victor. "État de nature et pacte de soumission chez Hegel." *Revue Philosophique de la France et de l'Étranger* 89 (1964): 45–65.

Grotius, Hugo. *De jure belli ac pacis*. Aalen: Scientia, 1993.

Gurvitch, Georges. *L'idée du droit social*. Paris: Sirey, 1931.

Habermas, Jürgen. "Arbeit und Interaktion." In *Technik und Wissenschaft als "Ideologie"?* 9–47. Frankfurt am Main: Suhrkamp, 1969.

———. *Legitimation Crisis*. London: Heinemann, 1976.

———. *Legitimationsprobleme im Spätkapitalismus*. Frankfurt am Main: Suhrkamp, 1973.

———. "Natural Law and Revolution." In *Theory and Practice*, 82–120. Boston: Beacon, 1973.

———. *The Theory of Communicative Action*. Vol. 2, *Lifeworld and System: A Critique of Functionalist Reason*. Boston: Beacon, 1987.

Hattenhauer, Hans, and Anton Friedrich Justus Thibaut, eds. *Thibaut und Savigny: Ihre programmatischen Schriften*. Munich: Vahlen, 1973.

Hauriou, Maurice, ed. *Aux sources du droit: Le pouvoir, l'ordre et la liberté*. Caen: Centre de philosophie politique et juridique, 1986.

———. "L'ordre social, la justice et le droit." In *Aux sources du droit: Le pouvoir, l'ordre et la liberté*, edited by Maurice Hauriou. Caen: Centre de philosophie politique et juridique, 1986.

———. *Principes du droit public*. Paris: Sirey, 1916.

Hayek, Friedrich August. *The Fatal Conceit*. Chicago: University of Chicago Press, 1989.

———. *Law, Legislation and Liberty: A New Statement of the Liberal Principles of Justice and Political Economy*. London: Routledge, 1977.

Haym, Rudolf. *Hegel und seine Zeit: Vorlesungen über Entstehung und Entwicklung, Wesen und Werth der Hegel'schen Philosophie*. Berlin: Rudolph Gaertner, 1857.

Hegel, G. W. F. *Die Vernunft in der Geschichte*. Hamburg: Felix Meiner, 1955.

———. *Gesammelte Werke*. Edited by Rheinisch-Westfälischen Akademie der Wissenschaften. 19 vols. Hamburg: Felix Meiner, 1968–.

———. *Hegel: Lectures on Natural Right and Political Science: The First Philosophy of Right*. Translated by Michael J. Stewart and Peter C. Hodgson. Oxford: Oxford University Press, 2012.

———. *Hegel: The Letters*. Translated by Clark Butler and Christiane Seiler. Bloomington: Indiana University Press, 1984.

———. *Hegel's Political Writings*. Translated by T. M. Knox. Oxford: Clarendon, 1964.

———. *Lectures on the History of Philosophy*. Vol. 3, *Medieval and Modern Philosophy*. Translated by Frances H. Simson and E. S. Haldane. Lincoln: University of Nebraska Press, 1995.

———. *Lectures on the Philosophy of World History*. Translated by Hugh Barr Nisbet. Cambridge: Cambridge University Press, 1975.

———. *Philosophie des Rechts: Die Vorlesung von 1819/20 in einer Nachschrift*. Frankfurt am Main: Suhrkamp, 1983.

———. *Vorlesungen über die Philosophie der Weltgeschichte*. Vol. 1, *Die Vernunft in der Geschichte*. Hamburg: Felix Meiner, 1955.

———. *Vorlesungen über Naturrecht und Staatswissenschaft (Heidelberg 1817/18)*. Hamburg: Meiner, 1983.

———. *Vorlesungen über Rechtsphilosophie*. 4 vols. Suttgart: Frommann-Holzboog, 1974.

———. *Werke in zwanzig Bänden*. Edited by E. Moldenhauer and K. M. Michel. Frankfurt: Suhrkamp, 1969–1971. CD-Rom, Berlin: Talpa.

Heller, Herman. *Gesammelte Schriften*. 3 vols. Leiden: Sijthoff, 1971.

Henrich, Dieter. "Hegels Theorie des Zufalls." In *Hegel im Kontext*, 157–86. Frankfurt am Main: Suhrkamp, 1971.

Henrich, Dieter, and Rolf-Peter Horstmann, eds. *Hegels Philosophie des Rechts die Theorie der Rechtsformen und ihre Logik*. Stuttgart: Klett-Cotta, 1982.

Heydenreich, Karl Heinrich. *Grundsätze des natürlichen Staatsrechts und seiner Anwendung nebst einem Anhange staatsrechtlicher Abhandlungen*. Leipzig: Weygandsche Buchhandlung, 1795.

Hirschman, Albert O. *The Passions and the Interests: Political Arguments for Capitalism before Its Triumph*. Princeton, NJ: Princeton University Press, 1997.

Hobbes, Thomas. *De Cive: English Version*. Oxford: Oxford University Prss, 1983.

———. *Hobbes: On the Citizen*. Cambridge: Cambridge University Press, 1998.

———. *Leviathan*. 3 vols. Oxford: Clarendon Press, 2012.

Hoffman, Hasso. *Repräsentation: Studien zur Wort und Begriffsgeschichte*. Berlin: Duncker und Humboldt, 1990.

Hoffmeister, Johannes, ed. *Briefe von und an Hegel*. 4 vols. Hamburg: Meiner, 1952–1961.

———, ed. *Dokumente zu Hegels Entwicklung*. Stuttgart: Fromann-Holzboog, 1974.

Honneth, Axel. *Freedom's Right: The Social Foundations of Democratic Life*. New York: Columbia University Press, 2014.

———. *The Struggle for Recognition: The Moral Grammar of Social Conflicts*. Cambridge, MA: MIT Press, 1996.

———. *Suffering from Indeterminacy: An Attempt at a Reactualization of Hegel's Philosophy of Right; Two Lectures*. Translated by Jack Ben-Levi. Assen, Netherlands: Van Gorcum, 2000.

Horstmann, Rolf-Peter. "Über die Rolle der bürgerlichen Gesellschaft in Hegels politischer Philosophie." *Hegel-Studien* 9 (1974): 209–40.

Hyppolite, Jean. *Introduction à la philosophie de l'histoire de Hegel*. Paris: Éditions du Seuil, 1983.

Jaeschke, Walter. "Hegel's Last Year in Berlin." In *Hegel's Philosophy of Action*, edited by Lawrence Stepelevich and David Lamb, 31–48. Atlantic Highlands, NJ: Humanities Press, 1983.

Jamme, Christoph. "Die Erziehung der Stände durch sich selbst." In *Hegels Rechtsphilosophie im Zusammenhang der europäischen Verfassungsgeschichte*, edited by Otto Pöggeler and Hans-Christian Lucas, 149–73. Stuttgart: Frommann-Holzboog, 1986.

Jamme, Christoph, and Elisabeth Weisser-Lohmann. *Politik und Geschichte: Zu den Intentionen von G.W.F. Hegels Reformbill-Schrift*. Bonn: Bouvier, 1995.

Jouanjan, Olivier. "État de droit, forme de gouvernement et représentation: A partir d'un passage de Kant." *Annales de la Faculté de Droit de Strasbourg* 2 (1998).

———. "Présentation." In *Figures de l'état de droit*, edited by Olivier Jouanjan, 7–62. Presses Universitaires de Strasbourg, 2001.

Kaser, Max. *Das römische Privatrecht*. 2 vols. Munich: Beck, 1955–1959.

Kelsen, Hans. *Pure Theory of Law*. Gloucester, MA: Smith, 1989.

Kervégan, Jean-François. "Société civile et droit privé: Entre Hobbes et Hegel." In *Architectures de la Raison: Mélanges Alexandre Matheron*, edited by Pierre-François Moreau, 145–64. Paris: ENS Editions, 1996.

Kiesewetter, Hubert. *Von Hegel zu Hitler: Die politische Verwirklichung einer totalitaren Machtstaatstheorie in Deutschland, 1815–1945*. Frankfurt am Main: Lang, 1995.

Klippel, Diethelm. "Die Historisierung des Naturrechts." In *Recht zwischen Natur und Geschichte*, edited by Heinz Mohnhaupt and Jean-François Kervégan, 103–24. Frankfurt: Klostermann, 1997.

———. "Naturrecht als Lehrfach an den deutschen Universitäten des 18. und 19. Jahrhunderts." In *Naturrecht, Spätaufklärung, Revolution*, edited by Otto Dann and Diethelm Klippel, 270–92. Hamburg: Meiner, 1995.

Koselleck, Reinhart. *Preussen zwischen Reform und Revolution*. Stuttgart: Klett, 1967.

Landau, Peter. "Hegels Begründung des Vertragsrechts." *ARSP: Archiv für Rechts-und Sozialphilosophie/Archives for Philosophy of Law and Social Philosophy* 59 (1973): 117–38.

Lardic, Jean-Marie. "La contingence chez Hegel." In Georg Wilhelm Friedrich Hegel, *Comment le sens commun comprend la philosophie*. Translated by Jean-Marie Lardic, 63–114. Arles: Actes Sud, 1989.

Locke, John. *The Second Treatise of Government*. London: J. M. Dent, 1993.

Losurdo, Domenico. *Hegel e la libertà dei moderni*. Rome: Editori Riuniti, 1992.

———. *Hegel und das deutsche Erbe*. Cologne: Pahl-Rugenstein, 1989.

Löwith, Karl. *Meaning in History: The Theological Implications of the Philosophy of History*. Chicago: University of Chicago Press, 1949.

———. *Sämtliche Schriften*. 9 vols. Stuttgart: J. B. Metzler, 1988.

Mabille, Bernard. *Hegel: L'épreuve de la contingence*. Paris: Aubier, 1999.

MacIntyre, Alasdair. *After Virtue*. Notre Dame, IN: University of Notre Dame Press, 1981.

———. *Whose Justice? Which Rationality?* Notre Dame, IN: University of Notre Dame Press, 1988.

Maier, Hans. *Die ältere deutsche Staats und Verwaltungslehre*. Munich: DTV, 1986.

Maine, Henry S. *The Ancient Law*. Boston: Beacon, 1963.

Manent, Pierre. *Tocqueville et la nature de la démocratie*. Paris: Fayard, 1993.

Marquard, Odo. "Hegel und das Sollen." In *Schwierigkeiten mit der Geschichtsphilosophie*, 37–51. Frankfurt am Main: Suhrkamp, 1964.

Marx, Karl. *A Contribution to the Critique of Political Economy.* Translated by N. I. Stone. Chicago: Charles and Kerr, 1904.

———. *Critique of Hegel's "Philosophy of Right."* Cambridge: Cambridge University Press, 1977.

———. *Economic and Philosophic Manuscripts of 1844.* Translated by Martin Milligan. Amherst, NY: Prometheus Books, 1988.

———. *Grundrisse: Foundations of the Critique of Political Economy (Rough Draft).* Translated by Martin Nicolaus. London: Penguin, 1973.

———. "On the Jewish Question." In *The Marx-Engels Reader,* edited by Robert C. Tucker, 26–53. New York: Norton, 1978.

———. *Theorien über den Mehrwert.* Vol. 1. Berlin: Dietz, 1965.

McDowell, John. *Having the World in View: Essays on Kant, Hegel, and Sellars.* Cambridge, MA: Harvard University Press, 2009.

———. *Meaning, Knowledge, and Reality.* Cambridge, MA: Harvard University Press, 1998.

———. *Mind and World.* Cambridge, MA: Harvard University Press, 1996.

Meier, Christian. *The Greek Discovery of Politics.* Cambridge, MA: Harvard University Press, 1990.

Meinecke, Friedrich. *Werke.* 9 vols. Munich: Oldenbourg, 1959.

Mommsen, Théodore. *Le droit public romain.* 7 vols. in 8. Paris: De Boccard, 1992.

Montesquieu. *Montesquieu: The Spirit of the Laws.* Translated and edited by Anne M. Cohler, Basia Caroly Miller, and Harold Samuel Stone. Cambridge: Cambridge University Press, 1989.

Moser, Johann Jacob. *Neues teutsches Staatsrecht: Von der Landeshoheit in Steuer-Sachen.* Metzler, 1773.

Müller, Adam Heinrich. *Die Elemente der Staatskunst.* 3 vols. Jena: Fischer, 1809.

Nicolin, Günter. *Hegel in Berichten seiner Zeitgenossen.* Hamburg: Meiner, 2013.

Nörr, Dieter. *Savignys philosophische Lehrjahre: Ein Versuch.* Frankfurt: Klostermann, 1994.

Nozick, Robert. *Anarchy, State, and Utopia.* New York: Basic Books, 1974.

Ottmann, Henning. *Individuum und Gemeinschaft: Hegel im Spiegel der Interpretationen.* Berlin: Walter de Gruyter, 1977.

Paine, Thomas. *Rights of Man: Common Sense, and Other Essential Writings.* Oxford: Oxford University Press, 1998.

Peperzak, Adriaan. "Zur Hegelschen Ethik." In *Hegels Philosophie des Rechts: Die Theorie der Rechtsformen und ihre Logik,* edited by Dieter Henrich and Rolf-Peter Horstmann, 103–31. Stuttgart: Klett-Cotta, 1982.

Petry, Michael J. "Hegel and the Morning Chronicle." *Hegel Studien* 11 (1976): 11–80.

Pinkard, Terry. *Hegel: A Biography.* Cambridge: Cambridge University Press, 2001.

———. *Hegel's Naturalism.* Oxford: Oxford University Press, 2012.

———. *Hegel's Phenomenology: The Sociality of Reason.* Cambridge: Cambridge University, 1996.

Pinkard, Terry, and H. Tristram Engelhardt. *Hegel Reconsidered: Beyond Metaphysics and the Authoritarian State.* Dordrecht: Kluwer, 1994.

Pippin, Robert B. *Hegel's Idealism: The Satisfactions of Self-Consciousness.* Cambridge: Cambridge University Press, 1989.

———. *Hegel's Practical Philosophy.* Cambridge: Cambridge University Press, 2008.

————. *Idealism as Modernism: Hegelian Variations.* Cambridge: Cambridge University Press, 1997.

Pocock, John Greville Agard. *The Machiavellian Moment.* Princeton, NJ: Princeton University Press, 1975.

————. *Virtue, Commerce, and History: Essays on Political Thought and History, Chiefly in the Eighteenth Century.* Cambridge: Cambridge University Press, 1985.

Pöggeler, Otto. "Hegel rencontre La Prusse." *Archives de Philosophie* 51 (1988): 353–83.

————. *Hegels Rechtsphilosophie im Zusammenhang der europäischen Verfassungsgeschichte,* edited by H. C. Lucas and O. Pöggeler. Stuttgart: Frommann-Holzboog, 1986.

Polanyi, Karl. *The Great Transformation: The Political and Economic Origin of Our Time.* Boston: Beacon, 1985.

Popper, Karl. *The Open Society and Its Enemies.* 2 vols. Princeton, NJ: Princeton University Press, 1966.

Pufendorf, Samuel von. *De jure naturae et gentium libri octo vol. 2: The Translation of the Edition of 1688.* Translated by C. A. Oldfather. Oxford: Oxford University Press, 1934.

Rehberg, August Wilhelm. *Untersuchungen über die französische Revolution.* 2 vols. Hannover: Ritscher, 1793.

Renault, Emmanuel. "La métaphysique entre logique et sciences particulières." In *Logique et sciences concrètes dans le système Hégélien,* edited by Jean-Michel Buée, Emmanuel Renault, and David Wittman, 13–32. Paris: L'Harmattan, 2006.

————. *Mépris social: Éthique et politique de la reconnaissance.* Bordeaux: Le Passant ordinaire, 2000.

Ricardo, David. *On the Principles of Political Economy and Taxation.* London: Penguin, 1971.

Riedel, Manfred. "Bürger, Staatsbürger, Bürgertum." In *Geschichtliche Grundbegriffe,* vol. 1, edited by Otto Brunner, Werner Conze, and Reinhart Koselleck, 672–725. Stuttgart: Klett-Cotta, 1974–1997.

————. "Hegels Kritik des Naturrechts." In *Zwischen tradition und revolution: Studien zu Hegels Rechtsphilosophie,* edited by Manfred Riedel, 170–203. Stuttgart: Klett-Cotta, 1982.

————, ed. *Zwischen Tradition und Revolution: Studien zu Hegels Rechtsphilosophie.* Stuttgart: Klett-Cotta, 1982.

Ritter, Joachim. "Hegel und die französische Revolution." In *Metaphysik und Politik,* 183–255. Frankfurt am Main: Suhrkamp, 2003.

————. "Moralität und Sittlichkeit: Zu Hegels Auseinandersetzung mit der Kantischen Ethik." In *Metaphysik und Politik: Studien zu Aristoteles und Hegel* 281–309. Frankfurt: Suhrkamp, 1969. Reprint, 2003.

Ritter, Joachim, Karlfried Gründer, Gottfried Gabriel, and Marcel Weber. *Historisches Wörterbuch der Philosophie.* Vol. 8, Basel: Schwabe, 1992.

Romano, Santi. *L'ordre juridique.* Paris: Dalloz, 2002.

Rosenkranz, Karl. *Hegels Leben.* Berlin: Duncker und Humblot, 1844.

Rosenzweig, Franz. *Hegel und der Staat (1920).* 2 vols. Aalen: Scientia, 1962.

Rousseau, Jean-Jacques. *Emile; or, On Education.* Translated by Christopher Kelly and Allan Bloom. Lebanon, NH: University Press of New England, 2002.

————. *Oeuvres complètes.* 5 vols. Paris: Gallimard, 1995.

————. *The Social Contract and the First and Second Discourses.* Translated by Susan Dunn and Gita May. New Haven, CT: Yale University Press, 2002.

Rückert, Joachim. *Idealismus, Jurisprudenz und Politik bei F. C. von Savigny.* Ebelsbach: Gremer, 1984.

Scheidemantel, Heinrich Gottfried. *Das Staatsrecht nach der Vernunft und den Sitten der vornehmsten Völker Betrachtet.* Cröcker, 1773.

————. *Repertorium des teutschen Staats- und Lehnsrechts.* Munich: Bayerische Staatsbibliothek, 1782.

————. *Schreiben an die Staats-und Lehenrechts-Gelehrten in Teutschland.* Munich: Bayerische Staatsbibliothek, 1782.

Schmalz, Theodor Anton Heinrich. *Das natürliche Staatsrecht.* Königsberg: Friedrich Nicolovius, 1794.

Schmalz, Theodor Anton Heinrich, and Friedrich Nicolovius. *Das reine Naturrecht.* Königsberg: Friedrich Nicolovius, 1792.

Schmitt, Carl. *The Concept of the Political.* Chicago: University of Chicago Press, 1996.

————. *Constitutional Theory.* Translated by Joseph W. Bendersky. Durham, NC: Duke University Press, 2008.

————. *Der Begriff des Politischen.* Berlin: Duncker und Humboldt, 1979.

————. *Der Nomos der Erde.* Berlin: Duncker und Humboldt, 1988.

————. *Die Hüter der Verfassung.* Berlin: Duncker und Humboldt, 1985.

————. "Nehmen, Teilen, Weiden: Ein Versuch der Grundfrage jeder Sozial-und Wirtschaftsordnung vom Nomos her richtig zu Stellen." In *Verfassungsrechtliche Aufsätze aus den Jahren 1924–1954: Materialien zu einer Verfassungslehre,* 489–504. Berlin: Duncker und Humbolt, 1953.

————. *The Nomos of the Earth.* New York: Telos, 2003.

————. *On the Three Types of Juristic Thought.* Translated by Joseph W. Bendersky. Westport, CT: Praeger, 2004.

————. *Political Theology.* Translated by Joseph W. Bendersky. Chicago: University of Chicago Press, 2005.

————. *Politische Theologie.* Translated by Joseph W. Bendersky. Berlin: Duncker und Humblot, 1990.

————. *Staat, Grossraum, Nomos: Arbeiten aus den Jahren 1916–1969.* Berlin: Duncker und Humboldt, 1995.

————. *Verfassungslehre.* Translated by Joseph W. Bendersky. Berlin: Duncker und Humboldt, 2003.

————. *Verfassungsrechtliche Aufsätze aus den Jahren 1924–1954: Materialien zu einer Verfassungslehre.* Berlin: Duncker und Humbolt, 1953.

Schneider, Hans-Peter. "Der Bürger zwischen Stadt und Staat im 19. Jahrhundert." *Der Staat* 8 (1988): 143–78.

Schröder, Jan, and Ines Pielemeier. "Naturrecht als Lehrfach an den deutschen Universitäten des 18. und 19. Jahrhunderts." In *Naturrecht, Spätaufklärung, Revolution,* edited by Otto Dann and Diethelm Klippel, 255–96. Hamburg: Meiner, 1995.

Schüler, Gisela. "Zur Chronologie von Hegels Jugendschriften." *Hegel-Studien* 2 (1963): 111–59.

Siep, Ludwig. "Der Kampf um Anerkennung: Hegels Auseinandersetzung mit Hobbes." *Hegel-Studien* 9 (1974): 155–207.

Sieyès, Emmanuel-Joseph. "Reconnaissance et exposition raisonnée des droits de l'homme et du citoyen." In *Écrits politiques*, edited by Roberto Zapperi. Paris: Éditions des Archives Comtemporaines, 1985.

———. *Qu'est-ce que le tiers état?* Geneva: Droz, 1970.

Smend, Rudolf. *Staatsrechtliche Abhandlungen: Und andere Aufsätze*. Berlin: Duncker und Humbolt, 1968.

Smith, Adam. *An Inquiry into the Nature and Causes of the Wealth of Nations*. Oxford: Oxford University Press, 1976.

———. *The Theory of Moral Sentiments*. Oxford: Oxford University Press, 1976.

Smith, Steven B. *Hegel's Critique of Liberalism: Rights in Context*. Chicago: University of Chicago Press, 1991.

Sobota, Katharina. *Das Prinzip Rechtsstaat*. Tübingen: Mohr, 1997.

Stern, Klaus. *Der Rechtsstaat*. Kölner Universitätsreden, n.s., 45. Krefeld: Scherpe, 1971.

Steuart, Sir James. *Untersuchungen über die Grundsätze von der Staatswissenschaft*. Vol. 2, Hamburg, 1796.

Stolleis, Michael. *Geschichte des öffentlichen Rechts in Deutschland*. 3 vols. Munich: Beck, 1988.

———. "Untertan-Bürger-Staatsbürger: Bemerkungen zur juristischen Terminologie im späten 18. Jahrhundert." In *Bürger und Bürgerlichkeit im Zeitalter der Aufklärung*, edited by Rudolf Vierhaus, 65–99. Heidelberg: Schneider, 1981.

Strauss, Leo. *Natural Right and History*. Chicago: University of Chicago Press, 1965.

———. *What Is Political Philosophy? And Other Studies*. Chicago: University of Chicago Press, 1988.

Talmon, Jacob L. *The Rise of Totalitarian Democracy*. Boston: Beacon, 1952.

Taminiaux, Jacques. "Commentaire." In *Naissance de la philosophie Hégélienne de l'état: Commentaire et traduction de la realphilosophie d'Iéna (1805–1806)*. Paris: Payot, 1984.

Tocqueville, Alexis de. *Correspondance*. Paris: Gallimard, 1983.

———. *De la démocratie en Amérique*. Pt. 1 of *Oeuvres complètes*. Paris: Gallimard, 1961.

———. *Democracy in America*. Translated by Arthur Goldhammer. New York: Literary Classics of the United States, 2004.

———. *L'ancien régime et la revolution*. Pt. 2 of *Oeuvres complètes*. Paris: Gallimard, 1952.

———. *Tocqueville: The Ancien Régime and the French Revolution*. Translated by Arthur Goldhammer. Cambridge: Cambridge University Press, 2011.

Topitsch, Ernst. *Die Sozialphilosophie Hegels als Heilslehre und Herrschaftsideologie*. 2nd ed. Munich: Piper, 1981.

Troeltsch, Ernst. *Der Historismus und seine Probleme*. Vol. 3 of *Gesammelte Schriften*. Tübingen: Mohr, 1922.

Troper, Michel. *La théorie du droit, le droit, l'état*. Paris: Presses Universitaires de France, 2001.

Villey, Michel. "Le droit romain dans la philosophie de droit de Hegel." *Archives de Philosophie du Droit* 16 (1971): 275–90.

Vlastos, Gregory. "Isonomia." *American Journal of Philology* 74, no. 4 (1953): 337–66.

vom Stein, Freiherr. *Briefwechsel, Denkschriften und Aufzeichnungen*. Berlin: Heymann, 1937.

Von Mohl, Robert. *Die Geschichte und Literatur der Staatswissenschaften.* 2 vols.. Erlangen: F. Enke, 1856.

von Ranke, Leopold. *Über die Epochen der Weltgeschichte.* Vol. 2 of *Aus Werk und Nachlass.* Munich: Historische Kommission bei der Bayerischen Akademie der Wissenschaften, 1971.

Von Stein, Lorenz. *Der Begriff der Gesellschaft, in Geschichte der sozialen Bewegung in Frankreich, von 1789 bis auf unsere Tage.* 3 vols. Leipzig, 1850.

Von Treitschke, Heinrich. *Historische und politische Aufsätze.* Leipzig, 1886.

Waszek, Norbert. "Hegels Exzerpte aus der Edinburgh Review 1817–1819." *Hegel-Studien* 20 (1985): 79–112.

———. "Hegels Lehre von der 'Bürgerlichen Gesellschaft' und die politische Ökonomie der schottischen Aufklärung." *Dialektik* 3 (1995): 35–50.

———. *The Scottish Enlightenment and Hegel's Account of "Civil Society."* Dordrecht: Kluwer, 2012.

Weber, Max. *Economy and Society: An Outline of Interpretive Sociology.* Berkeley: University of California Press, 1978.

Weil, Eric. *Hegel et l'état.* Paris: Vrin, 1994.

Weinacht, Paul-Ludwig. "Staatsbürger: Zur Geschichte und Kritik eines politischen Begriffs." *Der Staat* 8, no. 1 (1969): 41–63.

Wilhelm, Walter. "Savignys überpositive Systematik." In *Philosophie und Rechtswissenschaft: Zum Problem ihrer Beziehung im 19. Jahrhundert,* edited by Jürgen Blühdorn and Joachim Ritter, 123–36. Frankfurt: Klostermann, 1969.

INDEX